28198

OUT OF THE ORDINARY

OF THE ORDINARY

Robert Venturi
Denise Scott Brown
and Associates

ARCHITECTURE | URBANISM | DESIGN

David B. Brownlee, David G. De Long, and Kathryn B. Hiesinger

Checklist of projects and buildings by William Whitaker

Chronology by Diane L. Minnite

PHILADELPHIA MUSEUM OF ART

IN ASSOCIATION WITH YALE UNIVERSITY PRESS

Frontispiece: Denise Scott Brown and Robert Venturi reflecting upon the Hôtel du Département de la Haute-Garônne, Toulouse, France, 1999

Published on the occasion of the exhibition *Out of the Ordinary: The Architecture and Design of Robert Venturi, Denise Scott Brown and Associates*

Philadelphia Museum of Art
June 10, 2001, to August 5, 2001

Museum of Contemporary Art, San Diego
June 2, 2002, to September 8, 2002

The Heinz Architectural Center, Carnegie Museum of Art, Pittsburgh
November 7, 2002, to February 3, 2003

Exhibition organized by Kathryn B. Hiesinger with David B. Brownlee and David G. De Long, with the assistance of Diane L. Minnite and William Whitaker

In Philadelphia, the exhibition is supported by generous grants from the Philadelphia Exhibitions Initiative, a program funded by The Pew Charitable Trusts, and administered by The University of the Arts, Philadelphia; The Annenberg Foundation; the Robert Montgomery Scott Endowment for Exhibitions; The Women's Committee of the Philadelphia Museum of Art; Alcoa Foundation; Elise Jaffe and Jeffrey Brown; Frances Lewis; Mr. and Mrs. J. Roffe Wike II; and Marion Stroud Swingle.

Initial support was provided by The William Penn Foundation and the Graham Foundation for Advanced Studies in the Fine Arts. Additional funding was provided by Collab: The Group for Modern and Contemporary Design at the Philadelphia Museum of Art.

Produced by the Department of Publishing
Philadelphia Museum of Art
Benjamin Franklin Parkway at 26th Street
P.O. Box 7646
Philadelphia, Pennsylvania 19101-7646

Edited by George H. Marcus with Nicole Amoroso
Production managed by Richard Bonk
Designed by Malcolm Grear Designers, Providence, Rhode Island
Color separations by Professional Graphics Inc., Rockford, Illinois
Printed and bound by Arnoldo Mondadori Editore, S.p.A., Verona, Italy

Library of Congress Cataloging-in-Publication Data:
Out of the ordinary : Robert Venturi, Denise Scott Brown and Associates architecture, Urbanism, design / David B. Brownlee ... [et al.1.]
    p.cm.
Exhibition held at Philadelphia Museum of Art, June 10, 2001 to Aug. 5, 2001, Museum of Contemporary Art, San Diego, June 2, 2002 to Sept. 8, 2002, the Heinz Architectural Center, Carnegie Museum of Art, Pittsburgh, Nov. 7, 2002 to Feb. 3, 2003.
    Includes bibliographical references and index.
    ISBN 0-300-08995-3 (Yale) – ISBN 0-87633-148-7 (pbk.)
1. Venturi Scott Brown and Associates–Exhibitions. 2. Venturi, Robert–Exhibitions. 3. Scott Brown, Denise, 1931—Exhibitions. 4. Architecture—United States–20th century–Exhibitions. 1. Brownlee, David Bruce. II. Venturi, Robert. III. Scott Brown, Denise, 1931- IV. Philadelphia Museum of Art. V. Museum of Contemporary Art, San Diego. VI. Heinz Architectural Center.

NA737.V49 A4 2001
720'.92'9–dc21   2001032146

CONTENTS

vii   Preface

Anne d'Harnoncourt

2   Form and Content

David B. Brownlee

90   Seeking a Rational Mannerism

David G. De Long

182   Decorative Art and Interiors

Kathryn B. Hiesinger

244   Chronology

Diane L. Minnite

253   Project List

William Whitaker

269   Selected Bibliography

270   Acknowledgments

272   Index of Proper Names

PREFACE

This book accompanies an exhibition devoted to the celebrated architects and planners Venturi, Scott Brown, and Associates, who distinguish Philadelphia with their presence here. It is the third in an extended sequence of architecture exhibitions presented by the Philadelphia Museum of Art, beginning with the great nineteenth-century figure Frank Furness in 1973, and moving to Louis I. Kahn in 1991. Now it is a delight to salute Robert Venturi and Denise Scott Brown, two immensely creative and provocative forces in the history of architecture, during their lifetimes. This exhibition also joins a cycle of projects organized by the Museum around the year 2001, celebrating notable Philadelphia contributions to the history of painting, printmaking, and photography as well as architecture, all part of the Museum's celebration of its own 125th anniversary year.

The striking diversity of Venturi, Scott Brown's buildings and projects in Philadelphia, from the unprecedented Vanna Venturi house of 1959–64 to the bold renovation of Irvine Auditorium at the University of Pennsylvania in 2000, enables us to appreciate not only the range of the firm's accomplishments but also the intensity of their focus on both the pleasure and the difficulty inherent in each problem to be solved. The creation of profoundly original form, as in Robert Venturi's design for his mother's house in Chestnut Hill, is coupled with a keen understanding and sympathy for architecture of the past (the Fisher Fine Arts library at Penn so intelligently restored) and always allows for the new idea to preempt the cut-and-dried solution to a problem. For example: how to create a salute to Benjamin Franklin on the site of his long-demolished townhouse without undertaking a reconstruction. In Franklin Court, the firm's contribution to the Bicentennial, a cheerful white "ghost" framework rises amidst what remains of eighteenth-century Philadelphia, in no way disturbing the authenticity of the original structures and elegantly reminding us that Franklin's greatest contributions were in the realm of ideas.

Venturi, Scott Brown's invention of museum spaces, in which works of art and people come together, are among their contributions closest to a museum director's heart. The differences and similarities of their work for the Allen Memorial Art Museum in Oberlin and at the National Gallery, London, spring to mind, although separated by fourteen years and representing very different scales of opportunity. Both are deeply pondered additions to a beloved existing building: Cass Gilbert's Renaissance revival marble museum for an Ohio college town and William Wilkins's grandiose monument at the top of Trafalgar Square. Both new buildings play to and upon their very different contexts with wit, deference, and distinctness. And both provide deeply satisfying circumstances for looking at very different art—the high, clerestory-lit, single volume of space housing adventurous contemporary work near a quiet, tree-lined street and the noble, unfolding luminous galleries for Renaissance painting affording tranquil memories of Italian churches and palaces in the midst of the hurly burly of a great city. To our own Museum's building and planning, the contributions of Venturi, Scott Brown and Associates have included the exhibition design for "Philadelphia: Three Centuries of American Art" (1976), a comprehensive and intelligent master plan (1980) that brought the Museum's European galleries and period rooms into chronological sequence at last, and a striking redecoration of the West Foyer that furnished that formidable cube of space with a new information desk crowned by neon griffins, as well as jaunty, neoclassical benches (1989).

Venturi, Scott Brown's work is so rich in resonance, so imbued with response to the history of architecture on the one hand and twentieth-century popular culture on the other, that their architecture affords ample fare for analysis and debate on many levels. The experience of the buildings themselves—their use of light, their quality of space, their handsome proportions—often receives less attention from writers who focus on other aspects of their work. The cumulative report from those who use their buildings daily, however, is one of pleasure and a sense of needs thoughtfully attended to.

This book, and the exhibition it accompanies, present the architects' drawings to the public in unprecedented quantity. Robert Venturi draws as he thinks, with a bold grace even in his earliest notions for a project that always astonishes. The firm's love of color and feeling for typography infuse their renderings at later stages of a project with vivid character. Drawings in the exhibition range from pencil sketches on yellow-lined paper to formal presentation pieces; some demonstrate the firm's adeptness in the technology of architectural representation, most precociously perhaps, in the famous collage of panchromatic film, ink, pencil, and photographs on vellum produced for the National Collegiate Football Hall of Fame in 1967.

This retrospective exhibition is the result of the hard work and commitment of a team of colleagues devoted to the subject: David Brownlee, Professor of the History of Art, David De Long, Professor of Architecture, both at the University of Pennsylvania, and Kathryn Hiesinger, the Museum's Curator of European Decorative Arts and Design. Together with William Whitaker and Diane Minnite, they worked closely with the architects to select the projects to be included and to choose drawings, renderings, models, and decorative arts from a wealth of possibilities, with a view to presenting the work of the firm and its particular qualities of wit, grace, intelligence, love of ornament, and sensitivity to context. We are especially indebted to Julia Converse, Assistant Dean of the Graduate School of Fine Arts of the University of Pennsylvania, and Director of Penn's Architectural Archives, which plans to house the firm's archive, for her help and interest. William Whitaker, Collections Manager of the Architectural Archives, deserves special mention for heroically coordinating research on site and at the Manayunk office of Venturi, Scott Brown and Associates. Diane Minnite, Research and Collections Assistant in the Museum's Department of European Decorative Arts, coordinated all aspects of the exhibition and catalogue. She undertook the administration of this complex project under the guidance of Kathryn Hiesinger, whose enthusiastic scholarship in the field of twentieth-century design has resulted in so many distinguished exhibitions at the Philadelphia Museum of Art.

Without the financial support of an impressive array of public and private resources, this project could not have been realized. We are grateful to The William Penn Foundation and the Graham Foundation for Advanced Studies in the Fine Arts for their help during the initial research phase, and to the Philadelphia Exhibitions Initiative and The Annenberg Foundation for vital implementation grants. The Women's Committee of the Philadelphia Museum of Art gave generously as they have for so many of the Museum's exhibition and design projects. Additional funding came from the Robert Montgomery Scott Endowment for Exhibitions, and Collab: The Group for Modern and Contemporary Design at the

Philadelphia Museum of Art, and we were also happy to welcome the Alcoa Foundation as a first-time supporter. Marion Stroud Swingle, Museum trustee and longtime fan of the Venturi, Scott Brown firm, has provided wise counsel and generous assistance over the lifetime of this project; she is joined by Frances Lewis, Elise Jaffe and Jeffrey Brown, Mr. and Mrs. J. Roffe Wike II, and Joseph Allen.

The installation of an architecture exhibition is a particularly demanding challenge, and we are grateful to Tony Atkin of Atkin, Olshin, Lawson-Bell and Associates Architects, and his associate Donna Sink, for his thoughtful design of the show. Steven Izenour, longtime principal in the Venturi, Scott Brown firm, provided invaluable advice on all sorts of fronts, and the Museum's team, including Suzanne F. Wells, Coordinator of Special Exhibitions; Jack Schlechter, Installation Designer; Matthew Pimm, Director of Editorial and Graphics; and Diane Gottardi, guest graphic designer, rose to the occasion.

The creation of this book has been the last project undertaken by George H. Marcus before his retirement as Director of Publishing for the Philadelphia Museum of Art, a role he has played with panache for over thirty years. With his devotion to an elegant and appropriate design for each book and his concern for content both lively and scholarly, he has once again produced a handsome volume that makes a substantial contribution to the field. He, the authors, and I are grateful to Malcolm Grear Designers, and to the Museum's photographer, Graydon Wood, for his fine images of the decorative arts, and to Will Brown, who so sensitively photographed most of the drawings. The mix of imagination, dedication to the task, and hard work required to bring off a major exhibition and its catalogue demands much of the partnership between Museum staff and their counterparts outside the institution, and that partnership in this case extended to the subjects of retrospective itself: Denise Scott Brown, Robert Venturi, and so many members of their remarkable firm. We extend our profound and heartfelt thanks to them for their patience, their sharing of information and archives, and above all, for their extraordinary, ongoing contribution to the architecture of our time.

Anne d'Harnoncourt
The George D. Widener Director and Chief Executive Officer

OUT OF THE ORDINARY

Figure 1
Denise Scott Brown and Robert Venturi, c. 1968

FORM AND CONTENT

David B. Brownlee
Professor of the History of Art
University of Pennsylvania

Denise Scott Brown and Robert Venturi (fig. 1) met in 1960 and married in 1967, and during the first twenty years of their collaboration they literally invented the vocabulary with which we describe the "complexity and contradiction"[1] of late-twentieth-century culture. Out of these complexities, they also alloyed the most significant architecture and planning of their time. Venturi and Scott Brown's dual roles as cultural analysts and artists cannot easily be disentangled, nor can the separate contributions of the two artists be distilled. Their partnership has been as multidimensional and integrated as the challenges they have faced.

The world of the 1960s and 1970s, which Venturi and Scott Brown defined, was clouded by war, social unrest, and environmental crisis. But it was also brightened by the rekindling of American idealism and populist vitality. This was the era frozen by the Cold War, but the concomitant space race catapulted mankind to the moon. Americans went abroad to serve in the Peace Corps, but also to fight in Vietnam. The ills of a complacent society festered: Lyndon Johnson inaugurated the War on Poverty and Congress passed the Civil Rights Act, but America's ghettos erupted in riots. John F. Kennedy, Robert Kennedy, and Martin Luther King were assassinated, but not before they had brought to life new notions of public service.

During these decades, architecture and planning were also dislocated—wrenched from the seeming sureties of International Style modernism and propelled into an ill-defined territory. The validity of abstraction and the vitality of technological symbolism were questioned, while history and popular culture grew in influence. Perhaps most seriously, sociologists began to tally the negative societal consequences of modern design, and architects and physical planners were blamed. In 1972, dynamite toppled the International Style towers of the Pruitt-Igoe housing project in Saint Louis, emblematizing the fall of that superannuated species of modernism (fig. 2). Robert Venturi and Denise Scott Brown were among its severest critics.

In architecture, the most easily identified response to this criticism was the rise of a pretty style of historical

[1] Robert Venturi, *Complexity and Contradiction in Architecture* (New York: The Museum of Modern Art, 1966).

revivalism that simply abjured social responsibility and thus eluded the most serious, socially based antimodern arguments. By the mid-seventies, this phenomenon had taken root and was being called "post-modernism,"[2] a label that can only be tangentially associated with the use of the same term for post-structuralist and deconstructionist thinking in other disciplines, notably anthropology, literary studies, art history, and the new fields of women's and gay studies.

Scott Brown and Venturi were post-modernists in the larger, more important sense, notably, in their interpretation of architecture as a language of meaningful signs, in their respect for the judgments of the often ordinary viewer and user, and in their rejection of so-called master narratives of history, which favored certain outcomes and established lists of canonical works of art and literature. Morever, Venturi and Scott Brown never shrank from the social purpose of their work, further distancing them from the post-modernists of the pastel architectural variety—and indeed from most post-modernists. Sociologically astute as well as brilliantly visual, they worked to reconnect architecture and human purpose and place them on a new, more humane footing. As artists had done in other times of disturbing change—the Renaissance and the nineteenth century come to mind, for example—they embraced both the authority of history and the vitality of the real and the visible. The past and the present inspired them.

Riding Two Horses

Born an ocean apart, Robert Venturi and Denise Scott Brown (née Lakofski) came to their partnership already deeply involved in the debate about the future of architecture and with remarkably similar ideals. From their different experiences, however, they brought different but powerfully complementary training and skills. Denise Lakofski was born in Northern Rhodesia (now Zambia) in 1931. Her Jewish parents were the children of Latvian and Lithuanian émigrés. Her father was born in Southern Rhodesia (now Zimbabwe), and her mother had grown up in the unconventional freedom

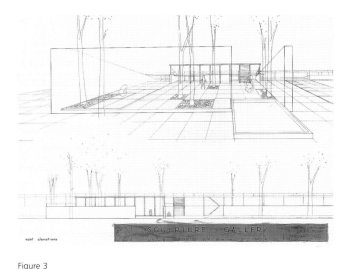

Figure 2
Demolition of the Pruitt-Igoe Housing Project, Saint Louis, 1972

Figure 3
Student Project for the Architectural Association, Sculpture Gallery, Lincoln's Inn Fields, London, 1953–54
East elevation and perspective. Diazo print with colored cut-paper title block, 21½ x 28⅛" (54.6 x 71.4 cm). Denise Lakofski

Collection of Venturi, Scott Brown and Associates, Inc.

[2] The style had just begun to be called "post-modern" when Charles A. Jencks wrote *The Language of Post-Modern Architecture* (New York: Rizzoli, 1977); see his "Footnote on the Term" in the fourth edition (1984) of that book, p. 8.

of the Zambian bush country, where she had dressed as a boy and had hunted. Later she had studied architecture for two years at the University of the Witwatersrand in Johannesburg, South Africa.

The Lakofskis moved to Johannesburg when Denise was two, and there her father prospered as a businessman. He built his family an International Style house with a flat roof, which served as a playground for his daughter.[3] Denise attended private school and took art lessons, and her art teachers encouraged her to study what was around her. The cosmopolitan culture of interwar Johannesburg—African, Afrikaans, and English, and increasingly filled with refugees from European intolerance—offered many subjects, both challenging and reassuring. This experience of cultural and artistic interaction she would later aver opened her eyes "to the vitality and poignance of 'impure' art."[4]

Her mother's example seemed to prove that architecture was women's work, and from the time she was five, Lakofski knew that she, too, would be an architect. She spent her summers working for architects and followed in her mother's footsteps to the University of the Witwatersrand, where she found liberal politics, but only a grudging acceptance of women, and a provincial architectural curriculum with little discussion of contemporary theory. In 1952 she moved to London, first working on housing in the office of the modernist architect Frederick Gibberd and then winning admission to the Architectural Association School, to learn "useful skills in the building of a just South Africa" as well as to find a richer intellectual milieu—and one more accepting of talented women.[5]

The Architectural Association was an exciting, unabashedly modernist place in the early 1950s, although its modernism was tempered by the humanity of the English town planning tradition and by a reviving interest in architectural history—highlighted by the work of John Summerson, the rising star among British architectural historians. Lakofski twice attended Summerson's course of lectures, which introduced her to mannerism, the distinctive, sometimes quirky,

classical architecture of Britain. The so-called New Brutalism was also beginning to make itself felt. Exemplified by Peter and Alison Smithson's rugged steel-framed Hunstanton School in Norfolk (1949–54), its tough, no-nonsense vocabulary was adapted from the latest rough-finished works of Le Corbusier and from the vigorous American buildings of Ludwig Mies van der Rohe. But it was more than a style. The Smithsons also embraced a realistic social vision, predicated, as Scott Brown later recalled, on "community life as it is, and not . . . some sentimentalized version of how it should be."[6] Although the Smithsons did not then teach at the Architectural Association, their philosophy, which they called "active socioplastics," also reached into the school, where Lakofski happily allied herself with "a group of students looking intensely at what was immediately around them—popular culture, the industrial and commercial vernacular, and neighborhood street life."[7]

Training at the Architectural Association retained some of the flavor of pre–World War II modernism, which Lakofski studied under the guidance of Arthur Korn, a German refugee, but her student art-gallery design of 1953–54 seemed to reflect the stylistic enthusiasms of the younger generation, for whom Mies was the hero of the day, combined with a manipulation of spatial sequences based on the temples of ancient Egypt (fig. 3). In her 1954 thesis project, criticized informally by the Smithsons, she and her thesis partner Brian Smith tackled a familiar type of problem (housing in a Welsh mining village) but solved it in an updated modern way with all residences kept close to the ground out of respect for the imagined desires of the inhabitants.

At the end of her studies, Lakofski was joined in London by the architect Robert Scott Brown, whom she had met during their student days at Witwatersrand. They married in 1955, and for three years they traveled and worked together in several leading architectural offices in Europe— including those of Ernö Goldfinger in London and Giuseppe Vaccaro in Rome—and South Africa. Much of

3 Denise Scott Brown, "A Worm's Eye View of Recent Architectural History," *Architectural Record*, vol. 172 (February 1984), p. 79; for her African memories, see also Denise Scott Brown, "Learning from

Africa" (interview by Evelina Francia), *The Zimbabwean Review*, July 1995, pp. 26–29.

4 Scott Brown, "Worm's Eye," p. 77.

5 Scott Brown, "Learning from Africa," p. 28.

6 Denise Scott Brown, "Learning from Brutalism," in David Robbins, ed., *The Independent Group: Postwar Britain and the Aesthetics of Plenty* (Cambridge and London: The MIT Press, 1990), p. 203.

7 Ibid.

the work was housing. The Scott Browns then turned to Peter Smithson for advice about their careers and further training, and he suggested that they go to the University of Pennsylvania in Philadelphia, where Louis Kahn was teaching at the Graduate School of Fine Arts. Kahn had recently burst onto the scene with a pair of strong buildings whose affinities with Brutalist ideals were apparent—the Yale University Art Gallery (1951–53) and the bathhouse of the Trenton Jewish Community Center (1954–55; see fig. 10).

The Scott Browns applied to Penn at the last minute in 1958, and, since there was no time to send the portfolio of drawings required for admission to the architecture department, they applied to the graduate program in land and city planning.[8] For idealistic young African architects, instilled with the idea of "socioplastics," city planning was not an unreasonable course, and it turned out to have enormous consequences for Scott Brown's future work and her partnership with Robert Venturi. Penn's Department of Land and City Planning in the 1950s was shaped by the controlled collision of two great forces, orchestrated by G. Holmes Perkins, dean of the Graduate School of Fine Arts, who had created the department when he arrived at the university in 1951.[9] The first of these forces was the gigantic work of urban renewal then under way in Philadelphia, which erected the office buildings of Penn Center adjacent to City Hall on the site of the former Pennsylvania Railroad station, "liberated" the eighteenth-century civic monuments of Independence National Historical Park from their nineteenth-century commercial setting, and revived Society Hill as a residential neighborhood, with restored eighteenth-century houses and carefully regulated new construction. This enterprise was launched by a series of reform-minded Democratic mayors and energetically and imaginatively executed by the city's planning commission, whose professional staff was led by Edmund Bacon. Bacon was the most effective city planner in the nation and an eloquent spokesman for the planner's ability to use visual thinking to capture public imagination and reshape the human experience. As chair of the planning

commission, Perkins worked with Bacon, and he saw to it that the persuasive physical reality of the new Philadelphia was reflected in what was taught at Penn and that the school's teachers participated in what was being built.

To balance this philosophy, Perkins had recruited from the University of Chicago a team of planners of a very different order, Martin Meyerson, Britton Harris, John Dyckman, and sociologist Herbert Gans, who brought to Penn a deep skepticism about the efficacy of formal design and a commitment to pushing city planning toward the social sciences. Indeed, the German-born Gans moved to Levittown, Pennsylvania, in the late 1950s, to understand better the reality of postwar American life.[10] Here was something akin to the Smithsons' "socioplastics," but now infused with real scholarship, and during their first semester at Penn, Denise and Robert Scott Brown took no studio courses—only housing, economics, statistics, and urban sociology (with Gans). "We didn't know how we could have lived our life till then without all that information," she recalled.[11]

The pattern of studio courses was established in their second semester, when the Scott Browns took David Crane's studio on the replanning of Chandigarh, where Le Corbusier and an international team of architects had only recently completed building a new capital for the Indian state of Punjab. The studio used "Le Corbusier's program but Penn's ideas."[12] What this entailed was a preliminary, interdisciplinary phase of research into the realities of Indian life (heavily weighted in the social sciences) before the design work began. And once pencils were put to paper, most of the attention was directed toward housing and very little toward the monumental buildings on which Le Corbusier had lavished his genius. When finally Scott Brown took a studio with Kahn, in her final semester, she found herself fighting with the great form maker about the appropriate balance between design ideas and social science.[13]

In the midst of this adventure, at the end of their first year at Penn, Robert Scott Brown was killed in an automobile accident, tearing apart the strong synthesis of love, life,

[8] Denise Scott Brown, "Denise Scott Brown," in Lynn Gilbert and Gaylen Moore, eds., *Particular Passions: Talks with Women Who Have Shaped Our Times* (New York: Clarkson N. Potter, 1981), p. 313.

[9] Ann L. Strong, "G. Holmes Perkins, Architect of the School's

Renaissance," in Ann L. Strong and George E. Thomas, *The Book of the School: 100 Years, The Graduate School of Fine Arts of the University of Pennsylvania* (Philadelphia, 1990), pp. 131–49.

[10] See Herbert J. Gans, *The Levittowners: Ways of Life and Politics*

in a New Suburban Community (New York: Pantheon Books, 1967).

[11] Quoted in Gilbert and Moore, *Particular Passions*, p. 313.

[12] Denise Scott Brown, "Between Three Stools: A Personal View of

Urban Design and Pedagogy," in *Education for Urban Design* (Purchase, N.Y.: Institute for Urban Design, 1982), p. 132; excerpted in Strong and Thomas, *The Book of the School*, p. 153.

[13] Scott Brown, "Between Three Stools," p. 140.

and work that had bound the young couple together. Denise Scott Brown completed her degree after another year of study, and, with the support of teachers who had recognized her incandescent intelligence, she was immediately hired as instructor and quickly promoted to assistant professor. She was then just twenty-nine, and she proved herself to be a superb teacher, applying the lessons that she had learned on three continents. She explained, "I lived . . . as a widow in sorrow and specialization. I put everything into teaching."[14]

As a young professor, as she had as a student, Scott Brown found herself at "the nexus between architecture and planning,"[15] right "in the middle between architects and planners, pulled and buffeted."[16] While she taught, the energy of the debate grew, crystallized for many in Jane Jacobs's *Death and Life of Great American Cities* (1961), a spirited attack on the bulldoze-and-rebuild urban-renewal projects created by architects and formal planners who thought visually rather than socially.[17] Scott Brown could sympathize with that position, and her first publication rather gently chided Philadelphia's great urban reshaper, Edmund Bacon, of whose work she wrote: "A 'design idea' can be good and able to be executed only if it is strongly tied to the city-building forces at play in the society."[18] But Scott Brown was also an architect, and while a member of the faculty, she also enrolled in the final studio needed to earn a second master's degree, in architecture. She was now teaching both architecture and city-planning students, trying to give the former an appreciation of the social sciences and the latter a respect for the essential role of physical design in the making of human environments. As Scott Brown would later say, she was "a circus rider trying to keep together the two horses—Architectural Formalism and Social Concern."[19]

In 1960, during Scott Brown's first year of teaching, Robert Venturi introduced himself after a faculty meeting at which she had denounced the idea, then mooted by campus planners, of demolishing Frank Furness's old university library building. Venturi had been too shy to voice his agreement publicly, but he now offered his support. He had been teaching architecture at Penn since 1954—first as Kahn's assistant—but, despite the vigorous debating and cross-departmental studio reviews, their paths had not previously crossed. Scott Brown and Venturi began to sit together at lectures and meetings, forming what he called "a coterie of two,"[20] and she audited the course on architectural theories that he had recently begun teaching. (He also taught regularly in the studio.) Between 1962 and 1964, she ran the theory course's seminars and workshops while he gave the lectures. Out of this first collaboration came Venturi's *Complexity and Contradiction in Architecture*, largely completed in 1962 but not published until 1966.

Nothing Is Fair or Good Alone

Robert Venturi was thirty-five when he met Denise Scott Brown. He had been practicing architecture since 1957, but only some renovation work had been built. Like Scott Brown, he was the child of immigrants. His father's father, a builder, had come in 1890 from Abruzzi to Philadelphia, where he established himself as a produce merchant. His father, who had been nine when the family immigrated, took over the business at sixteen when the elder Venturi died, and he became a prosperous wholesaler, moving to suburban Upper Darby when he married in 1924.

Venturi's maternal grandmother was from Puglia. His American-born mother was, like Scott Brown's, unconventional and powerful. A pacifist and a socialist who became a Quaker and voted for Norman Thomas, she sent her son to a Quaker elementary school and then to the aristocratic Episcopal Academy, not only for the excellence of the education but also to escape the mandatory flag saluting of public schools.

Again like Scott Brown, Venturi knew as soon as he knew almost anything that he wanted to be an architect. His parents shared their abiding interest in furniture, fashion, and architecture with their son, and he played with blocks and drew houses incessantly (fig. 4). His father pointed out

[14] Scott Brown, "An Interview" (interview by Linda Groat), *Networks* (California Institute of the Arts), no. 1 (1972), p. 54.

[15] Scott Brown, "Learning from Brutalism," p. 205.

[16] Scott Brown, "Worm's Eye," p. 75.

[17] Jane Jacobs, *The Death and Life of Great American Cities* (New York: Vintage Books, 1961).

[18] Denise Scott Brown, "Reviews: Form, Design, and the City," *Journal of the American Institute of Planners*, vol. 28 (November 1962), p. 298.

[19] Quoted in Joan Kron, "The Almost-Perfect Life of Denise Scott Brown," *Savvy*, vol. 1 (December 1980), p. 34.

[20] Quoted in Paul Goldberger, "Less Is More—*Mies van der Rohe*: Less Is a Bore—*Robert Venturi*," *New York Times Magazine*, October 17, 1971, p. 37.

Figure 4
House, c. 1930
Drawing. Crayon on construction
paper, detail. Robert Venturi
Collection of Venturi, Scott Brown
and Associates, Inc.

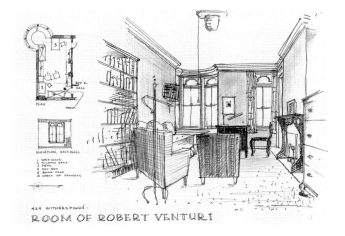

Figure 5
**Room at 424 Witherspoon Hall,
Princeton University, c. 1945**
Perspective, plan, and elevation. Pencil
on paper, 11 x 15" (27.9 x 38.1 cm)
Robert Venturi
Collection of Venturi, Scott Brown
and Associates, Inc.

Figure 6
**Half-way Cabin, Junior Sketch
Problem 1, Princeton University,
1945**
Aerial perspective, plan, and section
Ink, pencil, and gouache on board,
22 x 30" (55.9 x 76.2 cm). Robert
Venturi. Signed and dated December
18, 1945

Collection of Venturi, Scott Brown
and Associates, Inc.

buildings as they drove through Philadelphia, and Venturi remembered "the loathing and condescension" that the peculiarities of Furness's designs initially inspired in him, when he was still "an intolerant Colonial Revivalist, who doodled dream house plans on the backs of school books."[21] On Venturi's first trip to New York, his father impulsively ordered the cabdriver to stop outside McKim, Mead & White's Pennsylvania Station, so that he could show his son its imperial interior.[22] One high school summer was spent working for Ballinger Corporation, one of the largest local architectural firms.

Venturi went to Princeton, earning election to Phi Beta Kappa and his bachelor's in architecture, *summa cum laude*, in 1947. He continued his studies and received his master's of fine arts in 1950. While an undergraduate, Venturi lived in Witherspoon Hall, ultimately occupying a turreted corner room, which he selected for its architectural distinction (fig. 5). Down the hall lived Philip Finkelpearl, who later became a professor of English at Wellesley College and has been Venturi's lifelong friend. Surrounded by Princeton's beauty and comfort, he recalled rhapsodically, "I walked on air as I could discover multitudes of things within many disciplines hitherto not dreamt of in my philosophy."[23] In fact, notwithstanding its remoteness from the strenuous world of the 1940s, Princeton afforded Venturi, the Quaker produce-merchant's son, a continuing lesson in diversity.

Venturi's Princeton was notable for having resisted the modernizing trend in American architectural education, epitomized by Walter Gropius's transformation of Harvard into an American Bauhaus. Princeton's studios were still organized in the Beaux-Arts manner and overseen by Jean Labatut, trained in Paris in Victor Laloux's atelier. However, Labatut, who had started at Princeton in 1928, emphasized the problem-solving aspect of the Beaux-Arts system and never dictated the style of a building.[24] Indeed, Venturi's undergraduate and graduate projects were fluently modernist, with diagonally energized plans and rakish, single-pitched roofs (fig. 6), and until the early 1950s, his stylistic

21 Robert Venturi, "A Reaction to Complexity and Contradiction in the Work of Furness," *Pennsylvania Academy of the Fine Arts Newsletter*, Spring 1976, p. 5.

22 Robert Venturi, "Robert Venturi's Response at the Pritzker Prize Award Ceremony at the Palacio de Iturbide, Mexico City, May 16, 1991," in *Iconography and Electronics upon a Generic Architecture: A View from the Drafting Room* (Cambridge and London: The MIT Press, 1996), p. 98.

23 Ibid., p. 99.

predilection was for Frank Lloyd Wright, whom he had met when the architect visited the university in connection with the celebration of its bicentennial in 1947.[25]

Complementing Labatut's intelligent eclecticism was a rigorous curriculum in art and architectural history—the sort of thing that was being abandoned at more modern institutions. Professor Donald Drew Egbert taught the course in modern architecture undogmatically, enriching the story with a variety of unconventional detail and placing architectural history in the context of social and political forces. Egbert became Venturi's mentor, and thirty years later the architect reminisced:

> I took Donald Drew Egbert's course on the History of Modern Architecture four times. I sat in on it as a freshman, was the slide projectionist as a sophomore, took it for credit as a junior, and taught in it as a graduate student teaching assistant. Other architecture students at Princeton over several decades were also drawn to it, became devotés [sic], and were influenced by it. What attracted us was . . . his lack of jargon, the clarity and elegance of his plain talk, and the balance and common sense of his approach. . . .

> Egbert saw Modern architecture as a part of the complex of nineteenth- and twentieth-century civilization and his eyes were open to realities of that time that more doctrinaire historians, bent on proving points, couldn't see. For Egbert the influence of the Ecole des Beaux-Arts, for instance, was an important part of the complicated architectural history of the nineteenth and twentieth centuries. . . . Egbert's history of Modern architecture was inclusive—a complex evolution rather than a dramatic revolution made up of social and symbolic as well as formal and technological imperatives.[26]

In 1948, after a year of graduate study, Venturi traveled to Europe for the first time, and he took with him his Princetonian openness to a variety of inspirations. He toured through England (admiring the baroque architects John Vanbrugh and Nicholas Hawksmoor) and traversed France (sneaking in to see Le Corbusier's Villa Savoye), but the climax of his explorations began when he reached Rome, inaugurating a lifelong love affair with that city of baroque space, almost infinite layerings of history, and all of the varieties of classical architecture.

In 1950, at the end of his final year of graduate study, Venturi submitted his master's thesis, "Context in Architectural Composition." It was both the explication of a theoretical position and the presentation of a design for a new chapel for his alma mater, Episcopal Academy, and across the faces of more than two dozen sheets, he made his argument and presented his proposal. He began by explaining that his purpose was "to demonstrate the importance of, and the effect of setting on a building," and he laid out his twin premises: "Its context gives a building expression, its meaning" and "Change of context causes change in expression."[27] Venturi's interest in this subject derived from his frustration with student design assignments in which the setting was not described, and from the great satisfaction he derived from studying European buildings in their context in the summer of 1948. As a kind of motto, he quoted a passage from Ralph Waldo Emerson's "Each and All," which his mother had recommended, ending with the lines "All are needed by each one; Nothing is fair or good alone."[28]

The exemplars that Venturi attached to his argument came from two sources: the public monuments of Rome (which he just visited) and domestic American architecture—both subjects that would continue to hold his attention. From Rome, he chose to explicate the siting of the Trevi fountain (compared to the Saint Michel fountain in Paris), the Piazza S. Ignazio, the church of SS. Trinità and its relationship to the Spanish Steps, the Campidoglio (before and after Michelangelo, and before and after the Victor Emmanuel monument), and the Pantheon (compared to McKim, Mead & White's Girard Bank in Philadelphia and Thomas Jefferson's library at the University of Virginia). From American domestic architecture he selected Frank Lloyd Wright's Wingspread house for Herbert F. Johnson in Racine, Wisconsin (noting that his

[24] David Van Zanten, "The 'Princeton System' and the Founding of the School of Architecture, 1915–20," in Christopher Mead, ed., *The Architecture of Robert Venturi* (Albuquerque: University of New Mexico Press, 1989), pp. 40–42.

[25] Robert Venturi, "Frank Lloyd Wright Essay for the Pennsylvania Academy of the Fine Arts [1991]," in *Iconography and Electronics*, pp. 67–69.

[26] Robert Venturi, "Donald Drew Egbert—A Tribute," in Donald Drew Egbert, *The Beaux-Arts Tradition in French Architecture*, ed. David Van Zanten (Princeton: Princeton University Press, 1980), p. xiii.

[27] Robert Venturi, "Context in Architectural Composition: M.F.A. Thesis, Princeton University [1950]," in *Iconography and Electronics*, figs. 73–77 (Graphic presentation of M.F.A. thesis).

[28] Quoted in ibid., p. 344.

interest in context could be related to Wright's notions of the "organic"); the Federal-era Simpson-Hoffman house on Chestnut Street in Salem, Massachusetts; the International Style Koch house (designed by Carl Koch for his parents) in Belmont, Massachusetts; and Walter Gropius and Marcel Breuer's Aluminum City Terrace workers housing, built during World War II near Pittsburgh and compared to the Runtung housing estate, a Nazi-era development in Leipzig.

Venturi's thesis modestly foreshadowed the thinking that he would later wield against the architectural status quo. Its argument, which made some reference to Gestalt psychology, consisted chiefly of visual analysis applied to historical examples—a well-established methodology learned in hundreds of hours in art and architectural history classes. While this history-based approach was old-fashioned, now that modernism's antihistoricist rhetoric was well established, it sounded almost radical. Moreover, Venturi's celebration of context was at least by implication an attack on the International Style's proud commitment to universal architecture, unfettered by time and place.[29] Philip Johnson would make a similarly prescient presentation of his famous Glass House, full of historical comparisons, later that year.[30]

In light of the breadth of his later attack on the architectural status quo, it is important to note that the contextual issues treated in Venturi's thesis were only visual, and that it discussed meaning only as the product of physical conditions—form and placement. In this commitment to the analysis of the physical and visual, it maintained a footing within modernism, which Venturi would never abandon entirely. It would not be until his later collaboration with Denise Scott Brown that he extended his exploration of meaning beyond formalism and into the world of symbols and associations.

The proposed chapel for Episcopal Academy, with which he concluded his thesis, suspended a complex wood-trussed roof between windowless stone walls and brought indirect light onto the walls of the sanctuary through clerestories set in the outward slopes of the roof's two valleys (figs. 7, 8). The vocabulary of rough stone and the sculptural, although largely hidden, roof was vaguely Wrightian. Avowing that he had learned how to locate the building from his study of architectural context throughout history, Venturi posed the chapel and an adjacent memorial garden with studied casualness between the two late-nineteenth-century country houses that were the school's principal monuments. Episcopal Academy had recently adopted a plan to build a colonial revival chapel between the two houses, its facade aligned with theirs, and he offered this siting as a counterproposal. The school's design, he argued, would fail to create an architectural whole out of these disparate parts.

Venturi's thesis jury included Louis Kahn, whom he had met in the summer of 1947 while working in the building where Kahn had his office, and George Howe, senior statesman among American modernists and newly appointed chair of architecture at Yale, where Kahn was then teaching. Kahn was impressed by Venturi, and after graduation Venturi went to work for Oscar Stonorov, Kahn's former partner. He assisted Stonorov in the selection, design, and installation of the great Frank Lloyd Wright exhibition of 1951–54 that came to Gimbel's department store in Philadelphia. He never forgot the thrill of handling Wright's drawings of Falling Water. After a year, with Kahn's warm support, Venturi moved to Eero Saarinen's busy office in Bloomfield Hills, Michigan, where he spent two years in the company of Kevin Roche and Gunnar Birkerts. Venturi worked on the General Motors Technical Center and Milwaukee War Memorial Auditorium, although he never adopted as his own the modified Miesian and sculptural-concrete vocabularies that Saarinen employed—with his characteristic ambidexterity—for those projects.

Venturi came home to Philadelphia, where he faced a crisis in the family business. For eighteen months he took over from his ailing father and restored the firm to health. He became the company president after his father's death

[29] It must be observed that Le Corbusier himself skillfully used the visual analysis of ancient, medieval, and Renaissance architecture in arguing for abstraction in the 1920s. Moreover, Venturi's celebration of context began as a criticism not of the International Style but of the studio problems set at Princeton.

[30] Philip Johnson, "House at New Canaan, Connecticut," *The Architectural Review*, vol. 108 (September 1950), pp. 152–59.

Figure 7

Chapel for Episcopal Academy, Merion, Pennsylvania, Context in Architectural Composition: M.F.A. Thesis, Princeton University, 1950

Site plan. Ink on board, 29⅞ x 30½" (75.9 x 77.5 cm). Robert Venturi Signed and dated February 1950

Collection of Venturi, Scott Brown and Associates, Inc.

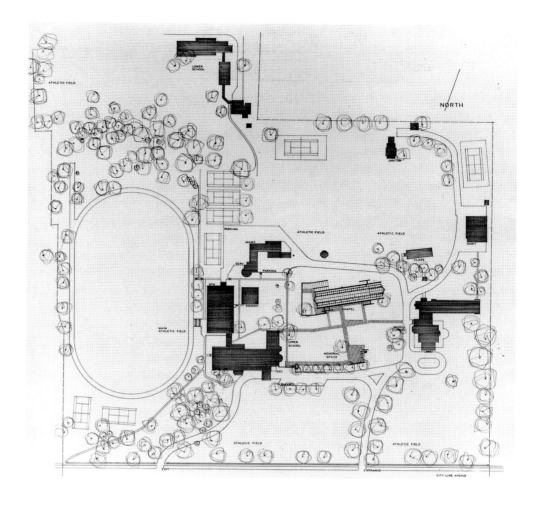

Figure 8

Chapel for Episcopal Academy, Merion, Pennsylvania, Context in Architectural Composition: M.F.A. Thesis, Princeton University, 1950

East perspective. Ink on board, detail. Robert Venturi. Signed and dated February 1950

Collection of Venturi, Scott Brown and Associates, Inc.

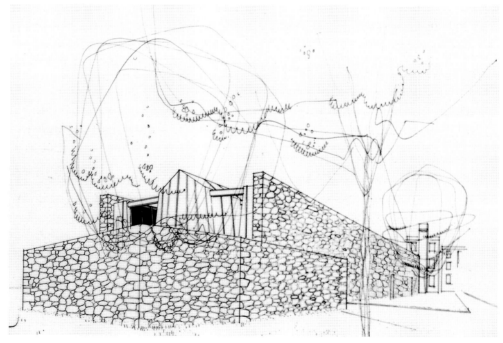

in 1959, and he continued to run the business at 1430 South Street until 1973. This practical business experience is an unacknowledged component of his later enthusiasm for the vernacular architecture of commerce and his sympathy for working people.

While running the business, Venturi also began to work part-time for Kahn and to teach at Penn as his assistant. He was thus engaged when, in February 1954, on his third try in three years, he won a Rome Prize Fellowship to the American Academy in Rome. (Kahn had written supporting letters before; that year he was on the jury.) Leaving the business in the hands of his cousins, Venturi left in October and spent the next two years in Italy. He continued the exploration that he had begun in 1948, but he significantly expanded its scope and the depth of his understanding. Already a confirmed eclectic, he immersed himself increasingly in all the varieties of Roman architecture—ancient to modern. His thesis research on Roman piazzas had made him aware of Armando Brasini (1880–1965), one of the classicists in Mussolini's stable of architects, and he now visited Brasini's buildings and met the architect himself— adopting a studious objectivity toward unfashionable subjects that he would carry with him for the rest of his career. Brasini's unfinished church of Il Cuore Immacolato di Maria Santissima (1931–38, work resumed 1950–54) in the Piazza Euclide fascinated him with its warring circular and Greek-cross plans.[31] Even more consequential for Venturi was Brasini's agriculture and forestry building for the Esposizione Universale di Roma (1940–42, now demolished), whose fragmentary, unfinished facade of layered arcades suggested a way to define space without contorting walls into sculptural shapes (fig. 9).

The second and third editions of Sigfried Giedion's *Space, Time and Architecture* were now available, and their enlarged argument about the baroque roots of modern space conceptions led Venturi to examine the familiar piazzas with new attentiveness. His inclination toward spatial analysis was shaped, too, by his appreciation of the energy

Figure 9
Armando Brasini, Agriculture and Forestry Building for the Esposizione Universale di Roma, Rome, 1940–42
Model. Photograph of lost original

Figure 10
Louis I. Kahn, Bathhouse, Jewish Community Center, Ewing Township, New Jersey, 1954–55
Central courtyard

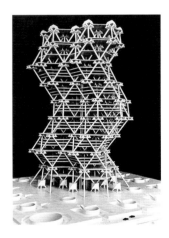

Figure 11
Louis I. Kahn, City Tower, Philadelphia, 1952–57
Model

---

[31] See Robert Venturi, "Armando Brasini Revisited [1993]," in *Iconography and Electronics*, pp. 59–61.

of abstract expressionism, bringing now, as he would later, an understanding of contemporary trends in painting to his architectural reflections. Space was also the hero in Vincent Scully's *Shingle Style* (1955), which Venturi read with avid interest while in Rome. Scully, who would become Venturi's firmest supporter and advocate, traced the origins of Frank Lloyd Wright's open planning to the late-Victorian architecture that he christened the "shingle style," along the way illustrating a cornucopia of engaging house forms and ingenious plans.

By far the most consequential discovery of Venturi's Roman sojourn, however, was mannerism. The visually imbalanced and apparently anxious art of the period between the High Renaissance and the baroque. This was a relatively new concept, having only been clearly defined by Walter Friedlaender in 1925—in German.[32] Venturi had first heard of it in undergraduate art history classes, and in 1946 Nikolaus Pevsner had explicated the matter in architectural terms with a brilliant essay.[33] Only in Rome, however, did he begin to see mannerism in a favorable light, guided by Philip Finkelpearl, who had studied this phenomenon in British literature during his graduate work at Harvard.[34] Venturi maintained that he only began looking at mannerist architecture during the last weeks of his fellowship, but it was an interest that he took home with him and never abandoned.[35]

Back home in August 1956, Venturi did what may have seemed almost inevitable for a bright Philadelphia architect—he resumed working for Louis Kahn. Over the next seven months, he contributed to a number of important projects, and he also rejoined Kahn in teaching at the University of Pennsylvania, where he would remain a member of the faculty until 1965. His warm relationship with Kahn continued into the 1960s, although his natural sensitivity about Kahn's appropriation of ideas from all of his associates led to later tension. In any case, at Penn and in Kahn's office, Venturi now found himself at the very center of the American reconsideration of architectural modernism—a position very comparable to that of Denise Scott Brown in her circle of friends from the Architectural Association and with the Smithsons.

Kahn's work in the mid-fifties was devoted to two simultaneous experiments with new architectural ideas, with the common aim of replacing the complacent picturesque of the now-commercialized International Style with something more principled and rewarding. One line of attack focused on reestablishing the preeminence in architectural planning of distinct rooms—each with its own function, structure, and light—to counter the drift toward the unstructured "openness" of contemporary design. The four separately roofed chambers of Kahn's bathhouse for the Trenton Jewish Community Center, built in 1955, epitomized his philosophy that "architecture comes from the making of a room" (fig. 10).[36] When Venturi joined Kahn, the older architect was working out this paradigm at a larger scale in designing the Research Institute for Advanced Science, a Baltimore-area think tank, for which Venturi prepared drawings.

Kahn's other line of investigation lay in structure, where, inspired by his collaborator Anne Tyng, he believed that an entirely consistent system of constructional order could banish willfulness and faddism. Investigation of polyhedral structures culminated in his great City Tower skyscraper project, and during Venturi's time in the office an enormous model of the tower was constructed (fig. 11). Venturi was responsible for many drawings during this phase of the project, in which every aspect of design—including floor spacing, window placement, and room division—was made subservient to the logic of construction.

From the Outside In and the Inside Out

Robert Venturi left Kahn's office in 1957 to launch his independent career, and after working a little with Mather Lippincott (whom he had met in Stonorov's office), in 1958 he established an association with Lippincott and his partner Paul Cope. Venturi's first works echoed Kahnian forms, but almost immediately, he established an independent position

[32] Walter Friedlaender, "Die Entstehung des antiklassischen Stiles in der italienischen Malerei um 1520," *Repertorium für Kunstwissenschaft*, vol. 46 (1925), pp. 49–86.

[33] Nikolaus Pevsner, "The Architecture of Mannerism," in Geoffrey Grigson, ed., *The Mint: A Miscellany of Literature, Art and Criticism* (London: Routledge and Sons, 1946), pp. 116–37.

[34] Scott Brown, "Worm's Eye," p. 77.

[35] Robert Venturi, "Notes for a Lecture Celebrating the Centennial of the American Academy in Rome Delivered in Chicago [1993]," in *Iconography and Electronics*, p. 53.

[36] Inscription on a drawing from 1971; in David B. Brownlee and David G. De Long, *Louis I. Kahn: In the Realm of Architecture* (Los Angeles: The Museum of Contemporary Art; New York: Rizzoli, 1991), fig. 215.

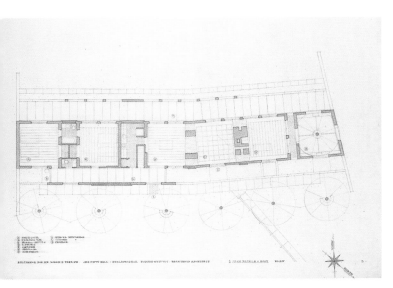

Figure 12
Pearson House, Philadelphia, 1957
Plan. Pencil and colored pencil on
vellum, 29 x 36" (73.6 x 91.4 cm)
Robert Venturi

Collection of Venturi, Scott Brown
and Associates, Inc.

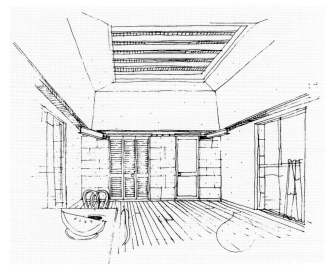

Figure 13
Pearson House, Philadelphia, 1957
Interior perspective. Robert Venturi
Whereabouts unknown

among the younger architects around Kahn whose critique of modernism would be labeled the "Philadelphia School."[37] As he and Scott Brown have pointed out, influences began to flow in both directions, from Kahn to Venturi and back.[38]

The large, unbuilt Pearson house (1957), which Venturi designed for a site in Philadelphia's in-city suburb of Chestnut Hill, was a bold beginning (figs. 12, 13). Big-boned and monumental, as were even Kahn's smallest buildings, it lined up five mighty Kahnian "rooms" railroad-car fashion, slightly bent between the second and third units and coupled by smaller rooms that Venturi called "servant spaces," adopting Kahn's own vocabulary for these spoilers of the open plan.[39] Kahn had for some years experimented with picturesque compositional strategies for such multipavilion designs, before asserting axial discipline with the Greek-cross plan of the Trenton bathhouse. Venturi took the experiment in another direction, adopting the linear scheme that Philadelphia architect Wilson Eyre had used in some of his seashore and suburban houses of the 1880s, illustrated in Scully's *Shingle Style*. But unlike Eyre's houses, the Pearson design's enfilade of great rooms ran between two long exterior screen walls, defining a corridor on one side and an open terrace on the other, where the house faced the quasi wilderness of the Wissahickon valley in Fairmount Park. Here was a layering of space such as Venturi had seen in Armando Brasini's agriculture and forestry building. Kahn would adopt this idea over the next few years as his own, using it in the double-skinned designs for warm climates that, he said, looked as though they were made by "wrapping ruins around buildings."[40]

With three other early commissions, Venturi showed even greater originality. In preparing the new home of the Institute of Fine Arts of New York University (1958–59), he chose to treat the interiors of Horace Trumbauer's Duke mansion, designed in 1912, with a degree of respect that was then unheard of for a monument of the early twentieth century. The projection equipment needed for classroom instruction was suspended in the ornate rooms without

[37] Jan C. Rowan, "Wanting To Be: The Philadelphia School," *Progressive Architecture*, vol. 42 (April 1961), pp. 130–63.

[38] See Scott Brown, "Worm's Eye," p. 73; and Robert Venturi, "Louis Kahn Remembered: Notes from a Lecture at the Opening of the Kahn Exhibition in Japan, January 1993," in *Iconography and Electronics*, p. 91.

[39] Venturi, *Complexity and Contradiction*, p. 104; Robert Venturi, "Program and Solution [Pearson House], September 2, 1958," VSB box 500 (Venturi, Scott Brown and Associates, Inc.; hereafter VSBA archives).

[40] Quoted in "Kahn," *Perspecta*, vol. 7 (1961), p. 9.

Figure 14

Fairhill Square, Philadelphia, 1958–59

Perspective of maintenance building. Pencil
and colored pencil on vellum, 16¾ x 21½"
(42.5 x 54.6 cm). Robert Venturi

Architectural Archives, University of
Pennsylvania, George E. Patton Collection

Figure 15
Beach House, New Jersey, 1959
Model. Cardboard and wood, 11¼ x 14¾ x 9½"
(28.6 x 37.5 x 24.1 cm)
The Museum of Modern Art, New York. Gift of Venturi, Rauch and Scott Brown, Inc.

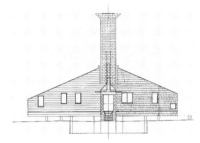

Figure 16
Beach House, New Jersey, 1959
Front elevation. Robert Venturi. Signed and dated December 22, 1959
Whereabouts unknown

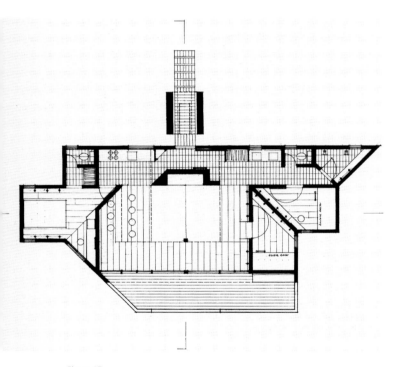

Figure 17
Beach House, New Jersey, 1959
Plan. Robert Venturi
Whereabouts unknown

harming their paneling and plasterwork, freestanding display panels and cases were simply installed in the unaltered entrance hall, and special brackets and footings kept the extensive system of steel book shelving off the walls and protected the floors. Throughout, the new was kept discretely and respectfully apart from the old. "Our technique" Venturi explained, "was to create harmony through contrast rather than similarity."[41]

At the same time, Venturi was sketching several whimsical alternative designs for a little maintenance building in Fairhill Square (1958–59) next to St. Christopher's Hospital for Children in Philadelphia (fig. 14). These tiny, lovingly drawn castles and cottages, sadly unexecuted, inaugurate an unbroken stream of such miniature *jeux d'esprit* within his oeuvre, entirely independent of Kahn's usually solemn example.

In their explicit historical referencing, the Fairhill Square designs also diverged from Kahn's practice, and this was a tack that Venturi took with increasing confidence and ever-increasing variety. Late in 1959, inspired by a possible commission from Thomas Fleming for a ski lodge, he designed another kind of vacation retreat, an ideal beach house to be set on the dunes of the Jersey shore, overlooking the Atlantic (figs. 15–17). As a boy, he had vacationed with his parents at Ocean City and Beach Haven, and seaside architecture would exercise an enduring hold on his imagination. The tall chimney of the beach house recalled that of the Pearson house, but the design vocabulary, while big-scaled, was no longer Kahn's. Instead, the tight skin of cedar shingles and the subsummation of all features beneath a single great roof overtly acknowledged the grand houses of Scully's *Shingle Style*, especially McKim, Mead & White's Low house in Bristol, Rhode Island (1887; fig. 18). But that was not the only historical reference: perched on pilings, with cars parked beneath, the beach house also bowed toward Le Corbusier's great Villa Savoye at Poissy-sur-Seine (1929–31), lofted on *pilotis*, or pillars, above its garage and vestibule.

[41] Robert Venturi, "Architect's Notes on the Renovations to the James B. Duke House," VSB box 500 (VSBA archives).

The cedar envelope of the beach house was perforated by all manner of openings, including a large belvedere, recessed in the roof on the seaward side. On its dune-top site, it faced two different environments, which helped to establish the markedly different character of the two facades: formal, private, and sparingly windowed on the inland side, and informal and extroverted as it faced the ocean, with sliding glass doors opening onto a large porch. This response to the character of the site was essential, Venturi proposed, extending the argument about context from his master's thesis. He rejected the mantra of modernists of all stripes that "honest" design had to proceed from the inside outward, and in his first published discussion of his own work, he explained: "I tend to design from the outside in as well as the inside out; the necessary tensions help make architecture."[42] If the conflict between different outside requirements and between inside and outside created complex, spatially layered facades, so much the better. With words that would be refined and amplified in subsequent writings, Venturi asserted: "The wants of a program, even with small buildings with simple materials, are diverse and conflicting. I welcome this. The building must do and be many things at once; tensions, ambiguities, and contrasts are results which make architecture; a work of architecture has subplots as well as a plot."[43]

The planning of the beach house, whose faceted exterior was projected inward by 45-degree walls, owed its character to Venturi's continued interchange with Kahn. In the first half of 1959 Kahn had designed the Goldenberg house, inventing the reentrant corner splays and diagonal internal walls that would be a signature feature of the Philadelphia School (fig. 19).[44] By splitting the corners open, Kahn boldly solved the famous "corner problem" of architecture, which had bedeviled the classicists of antiquity as they had sought to wrap the classical orders around buildings, and which had predisposed modernists toward dissolving corners with glass.[45] This hallmark of the Philadelphia School devolved into a meaningless stylistic wrinkle in lesser hands, but

Figure 18
McKim, Mead & White, Low House, Bristol, Rhode Island, 1887
Garden facade

Figure 19
Louis I. Kahn, Goldenberg House, Rydal, Pennsylvania, 1959
Plan. Pencil on vellum, 36¼ x 31"
(92.1 x 78.7 cm)
Louis I. Kahn Collection, University of Pennsylvania and the Pennsylvania Historical and Museum Commission

[42] Quoted in Rowan, "Wanting To Be," p. 154.

[43] Ibid., p. 157.

[44] See Brownlee and De Long, *Louis I. Kahn*, pp. 66–67.

[45] David B. Brownlee, "Turning a Corner with Louis I. Kahn," in Wolfgang Böhm, ed., *The Building and the Town: Essays for Eduard F. Sekler* (Vienna, Cologne, and Weimar: Böhlau Verlag, 1994), pp. 48–58.

Figure 20
**Foulkeways, Gwynedd Valley,
Pennsylvania, 1959–60**
Model. Photograph of lost original

Venturi comprehended the impulse "to make a series of spaces that go around the corners of the building continuously," and he identified the "exceptional diagonal" as another attractive variety of architectural complexity.[46] Judiciously employed, such contrasts were not disunifying; in the beach house, he argued, the "awkwardness of an insignificant part reinforces the meaning of the whole."[47]

Diagonals abound in two other Venturi designs of 1959. For Foulkeways, a retirement community designed for Quaker clients, he gathered seven clusters of apartments around cul-de-sacs, canting the end rooms in each block at a 45-degree angle to heighten the sense of enclosure and mark the entrance (fig. 20). The street-facing facades adopted the same silhouette as that of the beach house, a gable, topped by a tall chimney.

In the summer of 1959, Venturi began to design a house for his parents, who had acquired a lot in Chestnut Hill.[48] His first scheme compressed the Pearson plan into a square of six Kahnian rooms, framed on two sides by freestanding screen walls (figs. 21, 22). But he almost immediately cropped two of the corners and pieced the others with diagonals like those of Kahn's very recent Goldenberg house project, and it was apparently this revised design that he described to Kahn as "a great improvement" in September (fig. 23).[49] Following his father's death in December 1959, Venturi continued the project for his mother, experimenting with this species of plan for most of the house's long, three-year gestation period.

Closely related to these designs of 1959 was the small office building that Venturi built for the North Penn Visiting Nurses Association in Ambler, Pennsylvania, in 1961–63, where a jaunty diagonal extended the corner to greet the visitor and signal the way to the side entrance (figs. 24, 25). Oversized elements made the tiny building seem monumental, with a vocabulary and scaling that deserves some comparison with Kahn's Esherick house (1959–61), recently completed on a site near that selected by Venturi's mother. He layered the street elevation by pulling the upper windows behind the wall plane, and he applied decoration—

[46] Venturi, *Complexity and Contradiction*, p. 58.

[47] Robert Venturi, "Some Reasons for the Pointed Ends in the Gwynedd Project and the Beach House Project, December 22, 1966," VSB box 500 (VSBA archives).

[48] See Frederic Schwartz, ed., *Mother's House: The Evolution of Vanna Venturi's House in Chestnut Hill* (New York: Rizzoli, 1992); Alice T. Friedman, *Women and the Making of the Modern House: A Social and Architectural History* (New York: Harry N. Abrams, 1998),

pp. 188–213. My analysis of this design was aided by the research paper written by Rolando Corpus at the University of Pennsylvania, December 1998.

[49] Robert Venturi to Louis I. Kahn, September 21, 1959, "Venturi, Bob,"

box LIK 59, Louis I. Kahn Collection, University of Pennsylvania, and Pennsylvania Historical and Museum Commission (hereafter Kahn Collection). I am indebted to William Whitaker for this reference.

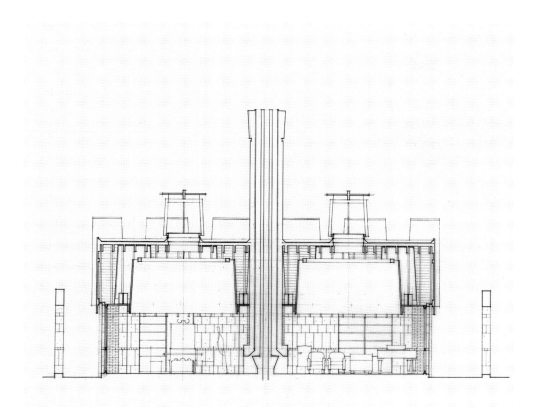

Figure 21
**Vanna Venturi House,
Philadelphia, 1959–64**

Section. Pencil on vellum, 22¼ x 30½"
(54 x 77.5 cm). Robert Venturi. Dated
c. July 1959

Collection of Venturi, Scott Brown
and Associates, Inc.

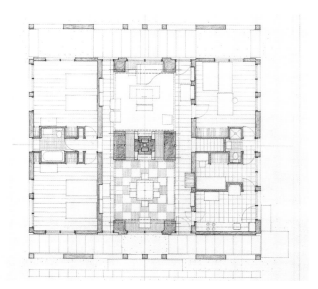

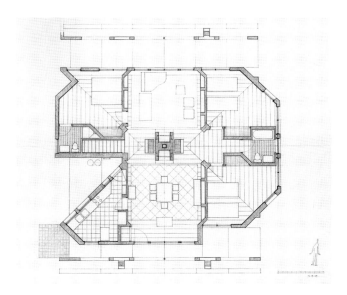

Figure 22
**Vanna Venturi House,
Philadelphia, 1959–64**

First-floor plan. Pencil and colored
pencil on vellum, 23⅜ x 21½"
(59.4 x 54.6 cm). Robert Venturi
Dated c. July 1959

Collection of Venturi, Scott Brown
and Associates, Inc.

Figure 23
**Vanna Venturi House,
Philadelphia, 1959–64**

First-floor plan. Pencil on vellum,
24¾ x 30¼" (62.9 x 76.8 cm). Robert
Venturi. Dated July 19, 1959

Collection of Venturi, Scott Brown
and Associates, Inc.

Figure 24
Headquarters and Clinic, North Penn Visiting Nurses Association, Ambler, Pennsylvania, 1961–63
Front and side facades

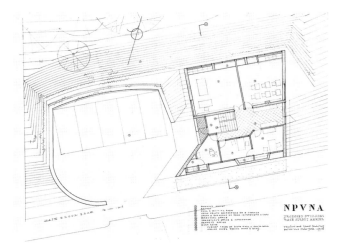

Figure 25
Headquarters and Clinic, North Penn Visiting Nurses Association, Ambler, Pennsylvania, 1961–63
Main-floor plan. Pencil on vellum, 24 x 36" (61 x 91.4 cm). Robert Venturi. Dated October 31, 1961
Collection of Venturi, Scott Brown and Associates, Inc.

moldings around the half basement windows and a giant arch over the small door—with heart-stopping disregard for the antidecorative ethos of modernism. A notice in *Architectural Forum* understandably ended with the question "Where does this kind of architecture go from here?"[50]

Complexity and Contradiction

By 1960, Robert Venturi was already a major contributor to the revision of modernism that centered on Louis Kahn. He had absorbed Kahn's notions of monumental scaling, room-based planning, and diagonal dissolution, and he had amalgamated these with the elements of his own personal style: explicit historical allusion, a rapt attentiveness to context, and the conception of the building perimeter as a layered zone in which interior and exterior forces achieved a complex spatial balance. As impressive as these accomplishments were—and as vital as they were to the conception of the Philadelphia School—in essence they only extended the formalist, design-centered critique of modernism that could be said to have started decades earlier. Vitally important to Venturi's further development as an artist, and central to the work created in collaboration with Denise Scott Brown, was the addition of a social dimension to this critique.[51]

In 1960, Venturi formed an architectural partnership with William H. Short, whom he first met when they were both graduate students at Princeton, and they set up an office in a row house at 333 South 16th Street in Philadelphia. John Rauch, who had been working for Cope and Lippincott since graduating from Penn in 1957, joined them. Even before this new partnership was in place, Venturi turned to Rauch for help with his entry in the competition for a national memorial dedicated to Franklin Delano Roosevelt. The site was between the Potomac River and the Tidal Basin in West Potomac Park, and although little attention was paid to the competition at the time—and nothing was built on the site for another forty years—Venturi's mention-winning design began to evince a new set of concerns. Created in collaboration with landscape architect George

[50] "Building in the News: Pennsylvania Clinic," *Architectural Forum*, vol. 119 (October 1963), p. 16.

[51] For Scott Brown's own analysis of the meeting of these two strains of architectural reformism, which she identifies as the New Brutalism and "An American Group" (that is, the Philadelphia School), see Denise Scott Brown, "Review Article: Team 10, Perspecta 10, and the Present State of Architectural Theory," *Journal of the American Institute of Planners*, vol. 33 (January 1967), pp. 42–50.

Patton and engineer Nicholas Gianopulos, the entry prefigured the large-scale earth sculptures and the environmental architecture of the next decade (fig. 26). It was, Venturi said, "several . . . things at once": for pedestrians, a marble promenade next to the river; for drivers, a roadway within "canyon-like walls" where cars could be parked out of sight; and for picnickers, a quiet spot on the edge of the Tidal Basin, framed by a protective grassy bank.[52]

Most notable for the future trajectory of Venturi's work was the giant text that he proposed to inscribe on the inclined, Potomac side of the marble wall that divided the parking area from the promenade. Consisting of quotations from Roosevelt's speeches and a catalogue of his achievements, this huge inscription immediately aligned Venturi, an inveterate doodler of letters and numbers, with contemporary artistic experiments with typography—like that which Jasper Johns had begun to conduct in the late fifties—and with the large-scale rhetoric of modern advertising. These areas of creativity had begun to converge as pop art. The scholarly concomitants of this phenomenon also bear consideration: notably the growing influence of semiotic analysis and the rising attention paid to the role of print and other media in shaping modern society, led by Marshall McLuhan in his *Gutenberg Galaxy: The Making of Typographic Man* (1962) and *The Medium Is the Massage* (with Quentin Fiore, 1967). But it is fair to say that while Venturi followed the general trends in contemporary painting, he did not know the pop artists, nor did he make media and semiotics the subject of systematic study.[53]

Implicit behind the large signage and public character of the Roosevelt memorial project was a new interest in the social function of art. This was certainly in keeping with the sociological bent of Penn's planning faculty, with whom Venturi now had increasing contact through his friendship with Denise Scott Brown, and it was also strongly allied with an enthusiasm for pop culture. Scott Brown had been photographing the commercial architecture of West Philadelphia, and that interest was converted into architecture in Venturi

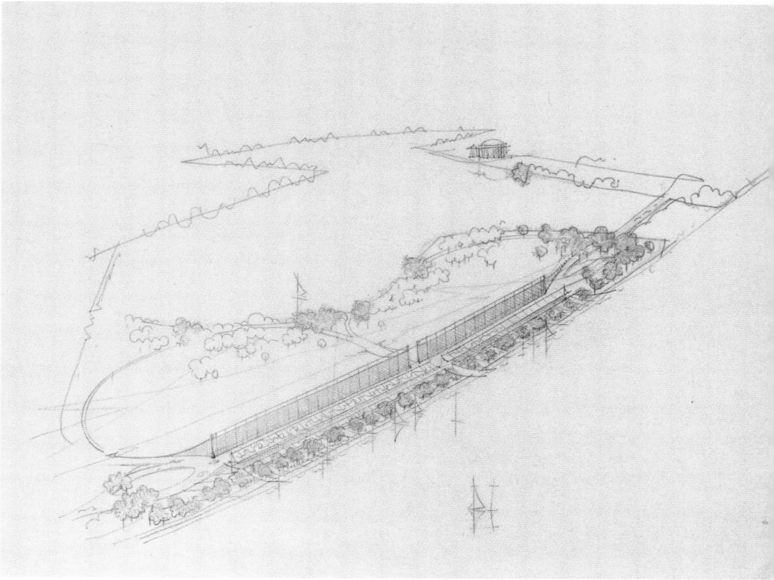

Figure 26
Franklin Delano Roosevelt Memorial, Competition, Washington, D.C., 1960
Aerial perspective. Pencil and colored pencil on yellow tracing paper, 29¾ x 38¼" (75.6 x 98.4 cm)
Robert Venturi
Collection of Venturi, Scott Brown and Associates, Inc.

Figure 27
Grand's Restaurant, Philadelphia, 1961–62
Perspective. Pencil on vellum, 24 x 34¾" (61 x 88.3 cm). Robert Venturi. Dated November 15, 1961
Collection of Venturi, Scott Brown and Associates, Inc.

[52] Robert Venturi, "3 Projects," *Perspecta*, vol. 11 (1967), p. 105.

[53] Denise Scott Brown and Robert Venturi, interview by students in History of Art 782, University of Pennsylvania, November 13, 1998; see also Stanislaus von Moos, *Venturi, Rauch & Scott Brown: Buildings and Projects*, trans. David Antal (New York: Rizzoli, 1987), pp. 51–57, 72 n. 81.

and Short's design for Grand's restaurant (1961–62), right in the heart of the Penn campus (fig. 27).[54] In this and many other projects from the sixties, the refined design sensibility of Gerod Clark can be detected.[55] A former student of both Scott Brown and Venturi, Clark was an avid collector—and creator—of pop cultural artifacts; as a wedding gift he gave the Venturis a giant industrial ventilation fan.[56]

For Harry and Marion Grand, the architects renovated the interiors of two adjacent buildings and created a new storefront, labeled inside and out with large, bright-colored lettering of the kind that would soon be called "super-graphics." A giant coffee cup, assembled out of yellow and blue panels, projected from the center of the sign, splitting the name of the restaurant in half (see fig. 303). Furnished with simple tables, booths, and bentwood chairs, and lit by prosaic industrial fixtures, Grand's evoked the simplicity of a working-class eatery, very much in the spirit of the latest Anglo-American critique of architectural arrogance. The Grands grew quickly unhappy with the splitting of their name, and they shifted the cup upward, out of the sign, ultimately installing a plastic, internally lit substitute for the name board as well. But the humble, lively project was widely seen, and it influenced much subsequent work. The architect Charles Moore, in most respects Venturi's closest ally during this period, claimed that "the whole business of paintings and flat-footed messages on the exterior and interior walls started with that restaurant."[57]

These new forces—social, symbolic, and popular—grew stronger in the young firm's next projects, and nowhere did they converge with more power and notoriety than in the federally subsidized apartment building for the elderly that they built for the Friends Neighborhood Guild, a nearly century-old Quaker community assistance organization. Guild House, designed in 1961–63 and built in 1965–66, was one of the first projects to be funded under Section 202 of the Housing Act of 1959.[58] Clark was the project manager, and the work was done in association with Cope and Lippincott. Mather Lippincott had been working for the Guild since 1949 and he helped them secure funding for the project.

The design began as a big-scaled, formal exercise in the manner of the Philadelphia School, as Venturi had helped to shape it. An early model shows a four-story building with the distinctive diagonal notchings in plan and a great, Roman thermal window, such as inspired both Palladio and Kahn, lighting the top-floor lounge, directly above the entrance (fig. 28). By 1963, the notches had disappeared, the height had grown to six stories, and the designers' interest had clearly shifted beyond the making of pure form to include other matters. Whereas Venturi had previously celebrated the visual context of architecture, Guild House now added an attachment to its social context. As completed, it not only responded to the rather humble wants of the residents, it also represented them. The building was both a social product and a social symbol.

Although user participation was not part of the design process, Guild House was conscientiously attuned to the architects' and client's rather thoughtful appreciation of the residents' actual needs. Apartment plans were of the familiar, old-fashioned kind, with real rooms rather than open planning, and an abundance of light brought in by the building's stepped-back south facade. The interior hallways snaked personally through the plan, abolishing the boring anonymity of ordinary modern apartment-building corridors (fig. 29). The comfortable ordinariness of these provisions for the residents was portrayed in the appearance of the building (fig. 30). Economy had dictated simple construction, and the architects did not resist for a moment, choosing to emphasize the "conventional" brick walls as a fitting representation of Guild House's prosaic reality.[59] Completing this picture were simple double-hung sash windows and a chainlink fence around the front gardens.

Some symbolic elements were adopted from popular culture. Above the door, a very large sign proclaimed "Guild House" in simple (but *gilded*) block letters, following the conventions of retail advertising, and glazed brick was

[54] My analysis of this design was aided by the research paper written by Ka-Kee Yan at the University of Pennsylvania, December 1998.

[55] John W. Cook and Heinrich Klotz, *Conversations with Architects* (New York: Praeger, 1973), pp. 260–61.

[56] Denise Scott Brown and Robert Venturi, interview by the author, Philadelphia, December 3, 2000.

[57] Quoted in Cook and Klotz, *Conversations*, p. 241.

[58] My analysis of this project was aided by the research of Rachel Iannacone, Ph.D. candidate at the University of Pennsylvania.

[59] Venturi, *Complexity and Contradiction*, p. 116.

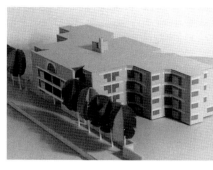

Figure 28

Guild House, Philadelphia, 1961–66

Early model. Photograph of lost original

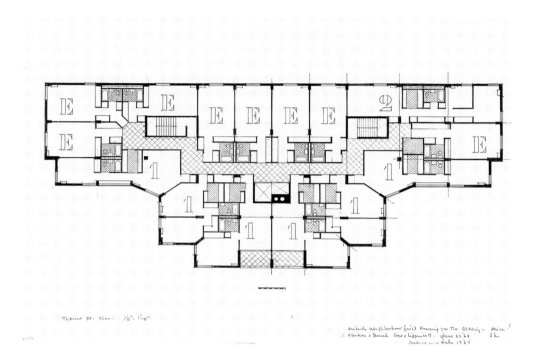

Figure 29

Guild House, Philadelphia, 1961–66

Floor plan. Pencil on vellum, 17⅞ x 24" (45.4 x 61 cm). Robert Venturi. Dated June 22, 1964; revised July 17, 1964

Collection of Venturi, Scott Brown and Associates, Inc.

Figure 30

Guild House, Philadelphia, 1961–66

Front facade

used for the ground floor of the entrance facade and for a single course at the fifth floor, in a cheapened, campy allusion to the usual classical demarcation of the top and bottom of a building. Most notoriously, the architects designed a gold-anodized aluminum sculpture, resembling a television antenna, for the center of the roof. Added to the project as the building was nearing completion, and after it had been determined that a functioning antenna could not meet their aesthetic standards, the sculpture precipitated a long argument with the otherwise very supportive client, Guild executive director Francis Bosworth. In the end the architects contributed 2,000 dollars toward the overall construction costs, in part because the Guild said that it had counted on such a contribution when it agreed to fabricate the metal ornament.[60] Playing the enfant terrible, Venturi explained that the sculpture was "a symbol of the aged, who spend so much time looking at T.V."[61] While this was a clear-eyed acknowledgment of a cultural reality, such as Herbert Gans was recording in Levittown, many saw the sculpture as a belittling statement about the occupants. But Venturi always insisted, "We didn't mean it that way. It's not for us to tell people that television is bad, and they should read books," and Scott Brown averred that the antenna was conceived "not hatefully, but lovingly; with tears maybe."[62] This unhappy misunderstanding would carry over into the interpretation of later, similar works.

The formal characteristics of Venturi's earlier architecture were not forsworn in favor of these new social and iconographic components, although explicitly Kahnian references grew fewer; nor was less painstaking attention given to formal design. Each detail, no matter how simple, was proportioned and positioned with a supremely high regard for its effect. The ordinary-seeming balconies participated with the large lounge window in a complicated program of spatial layering, and the centrally placed granite column in the doorway was cunningly contrived to create more of the intentional awkwardness and mannerist tension that Venturi had described in discussing the beach house. The column man-

aged both to block with stolid immobility the obvious path to the front door and to slip out from under the weight of the building as though it were an ephemeral object. Gerod Clark worked closely with Venturi to create these effects.[63]

This combination of formal acuity with new attention to social matters and their symbolic representation was also evident in the slow revision of the design for Venturi's mother's house, carried out at the same time.[64] In 1960–61, a great thermal window of Kahnian proportions was introduced, and the two-story public rooms began to be framed by gables (fig. 31), a motif that grew in significance through a sequence of revisions. In the first months of 1962, Venturi designed a house for Princeton art historian Millard Meiss in which the entire entrance facade was gathered beneath a great gable and centered on a chimney (fig. 32), reviving the formula he had used in 1959 in the beach house and on the end elevations at Foulkeways. In June 1962, the single dominant gable migrated to the Vanna Venturi house (fig. 33), and that fall, under budgetary pressure, the house shrank to its ultimate size, all gathered under one roof (fig. 34). Construction began in August 1963, and on April 1, 1964, the architect and his mother moved in.

This, the most significant house of the second half of the twentieth century, which has become known as the Mother's House, was first of all a triumph of formal design, embodying Venturi's ideas about context, mannerist complexity, and spatial layering. The house faced down the driveway toward its suburban environment with a large scale and a formality appropriate to the locale. At the rear, in private, the real complexity of the roof appeared, and the symmetrical accent was less (fig. 35). While apparently simple, the front facade was in fact riven by contrary forces: the gable was split at its apex like a mannerist pediment, the seemingly solid mass of the chimney revealed a window cut in its face, and the illusion of an axial door was soon dispelled.

The studied ambiguity of the design had an important spatial dimension, for the simple outer plane of the facade was cut away at the center to reveal the active architectural

[60] Israel Packel to Paul Cope Jr., February 8, 1968, "6104-FNG Correspondence / Mainly Friends Guild Rehab Program," VSB box 173 (VSBA archives).

[61] Venturi, *Complexity and Contradiction*, p. 116.

[62] Quoted in Cook and Klotz, *Conversations*, p. 262.

[63] Denise Scott Brown and Robert Venturi, interview by the author, Philadelphia, December 3, 2000.

[64] See note 48.

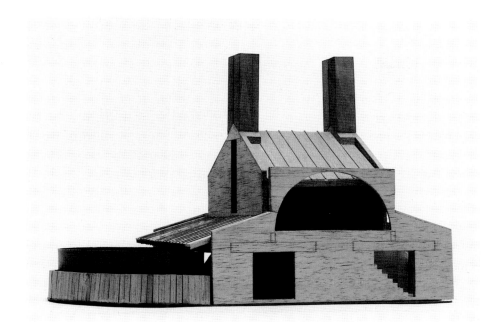

Figure 31
**Vanna Venturi House,
Philadelphia, 1959–64**

Model. Cardboard and balsa
wood, 9¼ x 14¼ x 9¾"
(23.5 x 36.2 x 24.8 cm)
Dated c. July 1959

The Museum of Modern Art,
New York. Gift of Venturi, Rauch
and Scott Brown, Inc.

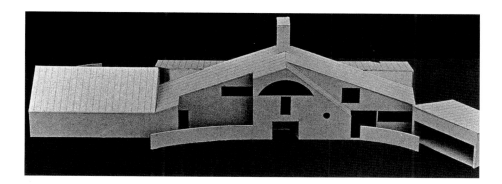

Figure 32
**Meiss House, Princeton,
New Jersey, 1962**

Model. Photograph of lost original

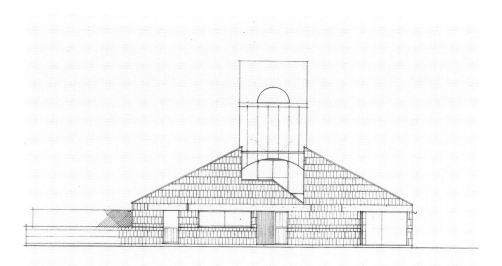

Figure 33
**Vanna Venturi House,
Philadelphia, 1959–64**

Front elevation. Pencil on vellum,
18 x 24" (45.7 x 61 cm). Robert
Venturi. Dated June 12, 1962

Collection of Venturi, Scott Brown
and Associates, Inc.

Figure 34
**Vanna Venturi House,
Philadelphia, 1959–64**
Front facade with Vanna Venturi
seated in the doorway

Figure 35
**Vanna Venturi House,
Philadelphia, 1959–64**
Rear facade

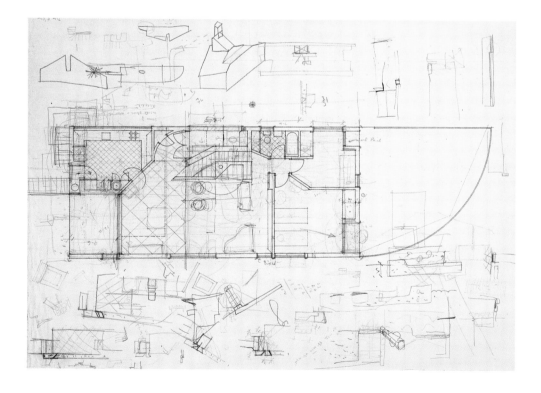

Figure 36
**Vanna Venturi House,
Philadelphia, 1959–64**

First-floor plan. Pencil, colored pencil,
and colored ballpoint pen on diazo
print, 17⅞ x 24⅜" (45.4 x 61.9 cm)
Robert Venturi. Dated December 8,
1962

Collection of Venturi, Scott Brown
and Associates, Inc.

work of the house going on a few feet behind it, reflecting a two-way struggle between inside and outside. Opening in the interstitial space between these two systems of order, the front door led inward to a rich experience of spaces that was guided by the familiar diagonal interior walls of the Philadelphia School, which now detached themselves from the corners to join the exciting promenade (fig. 36). Spatial exploration extended vertically as well, beginning in the swirl around the great chimney breast and the stair as they "compete[d]. . . for central position"[65] and then continuing upward as the stair ducked behind the fireplace and ascended.

A few years later, the play of vertical spaces in the Mother's House was recapitulated as the central theme in the diminutive four-story swimming pool pavilion that the architects designed for Mr. and Mrs. Bradford Mills in Princeton (fig. 37). The so-called Frug House, named for the dance craze of the Millses' children, consisted of almost nothing but the essential forms of the Venturi house: roof and central chimney outside, and inside a chimney intertwined by vertical ramps and stairs. For all of the flatness of the facades, this was an architecture of space.

Despite the virtuosity of these design elements, the Mother's House was far from being only an exploration of formal relationships. Like the Guild House, for which the design was evolving in tandem, it both served and symbolized a social fact, in this case the American family. Venturi explained that "the front, in its conventional combinations of door, windows, chimney and gable, creates an almost symbolic image of a house."[66] Despite his cautious "almost," the first and nearly all subsequent reviewers saw that the facade looked like a child's conception of home: a big roof to shelter, a towering chimney to warm, and a welcoming front door.[67] The most charming element of the domestic narrative that unfolded as one read these symbols was the tiny, nonfunctional "nowhere stair" that led upward from the architect's own studio/bedroom on the second floor to a nonexistent attic—to the notional realm of boyhood rainy days and make-believe.

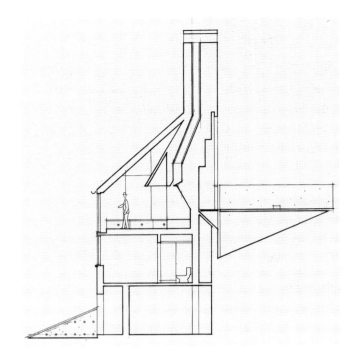

Figure 37
Mills Pool House, Princeton, New Jersey, 1966
Section. Pencil and transfer letters on vellum, 18 x 24" (45.7 x 61 cm)
Robert Venturi
Collection of Venturi, Scott Brown and Associates, Inc.

[65] Venturi, *Complexity and Contradiction,* p. 117.

[66] Ibid.

[67] [Ellen Perry Berkeley], "Complexities and Contradictions," *Progressive Architecture,* vol. 46 (May 1965), p. 168.

This general domestic symbolism was, true to Venturi's scholarly bent, richly woven into history. Palladio, as well as Kahn, was referenced in the thermal window atop the rear facade, and all kinds of other classical and mannerist features may be found after some scrutiny. Even the International Style, whose great, original monuments continued to hold Venturi's respect, was visible in the horizontal strip of windows, the general open plan of the public rooms, and the exposed steel column supporting the dining-room ceiling. However, the most important historical reference was to the iconic domestic architecture of the American shingle style. Early versions of this design, like the proposed beach house, had been drawn with cedar shingles, and, although the house was finally built of stuccoed concrete block, Venturi traced its formal and symbolic lineage to McKim, Mead & White's Low house, and its kin (see fig. 18).

Beyond history, the house associated itself with certain aspects of popular culture. Like houses in contemporary developments, it was ornamented, with prominent moldings (which wrapped around the windows and arched over the front entrance) and with even a kind of exterior chair rail girdling the house at the level of the windowsills. Like tract houses too, it was colorful. Although painted taupe gray when it was completed, Venturi had it painted pale green in 1967, ostensibly because the modernist architect Marcel Breuer had cautioned against the use of such natural colors.[68]

The Vanna Venturi house was only the architect's second complete building, but it was widely published and almost universally acclaimed, starting with the award of the sole honorable mention in the 1965 Art and Architecture Awards competition of the Architectural League of New York. The gold medal that year went to Harvard's Jose Luis Sert, and silver medals went to Eero Saarinen (posthumously, for the John Deere headquarters in Moline, Illinois) and Bertrand Goldberg, architect of Chicago's landmark Marina Towers. That a tiny building by a young architect was recognized amid this company was highly significant. Whereas the other celebrated works by young designers of the time

sounded a single note—the woody naturalism of Charles Moore's Sea Ranch (Gualala, California, 1965–66) and the revived Le Corbusian modernism of Richard Meier's Smith house (Darien, Connecticut, 1965–67)—Venturi's Mother's House was a symphony.

With Guild House and the Vanna Venturi house, the Venturi firm had found its voice. The powerful synthesis of new visual and new social thinking (with a concomitant appreciation of history and popular culture) became the foundation for all of their subsequent activity. Denise Scott Brown and Robert Venturi were now teaching together, and he regularly showed her the work that was in progress at the office. She offered her criticism and advice, and the maturity and multifaceted nature of these designs must be seen in conjunction with the beginnings of their collaboration. As though to describe the twin potencies of this new architecture, combining powerful forms and evocative symbols, Scott Brown wrote an essay in 1964 about the "meaningful city," in which messages were conveyed both by "*physiognomy*: that is, the sizes and shapes of buildings and the spaces around them" and by "*heraldry*—[that is] written and graphic signs."[69] One of the most significant partnerships in the history of art had been launched.

In 1964, with these projects on the boards, the firm was reorganized. William Short, who did not want to relocate from Princeton to the increasingly busy Philadelphia office, resigned, and John Rauch, a skillful designer and knowledgeable maker of buildings, moved up to the status of partner. Venturi dubbed him the "Rauch of Gibraltar."[70] In 1965–66, Scott Brown first appeared as a publicly acknowledged collaborator, in the competition for a new fountain at the end of the Benjamin Franklin Parkway in Philadelphia.

Cutting diagonally through William Penn's grid plan, the Benjamin Franklin Parkway extends the greenery of Fairmount Park into the heart of the city, from the Greco-Roman Philadelphia Museum of Art on the hill of Fairmount to the Second Empire–style City Hall. The new fountain was both to reinforce the City Hall end of the axis

[68] Schwartz, *Mother's House*, p. 25.

[69] Denise Scott Brown, "The Meaningful City," *AIA Journal*, vol. 43 (January 1965), p. 30. Scott Brown credits David Crane with coining "physiognomy" and "heraldry" as used here. Denise Scott Brown, interview by the author, Philadelphia, February 23, 2001.

[70] Quoted in Cook and Klotz, *Conversations*, p. 260.

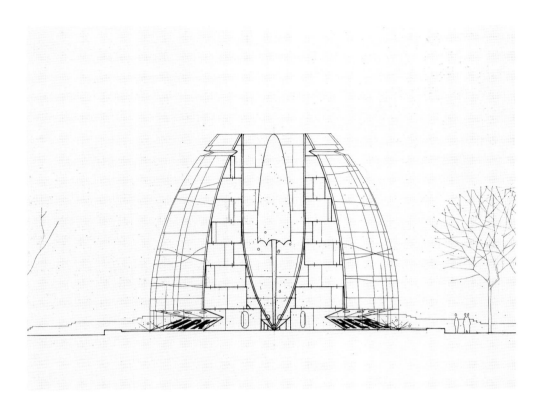

Figure 38
**Monumental Fountain on the
Benjamin Franklin Parkway,
Competition, Philadelphia, 1964**
Section. Robert Venturi
Whereabouts unknown

Figure 39
**Princeton Memorial Park,
Robbinsville, New Jersey, 1966**
Section and elevations of memorial
tower. Pencil and transfer letters on
vellum, 24 x 36" (61 x 91.4 cm)
Robert Venturi
Collection of Venturi, Scott Brown
and Associates, Inc.

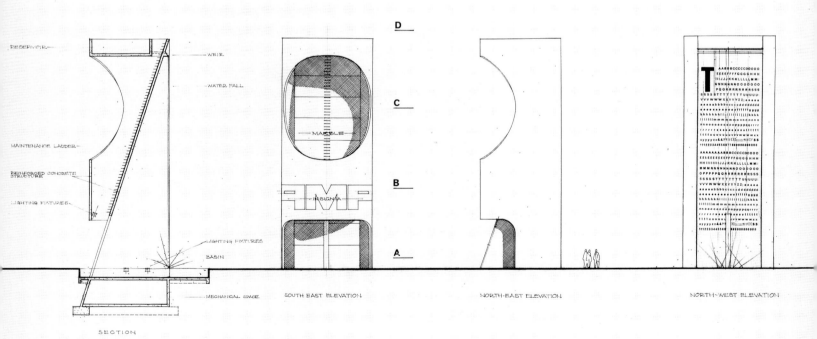

and to mark the beginning of the park, and to accomplish this, Venturi and Rauch proposed a very large piece of environmental art, almost on the scale of the Roosevelt memorial and with a similar dose of pop (fig. 38). During the mid-sixties other architects were designing large fountain projects, but this colossal bulb, shaped to give sympathetic form to the continuous sheeting of water on its exterior, was highly distinctive. From the inside a second water feature, a geyser sheltered from the wind by the structure, would be visible the entire length of the Parkway. A solemn inscription, screened by falling water, ran around the base: "Here Begins Fairmount Park." But when seen by motorists coming into the city, only the useful "Park Here" would be visible, signaling the presence of an underground garage. None of the fountain proposals was adopted.

During the summer of 1966, Venturi and Rauch adopted some of the same ideas in an unrealized design for a cemetery at Robbinsville, New Jersey, near Princeton and immediately adjacent to the New Jersey Turnpike. The site demanded forms that were both legible from afar and appropriately scaled for visitors on foot. The memorial tower (fig. 39), which would be visible from the highway, had to act at both scales. They designed a hollow cylinder of concrete with a raked slab inside that could be seen through giant perforations like those that Kahn was then including in his buildings in India and Pakistan. The upper face of the interior slab was revetted with alternating black and white marble, akin to the campanile of the cathedral of Siena, and lit at night. Its underside, screened by a sheet of falling water, was designed to be seen from nearby, and showing mistily through the water was the twenty-third psalm. Most of the graves were to be marked by bronze plaques set in the rolling lawns, in a scheme given shape by landscape architect Richard Cripps. A protective berm rose adjacent to the turnpike, like the screening feature in the Roosevelt memorial, with mausoleums set in its side. Intended chiefly for distant viewing were the gatehouse and administrative offices, clustered in a small brick box behind a marble wall—or sign-

board—proclaiming PRINCETON MEMORIAL PARK in huge letters. Although the materials were rich, and the landscape design was serene, some observers chafed at the large signs as they had at the Guild House antenna sculpture. An anonymous critic complained, "Venturi has great sport making fun of a lot of things . . . that some human beings feel a bit serious about. One happens to be death."[71] That was said by one of the jurors in *Progressive Architecture*'s 1967 annual design awards review, in which the Princeton Memorial Park was one of an astonishing three projects by the firm to be given awards. The others were the Frug House and a group of civic buildings for North Canton, Ohio.

North Canton was the American headquarters of the Hoover corporation, the appliance company that was almost synonymous with vacuum cleaners. Its small-town central square, at the intersection of Main and Maple streets, was dominated by the great bulk of the company's brick factory at the northeast corner. For the other three corners, Venturi and Rauch designed a city hall, library addition, and YMCA, and they sketched a shopping center.[72] The four designs, created in 1965–66, offered an encyclopedia of both the firm's physiognomic and heraldic architecture—combining provocative formal devices and pop signage.

The modest city hall adopted the false-front strategy of smaller commercial buildings on North Canton's Main Street to assert its importance in the presence of the large factory (fig. 40). The oversized cutout in its great marble screen wall again seemed Kahnian, but Venturi likened it to Louis Sullivan's big-featured small-town bank buildings,[73] like the National Farmers' Bank (Owatonna, Minnesota, 1907–8). Augmenting the effect of these large, abstract forms was a prominent symbol, an American flag, hung signlike from a horizontal pole over the sidewalk. The city hall was originally planned for a site directly across Main Street from the town square, but was shifted north when the original site was reconceived as a shopping precinct.

The YMCA and library were envisioned similarly, with freestanding screen walls that established their presence in

[71] "P/A Fourteenth Annual Design Awards Program," *Progressive Architecture*, vol. 48 (January 1967), p. 152.

[72] My analysis of this design was aided by the research paper written by Saiko Ito at the University of Pennsylvania, December 1998.

[73] Venturi, *Complexity and Contradiction*, p. 124.

Figure 40
**Redevelopment Plan, North
Canton, Ohio, 1965–66**

Perspective of city hall. Pencil on
vellum, 16½ x 36" (41.9 x 91.4 cm)
Robert Venturi

Collection of Venturi, Scott Brown
and Associates, Inc.

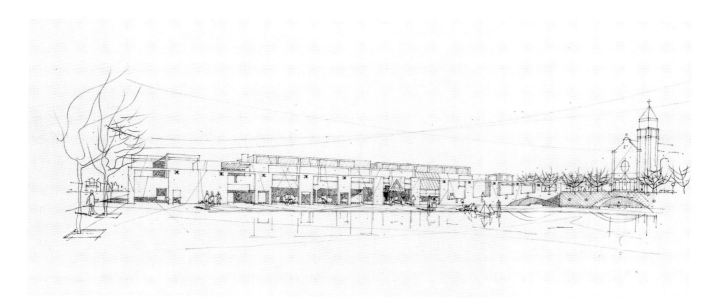

Figure 41
**Redevelopment Plan, North
Canton, Ohio, 1965–66**

Perspective of YMCA. Pencil on
vellum, 16¼ x 34½" (41.3 x 87.6 cm)
Robert Venturi

Collection of Venturi, Scott Brown
and Associates, Inc.

Figure 42
Redevelopment Plan, North Canton, Ohio, 1965–66

Perspective inside screen wall of YMCA. Pencil on vellum, 16½ x 30" (41.9 x 76.2 cm). Robert Venturi

Collection of Venturi, Scott Brown and Associates, Inc.

Figure 43
Redevelopment Plan, North Canton, Ohio, 1965–66

Plan of YMCA. Pencil and transfer letters on vellum, detail

Collection of Venturi, Scott Brown and Associates, Inc.

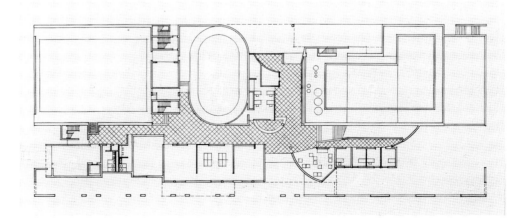

the townscape and as complicated buildings behind. Here there were no symbols or signs. The perforated screen walls were, of course, descended from Venturi's own Pearson house, but this form had been given monumental status in Kahn's recent designs for the conference center of the Salk Institute (La Jolla, California, 1959–65), Indian Institute of Management (Ahmedabad, 1962–74), and the East Pakistan capital complex (Dhaka, 1962–83).

The YMCA presented itself to the square with solemn formality, with a screen wall of dark brick and great regularity (figs. 41–43). But behind the wall, the architects created a lively space defined by the thrusts and jabs of the building's floor plan and conceived as both a warm-up area for ice skaters in the winter (there was even an outdoor hearth) and as a noble walkway from a parking lot to Main Street, aligned with an existing church. The library project wrapped a similar monumental screen around an existing building of 1954, which was to be augmented to the rear and side.

In creating what Venturi called a "contrapuntal juxta-position"[74] between the simple screen walls and the buildings behind them, the architects enlarged an existing theme in their work to a new scale. The plans of the North Canton buildings, full of irregularities suggested by the demands of the programs, also hearkened to the work of the Finnish architect Alvar Aalto, whose "barely maintained balance between order and disorder" Venturi celebrated.[75] A near contemporary of the great masters of the International Style, Aalto had managed to make architecture that was not only unconventionally planned, but also organic in form, region-alist in tone, and built of natural materials—all the while remaining affirmatively modern. These traits intrigued Venturi, and his slightly earlier entry in the competition for a new arts center at the University of California at Berkeley was even more explicitly Aaltoesque (figs. 44, 45).[76] The North Canton YMCA project fell victim to arguments about many details, including the relatively costly screen wall, and a neo-Georgian building was erected in 1969. Unspoken reservations also dogged the library and city hall

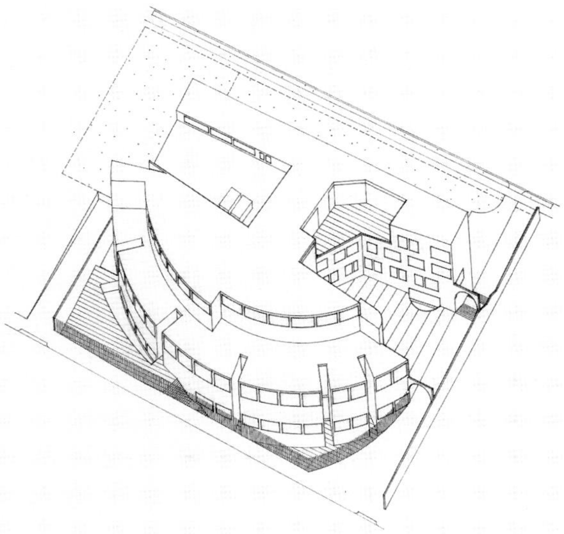

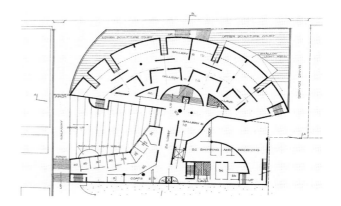

Figure 44
Arts Center, University of California at Berkeley, Competition, 1965

Axonometric. Pencil on vellum, 24 x 36" (61 x 91.4 cm)
Robert Venturi

Collection of Venturi, Scott Brown and Associates, Inc.

Figure 45
Arts Center, University of California at Berkeley, Competition, 1965

Entrance gallery floor plan. Pencil on vellum, detail. Robert Venturi

Collection of Venturi, Scott Brown and Associates, Inc.

[74] Ibid., p. 126.

[75] Robert Venturi, "Alvar Aalto [1976]," in Robert Venturi and Denise Scott Brown, *A View from the Campidoglio: Selected Essays, 1953–1984*, eds., Peter Arnell, Ted Bickford, and Catherine Bergart (New York: Harper & Row, 1984), p. 60.

[76] See von Moos, *Venturi, Rauch & Scott Brown*, pp. 33–36.

projects, and in the end, expansion of the library was postponed and the city government built itself a modestly modern building, across Main Street from the Hoover factory.

In 1965, both Venturi and Scott Brown left Penn. He would spend part of the next winter back in Rome as architect in residence at the American Academy, and in spring 1966, Yale named him and the English architect James Stirling as the new Davenport professors of architecture, a masterstroke in the campaign of the recently appointed architecture chair, Charles Moore, to diversify the department. Moore, a philosophical ally, called Venturi "one of the world's leading architectural intellectuals as well as a superb designer."[77] Scott Brown's assistant professorship was not renewed at Penn, and she left in some anger to take a visiting position at Berkeley. After a semester she moved to UCLA's new architecture school as co-chair of the urban design program. Despite these circumstances, this was a very happy transcontinental relocation, for at Penn she had learned—and taught—that the future lay in the new cities of the West: Los Angeles, San Diego, and Las Vegas. There, a new chapter of her work with Robert Venturi would begin.

While this transpired, the final words of their first chapter were being written and published. With the aid of a 1962 grant from the Graham Foundation, and with Scott Brown's criticism and encouragement, Venturi had assembled his lecture notes into a manuscript, and a long extract finally appeared in 1965 as "Complexity and Contradiction in Architecture."[78] Philip Finkelpearl had suggested this apt title,[79] which would also serve for the book-length version that was published a year later by the Museum of Modern Art. These writings recorded the thinking that Venturi had done at Penn, and the extract appeared in *Perspecta*, Yale's architecture journal, together with essays by his Penn colleagues Romaldo Giurgola and Louis Kahn. However, the publication of these works in New Haven rather poignantly signaled the end of the Philadelphia School. While this had never been more than a journalistic rubric for certain loosely associated people and ideas, it was now no longer

even a useful label. Tim Vreeland, another younger member of the "school," and Giurgola had already left for university administrative appointments at New Mexico and Columbia. Now Venturi was going to Yale to join a department headed by Moore, whose views coincided with the Philadelphians' in many respects and who had also contributed an essay to that signal volume of *Perspecta*. Yale architectural historian Vincent Scully wrote *Complexity and Contradiction's* introduction while his wife Marion helped Venturi prepare the manuscript for the press. Only Kahn and Robert Geddes, whose Philadelphia practices were prospering, remained at Penn.

Complexity and Contradiction summed up a remarkably fruitful decade of creative thinking and working. The structure of the argument was engagingly simple, designed to elucidate the different species of architectural ambiguity, duality, and controlled disorder. These phenomena were analyzed as they appeared in elevations, plans, the relationship between inside and outside, and the making of space. For those who had read the scattered writings that had already come from the office—and read between the lines—there was little that was entirely new. But taken as a whole, and explicitly positioned as "A Gentle Manifesto" in response to high modernism's absolutist rhetoric, the effect was breathtaking. Scully, in an impresario's introduction, was right to call it "probably the most important writing on the making of architecture since Le Corbusier's *Vers une Architecture*, of 1923."[80]

Long in preparation, *Complexity and Contradiction* was a palimpsest that recorded the evolution of Venturi's philosophy. It was, first of all, an extended exercise in the comparative visual analysis of historical precedents, assembled without regard for chronology. Examples from virtually every time and place of human artistry were adduced to support his thesis, although he showed favoritism for the Italian mannerists, Edwin Landseer Lutyens (the British twentieth-century classicist), Kahn, Le Corbusier, Aalto, Vanbrugh, and Hawksmoor. Venturi had learned this methodology from art historians, who hunted, selected, and organized images according to their visual properties. They,

[77] "Robert Venturi Is Appointed Davenport Professor at Yale," *Il Popolo Italiano* (Philadelphia), March 31, 1966.

[78] Robert Venturi, "Complexity and Contradiction in Architecture: Selections from a Forthcoming Book," *Perspecta*, vol. 9–10 (1965), pp. 17–56.

[79] See Scott Brown, "Worm's Eye," p. 77.

[80] Vincent Scully, introduction to Venturi, *Complexity and Contradiction*, p. 11.

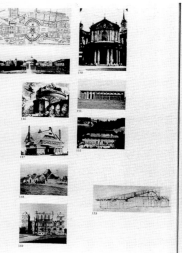

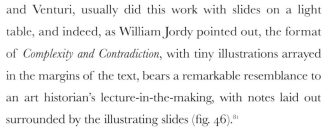

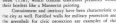

Figure 46

Pages from *Complexity and Contradiction in Architecture*, 1966

and Venturi, usually did this work with slides on a light table, and indeed, as William Jordy pointed out, the format of *Complexity and Contradiction*, with tiny illustrations arrayed in the margins of the text, bears a remarkable resemblance to an art historian's lecture-in-the-making, with notes laid out surrounded by the illustrating slides (fig. 46).[81]

Historical and visual, Venturi's foundational line of argument was rooted in the revisionist thinking of Princeton and Philadelphia. It was so old-fashioned that it seemed new, and he recognized the significance of what he was doing and took pains to demystify it for those for whom it might be unfamiliar. About history he said, "I try to be guided not by habit but by a conscious sense of the past— by precedent, thoughtfully considered."[82] And in explaining his focus on the visual traits of architecture, he was almost belligerent: "I make no special attempt to relate architecture to other things. I have not tried to 'improve the connections between science and technology on the one hand, and the humanities and the social sciences on the other . . . and make of architecture a more human social art' [quoting Robert Geddes]. I try to talk about architecture rather than around it."[83]

Given these pronouncements, which were noted by prominent reviewers,[84] the book's thin but critically important second layer of analysis came as a surprise. *Complexity and Contradiction* concluded not with a picture of a mannerist doorframe, but with a photograph of the messy commercialism of an American Main Street; moreover, Main Street was compared favorably to Jefferson's great lawn at the University of Virginia. And the last two pages of the essay proposed that both Main Street and the commercial strip were "almost all right,"[85] implying that they not only possessed visual interest, but that the social forces that produced them were worthy of study and respect. In short, at this critical point, Venturi overlaid his historical and formalist argument with a dose of popular culture and an acceptance of the nonjudgmental, sociological bent of recent planning. Thus did Denise Scott Brown's experience

81 See von Moos, *Venturi, Rauch & Scott Brown*, p. 13.

82 Venturi, *Complexity and Contradiction*, p. 18.

83 Ibid., p. 20.

84 See, for example, Colin Rowe, "Waiting for Utopia," *New York Times Book Review*, September 10, 1967, pp. 18–22.

85 Venturi, *Complexity and Contradiction*, pp. 102–3.

86 Denise Scott Brown and Robert Venturi, interview by the author, Philadelphia, December 3, 2000.

87 Quoted in Gilbert and Moore, *Particular Passions*, p. 316; see also Kron, "The Almost-Perfect Life of Denise Scott Brown," p. 32.

with the Smithsons in London and with Gans at Penn combine with Robert Venturi's appreciation of the lessons learned from Egbert at Princeton and Kahn in Philadelphia. The next stop for them, together, was Las Vegas.

Learning from Everything

Denise Scott Brown's parents had vacationed in Las Vegas in the 1950s, and they were unabashed admirers of its glittering attractions. She followed in their track, stopping off in the casino city on her way to California in 1965, when she leapfrogged across the country by plane, also visiting Miami, San Antonio, and Phoenix.[86] In 1966–67 she invited Venturi to UCLA as a visiting critic, and while her students worked on a four-day sketch problem in Los Angeles, she took him back to Las Vegas, where they rented a car, and with its radio blaring rock-and-roll, they toured the strip. "We rode around from casino to casino," she remembered. "Dazed by the desert sun and dazzled by the signs, both loving and hating what we saw, we were jolted clear out of our aesthetic skins" (fig. 47).[87] They were also jolted into love for each other, and on July 23, 1967, they were married on the front porch of her bungalow in Santa Monica. A member of the firm informally at first, she became a partner in 1969.

Their first forays to Las Vegas were chronicled in a pair of coauthored articles in 1968,[88] the second of which was expanded in 1971.[89] These were assembled in the book *Learning from Las Vegas*, published in 1972, and by that time their ideas were beginning to be well known—even notorious. Venturi and Scott Brown's study of Las Vegas reversed the order of the arguments in *Complexity and Contradiction*. Whereas the earlier work had begun on the foundation of Venturi's formal analysis, ending with an appreciation of popular culture—where Scott Brown's interest was greater, the Las Vegas essays started by proclaiming the importance of the commercial vernacular and by asserting that one of the social functions of architecture—communication—was more important than the formal manipulation of mass and space. Only after these premises had been established did

Figure 47
Robert Venturi and Denise Scott Brown in Las Vegas, 1966

[88] Robert Venturi and Denise Scott Brown, "A Significance for A&P Parking Lots or Learning from Las Vegas," *Architectural Forum*, vol. 128 (March 1968), pp. 37–43; Denise Scott Brown and Robert Venturi, "On Ducks and Decoration," *Architecture Canada*, October 1968, pp. 48–49.

[89] Robert Venturi and Denise Scott Brown, "Ugly and Ordinary Architecture or the Decorated Shed: 1. Some Definitions Using the Comparative Method," *Architectural Forum*, vol. 135 (November 1971), pp. 64–67; Robert Venturi and Denise Scott Brown, "Ugly and Ordinary Architecture or the Decorated Shed: 2. Theory of Ugly and Ordinary and Related and Contrary Concepts," *Architectural Forum*, vol. 135 (December 1971), pp. 48–53.

Figure 48
"Duck" and "Decorated Shed." From
***Learning from Las Vegas,* 1972**

Figure 49
**National Collegiate Football Hall
of Fame, Competition, Piscataway,
New Jersey, 1967**
Model. Photograph of lost original

Venturi and Scott Brown apply the comparative method of the art historian, and even then they examined Las Vegas with an eye to the functioning of signs and symbols rather than the making of forms. It was Scott Brown who invented their taxonomy for roadside communication, modifying the "physiognomic" and "heraldic" nomenclature for the analysis of urban environments that she had already published. Thus was born the famous distinction between "ducks" and "decorated sheds": the sculptural buildings that embodied their message and the utilitarian structures that spoke with signs (fig. 48). It was the decorated sheds of Las Vegas that they judged to be the most relevant architecture for the time.

The work that Venturi created in the late 1960s, as an increasing number of commissions came into the office, reflected these discovered phenomena and invented typologies with spritely literalness. Two fire stations, quintessential decorated sheds, are exemplary of this work.[90] Fire Station No. 4 in Columbus, Indiana (1966–68)—sponsored like many of Columbus's extraordinary collection of buildings by the Cummins Engine Foundation—adopted the small-town false front of the North Canton city hall both to achieve monumentality and to disguise the unequal ceiling heights of the garage and the sleeping quarters (fig. 50). A symbolically important and eminently practical hose-drying tower rose at the center, lofting identifying supergraphics above the midwestern town. (Pop enthusiast Gerod Clark was the project architect.) The Dixwell Fire Station in New Haven, Connecticut (1967–74), wrapped itself in a vivid red-brick signboard—redder than a fire engine—with an Art Moderne curve that peeled off of the facade to cantilever above the corner entrance (fig. 51).

The prizewinning entry in the National Collegiate Football Hall of Fame competition took this genre of architectural signography to an extreme (fig. 49). A "Bill-Ding-Board," Venturi called the 1967 design, aptly eliding the difference between architecture and advertisement for what was described as the National Football Foundation's "Ideological Center." Conceived, according to the foundation,

[90] My analysis of these designs was aided by the research paper written by Rachel Iannacone at the University of Pennsylvania, June 1999.

Figure 50
**Fire Station No. 4, Columbus,
Indiana, 1966–68**
Front facade

Figure 51
**Dixwell Fire Station, New Haven,
1967–74**
Front facade

Figure 52
**National Collegiate Football
Hall of Fame, Competition, Piscataway,
New Jersey, 1967**

Interior perspective. Panchromatic
film, ink, pencil, and photographs on
vellum, 27⅞ x 23¾" (70.8 x 60.3 cm)
Robert Venturi and Gerod Clark

Collection of Venturi, Scott Brown
and Associates, Inc.

"at a time of the long hair, beard, beatnik revolt on the campus," it was to promote football as "the biggest and best classroom in the nation for teaching leadership."[91] Facing the parking lot, picnic ground, and the nearby Rutgers Stadium was a stupendous signboard, proportioned like a football field, with 200,000 programmable lights that could recreate the great moments of historic games. This false front, Venturi said, was like the facade of a cathedral, while behind it was an externally simple "shed," with bleachers at the back facing a real practice field. In the more complex interior, the relics of football were to be displayed in chapel-like side chambers adjacent to a two-story great hall, where movies were to be splashed on the vaulting above (in a manner that Venturi likened to the painted ceilings of baroque churches) and on the parapet of the balcony, and the long wall opposite the chapels was to flicker with a mosaic of rear-projection screens (fig. 52). The National Football Foundation's plans were inchoate, and this design and the New Jersey site were ultimately abandoned. But when the Hall of Fame was later built in South Bend, Indiana, its football-shaped building ironically recalled a "duck" that Venturi had first sketched for the project.

Although exaggerated scale was an essential ingredient in projects of this kind, the absolute size was rarely large, and two of their most memorable decorated sheds were very small indeed. The little medical office building created for Dr. George Varga and Dr. Frank Brigio (1966–68) across the street from a hospital on a suburban street corner in Bridgeton, New Jersey, had a Philadelphia-style acute angle at one end and a front facade that assembled big features. A gigantic arched doorway (most of it a false-front screen wall) took its place beside several large and nearly, but not quite, square windows, divided into four lights to resemble old-fashioned double-hung sash. This window type was reprised in many designs from the Vanna Venturi house onward and taken up by other architects.

For the Nathaniel and Judy Lieb house (1967–69), set among nondescript postwar beach cottages on Long Beach Island at Barnegat Light, New Jersey, the compositional strategy was even bolder (figs. 53, 54).[92] To take advantage of the ocean view across the yard of a neighboring house, the living room shared the top floor with a porch that was bracketed between a stepped-back wall of windows and a parapet. All of this acted as a giant sculptural incident within the blocky profile of the trapezoid-planned house, which was also enlivened by a two-story, three-quarter-circle window that lit the interior stair. The front door stood atop a broad stoop that stretched the width of the house, designed as much for sitting and sunning as for entry, with a supergraphic house number painted beside the door. These devices combined to make the small seem large and the ordinary, unusual. With the sharper rhetoric that he had begun to adopt to describe these pop-inspired projects, Venturi called it "a kind of bold little ugly banal box."[93]

This group of designs, closely allied with Venturi and Scott Brown's investigation of the symbolic language of Las Vegas, earned the firm a reputation for doing simple projects with ingenuity and artistry. However, a series of larger designs from the same period, whose laconic "shed" style was devoid of supergraphics and symbolism, suffered seriously at the hands of hostile and uncomprehending critics, and most of them remained unbuilt. With their beautifully composed facades and Aalto-like planning complexities, they deserved better.

Venturi and Rauch's proposed Transportation Square Office Building (1967–69) won the competition conducted by the Washington Redevelopment Land Agency for part of the revitalization of southwest Washington, D.C. Designed for developer Mallory Walker (who was later bought out by the Martin Marietta corporation's development division), the slablike office building was to be clad in marble in deference to its location among government buildings, but its ribbon windows and flat roof acknowledged, like Guild House, the ordinary modernism that sheltered American life in the late twentieth century. Modernism was among the things that were almost all right, and the architects explicitly

[91] Robert Venturi, "A Bild-Ding-Board Involving Movies, Relics and Space," *Architectural Forum*, vol. 128 (April 1968), p. 75.

[92] My analysis of these designs was aided by the research paper written by Nicholas Sawicki at the University of Pennsylvania, December 1998.

[93] Quoted in "Ordinary as Artform," *Progressive Architecture*, vol. 51 (April 1970), p. 108.

Figure 53
Lieb Beach House, Barnegat Light, New Jersey, 1967–69
East and street facades

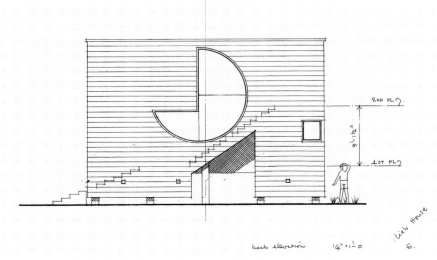

Figure 54
Lieb Beach House, Barnegat Light, New Jersey, 1967–69
West elevation. Pencil on vellum,
12 x 18½" (30.5 x 47 cm)
Robert Venturi

Collection of Venturi, Scott Brown and Associates, Inc.

acknowledged an indebtedness to the window pattern of Edward Larrabee Barnes's new 20 State Street building in Boston.[94] The design was remarkably subtle, with a rear corner stepped back to clear a railroad line, like Aalto's Social Security Office in Helsinki (1952–56), and an entrance forecourt, which shrank as it receded between framing walls of verd antique, like a baroque stage (fig. 55). The three-story buildings that defined the forecourt also established the building's relationship to the pedestrian environment of Maryland Avenue and reinforced the street's diagonal focus on the dome of the Capitol. These subtleties eluded the Fine Arts Commission, whose charge it was to review all architecture in the ceremonial heart of the capital city, and Venturi's celebration of the mundane profoundly displeased them. Commissioner Gordon Bunshaft, design partner in Skidmore, Owings & Merrill, took the lead in attacking the design as "ugly and ordinary," an epithet that Venturi and Scott Brown subsequently bore as a badge of honor, flourishing it in their more strident writings.[95] In the end, the building was redesigned as directed by the commission, eliminating the stepped corner and forecourt buildings, but then it no longer provided the capacity required by the developer and was not built.

The firm also entered a competition for middle-income housing at Brighton Beach in Brooklyn (1967–68) with a design that dealt brilliantly with the challenging program but badly split the jury of seven evaluators (fig. 56). Their entry consisted of two towers, arranged so that all but two apartments looked toward the sea. Interference with views from the existing six-story buildings was minimized, and row houses between and beside the towers continued the pedestrian-scale environment of the local streets to the boardwalk. This cleverness was disguised to many of the jurors by the ordinary modernity of the facades, and Philip Johnson, the chair of the jury, spoke for a majority when he called the proposal "a pair of very ugly buildings."[96] Johnson professed himself "taken by surprise" when the designers of the anonymously submitted entry were

Figure 55
Transportation Square Office Building, Competition, Washington, D.C., 1967–69
Model. Plexiglass, paint, and wire, 4½ x 17 x 17½" (11.4 x 43.2 x 44.5 cm)
Collection of Venturi, Scott Brown and Associates, Inc.

Figure 56
Middle-Income Housing Development for Brighton Beach, Brooklyn, Competition, 1967–68
Model. Photograph of lost original

[94] Robert Venturi, Denise Scott Brown, and Steven Izenour, *Learning from Las Vegas* (Cambridge and London: The MIT Press, 1972), p. 139.

[95] Ibid., p. 141.

[96] "Jury's Report: Letter, Philip Johnson to Jason R. Nathan," in *Record of Submissions and Awards: Competition for Middle-income Housing at Brighton Beach, Brooklyn, 1968* (New York: Housing and Development Administration, 1968), n.p.

Figure 57
Mathematics Building, Yale University, Competition, New Haven, 1969–70

Perspective. Ink on mylar, 30 x 40"
(76.2 x 101.6 cm). W. G. Clark

Collection of Venturi, Scott Brown and Associates, Inc.

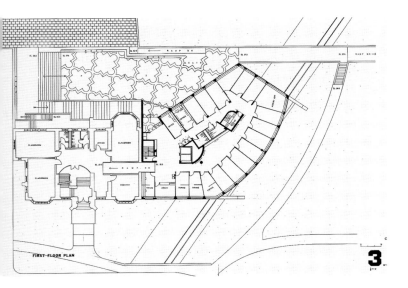

Figure 58
Mathematics Building, Yale University, Competition, New Haven, 1969–70

First-floor plan. Ink on mylar, 32½ x 42" (82.6 x 106.7 cm)

Collection of Venturi, Scott Brown and Associates, Inc.

revealed, identifying Venturi as "not only a great friend of mine, but certainly the leading theoretician of the younger architects of this country."[97]

Three of the jurors (Columbia architecture chair Romaldo Giurgola, MIT architecture chair Donlyn Lyndon, and contractor Richard Ravitch) had, however, voted to award the architects first prize. Giurgola, a leader of the erstwhile Philadelphia School, argued, "Beauty becomes an incomprehensible abstraction when it is separated from the world of life—from the world of everyday life that is," and went on to praise "the simple, dignified and clear statement of human purpose" embodied in their entry.[98] One of Lyndon's partners, Charles Moore, had been on the jury that gave the Venturi firm three *Progressive Architecture* awards the previous year, and Lyndon now celebrated the design that did not "detract from or demean the surrounding neighborhood" and that "offers real benefits for the people who might occupy it rather than polemic satisfaction to those who consider it."[99] In the end, the sharply divided jury gave third prize to the proposal.

In 1970, the minority view at Brighton Beach became the majority opinion in the competition for a new Mathematics Building at Yale—an expansion of historic Leet Oliver Memorial Hall (1908; figs. 57, 58). Charles Moore himself, still chair of architecture at Yale, was the professional advisor for the contest, and the jury comprised Giurgola, Scully, Barnes, and Roche, as well as the chairman of mathematics, an architecture student, and the director of campus planning. After reviewing the 479 entries, they unanimously selected the serious and quiet design submitted by Venturi and Rauch.

This was a triumph for what was beginning to be called "contextual" or "inclusivist" architecture, and it reflected the widening acceptance of Venturi and Scott Brown's thinking. Only a few months earlier, Charles Moore's own understated residence hall for Brown University had won the top prize in *Progressive Architecture*'s annual awards, for which Venturi served on the jury. Venturi had praised it for

[97] Ibid.

[98] "Jury's Report: Letter, Romaldo Giurgola to Jason R. Nathan," in *Record of Submissions and Awards*, n.p.

[99] "Jury's Report: Letter, Donlyn Lyndon to Jason R. Nathan," in *Record of Submissions and Awards.*, n.p.

being "on the one hand, dumb and ordinary, and on the other hand, very sophisticated, sensitively, and unusually done."[100] The editors had summed up the awards as "an apotheosis of the ordinary," noting that "the heroic, monumental idiom of past decades was eschewed."[101]

The Mathematics Building judging took place during the spring of 1970, while campuses nationwide, Yale among them, were swept by antiwar demonstrations, and the Venturi firm's design captured both the time's contempt for bombast and the preference that the writers of the building program had expressed for "workable, economical, generally nonmonumental space" and "the integration of new buildings into the strong existing fabric."[102] Venturi and Rauch's entry discreetly attached itself to the end of the older building and spanned the adjacent railroad track with a large but quiet wing that provided needed circulation space, a new library, large lounges, and faculty offices. The major entrance was left in Leet Oliver hall, and the simple, curved facade that faced Hillhouse Avenue recalled both Aalto's unusual planning geometry and his understated vocabulary. A rearward extension of the basement accommodated the needed lecture halls, made accessible by a wide outside stair whose window-cut walls also brought light into the underground public spaces. Above the lecture halls a plaza was paved with a quatrefoil pattern, a historic allusion that was also picked up briefly in a concrete screen of Gothic tracery over the rear entrance, located where old and new buildings met. This allusion to the neo-Tudor forms of Leet Oliver was Venturi's most notable historical reference since his shingle-style house designs of the early sixties. Yale architectural historian George Hersey was then deeply engaged in the study of such historical "associationism" in Victorian architecture, and Venturi had designed a little vacation house for him in 1967–68.[103]

While the Mathematics Building design was warmly appreciated by like-minded colleagues along the vaguely defined but long-established Yale-Penn axis, which now subsumed the Philadelphia School, opposition for this species of architecture had also crystallized. This opposition centered among the "New York Five" (Peter Eisenman, Richard Meier, Charles Gwathmey, John Hejduk, and Michael Graves), whose exhibition at the Museum of Modern Art in 1969 had brought the first focused attention to their enthusiastic revival of 1920s modernism. But it also ran much more broadly among those who could not comprehend the beauty of the ordinary. Consequently, the Mathematics Building attracted the same criticism that the Transportation Square building and the Brighton Beach apartments had suffered, and the attacks were more public. Dissenting readers of *Architectural Forum* responded to that journal's enthusiastic account of the competition by labeling the design "a piece of Junk" and "the architecture of the absurd."[104] A few even attacked the credibility of the competition process, given the strong collegial and philosophical connections among contestants and judges. Yale formally adopted the Mathematics Building project and publicized it with a brochure in which future architecture critic Paul Goldberger, Class of 1972, wrote an appreciative essay.[105] But the necessary funds were not raised, leaving it to Charles Moore and his co-editor Nicholas Pyle to give the project immortality in a book about the competition.[106]

At the new Purchase campus of the State University of New York, they at last got to build two quiet examples of what they had called "architecture for a time of questioning."[107] The Humanities (1968–73) and Social Science (1970–78) buildings were largely *un*-decorated brick sheds that stood deferentially, screened by the system of covered walkways established by Edward Larrabee Barnes's master plan. Behind their plain facades, the buildings' rich plans orchestrated a cacophony of room types, all assembled around systems of streetlike corridors that widened at opportune places to provide for meeting and lounging (fig. 59). These street corridors inaugurated a potent constituent of Venturi and Scott Brown's subsequent work, pushing beyond the Aaltoesque formulas that had shaped their planning to this point.

[100] Quoted in Ada Louise Huxtable, "Heroics Are Out, Ordinary Is In," *New York Times*, January 18, 1970.

[101] "The Jury Discusses the Present State of the Art and Trends toward the Future," *Progressive Architecture*, vol. 51 (January 1970), p. 78.

[102] Venturi, Scott Brown, and Izenour, *Learning from Las Vegas*, p. 150.

[103] See George Hersey, "J. C. Loudon and Architectural Associationism," *Architectural Review*, August 1968, pp. 88–92.

[104] "Mathematics at Yale: Readers Respond," *Architectural Forum*, vol. 133 (October 1970), p. 65.

[105] Paul Goldberger, "About the Architect," in *A New Mathematics Building at Yale* (New Haven: Yale University, n.d.), n.p.

[106] Charles W. Moore and Nicholas Pyle, eds., *The Yale Mathematics Building Competition: Architecture for a Time of Questioning* (New Haven: Yale University Press, 1974).

[107] Venturi, Scott Brown, and Izenour, *Learning from Las Vegas*, p. 150.

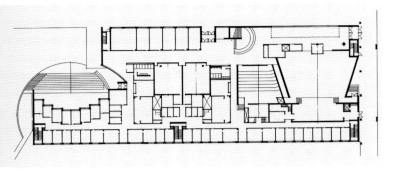

Figure 59
Humanities Building, State University of New York at Purchase, 1968–73
First-floor plan. Dated January 17, 1969; revised January 30, 1969
Whereabouts unknown

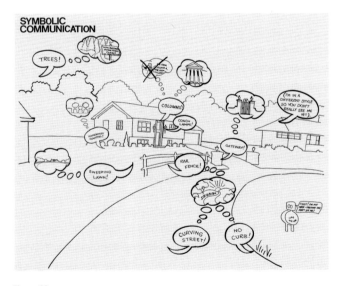

Figure 60
"Precedents of Suburban Symbols," from the "Learning from Levittown Studio," Yale University, 1970. From *Learning from Las Vegas*, 1972

While these university projects were being designed, Venturi and Scott Brown were teaching together at Yale, where he had been appointed in 1966 and she, quitting her professorship at UCLA after their marriage, had accepted a visiting position. They taught a celebrated trio of studios: the New York City subway, in 1967; Las Vegas, in 1968; and Levittown, in 1970. Scott Brown established the pedagogical structure of these courses, which grew from the model that she had learned from David Crane at Penn: each began with a lengthy period of interdisciplinary research—leaning heavily on architectural history and the social sciences, followed by a period of fieldwork—inclined sharply toward formal analysis, and ended with synthesis and design. The Las Vegas study, founded on their own previous investigation and writing and monumentalized in their book of 1972, was rightly the most famous, but the group of projects needs to be seen together in order to understand the range of their interests. For while the Las Vegas studio concentrated on iconography—and necessarily on what could be seen as the rather unsavory manipulation of common people by cunning advertisers—the subway and Levittown case studies sympathetically examined the success of residents and users in navigating and shaping the environments in which they found themselves.

The studio devoted to the Herald Square subway station, planned by Scott Brown, although she was not yet formally appointed at Yale, took place in the fall semester of 1967. She stipulated that they begin "by looking (non-judgmentally at first) at what is there."[108] Those transiting the labyrinthine, three-story complex of platforms, stairs, and tunnels were counted and observed, and their "decision points" and "desire lines" were mapped according to a methodology that Scott Brown adapted from city planning and urban design. In the end, the recommended design solutions were adjustments rather than remakings, derived from the more successful parts of the existing station. Circulation patterns were simplified and underused areas were closed off. Lighting was carefully varied, not washing all surfaces with

108 Denise Scott Brown, "Program Extracts: Introduction and First Phase," *Perspecta*, vol. 12 (1969), p. 50.

uniform brightness but modulated to help to define space. The architects depended heavily on signs, allowing commercial signage to be large, omnipresent, and bright, and organizing directional signage around a network of lighted color "threads" to guide passengers to their trains. Added to these visual stimuli were the sounds of different types of music and the smells of food and perfume, organized to define the character of different geographies. Venturi explained, "I think the value of our architectural study came from not trying to make architecture. The architect has limited control in the first place over the shapes of subway spaces which are constrained by the street above, the basements of buildings and the underground utilities. But he can work with lighting and the words and symbols of advertising as well as with assemblages of conventional subway elements such as gum machines."[109]

The famous fall 1968 Las Vegas studio, renamed by the students "The Grand Proletarian Cultural Locomotive" in the spirit of the times, was similarly sympathetic to the lessons to be learned from ordinary experience. But while it produced a wealth of further analysis of the system of signs and sheds as they functioned on the Strip, the studio did not alter Venturi and Scott Brown's already published interpretation of this environment and its significance. It did, however, add Steven Izenour to their team. A student of theirs at Penn, he was then completing his master's degree in environmental design at Yale, where he served as their teaching assistant. Izenour joined the firm the next year and joined them on the title page of the Las Vegas book when it appeared in 1972, permanently adding his breezy confidence and his special enthusiasm for the technologies of modern communication, theater, and exhibition design to the mixture of talents in the office.

The Levittown studio of 1970, promptly christened "Learning from Levittown," was their last collaborative teaching at Yale. It broke important new ground by focusing not on the original creators of the postwar suburb—builders like the Levitts—but, in the spirit of Herbert Gans,

on those who lived in such communities and the changes they wrought. Here was a sign system more subtle and personal than those of Herald Square and Las Vegas, which made it much more appealing (fig. 60). Although some of their Levittown findings appeared in *Learning from Las Vegas*, the hoped-for book never materialized, and it was only in the "Signs of Life" exhibition of 1976 at the Renwick Gallery in Washington that their wise and witty decoding of the suburban landscape was made available to the general public.[110]

The spirit of these studios was very directly transferred into a group of planning projects with which the firm was grappling at the same time. Closest to the tenor of sixties activism was the work they donated in 1968–72 to the Citizens Committee to Preserve and Develop the Crosstown Community, a Philadelphia grassroots organization that, like similar groups across the country, was battling against the encroachment of highway projects in poor neighborhoods.[111] The roadway in question was the proposed Crosstown Expressway, which was to cut a two-block swath through a faded commercial and residential district along South Street in order to complete a highway loop around Center City. Part of this area was a center of African-American life and commerce, and not entirely coincidentally, it also included the headquarters of the Venturi produce business at 1430 South Street. The sunken road would sharply divide black neighborhoods in the south from white neighborhoods to the north, leading George Dukes, president of the South West Central Residents Association, to label it "the Mason-Dixon Line."[112] Denise Scott Brown called it simply "an immoral act,"[113] and she took up the project not as a technocratic assignment but as a political cause. Mayor James Tate was already holding up the expressway in deference to credible threats of racial violence, giving Scott Brown (who was assisted by Izenour and a team of volunteer lawyers) time to prepare a counterproposal that they presented in September 1968 (fig. 61). It depicted what could be seen if the expressway were stopped: preserved nineteenth-century storefronts and revitalized businesses on

[109] Robert Venturi, "Mass Communication on the People Freeway or Piranesi Is Too Easy," *Perspecta*, vol. 12 (1969), p. 49.

[110] *Venturi, Scott Brown & Associates: On Houses and Housing*, Architectural Monographs, no. 21 (New York: St. Martin's Press, 1992), pp. 50–65; Venturi & Rauch, Architects, "Signs of Life: Symbols in the American City," *Aperture*, no. 77 (1976), pp. 49–65.

[111] Venturi, Scott Brown, and Izenour, *Learning from Las Vegas*, pp. 126–33; Lenora Berson, "The South Street Insurrection," *Philadelphia Magazine*, September 1969, pp. 87–92, 174–78, 181–82; Michelle Osborn, "The Crosstown Is Dead: Long Live the Crosstown," *Architectural Forum*, vol. 135 (October 1971), pp. 38–41.

[112] Quoted in Berson, "South Street," p. 92.

[113] Quoted in Cook and Klotz, *Conversations*, p. 265.

Figure 61

**South Street from the Philadelphia
Crosstown Community Planning
Study, 1968**

Whereabouts unknown

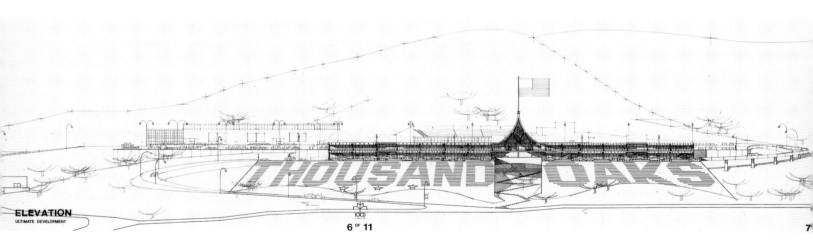

Figure 62

**Thousand Oaks Civic Center,
Competition, Thousand Oaks,
California, 1969**

Elevation. Ink, pencil, and transfer
letters on mylar, 21 x 81⅜"
(53.3 x 207.3 cm). Robert Venturi,
Steven Izenour, Arthur Jones, John
Anderson, and W. G. Clark

Collection of Venturi, Scott Brown
and Associates, Inc.

South Street, sympathetically enhanced residential blocks south of South, and two nodes of community services (with small school, clinic, recreational and meeting facilities). This vision, modest and closely meshed with what Scott Brown had learned through consultation about the neighborhood's sense of itself, was sufficiently vivid to hold its own when the chamber of commerce returned with a plan to resuscitate the expressway by covering it with a deck. A new team of consultants, who unlike Scott Brown were well paid, recommended against that expensive strategy in December 1970, and South Street was preserved. Scott Brown's proposed community service centers were not built, however.

The defenders of South Street had come to Scott Brown because her work in Las Vegas proved that she could appreciate the ordinary commercial vernacular, but the scale and structure of the Las Vegas strip offered little that was directly relevant to the Crosstown study. Not so in the 1969 competition for the Thousand Oaks Civic Center, for which they won an honorable mention. For the hillside site overlooking the Ventura Freeway just northwest of Los Angeles, they devised a simple steel-framed building with gigantic signage, inflating the typology of the North Canton city hall to the scale of the American highway (fig. 62). Robert Venturi's sense of humor was reflected throughout the design: in the flared, neon-lit legs of a giant flagpole, which recalled the shape of the live oak trees that gave the booming suburb its name in the lettered hillside; and in the notion that the individual government offices should be advertised to those arriving from the adjacent parking lot by "tastefully lettered signs on the balconies and fascias, to be read like today's special on the A&P windows."[114]

At California City, however, Scott Brown did not have to compete to work. The developer, Great Western United Corporation, recognized the relevance of their Las Vegas studies, and they turned to her in 1970–71 for help in reshaping the form and image of the sprawling, 100,000-acre subdivision-as-city, located near Edwards Air Force Base in the Mojave Desert. Much of the land had been sold, but only two thousand residents had settled there—mostly in trailers —while most lot owners waited for retirement or an eager buyer. Scott Brown recommended an ecological study, but she did not propose any significant recasting of the master plan. However, she and Venturi did devise various ways to increase the visual interest of this largely empty landscape, most notably a system of gigantic roadside signs for the Twenty Mule Team Parkway, the straight, twelve-mile road that led from the town center to a hilltop recreation center (figs. 63–66). Desert flower forms were chosen because they were "beautiful" and "uncommercial" and because they softened the harshness of the scene for desert-shy visitors.[115] At the town end of the Parkway, they designed a building for the town government and the developer's staff, containing these functions within a gold-mirrored glass cube that would shimmer with disconcerting scalelessness across the twelve miles of paving (fig. 67).[116] Signs and symbols were not always needed.

Taken as a whole, Venturi and Scott Brown's work of the late sixties demanded a great deal of its viewers. As Vincent Scully said, they had "broken through a haze of superficial idealism to the core of what is real in the present day,"[117] and there were many for whom the lessons to be learned from ordinary and real office buildings, apartment houses, suburban shopping centers, urban commercial districts, and tract developments were unpalatable. Compounding the problem was their now sharper rhetoric and the fact that many did not accept that one could study Levittown and Las Vegas without endorsing the capitalists who promoted suburban sprawl and invested in the gambling industry. The architectural historian Kenneth Frampton castigated them for adopting "a marginally tolerant attitude towards those values which are already desecrating large tracts of our physical environment."[118]

However, in the antiheroic climate of the time, Venturi and Scott Brown's work also found notable champions. In Robert Stern's *New Directions in American Architecture* and Vincent Scully's *American Architecture and Urbanism* (both published in 1969), Venturi and Scott Brown were identified as

[114] Steven Izenour and Denise Scott Brown, "Civic Center Competition for Thousand Oaks, California," *Architectural Design*, vol. 41 (February 1971), p. 113.

[115] Venturi, Scott Brown, and Izenour, *Learning from Las Vegas*, p. 181.

[116] Ibid., pp. 185–87.

[117] Vincent Scully, *The Work of Venturi and Rauch, Architects and Planners*, exh. brochure (New York: Whitney Museum of American Art, 1971), n.p.

[118] Kenneth Frampton, "America, 1960–1970: Notes on Urban Images and Theory," *Casabella*, vol. 35 (December 1971), p. 33.

Figure 63

**General Plan, California City,
California, 1970–71**

Windshield view of Twenty Mule
Team Parkway. Marker and pencil
on vellum, 14 x 28″ (35.6 x 71.1 cm)
Robert Venturi. Signed and dated
July 17, 1970

Collection of Venturi, Scott Brown
and Associates, Inc.

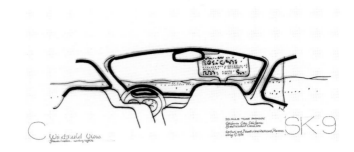

Figure 64

**General Plan, California City,
California, 1970–71**

Roadside flowers on Twenty Mule Team
Parkway. Marker and colored marker
on yellow tracing paper, 12 x 28″
(30.5 x 71.1 cm). Robert Venturi

Collection of Venturi, Scott Brown and
Associates, Inc.

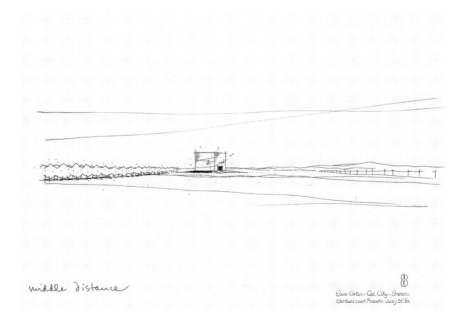

Figure 65

**General Plan, California City,
California, 1970–71**

Perspective with city hall in the middle
distance. Marker and pencil on vellum,
18 x 24″ (45.7 x 61 cm). Robert Venturi
Dated July 31, 1970

Collection of Venturi, Scott Brown
and Associates, Inc.

Figure 66

**General Plan, California City,
California, 1970–71**

Roadside flowers on Twenty Mule Team
Parkway. Marker and colored marker
on yellow tracing paper, 12 x 27¼"
(30.5 x 69.2 cm). Robert Venturi

Collection of Venturi, Scott Brown and
Associates, Inc.

Figure 67

**General Plan, California City,
California, 1970–71**

Southwest elevation of city hall
Panchromatic film on photomechanical
print, 20½ x 31¼" (52.1 x 79.4 cm)
Terry Vaughn and W. G. Clark. Dated
May 7, 1971

Collection of Venturi, Scott Brown
and Associates, Inc.

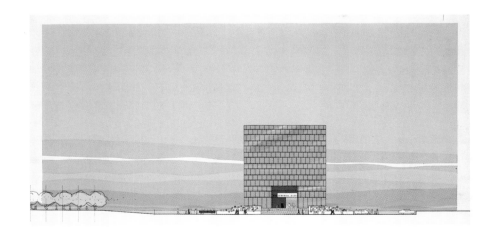

highly significant contemporary designers, and in October 1971, the Japanese journal *Architecture and Urbanism* devoted an entire issue to their work—the first such recognition. That was also the month in which, at the invitation of the Whitney Museum of American Art, they installed an exhibition of their own designs and projects. Highlighting the most recent and controversial works—the Las Vegas and Levittown studios, the Mathematics Building at Yale, and the Transportation Square building—and presenting them on two bold, billboard-sized backlit panels (executed by Steven Izenour and Gerod Clark), the Whitney show naturally attracted critical attention. But the general tone was remarkably respectful, even among those who were not fully convinced, and the quantity of reporting for what was actually a very modest, month-long display was remarkable. The *New York Times* devoted five articles to the show, including the longest and most insightful discussion of their work to date, written by Paul Goldberger and published in the Sunday magazine section.[119] Ada Louise Huxtable, the *Times*'s architecture critic, wrote about the show twice, and while she voiced some misgivings along the way, she called their Las Vegas and Levittown studios "brilliant" and their architecture "eye-opening and catalytic."[120] She summarized: "Today, not only art but truth is complex and contradictory, values are inverted and humor is black. Necessary change comes through the shock of recognizing the irrationality of reality."[121]

Coming Home

In 1969, when Scott Brown became a partner in the firm, Steven Izenour, fresh from the Las Vegas studio, also came to work for them. David Vaughan, who completed his architectural training under Kahn at Penn in 1968, joined the office in 1970. That year Scott Brown and Venturi both stopped teaching to devote themselves entirely to the practice.

The Venturis had lived with Vanna Venturi when they married in 1967, but after a few months, they moved to I. M. Pei's Society Hill Towers, where ensconced in a building for which they had little affection, they could look down on the patterns of the city that they loved. In May 1971 they adopted their son James—called Jimmy—who imposed substantial burdens on his very busy parents but also greatly enriched their lives. Hoping now to be able to combine home and office, they went house hunting, and while they could not arrange to live and work under one roof, they found a splendid home. Designed in 1909 by Milton Medary, it stood with formal symmetry at the end of a private lane in the leafy, in-city suburb of Mount Airy. They were especially captivated by its exceedingly rare Art Nouveau details. They moved in in 1972, and commenced, through decoration and furnishing, to make the house their own. That year, when Scott Brown was asked if she were interested in the deanship of the School of Architecture at Yale, she declined the invitation.

The work that they did together over the next several years seemed to draw energy from these new professional and personal relationships. To be sure, skirmishing and anguishing over their investigations of popular culture continued, and the publication in 1972 of *Learning from Las Vegas* stirred a considerable tempest. James Marston Fitch excoriated "that desert hell-hole,"[122] and Fred Koetter lashed out at them for "enjoy[ing] not only the formal idiosyncrasies of the strip, but its message of popular commerce and public license as well."[123] While the continuing influence of popular culture over their work was palpable, however, it now took its place beside other themes. In December 1971, Scott Brown had conceded, "Facing the implications of Las Vegas in our work is proving much more difficult than describing Las Vegas,"[124] and they seemed glad to take up other challenges.

The mood of Scott Brown and Venturi's work in the early 1970s was captured in two of the most distinctive buildings of the twentieth century: the pair of little beach houses built side by side on the coast of Nantucket for the families of law professor David Trubek of Yale and his brother-in-law George Wislocki, an environmentalist (fig. 68).[125] Trubek had taken Vincent Scully's advice in coming

119 Goldberger, "Less Is More," pp. 34–37, 102–6.

120 Ada Louise Huxtable, "Plastic Flowers Are Almost All Right," *New York Times*, October 10, 1971.

121 Ada Louise Huxtable, "Celebrating 'Dumb, Ordinary' Architecture," *New York Times*, October 1, 1971.

122 James Marston Fitch, "Single Point Perspective: Learning about Las Vegas . . ." *Architectural Forum*, vol. 140 (March 1974), p. 89.

123 Fred Koetter, "On Robert Venturi, Denise Scott Brown, and Steven Izenour's Learning from Las Vegas," *Oppositions*, vol. 3 (May 1974), p. 100.

124 Denise Scott Brown, "Pop Off: Reply to Frampton [1971]," in

Venturi and Scott Brown, *View from the Campidoglio*, p. 37.

125 My analysis of these designs was aided by the research paper written by Nicholas Sawicki at the University of Pennsylvania, December 1998.

Figure 68
**Trubek and Wislocki Houses,
Nantucket, Massachusetts,
1970–72**
Front facades

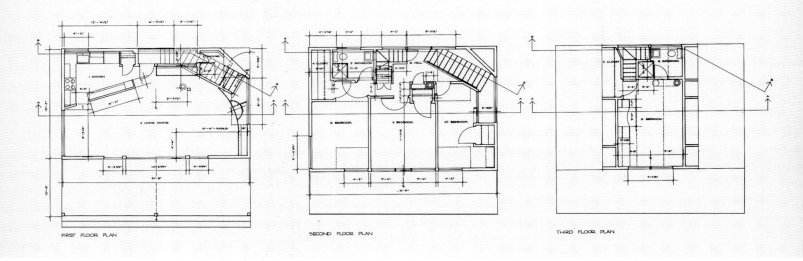

FIRST FLOOR PLAN   SECOND FLOOR PLAN   THIRD FLOOR PLAN

Figure 69

Trubek and Wislocki Houses, Nantucket, Massachusetts, 1970–72

First-, second-, and third-floor plans of the Trubek house. Ink on mylar, details. Dated July 1, 1971

Collection of Venturi, Scott Brown and Associates, Inc.

Figure 70

Coxe and Hayden House and Studio, Block Island, Rhode Island, 1979–80

Rear facades

to the firm to create two cottages so that the five Trubek and Wislocki children could spend their vacations together. Designed quickly in the winter of 1970–71, the houses started in Venturi's mind as children of his tall-chimneyed shingle-style beach house project of 1959, but the realities of Nantucket construction costs shrank them. They did evince a Philadelphia School bigness of details, which were organized with telling precision on the small facades, but unlike the similarly big, but diminutive, Lieb house, the Trubek and Wislocki houses were covered in cedar shingles, and the chosen context was not pop art but architectural history— a form of referencing that the architects had recently reintroduced in their design for the Yale Mathematics Building. While shingled, the historical models for these cottages were not the great houses of the shingle style; in scale, if not in detail, they were more like the humble nineteenth-century fishermen's dwellings in the village of Siasconset on Nantucket. The architects could not help but point out that the studied misalignment of the siting of these gable-ended buildings was like that of the Greek temples at Selinunte, in Sicily,[126] and while the casual visitor may not identify that reference, there is something ineffably heroic about these little buildings on the edge of the sea. The optimism with which they face a vast world seems particularly American.

The slightly larger Trubek house was big enough for some of the spatial layering and vertical integration that had marked Venturi's earlier houses (fig. 69). The front door was pulled into a niche behind the skin of the building, and when opened, it deposited the visitor in an already moving swirl of diagonal activity. In one corner, the stair to the bedrooms rose obliquely from a curvilinear bench-cum-step, its trajectory explaining—but not perfectly matching—the cropped southwest angle of the house. From the second floor, a tinier stairway—hidden behind what looked like a closet door—led to the master bedroom under the roof.

Completed in 1972, the houses were warmly received, which went a little way toward balancing the consternation with which *Learning from Las Vegas* was greeted in some circles.

In *House & Garden*, George Wislocki enthused, "Plainly we are in love with those houses,"[127] and Vincent Scully lionized them in *The Shingle Style Today: Or, The Historian's Revenge* (1974), where they appeared on the cover. Four years later they were featured in the *New York Times Magazine*, where Paul Goldberger praised them as "serene and restful places, full of understanding of the nature of their island"—hardly something that was said of the firm's Las Vegas–inspired work.[128]

So prominent were these two small houses in reshaping public understanding of Venturi and Scott Brown's work that the architects were commissioned in 1979 to create a similar pair on Block Island for the extended family of Weld Coxe and Mary Hayden (fig. 70). Both Coxe and Hayden were architectural marketing consultants who worked occasionally for the firm. This time, the smaller building was a workshop with two guest rooms above, but the successful Nantucket formulas were repeated: big windows carefully assembled within a vernacular frame, and studied placement of the two small buildings in dialogue with each other and the sea.

In the same year that they began the Trubek and Wislocki houses, Venturi and Scott Brown also started to work for Peter and Sandy Brant. Their association with these wealthy collectors of pop art—and the publishers of *Art in America* and *Antiques*—would create three buildings and two important unbuilt projects, all of which helped their star to ascend during the 1970s. The first project was a country house on a horse farm near Greenwich, Connecticut. Designed in 1971–73 and completed in the spring of 1974, this first Brant house provided the collectors with wall space for their large paintings and a suitable setting for their collection of Art Deco furniture (fig. 71).[129] Like the little houses in Nantucket, it alluded to history with new enthusiasm, referencing the symmetrical bow-fronted country houses of the British Regency and American Federal periods, and in particular Gore Place in Waltham, Massachusetts. In fact, Venturi waggishly labeled the house "Brant's Place." But many other sources were tapped for the design, including

[126] Venturi, Scott Brown, and Izenour, *Learning from Las Vegas*, p. 169.

[127] Quoted in "Sharing Land the Compound Way: A Pair of Seaside Summer Cottages Designed to Match the New England Seascape,"

House & Garden Second House, Spring/Summer 1974, p. 70.

[128] Paul Goldberger, "Siblings by the Seaside," *New York Times Magazine*, May 21, 1978, p. 84.

[129] My analysis of this design was aided by the research paper written by Isabel Taube at the University of Pennsylvania, December 1998.

Figure 71
**Brant House, Greenwich,
Connecticut, 1970–74**
Front facade

Figure 72
**Brant House, Greenwich,
Connecticut, 1970–74**
First-floor plan. Ink on mylar,
24 x 36" (61 x 91.4 cm)
Collection of Venturi, Scott Brown
and Associates, Inc.

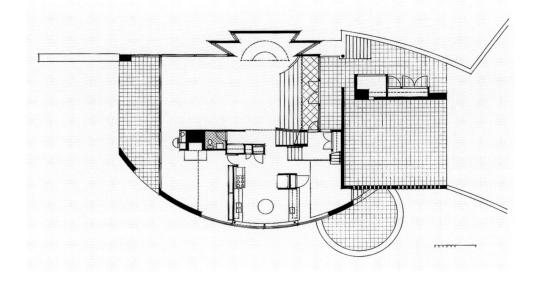

Figure 73

Brant House, Greenwich, Connecticut, 1970–74

Entrance stairway and dining area

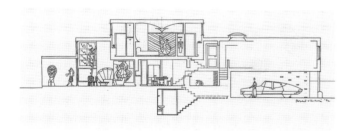

Figure 74

Brant House, Greenwich, Connecticut, 1970–74

Section. Pencil on vellum, detail
Robert Venturi. Signed and dated
January 25, 1972

Collection of Venturi, Scott Brown
and Associates, Inc.

the lessons learned in Levittown, which taught that Americans now entered their homes through their garages. Accordingly, the Brant house turned its garage toward the arriving visitor, and as at Le Corbusier's Villa Savoye, the owners pulled in beneath a hovering ribbon-windowed facade. Those who parked in the driveway entered along a walkway to the right of the garage, joining the path that the owners would take directly from their car (fig. 72).

Inside, the house dealt ingeniously with the clients' program while creating a spatial adventure. Arriving at the front door, whether directly from the garage or by passing around it, one encountered a broad but shallow vestibule and then a sweeping stair of alternating black and white marble steps (fig. 73). Ahead and up half a flight, the two-story height of the living and dining room opened serenely toward a wall of windows, but there was ample wall space on all other sides for big paintings by the Brants' friend Andy Warhol. A side-lit alcove, topped by a sculptural, Decolike lighting baffle, provided a showcase for their period dining furniture, and the sleek, mildly modern lines of the house were generally sympathetic to their collection. To the left of the entrance was the kitchen, unexpectedly but rightly filling the house's front bow and establishing the modern kitchen at the center of domestic life, as Frank Lloyd Wright had done in his Usonian houses. The private areas of the house were masterfully contrived as interlocking layers of vertically integrated space (fig. 74). Next to the kitchen was a sunny, two-story playroom for the Brants' children, connected by its own stairway with their bedrooms over the garage and thus creating a separate zone for the younger members of the family. This back stair met the front stair on a skylit landing, where the guest room was also located. From the landing a private stairway ascended to the third floor and the master bedroom, which, like Venturi's own room in his mother's house, was a privileged realm atop the whole.

The planning, massing, and historical references of the Brant house owed a good deal to two unbuilt projects. For

Figure 75
D'Agostino House, Clinton, New York, 1968–73
Model. Photograph of lost orginal

Figure 76
Wike House, Willistown, Pennsylvania, 1968–69
Model. Chipboard and colored paper, 6½ x 30¾ x 22½″ (16.5 x 78.1 x 57.2 cm)
Collection of Venturi, Scott Brown and Associates, Inc.

Anthony and Muriel D'Agostino, Venturi had designed a house in 1968 that also greeted visitors in a grandiose garage and then led them upward via a gigantic flight of stairs to an elevated suite of rooms, from which to view the snowy plateau of upstate New York (fig. 75). Atop the house was a master bedroom capped in wood vaulting, which was likened to "Polish synagogues of the eighteenth century," while the house's stepped gable was described as Dutch and its gray brick was compared to the color of a weathered barn that stood nearby.[130] The D'Agostino project advanced through the drafting of construction documents in 1971, but although discussions continued, it went no further.

A larger, but similarly disposed, house had been designed for their friends Roffe and Penny Wike in 1968–69. Arriving visitors would have found a welcoming garage and an adjacent loggia, sheltered at the base of the house's bow front (fig. 76). From the loggia, an astonishingly extravagant, exterior stairway cut through the entire house to raise visitors to an entrance porch at the level of the main floor. The upper floors were layered together in a complicated section and connected by multiple stairs, and, once more, a single bedroom occupied the uppermost floor. The house was designed to complement the couple's eighteenth-century antiques, and the architects attributed the inspiration for the bold main elevation to Vanbrugh, and specified yellow brick to recollect the tawny stone of the neo-Palladian Holkham Hall (Norfolk, England, 1734–61).[131]

As had been intended for these unbuilt precursors, the Brant house was constructed of brick. The major facade was laid up in two shades of blue-green, assembled in a subtle pattern that was the subject of almost endless study in the first months of 1973, toward the end of the design process (fig. 77). While perhaps inspired by the nineteenth-century polychromy that George Hersey discussed in *High Victorian Gothic: A Study in Associationism* (1972), the effect was eerily naturalistic, with the two tonalities echoing the color variations of the surrounding lawns and bushes. It was clear that this pattern was not meant to be a legible sign or symbol;

[130] Venturi, Scott Brown, and Izenour, *Learning from Las Vegas*, p. 164.

[131] Ibid., p. 167.

[132] Paul Goldberger, "Tract House, Celebrated," *New York Times Magazine*, September 14, 1975, pp. 68–69, 74; Yukio Futagawa, ed., *Global Architecture*, vol. 3, *Modern Houses* (Tokyo: A.D.A. Edita, 1981).

[133] Denise Scott Brown and Robert Venturi, interview by students in History of Art 782, University of Pennsylvania, November 13, 1998.

its interest was purely visual, in this case, aiming to establish a visual connection between the house and its surroundings.

Like the Trubek and Wislocki houses, the Brant house was widely and favorably noticed, helped no doubt by the prominence of its owners. Paul Goldberger, the youthful but now perennial champion of Venturi's work, wrote it up glowingly in the *New York Times Magazine* in 1975, and in 1981 it was given a lavish color presentation in the third volume of Yukio Futagawa's "Global Architecture" series.[132]

These well-regarded residential projects were soon joined by what Robert Venturi called the firm's "first high-falutin job"—the large addition to Oberlin College's Allen Memorial Art Museum, which they built in 1973–77.[133] When its director Richard Spear was newly appointed in 1972, he immediately began to search for an architect to undertake the long-contemplated expansion of Cass Gilbert's elegant quattrocento-style building (1915–17), facing Tappan Square—the green common shared by the town and the college. A search committee dominated by art historians unanimously chose Venturi, of whom Spear wrote, "His writings may have created a controversial image for some, but his personality, his intelligence, his sensitivity, and his architecture convince us that he is ideally suited to Oberlin's needs."[134] Spear and Venturi got along famously and became good friends.

Venturi likened the challenge of adding a side wing to the symmetrical renaissance museum to placing "a bowler hat on a Venus," and throughout the summer and fall of 1973 the office worked to design the most sympathetic placement of the needed additional gallery space, classrooms, studios, conservation laboratories, and library.[135] The adopted solution linked the old building and the new educational and laboratory wing with a single, two-story, Kahnian gallery "room," whose corners were cropped in Philadelphia Style deference to their neighbors (fig. 78). Never before had the architects' respect for context been put to such a test, and they reveled in it. For Venturi, this meant respectful treatment of both the "plain" and

Figure 77
Brant House, Greenwich, Connecticut, 1970–74
Elevation studies (overlay). Marker and colored marker on yellow tracing paper, 12 x 28¾" (30.5 x 73 cm)
Robert Venturi
Collection of Venturi, Scott Brown and Associates, Inc..

My analysis of this design was aided by the research paper written by Kelly McCullough at the University of Pennsylvania, December 1998.

[134] Richard Spear to Robert Fuller [President of Oberlin College], March 27, 1973. Courtesy of Richard Spear.

[135] Robert Venturi, "Plain and Fancy Architecture by Cass Gilbert and the Additions to the Allen Memorial Art Museum by Venturi and Rauch, at Oberlin [1976–77]," in Venturi and Scott Brown, *View from the Campidoglio*, p. 51.

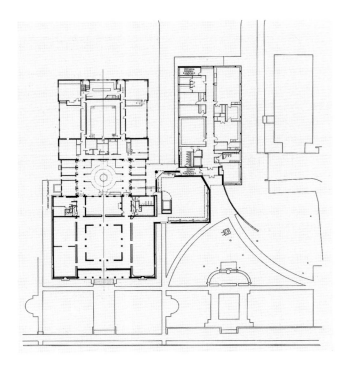

Figure 78
**Allen Memorial Art Museum,
Oberlin College, Ohio, 1973–77**
First-floor plan
Whereabouts unknown

"fancy"—both Cass Gilbert's palazzo and the modest Midwest town in which it was built, where a gas station stood just across Lorain Street from the museum.[136] The resulting design was a decorated shed that managed to be deferential to all while speaking in its own voice. The academic/laboratory wing was pulled back to align itself with the service wing of the adjacent Hall Auditorium (Wallace Harrison, 1953), and it adapted that building's brick facade and ribbon windows. The linking gallery room carried a clerestory across the top of its facade, echoing the windows of the new wing's top-floor library, while its facade veneer of rose granite and cream limestone repeated Cass Gilbert's colors of 1917.

Great care was given to designing the masonry pattern of the main facade, which was undertaken in the same year that the facade patterns of the Brant house and the Hartford Stage Company Theater were worked out. After sketching diaper patterns and experimenting with a flecked pattern of scattered rose granite, the architects settled on a not-quite-square and not-quite-aligned checkerboard (figs. 79–81). This gave a balance of color nearly equal to that in the original facade without imitating it. The pattern could be proportioned in such a way that it met certain key points of the earlier building's detailing (at the cornice and water table) and then studiously failed to match at other locations, preserving the necessary distinction of the new. The pattern was a purely formal solution to a demanding visual problem (fig. 82), but Venturi and Scott Brown's rhetoric invited onlookers to imagine its symbolism. The trademark red-and-white checkerboard of Ralston Purina Corporation prompted wags to dub the museum "Purina Art Chow."

Venturi was determined to create excellent natural lighting in the two-story gallery. He visited Philip Johnson for advice (Johnson liked skylights but said they were impractical),[137] and he and Scott Brown went to see Kahn's recently completed Kimbell Museum in March 1974, only days after the architect's death. They found the silvery skylighting especially magical, but they preferred more ordinary lighting and

[136] Ibid.

[137] Philip Johnson and Robert Venturi, Minutes of meeting conference, February 28, 1974, "3.3 Program Meeting Min.," VSB box 55 (VSBA archives).

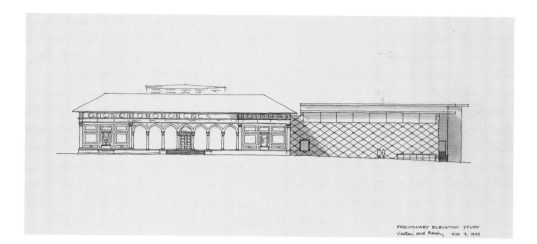

Figure 79

Allen Memorial Art Museum, Oberlin College, Ohio, 1973–77

Preliminary elevation study. Marker and colored marker on yellow tracing paper, 18 x 36¾" (45.7 x 93.3 cm) Robert Venturi. Dated August 7, 1973

Collection of Venturi, Scott Brown and Associates, Inc.

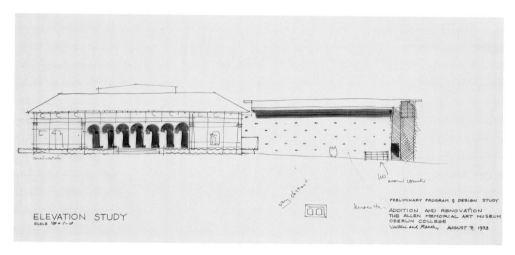

Figure 80

Allen Memorial Art Museum, Oberlin College, Ohio, 1973–77

Preliminary elevation study. Marker on yellow tracing paper, 18 x 36" (45.7 x 91.4 cm). Robert Venturi Signed and dated August 7, 1973

Collection of Venturi, Scott Brown and Associates, Inc.

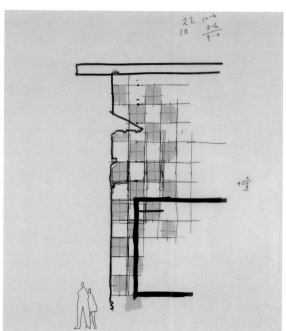

Figure 81

Allen Memorial Art Museum, Oberlin College, Ohio, 1973–77

Elevation. Marker and colored marker on yellow tracing paper, 24 x 22½" (61 x 57.2 cm). Robert Venturi

Collection of Venturi, Scott Brown and Associates, Inc.

Figure 82

Allen Memorial Art Museum, Oberlin College, Ohio

Cass Gilbert's building (1915–17) with gallery addition (1973–77) at right

Figure 83
**Allen Memorial Art Museum,
Oberlin College, Ohio, 1973–77**
Gallery interior

Figure 84
**Allen Memorial Art Museum,
Oberlin College, Ohio, 1973–77**
Ionic column, detail

they knew that they could not accomplish Kahn's effects without a "Texas-size budget."[138] This firmed their resolve to light the space with a clerestory of conventional windows, but by locating them in a coved recess above the plane of the ceiling and by baffling their light with frosted plexiglass "curtains," they were able to create their own magic (fig. 83).

Although the big gallery was the physical connector of the old building and the new wing, for security reasons, it could only be entered from the old building and therefore was not a thoroughfare. Students and staff passing between the new facilities and the teaching spaces at the back of the old museum had to traverse a covered walkway attached to the rear of the linking gallery. This route passed outside the window set in the gallery's cropped northeast corner, and at this location in June 1976, only months before the building was completed, the architects added one of its most celebrated features, a Greek Ionic column (fig. 84). Avowedly classical, this detail did not pay homage, however, to Gilbert's cool Tuscan Renaissance; the spiritual brothers of this squat and wooden Ionian were the porch columns on the houses across Lorain Street. Unlike the works of conventional postmodernists, which would soon fill the pages of architectural magazines, Venturi's classicism was never literal.

The apparent ease with which this strong design took its place among its neighbors was repeated in the architects' other major academic commission of this period, the Faculty Club for the Pennsylvania State University (1973–76).[139] Here the context, at the edge of the campus, was the neo-colonial white-brick Nittany Lion Inn and, to the south, a vista through a grove of oaks and across North Atherton Street and a golf course to the low mountains of central Pennsylvania. At the heart of the architects' conception was a medieval-like two-story dining hall, which they preserved throughout several revisions. At first, in April 1974, their proposal was a two-story building with the major dining room on the upper floor. Its white brick would have been consonant with the inn, but its big-windowed, flat-roofed, vocabulary seemed more modern and marked it as coeval

[138] Robert Venturi and Denise Scott Brown, "Notes of visit to the Kimbell Art Museum," March 21, 1974, "3.3 Program Meeting Min.," VSB box 55 (VSBA archives).

[139] My analysis of this design was aided by the research paper written by Ka-Kee Yan at the University of Pennsylvania, December 1998.

with the academic wing of the Oberlin museum (fig. 85). In July, warned that they must reduce the size of the building to meet the budget, they not only radically reconfigured the program arrangement—shrinking the main dining room, dropping it to ground level, and banishing the smaller meeting rooms and the bar into the basement—but they also reconceived the exterior treatment. Rather than looking to the Nittany Lion Inn to define the character of the design, they now turned to the forested lot and redesigned the building as a woody shingle-style house, all hatted under a great, low-slung roof of cedar (fig. 86). Although other architects had by now begun to take up Venturi's suggestive experiments with a shingled vocabulary, most had focused on the pretty, picturesque character of the style. Venturi, however, followed Nikolaus Pevsner's and Vincent Scully's predilection for the more severe, abstract variations of the genre, like H. H. Richardson's Stoughton house (Cambridge, Massachusetts, 1882–83), as bespoken in the Penn State Faculty Club's taut composition of vast, shingled planes and large, simple windows. This revision, with the clerestory-lit dining commons painted light green to intensify the effect of the surrounding trees, was constructed in 1975–76. But the club could never obtain a liquor license, and that, combined with its location on the edge of the campus, led to its rather quick abandonment and its transformation into a conference center.

Their woody idiom, more abstract than most acknowledge but still identifiably linked to historical precedents, spawned two smaller offspring in the mid-seventies. Just when the design of the Faculty Club was turning toward the shingle style in 1974, Venturi was beginning to sketch a small weekend house for *Village Voice* theater critic and columnist Carll Tucker on his parent's estate in Katonah, New York (fig. 87).[140] It was a cedar-shingled tower whose big external features and combative interplay of vertical spaces, wrapped around the chimney, hearkened back to the Frug House. Inside, the Spartan plan provided only a small bedroom, bath, and kitchen at ground level, from

[140] My analysis of this design was aided by the research paper written by Isabel Taube at the University of Pennsylvania, December 1998.

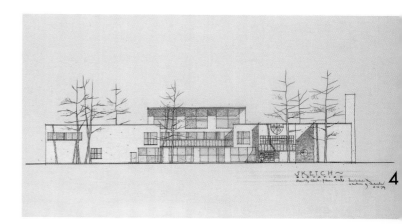

Figure 85

Faculty Club, The Pennsylvania State University, University Park, Pennsylvania, 1973–76

Elevation. Marker, pencil, colored pencil, and transfer letters on yellow tracing paper, 18 x 36" (45.7 x 91.4 cm)
Robert Venturi. Dated April 16, 1974
Collection of Venturi, Scott Brown and Associates, Inc.

Figure 86

Faculty Club, The Pennsylvania State University, University Park, Pennsylvania, 1973–76

Perspective. Marker and transfer letters on vellum, 24 x 36" (61 x 91.4 cm)
Collection of Venturi, Scott Brown and Associates, Inc.

Figure 87
**Tucker House, Katonah, New York,
1974–76**
Front facade

Figure 88
**Tucker House, Katonah, New York,
1974–76**
Living room with fireplace

which a narrow stair led up behind the chimney to a single, two-story room, girdled by a library balcony and centered on a great fireplace that echoed the symbolic gable of the house's profile (fig. 88). Large windows on three walls and a great oculus, expressed externally as a dormer, lit this small, tall aerie, bringing in the woods and allowing outside viewers to see right through the house. Tucker knew what he wanted—"irony, anguish, wit, a yearning for a monumental certainty and the awareness that such certainty is and always was . . . a grand illusion"—and he got it.[141]

A year later, in 1975, Venturi worked out a similar solution for the more ambitious program that the Brants set for a ski lodge in Vail, Colorado, to be shared with Jed Johnson, Andy Warhol's art director, cameraman, and close friend (fig. 89).[142] The tower was four stories tall this time, and the vertical spatial routing was enormously complex, beginning with a grand axial stair rising from the ground floor (with its sauna and storage room) to a floor of simple, cramped bunkrooms (fig. 90). From there, a stairway wedged tightly into the corner—as in the Wislocki house—rose to the kitchen/dining floor (where there was also a guest bedroom) and on up to the atticlike living room at the top of the house (fig. 91). Inside and out, the house was made of wood, and the living room, with its wooden groin vault, was an especially congenial setting for the Brant's collection of Mission and Stickley furniture. The Brant-Johnson house professed no specific historical pedigree, but it seemed to know history very well. Venturi avowed, "We thought of an Art Nouveau grandfather clock with arts and crafts overtones."[143]

At the same time the Brants also asked for a large house in Tucker's Town, Bermuda, where they had begun to vacation.[144] Above the pink beaches of Castle Harbour Bay on one side and the Atlantic Ocean on the other, they created an almost phantasmagoric house in white stucco, washed and warmed by history and climate alike (fig. 92). Deferring to the locale and the design review authority of the Mid Ocean Club, which controlled the land, the house reverberated to the gentle rhythms of the island's traditional

[141] "Tucker House, New York 1975," *L'Architecture d'aujourd'hui*, no. 197 (June 1978), p. 20.

[142] My analysis of this design was aided by the research paper written by Isabel Taube at the University of Pennsylvania, December 1998.

[143] Quoted in N.M. [Nori Miller], "Forceful Gesture on a Wooded Hillside," *AIA Journal*, vol. 67 (mid-May 1978), p. 103.

[144] My analysis of this design was aided by the research paper written by Isabel Taube at the University of Pennsylvania, December 1998.

Figure 89
Brant-Johnson Ski House, Vail, Colorado, 1975–77

Perspective. Panchromatic film on photomechanical print, 22 ¼ x 28 ¾"
(56.5 x 73 cm). Robert Venturi
Signed and dated 1975

Collection of Venturi, Scott Brown and Associates, Inc.

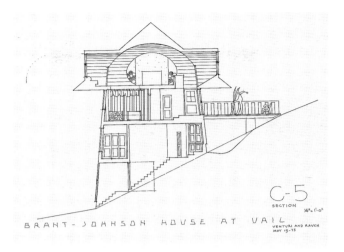

Figure 90
Brant-Johnson Ski House, Vail, Colorado, 1975–77

Section. Pencil on vellum, 18 x 24"
(45.7 x 61 cm). Robert Venturi
Dated May 19, 1975

Collection of Venturi, Scott Brown and Associates, Inc.

Figure 91
Brant-Johnson Ski House, Vail, Colorado, 1975–77

Top floor

Figure 92
Brant House, Tucker's Town, Bermuda, 1975–77

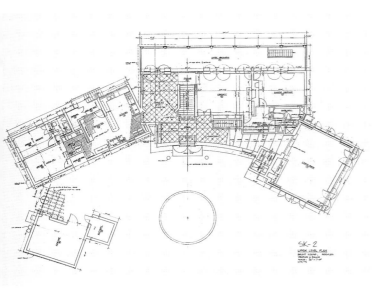

Figure 93
Brant House, Tucker's Town, Bermuda, 1975–77

Upper-level plan. Pencil on vellum, 30 x 42" (76.2 x 106.7 cm)
Dated January 9, 1975

Collection of Venturi, Scott Brown and Associates, Inc.

architecture. But underneath lay a remarkably sophisticated plan and spatial system, with its top-floor entry and a main stair leading downward toward the bedrooms and the sea in a manner indebted to George Howe's High Hollow house (Philadelphia, 1914–16), and its master-bedroom suite and service functions housed in two distinct blocks attached obliquely to the main body of the house (fig. 93). The latter arrangement echoed, without apparent knowledge, the plans that Kahn had proposed for Saint Andrew's Priory (Valyermo, California, 1961–67) and the Dominican Motherhouse of Saint Catherine de Ricci (Media, Pennsylvania, 1965–66), where the various functions of the program were expressed as individual pavilions, which "make up their minds where their positions are."[145]

Completed in 1977, this third Brant house was published in *Architectural Digest*—the glamorous mass-circulation magazine—as the Tucker house had been.[146] The easy-to-like forms of these latest houses and the notable absence of an accompanying polemic from their designers earned them a wide audience. While by no means forswearing the philosophical bases of their architecture, in an interview in 1972, Scott Brown allowed that a new mood had taken hold: "Our work in the firm changes with maturing, with success, with the advent of new people, and in general with living our lives. Bob's work is tense and brittle and it will always be; that's one of its strengths. But it becomes less stridently so. It becomes easier. The irony which is in it shifts to another plane. It becomes greater through letting in the humanity, letting in the love, through not being quite as brittle about human relationships."[147]

Revolutionary Times and the Silent Majority

Although somewhat overshadowed by these significant new themes, Venturi and Scott Brown's social activism and the pop cultural enthusiasm, which had marked their Yale studios, the Thousand Oaks and California City plans, and the South Street project, did not disappear during these years. Indeed, had more of the proposals that they prepared

[145] Louis I. Kahn, *Architecture: The John Lawrence Memorial Lectures* (New Orleans: Tulane University School of Architecture, 1972), n.p.

[146] Carol Vogel, "Architecture: Robert Venturi," *Architectural Digest*, vol. 37 (October 1980), pp. 88–95; Paul

Goldberger, "Architecture: Venturi and Rauch," *Architectural Digest*, vol. 35 (January/February 1978), pp. 100–7.

[147] Scott Brown, "An Interview" (interview by Linda Groat), p. 55.

during the early seventies for the celebration of the American Bicentennial in Philadelphia been executed, the Trubek and Wislocki houses, the Brant houses, and the Allen Memorial Art Museum would have stood together with a greater variety of other projects. As it was, Venturi and Scott Brown completed only a few works in conjunction with the two-hundredth birthday of the nation, most notably Franklin Court in Philadelphia and the "Signs of Life" exhibition in Washington, D.C., but these very significant undertakings furthered a new public appreciation of their art.

In 1968–69, disappointed by the generally vapid architecture of Expo '67 in Montreal and dismayed by the unremedied injustices and strife of American society, Scott Brown had begun to make suggestions for the international exhibition that many assumed would mark the Bicentennial in Philadelphia. She burst the balloon of pompous world's fair rhetoric ("Man and His World" had been the Montreal theme), decreeing that the times were "non-heroic . . . , non-universalist, anti-architectural."[148] In such an era, and with such challenges before the nation, it would be far better if the fair adopted the modest motto "House in Order by 1976," under which the "celebration [of] social innovation would overshadow architectural innovation." She and Venturi laid out a thoughtful plan for a fair that brought economic benefit to black neighborhoods, trained the unemployed for good jobs, created new housing, and tactfully asked other nations to showcase their successes in public transportation, schools, and trash collection. The architecture of this socially responsible fair would necessarily consist of "modest buildings with big signs"—that is, decorated sheds.[149]

So widespread was the acceptance of such antiestablishment sentiment at the time that Venturi and Scott Brown were commissioned to develop this thinking further.[150] In January 1972 they were among a consortium of six Philadelphia architectural firms, headed by Louis Kahn, who were hired by the Philadelphia 1976 Bicentennial Corporation to prepare a proposal for submission to the American Revolution Bicentennial Commission, which

would decide which events would receive federal funds. In February, after the site of the fair, on industrial land near the mouth of the Schuylkill, was selected, they worked quickly through the spring to design a linear fairground organized around what they nicknamed the "Streep"—a hybridized street and commercial strip that clearly revealed the lessons learned in Las Vegas (fig. 94). Dubbed "The Street of the World," it was to be overhung by gigantic multimedia signs and lined by simple sheds with spectacular facades. Steven Izenour was the project manager, and Scott Brown was heavily involved in framing this conception. Kahn's own design, the famous Forum of the Availabilities, evidently drew some of its streetlike character from their thinking, but, despite its combined energies, the Philadelphia proposal was rejected by the commission in May, ending the city's hopes for a world's fair. The federal authorities balked at assigning world's fair status to any single city.

This left Philadelphia's Bicentennial celebration in the hands of local organizations, and that fall, the Greater Philadelphia Cultural Alliance asked Venturi and Scott Brown to make plans for adapting the Benjamin Franklin Parkway, Philadelphia's boulevard of museums, as a venue for cultural events and performances. Judging that the existing character of the broad roadway was already well-suited to these activities, Venturi, Scott Brown, and Izenour presented a plan in December that proposed only the addition of small, false-fronted temporary buildings for exhibits and vending, supplemented by portable stages and truck-mounted displays and food services. A more profound change was proposed at night, however, when the Parkway was to be canopied with moving lights and dazzled by fireworks (fig. 95). This project also foundered when federal funding did not materialize, although a performance tent inspired by the structures of the German architect Frei Otto and designed by others was erected in 1976 at the art museum end of the Parkway.

One of the six partner firms in the unsuccessful presentation to the federal Bicentennial planners had been

---

[148] Denise Scott Brown, "Observing Architecture: The Bicentennial's Fantasy Stage," *Philadelphia Evening Bulletin*, March 8, 1968.

[149] Denise Scott Brown and Robert Venturi, "The Bicentennial Commemoration, 1976," *Architectural Forum*, vol. 131 (October 1969), p. 66.

[150] My analysis of these designs was aided by the research paper written by Susanna Williams Gold at the University of Pennsylvania, December 1998.

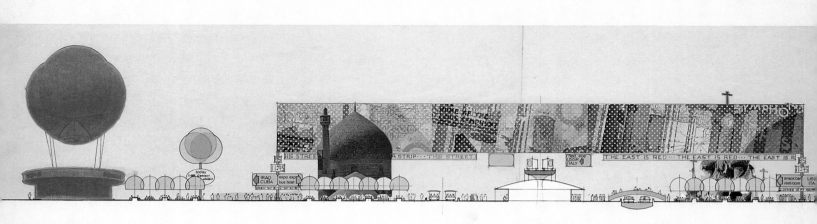

Figure 94

**International Bicentennial
Exposition Master Plan,
Philadelphia, 1971–72**

Street section, Eastwick site
Photomontage, 12½ x 53½"
(31.8 x 135.9 cm). Steven Izenour
Signed

Collection of Venturi, Scott Brown
and Associates, Inc.

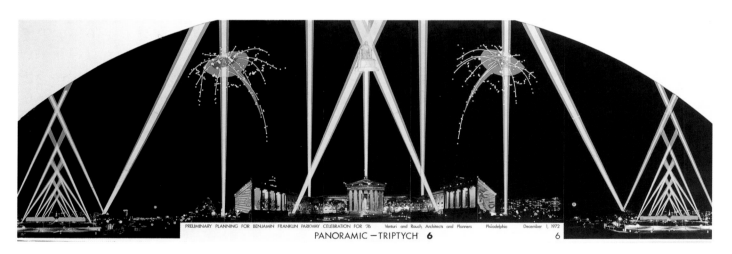

Figure 95

**Celebration 76 Exposition Master
Plan, Philadelphia, 1972–73**

Panoramic triptych. Panchromatic film on
photograph, 24 x 60" (61 x 152.4 cm)
Steven Izenour. Dated December 1, 1972

Collection of Venturi, Scott Brown
and Associates, Inc.

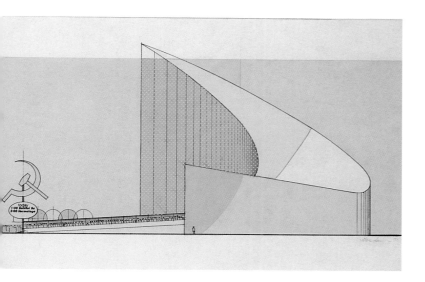

Figure 96
**Schuylkill River Corridor
Study (City Edges Program),
Philadelphia, 1973–74**

Photomontage, 11½ x 18"
(29.2 x 45.7 cm). Steven Izenour
and Paul Hirshorn

Collection of Venturi, Scott Brown
and Associates, Inc.

Murphy Levy Wurman, headed by Richard Saul Wurman, a former pupil of Kahn. In 1973–74, Venturi and Scott Brown teamed with Wurman again under contract with the city to design improvements to Philadelphia's automobile approach routes, funded by a grant from the City Edges program of the National Endowment for the Arts (NEA). The proposal was crafted by a team under Scott Brown's leadership, and it resembled the Twenty Mule Team Parkway design, which had adopted the highway medium of billboard communication while rejecting its commercial messages. In Philadelphia, informational billboards would advertise the attractions of the city to Bicentennial visitors—while also providing some visual relief from the bleak postindustrial landscape through which many of the approach roads passed (fig. 96). In the end only some of the smaller, directional signs described in the plan were implemented.

These disappointments must have been largely offset by one stunning, fully executed Bicentennial project in the city of Philadelphia, Franklin Court, on the excavated site of Benjamin Franklin's home. Lacking sufficient documentation for the accurate recreation of Franklin's long-demolished house, the National Park Service called only for the restoration of the adjacent row of houses that Franklin had owned on Market Street. At the location of his own house, they specified a museum. Commissioned in 1972 and largely designed in spring 1974, the plan by Venturi and Scott Brown pushed the museum underground and erected a steel skeleton to represent the house where it had once stood (fig. 97). To bring this "ghost" house to life, viewing ports showed the underlying excavations, and excerpts from the many letters and household records that described the dwelling were inscribed in the paving. Although not immediately apparent, Franklin Court was shaped by the ideals of Venturi and Scott Brown's other contemporary work: history was treated with both reverence and imagination, and architecture was replaced by words—albeit words carved in the pavement rather than mounted on billboards.

Figure 97
**Franklin Court, Philadelphia,
1972–76**

The large open area surrounding what Venturi called the "modern sculpture" of the Franklin house was densely filled with recreated eighteenth-century gardens and furnished with oversized benches and pergolas.[151] Venturi was famously averse to the windy, underused plazas typical of urban renewal projects, having said in conjunction with his 1965–66 plan to fill Boston's Copley Square with a miniature of the city's grid plan that "Americans feel uncomfortable sitting in a square: they should be working at the office or home with the family looking at television."[152] Franklin Court gave Americans something to sit outdoors for. The Franklin house and museum were very warmly received, being featured in *Progressive Architecture*'s April 1976 coverage of the otherwise rather unremarkable new buildings in the nation's Bicentennial city. The magazine acknowledged that the Philadelphia School, which it had christened in 1961, was no longer a definable presence, but it saw in the work of a younger Philadelphia generation, now led by Venturi and Scott Brown, the broadening and strengthening of many of its ideals.[153]

Bicentennial visitors to Philadelphia could also see exhibitions designed by Venturi and Scott Brown in the city's two major art museums. "In this Academy: The Pennsylvania Academy of the Fine Arts, 1805–76," and "Philadelphia: Three Centuries of American Art" at the Philadelphia Museum of Art were both installed in a subdued, respectful style that did not, however, seem imitatively historical. They matched the confident spirit of Franklin Court, but they attracted little attention as designs per se. More notice was paid to the two other major exhibitions that the firm created that year, in New York and Washington. For "200 Years of American Sculpture" at the Whitney Museum of American Art, the firm devised historically appropriate, almost theatrical, settings for the 345 objects. Neoclassical statues stood in a mauve environment, their marble brightly lit, with walls painted to suggest paneling. David Smith's modern sculpture was placed before a 50-foot photomural of a grassy hillside, evoking the setting of his studio in Bolton Landing, New York. Plain white studio space was set aside for the most recent works, because it was in such rooms that they were created and first displayed. And, attached to the front of the museum, a 26-foot photo placard of Hiram Powers's *Greek Slave* (c. 1843) signposted the show. These efforts won few compliments. In the *New York Times*, Hilton Kramer blasted "the designers' indulgence in a retrograde taste for drab color, for higgledy-piggledy display, and for a mode of 'lighting' (it really ought to be called darkening) that can be counted on to obscure more than it reveals."[154] Thomas Hess opined for *New York* that the show "almost sinks out of sight in Pop-arch Plexiglas and plasterboard installations."[155] Izenour admitted, "If we have any philosophy of exhibit design at all . . . it's one of a kind of overload; we walk a thin line when it comes to boggling people's minds by offering lots of choices through juxtaposition— and maybe sometimes we fall over."[156]

Happily, "overload" was generally judged to be exactly the right philosophy for the fourth and most celebrated exhibition that they created for the Bicentennial, "Signs of Life: Symbols in the American City," which was shown in Washington, D.C., at the Renwick Gallery of the Smithsonian Institution. There, in a display executed by Steven Izenour, Venturi, and Scott Brown, they assembled in one place the various "lessons" that they had learned from popular culture about the iconography of architecture. The three sections of the show were devoted to "The Strip" (a dazzling display of signs from the roadside, á la Las Vegas), "The Street" (a historical survey of outdoor advertising on Main Street—or South Street—America), and "The Home" (where the Levittown material was finally presented comprehensively; figs. 98, 99). The Home was by far the most widely noticed and admired component of "Signs of Life," in part because it was their least familiar work, but also because of the wry humor with which it presented the ideals and fantasies that Americans attached to their homes. Scott Brown had always maintained that they looked at the tastes and foibles of ordinary people with affection, and that affection was

[151] Thomas Hine, "An Appraisal: Franklin Shrine to Center on Abstract 'Ghost' Home," *Philadelphia Inquirer*, July 19, 1974.

[152] Venturi, *Complexity and Contradiction*, p. 133.

[153] Robert Coombs, "Philadelphia's Phantom School," *Progressive Architecture*, vol. 57 (April 1976), pp. 58–63.

[154] Hilton Kramer, "Art View: A Monumental Muddle of American Sculpture," *New York Times*, March 28, 1976.

[155] Thomas B. Hess, "Art: White Slave Traffic," *New York*, vol. 9 (April 5, 1976), p. 62.

[156] Quoted in Teresa Reese, "Rude Graphics, or Learning to Love Las Vegas," *Print*, vol. 34 (September/October 1980), p. 45.

Figure 98

"Signs of Life: Symbols in the American City," Renwick Gallery, Smithsonian Institution, Washington, D.C., 1974–76

Installation view of "The Street"

Figure 99

"Signs of Life: Symbols in the American City," Renwick Gallery, Smithsonian Institution, Washington, D.C., 1974–76

Installation view of "The Home"

easy to see in the cartoon bubbles in which the furnishings and fittings of the houses "spoke" their minds.

"Signs of Life" received more attention and more uniformly favorable notice than anything they had previously done. Long extracts from the exhibition catalogue were reprinted in both *Progressive Architecture* and *Architectural Design* in August.[157] Ada Louise Huxtable called it "the kind of show that changes the way you look at the world" in the *New York Times*; the *New Yorker* gave more than a cheerful page to it in the "Talk of the Town"; *Newsweek* trumpeted, "schlock is beautiful"; and Sunday magazines from coast to coast delighted in telling their readers about the delicious awfulness that the Smithsonian had legitimized.[158]

The complaints about the show focused on a single theme, what Dean James Polshek of Columbia University, a persistent foe, called "the relatively uncritical acceptance of many of the dehumanizing aspects of our suburbs."[159] Paul Goldberger, deciding to temper his usual enthusiasm for Venturi and Scott Brown, agreed that "the exhibition's absolute refusal to be judgmental is one of its most serious problems."[160] This was not a new line of criticism, and Venturi, whose fascination with the suburbs and the strip had never constituted an uncritical acceptance of either the social or the visual status quo, had long ago formulated a standard—if now exasperated—response. As Denise Scott Brown put it, "We don't say, 'Don't judge.' We use non-judgmentalism as a technique for sharpening our aesthetic sensibilities. We, like all other architects, are judges. We judge in order to act."[161] After second editions of both *Learning from Las Vegas* and *Complexity and Contradiction* appeared in 1977, and the same plaint was heard, Venturi put it simply: "Remember, the title of the book is *Learning from Las Vegas*, not *liking* Las Vegas."[162]

These countercurrents notwithstanding, the late seventies were kind to Venturi and Scott Brown. Their office was busy and the journals were full of news about their work. *Progressive Architecture* featured them in an entire issue in October 1977, in which John Morris Dixon said recent evidence "convinces

[157] "Symbols in the Home: A House Is More Than a Home," *Progressive Architecture*, vol. 57 (August 1976), pp. 62–67; "Signs of Life—Venturi/Rauch," *Architectural Design*, vol. 46 (August 1976), pp. 496–98.

[158] Ada Louise Huxtable, "Architecture View: The Pop World of the Strip and the Sprawl," *New York Times*,

March 21, 1976; "Talk of the Town: Symbols," *The New Yorker*, vol. 52 (March 15, 1976), pp. 27–29; Maureen Orth with Lucy Howard, "Schlock Is Beautiful," *Newsweek*, vol. 87 (March 8, 1976), p. 56.

[159] Quoted in Beverly Russell, "Real Life: It's Art," *House & Garden*, vol. 148 (August 1976), p. 107.

us that the firm's work has a real superiority"—and even possesses "eternal values."[163] Acclaim came from abroad as well. *Werk/Archithese* (Switzerland) devoted its July–August 1977 volume to them; *Architecture and Urbanism* (Japan) followed with special issues in January 1978 and December 1981, as did *L'Architecture d'Aujourd'hui* (France) in June 1978. In 1978 *Architectural Design* (England) launched its new monograph series with *Venturi and Rauch: The Public Buildings*.

Against this backdrop, there was general astonishment when the American Institute of Architects solicited but then rejected Venturi's application to become a fellow of the Institute in 1977. There was talk of blackballing, and as a mark of disapproval, Vincent Scully publicly declined to accept an award that the AIA had proposed to give him. In 1978 everyone politely pretended that nothing had happened when Venturi was made a fellow.

That Venturi and Scott Brown had achieved so much was a testament to the persuasiveness of their art and their argument, for they had not chosen the easy route. On the one hand, their commitment to a socially founded design method parted them from the new "post-modern" kind of aesthetes, who were losing themselves in the prettiness of drawings—notably, the sumptuous renderings of the Ecole des Beaux-Arts displayed in New York at the Museum of Modern Art in 1975. On the other hand, their commitment to the objective analysis of the suburbs and shopping centers of capitalist society cut them off from the "radical chic" architects of the Left. For them, architecture was *both* social and visual; neither was easy by itself, and the combination of the two was even harder. As Scott Brown wrote, "A basic question is: can architects' concerns with form and its aesthetics be reconciled with their social concern and social idealism? My aim is to show that they can."[164] And she did.

The Presence of Post-Modern

"Is not Main Street almost all right?" Robert Venturi had asked on the penultimate page of his essay in *Complexity and Contradiction*.[165] In the same year (1966), Congress passed a

new tax law favorable to historic preservation. Over the next decade, revisionist thinking about the making of new architecture and about preserving old architecture converged, and in the later seventies, Venturi and Scott Brown received a wave of commissions to advise those who were making use of federal programs to revitalize America's Main Streets. Scott Brown played a leading role in these projects, and her flexible and inventive approach expanded the themes established at Franklin Court and steered American preservation practices away from phony authenticity. At the same time, their designs for new buildings—full of commercial, historical, and purely formal vitality—distinguished themselves from the pedigree-seeking work of the increasingly visible post-modernists.

Venturi and Scott Brown's most glamorous project during this period was the remaking of America's Main Street, Pennsylvania Avenue in Washington, D.C., traversed on every Inauguration Day by the first family as it made its way home to the White House from the ceremonies at the Capitol. Here, in collaboration with landscape architect George Patton, they created Western Plaza (renamed Freedom Plaza) at the White House end of the great boulevard. The design made amends for the violence done to L'Enfant's plan in the nineteenth century, when the Treasury Building was allowed to push its portico into the sight line (and roadway) connecting the Capitol and White House.[166] As worked out in the first months of 1978, their plan called for a raised square between Thirteenth and Fourteenth streets, paved with a portion of L'Enfant's imperfectly realized plan for the city and so placed that the miniature Pennsylvania Avenue of the map and the real avenue were aligned (fig. 100). Three-dimensional models of the White House and Capitol were to take their appropriate places on the map, within sight of their real counterparts (fig. 101), echoing their plan for Boston's Copley Square in 1965–66, which had included a miniature Trinity Church. As subsequently developed, the black granite and white marble paving was inscribed, as at Franklin Court,

[160] Paul Goldberger, "How to Love the Strip: 'Symbols in the American City,'" *ARTnews*, vol. 75 (September 1976), p. 50.

[161] Scott Brown, "An Interview" (interview by Linda Groat), p. 52.

[162] Quoted in Jerry Bowles, "Building in the Vernacular," *Today: The Inquirer Magazine*, September 23, 1979, p. 34.

[163] John Morris Dixon, "Venturi & Rauch: Introduction, Realization of Symbols," *Progressive Architecture*, vol. 58 (October 1977), p. 49.

[164] Denise Scott Brown, "On Architectural Formalism and Social Concern: A Discourse for Social Planners and Radical Chic Architects," *Oppositions*, vol. 5 (Summer 1976), p. 101.

[165] Venturi, *Complexity and Contradiction*, p. 102.

[166] My analysis of this project was aided by the research of Rachel Iannacone.

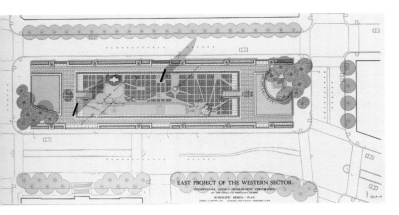

Figure 100
Freedom Plaza, Washington, D.C., 1977–79
Schematic design and plan
Panchromatic film on photomechanical
print, 39⅞ x 80¼" (101.3 x 203.8 cm)
James H. Timberlake, Steven Kieran,
Frederic Schwartz, and Steven Izenour
Dated September 8, 1978
Collection of Venturi, Scott Brown
and Associates, Inc.

Figure 101
Freedom Plaza, Washington, D.C., 1977–79
Plaza with mock-up miniature
buildings

with thirty-nine quotations about the city. This wonderful juxtaposition of scales, interwoven with graphics and historical sensibility, filled what would otherwise have been a rather bleak and empty plaza. Rising above it, two great pylons were to frame the view of the Treasury Building at the end of the avenue, at last establishing a suitable terminus and anchoring the design to the city itself.

The three-dimensional elements of Western Plaza proved to be very controversial. The initial commission included the sculptor Richard Serra, although it is difficult to understand how the Pennsylvania Avenue Development Corporation (PADC), the client entity, imagined that Serra's large, site-specific minimalism and Venturi and Scott Brown's architecture would coexist. Indeed, they could not. Serra wanted to place a large, multipart sculpture on the main axis, blocking the vista that Venturi and Scott Brown hoped to frame with pylons. In a series of increasingly nasty meetings, Serra and Venturi clashed, with the sculptor likening Venturi's respect for the monumental classicism of Pennsylvania Avenue to fascism. J. Carter Brown, director of the National Gallery of Art and chair of the Fine Arts Commission (which had to approve the design), supported what he called Venturi's "brilliant solution," and at the end of March, Serra was told that he must redirect his energies to a smaller, horizontal work.[167] He then quit.

Venturi and Scott Brown's victory was incomplete, for although Brown and both the PADC and the Fine Arts Commission admired the underlying rationale of the twin-pylon scheme, they could not agree on the character of these two tall markers. The proposed pylons were successively inscribed and colored, and then replaced by flagpoles, without winning consensus, and so, in February 1979, they were stricken from the plan—with the hollow promise that they might be added later. The miniature White House and Capitol suffered a similar fate in May, when they were replaced with bronze plans, inlaid in the paving. Dedicated in November 1980, this two-dimensional reduction, while still witty and urbane, disappointed the fans of the original

[167] Grace Glueck, "Art People: A Tale of Two Pylons," *New York Times*, April 7, 1978; Paul Richard, "New Design for a 'National Square,'" *Washington Post*, May 24, 1978;

Jeremy Gilbert-Rolfe, "Capital Follies," *Artforum*, vol. 17 (September 1978), pp. 66–67.

plan, with Paul Goldberger lamenting its necessarily "flat reception."[168]

The intended character of Western Plaza was partially achieved in Philadelphia in 1979–83, when Welcome Park was created on the site of the Slate Roof House, William Penn's residence (fig. 102). Its paving replicated the grid of Penn's plan for the city, with a statue of Penn on a pedestal at the center—where, in the real city, a much larger statue of the founder surmounts City Hall—and a bronze model of the Slate Roof House marking its historic location. The four leafy squares of the Philadelphia plan were each planted with a single tree.

While historically referenced, neither Western Plaza nor Welcome Park dealt with the preservation and revitalization of old buildings, but that was a central theme of a series of important projects by Scott Brown that kept the office busy during these years. Galveston, Texas, the once important seaport city whose star had been eclipsed by the inland capitals of oil and cattle, hired the firm in November 1974, using money from the NEA's City Options program. Five blocks of The Strand, lined with nineteenth-century iron fronts and early twentieth-century lofts and ending in the vast Art Deco Santa Fe railway terminal, were identified as the starting point for a restoration campaign, for which the architects would provide guidelines. Scott Brown's immediate responses to the challenges of The Strand guided their report. She told an inquiring reporter, "We see The Strand not as a dead architectural museum but as a lively place melded imaginatively with the right commercial enterprises."[169] In keeping with that philosophy, The Strand "Action Plan" of 1975 allowed extensive interior renovations, so that new uses could fill the buildings, and structures of all vintages were to be treated with similar respect. The intended effect was "artful but impressionistic . . . eclectic rather than pure."[170] Approved facade colors, allowing for substantial variety, were identified, and the plan prescribed an integrated system of signs in which neon, appropriate on the strip but not in a turn-of-the-century warehouse district,

Figure 102
Welcome Park, Philadelphia, 1979–83

[168] Paul Goldberger, "Western Plaza in Washington Gets a Somewhat Flat Reception," *New York Times*, December 18, 1980.

[169] Quoted in Ann Holmes, "The Pop Artist Who Isn't Kidding Plans to Give Vitality to The Strand," *Houston Chronicle*, November 24, 1974.

[170] Robert Venturi and John Rauch quoted in Peter Papademetriou, "News Report: Report from Galveston," *Progressive Architecture*, vol. 57 (December 1976), p. 26.

Figure 103
The Strand District Comprehensive Plan, Galveston, Texas, 1974–76
Perspective
Whereabouts unknown

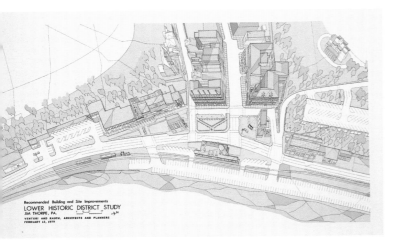

Figure 104
Lower Historic District Planning Study, Jim Thorpe, Pennsylvania, 1977–79
Aerial perspective. Dated February 13, 1979
Whereabouts unknown

was not allowed (fig. 103). The nineteenth-century commercial district of Philadelphia, called "Old City," was the subject of a similar plan in 1976–78.

The firm undertook a smaller-scale version of such a project, with larger consequences, in Jim Thorpe, Pennsylvania, a down-at-the-heels Victorian resort-turned-mining-town in a spectacular mountain setting (1977–79). Assisted by David Marohn, an architecture graduate of the University of Pennsylvania, one of several young designers who joined the firm during this active period and stayed on to shape its future, Scott Brown once again prepared "an historical preservation study that did not try to rebuild the town to look the way it used to look."[171] Bolstered by economic, transportation, and demographic analyses, the architectural recommendations focused on the ailing main street. She defined a program of directional and informational signage and a strong yet flexible set of preservation guidelines that became the foundation of Jim Thorpe's remarkable resurgence as a tourist destination (fig. 104).

An entirely different variety of architecture was treated with similar sensitivity and good sense in the "Action Plan" that Scott Brown wrote in 1978–79 for Washington Avenue, the main street of the just-created Art Deco historic district in Miami Beach. Most of its small hotels and commercial buildings dated from the 1920s and 1930s—a vintage that was then neither universally respected nor well studied—and the Scott Brown report advanced both causes. As was often the case, the preliminary survey found much that was already "almost all right" about Washington Avenue: "its human scale, its interesting variety of stores, its architecturally important buildings."[172] What was needed was a better mixture of retail offerings and improved pedestrian amenities, and the plan outlined these opportunities and proposed new signage that captured the spirit of Art Deco design (fig. 105). Scott Brown, whose parents were early enthusiasts for Art Deco, had vacationed in Miami Beach, and had touted the attractions of the city before working there. She rightly forecast the attractiveness of the city's

171 Quoted in Jim Quinn, "Jim Thorpe Is Alive and Well and Blooming in Pennsylvania," *Philadelphia Magazine*, November 1979, p. 283.

172 Denise Scott Brown, "Practice: Revitalizing Miami, A Plan for Miami Beach's Washington Avenue," *Urban Design International*, vol. 1 (January/February 1980), p. 24.

small hotels to a new type of American and European traveler, and there, as in Jim Thorpe, tourism and preservation soon soared together.

Atlantic City, New Jersey, another seaside resort that had passed its prime, would have seemed to be a likely candidate for a similar transformation. But the legalization of gambling in that city had spawned a boom in the construction of large casino hotels, and without any effective controls in place, many of the most significant older buildings were demolished, among them the Traymore Hotel, the 1914–15 masterpiece by Philadelphia's proto-modernist architect William Price. On the eve of its destruction in 1972, Venturi and Scott Brown purchased chairs from the hotel's dining room to furnish their newly aquired Mount Airy home. In 1977 the appointed time seemed to have come for the Blenheim Hotel (William Price, 1905–6) to meet the implosion experts, but its owner, Reese Palley, while leasing the site to the Bally gambling empire, hired Venturi and Scott Brown to plan the adaptation of the old building to serve its new masters. Their design preserved the domed, vaguely Moorish central pavilion of the historic building, behind which a gigantic hotel and casino complex rose in a semicircle—letting the historic building provide decoration for the commodious, modern shed (fig. 106). Palley, however, had not stipulated that Bally follow his architectural lead, and the Blenheim was destroyed to make way for Bally's Park Place. All that was left in Atlantic City was the opportunity to study, and in 1979, Izenour conducted a studio at Penn devoted to the city, much in the manner of the Las Vegas and Levittown projects.

This preservation-related work did nothing to diminish the enthusiasm of Scott Brown, Venturi, and their collaborators for the commercial vernacular of the present, and probably their best-known projects from the late seventies were bold additions to the history of the American strip. In 1973–74 Venturi and Rauch began to talk about possible work with Frances and Sydney Lewis, president of Best Products, a chain of catalogue showrooms.[173] The Lewises were notable

[173] My analysis of this project was aided by the research of Rachel Iannacone.

Figure 105

Washington Avenue Revitalization Plan, Miami Beach, 1978–79

Elevation of shop fronts. Marker and colored marker on diazo print, detail
Steven Izenour and Janet Colesbury
Collection of Venturi, Scott Brown and Associates, Inc.

Figure 106

Park Place Hotel and Casino, Atlantic City, New Jersey, 1977

Perspective. Panchromatic film, ink, and cut paper on foam core, 21¾ x 36½" (55.2 x 92.7 cm)
Robert Venturi
Collection of Venturi, Scott Brown and Associates, Inc.

Figure 107
**Showroom, Best Products
Company, Langhorne,
Pennsylvania, 1973–79**
Side facade

Figure 108
**Headquarters, Institute for
Scientific Information,
Philadelphia, 1977–79**
Front elevation. Panchromatic film
on photomechanical print mounted
on foam core, 29⅛ x 56¼"
(74 x 142.9 cm). James H. Timberlake
and Paul Muller. Dated October 1978

Collection of Venturi, Scott Brown
and Associates, Inc.

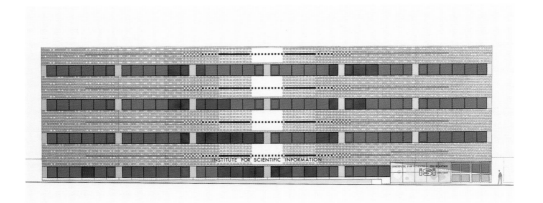

collectors of twentieth-century art and design who—like the Venturis—saw artistic opportunity in the shopping centers of suburbia. Best had already commissioned sculptor James Wines and his iconoclastic SITE (Sculpture In The Environment) group to design a store in Richmond, Virginia. There, in an ordinary suburban parking lot, the Best store seemed to be collapsing as a thin veneer of brick peeled away from the structure. Here was a decorated shed in decay.

Venturi and the Lewises remained in contact for several years, discussing various possibilities, including a store with an allover appliqué of a floral pattern inspired by the commercial wallpaper that he and Scott Brown had chosen for their bedroom.[174] The experiments with facade designs for the Allen Memorial Art Museum and the Brant house also occurred during this period. Best looked for some time to find a site for this attractive idea, settling on the Oxford Valley Mall in Langhorne, Pennsylvania, just north of Philadelphia. Like a vertical projection of the wildflowers that grew in the surrounding scruffy fields, the boxy showroom, clad in enameled panels, bloomed there in 1979 (fig. 107). In the winter of 1979–80, the Oxford Valley building and several designs by SITE were featured in an exhibition at the Museum of Modern Art, along with specially invited Best showroom designs by Michael Graves, Allan Greenberg, Anthony Lumsden, Charles Moore, Robert Stern, and Stanley Tigerman. In his introduction to the exhibition catalogue, Philip Johnson described the various proposals as "all aimed at decorating a 'shed.'"[175] Venturi and Scott Brown's language was the only way to describe this new phenomenon.

BASCO, a similar catalogue-showroom business, was also working with Venturi and Scott Brown at this time. In 1977 they had two stores under construction and a third, fully developed, design that went unbuilt. The unrealized design for the Philadelphia suburb of King of Prussia was to be a Best-like box, ornamented with a fictive trellis and fruit trees. For Wilmington, Delaware, they built a simple striped

Figure 109
**Showroom and Warehouse,
BASCO, Inc., Philadelphia, 1977–78**
Front facade

[174] Robert Venturi to Andrew Lewis, November 24, 1976, "2.1 BEST Correspondence, Best," VSB box 142 (VSBA archives).

[175] Philip Johnson, foreword to *Buildings for Best Products* (New York: The Museum of Modern Art, 1979), n.p.

shed with BASCO spelled out in widely spaced letters across the upper facade (1976–78). Even more elemental was the renovation carried out for the company on Roosevelt Boulevard in Northeast Philadelphia. BASCO had acquired an abandoned shopping-center building that was 1,110 feet long and only 16 feet high, which was simply painted blue before the company's name was erected in 34-foot-high three-dimensional red aluminum letters in front of its facade (fig. 109). BASCO president Alex Egyed was delighted. "I just drive down and look at the sign," he said. "It makes me feel good."[176]

Another satisfied decorated-shed client was Eugene Garfield, founder and president of the innovative Institute for Scientific Information (ISI), a Philadelphia organization that might rightly claim to have invented the information age. Starting in the 1950s, *Current Contents*, the ISI flagship publication, and its progeny established a new standard for the sorting and indexing of published information, and by 1979, ISI reached the point of indexing 900,000 items from 6,200 journals and 4,200 books.[177] By 1977, the company had outgrown its rented quarters and Garfield took the suggestion of Martin Meyerson, then president of the University of Pennsylvania, to ask Venturi and Scott Brown to design him a new building in Philadelphia, which would house 350 employees when it was completed. Garfield had wanted "a building that everyone would recognize as a lively and distinctive contribution to the community,"[178] and in return Venturi created a decorated shed with the most complex facade pattern to date (fig. 108). "We decided," he said, "it was time for buildings to be pretty again."[179] At the doorway of the building, on Market Street, raked under the southeast corner at a distinctive angle, the wall was paneled with flowers like those on the Best store at the Oxford Valley Mall. But the breadth of the main facade vibrated with a geometric pattern of colored tiles and enameled spandrel panels. Inevitably, given ISI's data business and Venturi and Scott Brown's avowed dedication to symbolism, observers likened the pattern to an (embarrassingly obsolete)

computer punch card. In truth the design was an extended exercise in abstraction, based on a Victorian pattern book and intended to subvert the dour, corporate environment established by its neighbors in the University City Science Center. Venturi confessed, "We had lots of fun, with these rhythms," and he called the composition "a kind of fugual or counterpoint rhythm with space."[180]

There was no mistaking a series of other, nearly contemporary works as abstract exercises in form and color. Not ducks, precisely, these examples of superior roadside architecture were more like highly physiognomic and explicit billboards. For the Discovery Place Museum of Science and Technology in Charlotte, North Carolina (1976–81), the firm conceived a building that literally represented the geology of the earth and its inhabitants, with a stratified cliff as the facade and a dinosaur stalking on the roof (fig. 110). (Venturi and Rauch only served as consultants for the less-striking design that was finally executed.) For a gas station, to be converted into a branch office of County Federal Savings and Loan Association in Fairfield, Connecticut (1977), they proposed an oversized colonial-revival cupola. This was a suitable signpost, the architects thought, for its conservative neighborhood, but it was judged too "vulgar" by the local Fine Arts Commission (fig. 112).[181] In the end a simple cottage, designed by others, was permitted. To make the Regional Visitor Center at Hartwell Lake, South Carolina, visible to motorists on nearby I-85, their unchosen 1977–78 competition entry proposed a little building with a blue roof surmounted by a giant red castle—the emblem of the client, the Army Corps of Engineers (fig. 111). And a scheme for a jazz club for an unspecified suburban site near Houston, commissioned by the Nichol's Alley Company (1977–78), occasioned a model frigate in full sail on the roof of a one-story classically detailed shed, wherein a nautical theme was expected to be carried out with projected images and displays (fig. 113).

During November and December 1975, the Museum of Modern Art in New York had hosted a dazzling exhibition

[176] Quoted in Thomas Hine, "Basco Gives the High Sign," *Philadelphia Inquirer*, November 6, 1978.

[177] "New Building Highlights ISI's Growth," *ISI Alert*, vol. 3 (1979), p. 1; Eugene Garfield, "New Year, New Building," *Current Comments*, no. 1 (January 7, 1980), p. 5.

[178] Garfield, "New Year," p. 6.

[179] Quoted in Jim Quinn, "Computer Chic Enters the Building Scene, Courtesy of Venturi and Rauch," *Philadelphia Magazine*, January 1979, p. 91.

[180] Ibid.

[181] Von Moos, *Venturi, Rauch & Scott Brown*, p. 226.

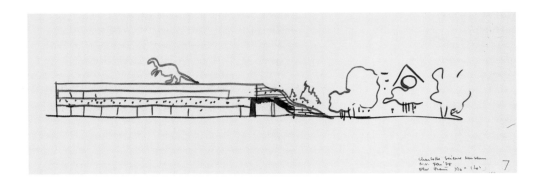

Figure 110
Discovery Place Museum of Science and Technology, Charlotte, North Carolina, 1976–81

Elevation. Marker on yellow tracing paper, 9½ x 29½" (24.1 x 74.9 cm) Robert Venturi. Signed and dated February 1978

Collection of Venturi, Scott Brown and Associates, Inc.

Figure 111
Hartwell Lake Regional Visitor Center, Hartwell Lake, South Carolina, 1977–78

South elevation. Panchromatic film on photographic print mounted on foam core, 18 x 26" (45.7 x 66 cm) Frederic Schwartz. Dated August 1978

Collection of Venturi, Scott Brown and Associates, Inc.

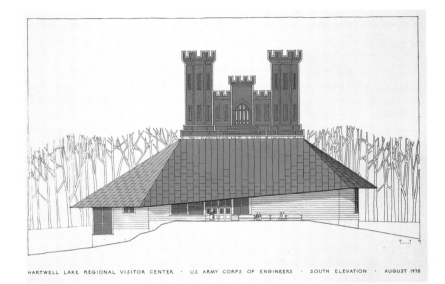

HARTWELL LAKE REGIONAL VISITOR CENTER · U.S. ARMY CORPS OF ENGINEERS · SOUTH ELEVATION · AUGUST 1978

Figure 112
Branch Office, County Federal Savings and Loan Association, Fairfield, Connecticut, 1977

West elevation. Panchromatic film on photomechanical print mounted on foam core, 26 x 26" (66 x 66 cm) Stanford Hughes. Dated April 4, 1977

Collection of Venturi, Scott Brown and Associates, Inc.

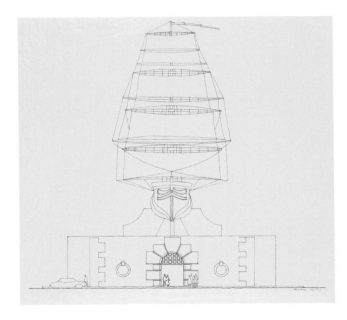

Figure 113
Jazz Club, Houston, 1977–78

Elevation. Marker on yellow tracing paper, 35¾ x 41" (90.8 x 104.1 cm) Steven Izenour and James H. Timberlake

Collection of Venturi, Scott Brown and Associates, Inc.

FAMOUS ARCHITECTURE IN THE WORLD
ELEVATION
WEST WALL OF MILLER BUILDING
NOTE: INTERRUPTIONS IN FRIEZE PANELS WILL ACCOMMODATE EXIT DOORS THERE.

SCALE 3/16" = 1'-0"

DOWNTOWN
SCRANTON
MVRAL-PROJECT

2

Venturi and Rauch, Architects + Planners
September 23, 1976

Figure 114

Downtown Mural Art Project, Scranton, Pennsylvania, 1976–77

Elevation. Panchromatic film on photomechanical print, 18 x 40" (45.7 x 101.6 cm). Robert Venturi. Color rendering by Steven Izenour. Dated September 23, 1976

Collection of Venturi, Scott Brown and Associates, Inc.

of unexpected beauty: student works from the long history of the Ecole des Beaux-Arts in Paris, the institutional guardian of the academic tradition in French architecture. The huge, exquisitely colored drawings created a stir among those architects who were already inclined to revalue the historicism of the nineteenth century and to elevate the status of architectural drawings per se. Post-modernism began to anchor itself to these seductive, classical renderings, which were echoed in various keys by the increasingly classical work of Michael Graves, Allan Greenberg, and Robert A. M. Stern. The Museum of Modern Art itself, where the International Style had been christened and made historical, now seemed to do almost as much for the post-modern, and the belated appearance of the lavish catalogue in 1977 (the same year as Charles Jencks's *The Language of Post-Modern Architecture*) reinforced and enlarged these impressions.[182] Celebration and condemnation swirled around the show, and later the book, as though they were post-modernism itself.

Venturi and Scott Brown, whose work was ornamented, colorful, and historically rooted, were naturally expected to be allies of the post-modernists in this discussion, and they were usually identified as their artistic parents. But the foundation of their art lay in a profound critique of modern society, which the post-modernists abjured, and in a formally based restudy of modern architecture, which the post-modernists attacked. Accordingly, when they were invited to comment on the Beaux-Arts phenomenon, they took pains to distance themselves from it. In a forum sponsored by the Institute for Architecture and Urban Studies in New York and again at the Architectural Association in London, Scott Brown soberly warned that the celebrated respect for urban setting and history of the Beaux-Arts was too easily transmogrified into support for "ruling-class architecture set in plazas," and she expressed her fear that the "current establishment interest in the Beaux-Arts will be a fad and an evasion."[183]

In fairness, the visual character of some of Venturi and Scott Brown's work from the late 1970s certainly con-tributed to the widespread misunderstanding of their position. Their whimsical 1976–77 proposal for a freestanding "mural" in Scranton, Pennsylvania, that depicted great monuments of architectural history—from a temple at Luxor to the arches of McDonalds—was susceptible to being misread as a conventional post-modernist exercise (fig. 114). The stylistic rootlessness of his Eclectic House series of 1977 seemed to fit the bill even more closely (fig. 115), but this trait was never evident in real commissions, as several houses from this period demonstrate.

In the ineffably gentle hills of northern Delaware, Venturi created a home for Peter and Karen Flint in 1978–80 that absorbed the tonalities of the surrounding eighteenth-century architecture and reflected them back, slightly skewed, with charm (figs. 116, 117). While the sheltering roof recalled the elemental forms of the shingle style, the wide portico playfully exaggerated the proportions of colonial classicism and converted it into an artistically disciplined two-dimensional diagram. The requirement of a large room for Karen Flint's organ, harpsichord, and two pianos invited a renewed exploration of the vertical layering of domestic space, with the vaulted, two-story music room placed atop the living room—from which vantage it looked into the top of the tall dining room. Stairways rose on both sides of the living room, permitting separate access to the children's bedrooms when desired. For all its sophistication, it was unquestionably a *country* house, with a lack of affectation that Vincent Scully rightly likened to a dollhouse.[184]

At about the same time, the architects were designing a very different house for Irving and Betty Abrams, collectors of modern art in Pittsburgh (1979–81). There, spanning a rivulet on a narrow, valley floor site in an exclusive suburb, they placed a spiritedly moderne house with a humpbacked roofline that mimicked the profile of an adjacent stone bridge. Inside, the simple but strongly stated requirements of a retired couple were accomplished almost entirely on one floor, with a two-story living room in the center, a master bedroom and indoor exercise pool at one end, and an

182 Arthur Drexler, ed., *The Architecture of the Ecole des Beaux-Arts* (New York: The Museum of Modern Art; Cambridge and London: The MIT Press, 1977).

183 Denise Scott Brown, "Learning the Wrong Lessons from the Beaux-Arts [1978]," in Venturi and Scott Brown, *View from the Campidoglio*, pp. 68–69; see also Denise Scott Brown, "Forum: The Beaux-Arts Exhibition," *Oppositions*, vol. 8 (Spring 1977), pp. 165–66.

184 Vincent Scully, "Architecture: Venturi, Rauch and Scott Brown," *Architectural Digest*, vol. 42 (March 1985), pp. 184–91, 236, 243.

Figure 115
Eclectic House Series, 1977
Elevations. Robert Venturi
Whereabouts unknown

Figure 116
Flint House, Greenville, Delaware, 1978–80
Front facade

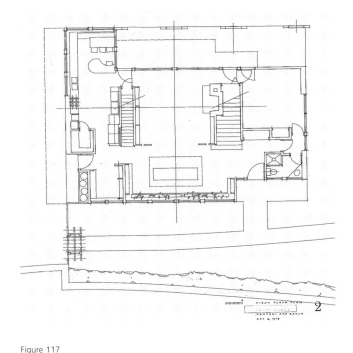

Figure 117
Flint House, Greenville, Delaware, 1978–80
First-floor plan. Pencil on vellum, 22½ x 24" (57.2 x 61 cm). Dated October 6, 1978
Collection of Venturi, Scott Brown and Associates, Inc.

enormous kitchen for Betty Abrams's serious avocation at the other. A partial second floor, looking out into the living room from a balcony (like that of Le Corbusier's Maison Citrohan), contained only a spare bedroom and a utility room. In the spirit of their recent Miami and Atlantic City work, the two principal facades were organized as sweeping Art Deco sunbursts, which gave shape to the large windows that lit the living room and the jazzy paint scheme in several shades of green (fig. 118).

It was at this time, too, that Peter and Sandy Brant, with new triplets and a new enthusiasm for eighteenth-century antiques and for horses, asked for changes in their house in Greenwich. True to the tenor of their interests, in 1978–79 the architects devised two solutions. The first was a red-brick, slightly exaggerated, Federal-style addition to the rear of the existing house, with a formal, symmetrical entrance at the center. However, judging that the Brants no longer wanted "Mannerist complexity" and that they had "lost interest in the architectural symbolism that formed the basis of the original house," they went on to conceive an entirely new design based on George Washington's house, Mount Vernon (fig. 119).[185] But true to themselves, rather than smooth out the asymmetries—markers of its humble origins—that Washington had allowed to remain while enlarging his house, the Venturis exaggerated these idiosyncrasies and played with the scale of elements to make the big house seem somewhat smaller than it was. The Brants did not find this exploration interesting, and they turned to Allan Greenberg for a more correct and rather pallid interpretation of the first president's Potomac house.

A similarly serious irreverence pervaded the historical detailing that Venturi brought to the Knoll furniture and fabric showroom in New York that he created in 1979–80, when he was also beginning to design furniture for the firm. Arranged on the second and third floors at 655 Madison Avenue, the display rooms were low-key out of respect for the classic modern furniture, save for a luscious, multicolored cascade of velvety cloth that dropped through an

185 Robert Venturi, "*Il Proprio Vocabolario*: Four Houses for *Gran Bazaar* [1982]," in Venturi and Scott Brown, *View from the Campidoglio*, p. 101.

Figure 118
Abrams House, Pittsburgh, 1979–81

North elevation. Marker, colored marker, and pencil on yellow tracing paper, 12 x 24" (30.5 x 61 cm) Robert Venturi. Dated July 1979

Collection of Venturi, Scott Brown and Associates, Inc.

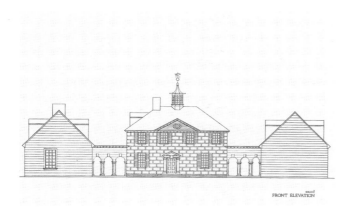

Figure 119
Brant House, Greenwich, Connecticut, 1978–79

Front elevation. Pencil and transfer letters on vellum, 36½ x 49½" (92.7 x 125.7 cm). James H. Timberlake

Collection of Venturi, Scott Brown and Associates, Inc.

opening in the intervening floor to greet the visitor. Architectural invention was saved for the conference room, where Venturi adopted what he called "a good classic-modern architectural device, the illuminated plastic ceiling" (such as the suspended ceiling system that Eero Saarinen had put into use when Venturi was working in Bloomfield Hills), and had it silkscreened with a pattern adapted from the low-relief stucco ceilings of the eighteenth-century architect Robert Adam (fig. 120).[186] Here were modern classic and neoclassical in an unrehearsed duet, the boldness of which Venturi would also harness in his Knoll furniture designs.

These special, sometimes unsettling, escapades with historical precedent were quite unlike the work that Robert Stern and Allan Greenberg were doing during the same time. Even more dissimilar was Venturi and Scott Brown's continuing commitment to creating intelligent but ordinary architecture when the setting seemed to demand it. This was evident in two nearly contemporary competitions, for a new Australian parliament building in Canberra (1979) and the Museum für Kunsthandwerk in Frankfurt, Germany (1979–80).

The Australian competition drew proposals from around the world, and the entry devised by a team under the management of Steven Izenour chose to underplay the symbolism that other contestants employed—some no doubt inspired by the firm's own championing of iconographically rich architecture. Instead, the architects created a sculptural and spatial form attuned to the program and to the geometries of both Walter Burley Griffin's neobaroque city plan and the powerful surrounding landscape (fig. 121). The design was laconic in detail but strong in forms, with a simple arch marking the main axis between the House and Senate chambers and a gently bowed facade looking down the hill and over the old "temporary" parliament house that had served since 1927 and was now to be preserved. Ironically, the winning design by Romaldo Giurgola flew an enormous Australian flag from its central mast—just like Venturi's proposal for a giant flagpole for the Thousand Oaks Civic Center in 1969.

[186] Andrew MacNair, "Venturi and the Classic Modern Tradition," *Skyline*, March 1980, p. 5.

Figure 120
**Offices and Showroom, Knoll
International, New York, 1979–80**
Conference room

Figure 121
**Commonwealth Parliament
House, Competition, Canberra,
Australia, 1979**
Aerial perspective. James H. Timberlake
Whereabouts unknown

On the Main River in Frankfurt, the site for the Museum für Kunsthandwerk lay among handsome early nineteenth-century houses, one of which, the Villa Metzler, was to be incorporated in the design (figs. 122, 123). The large park west of the Villa Metzler was a much appreciated open space on the river, but the addition committed itself "to hold the line of the street," and so pushed across the park with its facade plane and cornice height aligned with those of the villa.[187] The facade itself was intentionally prosaic, with windows approximating the size of the old house and a marble wall veneer and red stone plinth emulating its coloration. Only around the entrance at the west end of the new wing did the designers venture a stronger statement. There, a low, columnar portico was opened beneath the facade, framed at one end by an expanse of rusticated red stonework and a single Renaissance window. Behind this quiet front, the plan mobilized itself to make familiar, Aalto-like accommodations for varied room sizes and shapes. A service core ran through the center of the building, and the galleries, usefully arranged in suites, were carefully planned to admit only the prescribed amounts of light. The design placed second in the limited competition behind that of Richard Meier, whose severe exercise in revived Le Corbusian geometries wrapped itself behind the Villa Metzler to preserve more parkland along the river.

The Frankfurt competition designs were due in March 1980, and even before they shipped, the office was busy with its presentation for that summer's Venice Biennale, where an architectural exhibition under the motto "The Presence of the Past" was to be mounted in the long ropeworks building of the Arsenal. As the motto suggested, the Biennale was conceived as a demonstration of the ascendancy of post-modern historicism, building on the foundation laid by the Ecole des Beaux-Arts show at the Museum of Modern Art. Alcoves along what was called the "Strada Novissima," designed by Michael Graves, Robert Stern, Charles Moore, Hans Hollein, Ricardo Bofill, Leon Krier, and Allan Greenberg, among others, went some way

[187] [Denise Scott Brown],
"Competition Feature: Venturi,
Rauch and Scott Brown, Arts and
Crafts Museum, Frankfurt am
Main," *Architectural Design*, vol. 51
(December 1981), p. 124.

NORDANSICHT

MUSEUM FÜR KUNSTHANDWERK · FRANKFURT am Main

Figure 122
**Museum für Kunsthandwerk,
Competition, Frankfurt am Main,
West Germany, 1979–80**

North elevation. Ink on mylar, detail
James Bradberry

Collection of Venturi, Scott Brown
and Associates, Inc.

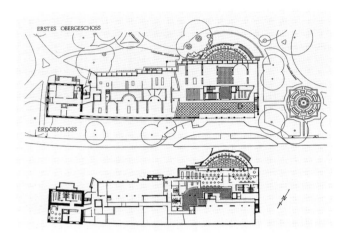

Figure 123
**Museum für Kunsthandwerk,
Competition, Frankfurt am Main,
West Germany, 1979–80**

Site plan. Ink on mylar, detail

Collection of Venturi, Scott Brown
and Associates, Inc.

Figure 124
**Strada Novissima, Biennale,
Venice, 1980**

The Venturi Scott Brown facade
is at left

toward that goal (fig. 124). Venturi and Scott Brown were there, too, and they must have viewed their situation with some dismay, for, like the Museum of Modern Art exhibition, this was congenial but not entirely comfortable company. As a kind of commentary on its neighbors, the facade of their alcove was a version of the Doric variant from the Eclectic House series, a preposterous three-columned portico that, like Guild House, planted a column firmly in the approach axis. (In Venice, the problem of entrance was eliminated, for the whole facade lifted up like a curtain to allow admission to the alcove.) Inside, the Mother's House lay directly ahead, an iconic reminder that whatever it was that post-modernists were doing in 1980, significant new directions for late-twentieth-century architecture had been signposted nearly two decades earlier. And to show that not everyone agreed that only classicism was almost all right, the two side walls of their alcove were covered with large photographs of the beflowered Best store at the Oxford Valley Mall and the red-lettered BASCO in Northeast Philadelphia.

Venturi and Scott Brown attached words to this criticism of the post-modern. In his Walter Gropius Lecture at Harvard in 1982, Venturi returned to the themes of Scott Brown's critique of the Beaux-Arts show, railing against the new tyranny of "parvenu Classicism."[188] Arguing against the claimed originality of the new fad, he explained that the term "post modern architecture" had already been used in the 1940s by his old studio teacher Jean Labatut, to describe more generally the new circumstances of postwar design.[189] But his chief criticism was that post-modernists were devoting too much energy to theory. In his Annual Discourse before the Royal Institute of British Architects in London in 1981, he said, "now is the time to do more and speak less, to concentrate on quality in practice rather than ideology in words."[190]

That was an unexpected pronouncement from an architect who for the first decade and more of his independent practice had made his reputation as a cogent and witty writer. But in the 1970s, as their architectural work became more abundant, Robert Venturi and Denise Scott Brown had written less and built more. In 1980 they renamed the firm "Venturi, Rauch and Scott Brown," and (fittingly) they moved their enlarged staff to the three-story industrial building on Main Street in Manayunk—an industrial village of the nineteenth century now contained within the city of Philadelphia. They had just been approached by Princeton University, Venturi's alma mater, to renovate old buildings and design new ones in support of a new system of undergraduate residences. In the years ahead, Princeton would become their greatest and wisest patron, establishing the enlarged scale and many of the new program types of their subsequent work.

[188] Robert Venturi, "Diversity, Relevance and Representation in Historicism, or *Plus ça Change. . . Plus a Plea for Pattern All Over Architecture with a Postscript on My Mother's House* [1982]," in Venturi and Scott Brown, *View from the Campidoglio*, p. 113.

[189] Quoted in MacNair, "Venturi and the Classic Modern Tradition," p. 4.

[190] Robert Venturi, "The RIBA Annual Discourse [1981–82]," in Venturi and Scott Brown, *View from the Campidoglio*, p. 104.

Figure 125
**Gordon Wu Hall, Princeton
University, New Jersey, 1980–83**

SEEKING A RATIONAL MANNERISM

David G. De Long
Professor of Architecture
University of Pennsylvania

Figure 126
Robert Venturi and Denise Scott Brown, c. 1983

By the early 1980s, Robert Venturi and Denise Scott Brown (fig. 126) had achieved international fame. Critics described them as America's most influential, and most closely followed, architects,[1] and they continued to augment this position through a practice that reflected a clear, consistent approach, one remarkably congruent with their widely published theories of design. Opportunities increased with the new commissions that came to the firm during these years, their growing numbers a predictable result of widespread publicity. These commissions fall into easily identifiable typologies, which provide a structure for the study of their later practice: buildings for universities, museums, and other civic institutions; designs for public monuments, commercial structures, and houses. Themes transcending these typologies can also be discerned. This is shown by a cluster of recent buildings—one commercial, one civic, and one academic—that reflects an increasing concern with patterns of movement as they relate to a broader social and cultural context, in which the physical context itself has needed reinforcement. These buildings, which define streets with an authoritative presence less evident in earlier examples, could signal the beginning of a new phase in the ongoing work of Venturi, Scott Brown and Associates.

As in any successful architectural practice, Venturi and Scott Brown's accomplishments depended on the creative energies of dedicated associates. Steven Izenour, a principal and veritable fixture in the firm, continued to provide vitalizing energy, joined in these years by his son, John. David Vaughan, another principal, was a key member until his retirement—a reminder of the firm's longevity. Others chose the professional route of remaining partly in the background, providing what Scott Brown describes as having "brilliances that can be sectionalized."[2] Without the likes of David Marohn, John Hunter, and John Bastian, among the many in this group, much less would have been realized. While some, such as Nancy Rogo Trainer, Jaimie Kolken, and Eva Lew, were lured away by other offices, their energies helped sustain the firm, even if briefly. Still others left to

[1] See, for example, Robert Bruegmann, "Two Post-Modernist Visions of Urban Design," *Landscape*, vol. 26, no. 2 (1982), pp. 31–37; Martin Filler, "Learning from Venturi," *Art in America*, vol. 68 (April 1980), pp. 95–101.

[2] Denise Scott Brown, interview with the author, Philadelphia, March 15, 2001.

Figure 127
**Robert Venturi and colleagues
in studio of office in Manayunk,
c. 1997**

Figure 128
Venturi Scott Brown House, c. 2000
Living room

establish firms of their own, producing work so varied that it distinguishes the Venturis' office as a stimulus to independent thought rather than as a maker of rubber stamps. One has only to look at the work of Paul Hirshorn, Stephanie Christoff, and Ron Evitts to sense the Venturis' role in encouraging a younger generation of architects to move in new directions.

But substantial change came to their office also; John Rauch's unofficial departure in November 1987 provided the most visible sign, and in 1989 the firm changed its name from Venturi, Rauch and Scott Brown to Venturi, Scott Brown and Associates. Otherwise, calm seemed to prevail within their Manayunk building, ever-more crowded with stacks of drawings, discarded study models, old prototypes, an occasional dog or parrot, and kids on weekends (fig. 127). Its informal atmosphere reinforces the feeling of the family business that it is, although a comparatively large one, with a staff of anywhere from thirty-five to fifty (and occasionally more) working there at any one time.

The Venturis remained comfortably settled in their home as well, made quieter still by the fact they are seldom there, returning for late suppers and adding to towering piles of books yet to be read (fig. 128). For when they are not in their office, they are on the road, tending commissions across the globe, interviewing for new jobs, dealing with endless invitations to lecture and teach, and accepting a multitude of awards. These include Venturi's Pritzker Architecture Prize (1991) and their joint National Medal of Arts (1992), along with countless others, and between them they have received nineteen honorary degrees since 1980. They continue to write extensively, although understandably in shorter segments; the three major publications to appear after 1980, *A View from the Campidoglio* (1984), *Urban Concepts* (1990), and *Iconography and Electronics upon a Generic Architecture* (1996), are mostly compilations of earlier essays, but with biting commentary that sharpens critical perspective.[3]

[3] Robert Venturi and Denise Scott Brown, *A View from the Campidoglio: Selected Essays, 1953–1984*, eds., Peter Arnell, Ted Bickford, and Catherine Bergart (New York: Harper & Row, 1984); Denise Scott Brown, *Urban Concepts*, Architectural Design, profile 83 (New York: St. Martin's Press, 1990); Robert Venturi, *Iconography and Electronics upon a Generic Architecture: A View from the Drafting Room* (Cambridge and London: The MIT Press, 1996).

Accommodating Shapes for Academia

In the 1980s, commissions from universities came to constitute a major segment of the firm's later work, beginning with those from Princeton in 1980. After the university decided to establish a system of residential colleges, existing facilities had to be adapted to provide additional commons and to create more visible identities for each of them. The Venturis were involved with several of these conversions, including Rockefeller and Mathey colleges, both 1980–83, and Blair Hall, 1981–84. Butler College was different, however, requiring a major addition to enhance its existing building. To be named Gordon Wu Hall (fig. 125), this addition was to contain an appropriately collegial dining hall and related commons and to become a ceremonial entrance to the college itself.

Programming for Wu Hall began in May 1980; schematic designs were approved that October, final designs by March 1981, and working drawings by July of that year.[4] Construction began in August 1981 and was completed by April 1983. The building was widely praised, which undoubtedly reinforced Princeton's decision to offer ongoing commissions to the firm of a prominent alumnus. The Venturis benefited in other ways as well, for Princeton had proved to be an unusually sympathetic client. Looking back on the occasion of receiving the Pritzker prize in 1991, Venturi celebrated the university's support: "William Bowen and Neil Rudenstine, as, respectively, recent President and recent Provost of Princeton . . . have been the Lorenzo de' Medicis of our office as patrons—full of grace, discerning and appreciative."[5]

Wu Hall contains as its main space a navelike dining hall (fig. 129) configured in the manner of the earlier faculty club at Penn State (1973–76; see fig. 301). Along the north and east, the dining hall is pulled free of the exterior walls, which assume their own profile in response to the adjoining wings of Wilcox Hall (fig. 130). This allows a gracefully shaped courtyard to be formed, not rigidly framed but instead suggestively opened, somewhat in the spirit of Alvar Aalto, one

Figure 129
Gordon Wu Hall, Princeton University, New Jersey, 1980–83
Dining hall

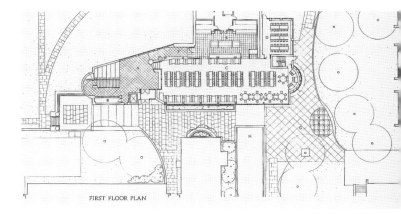

FIRST FLOOR PLAN

Figure 130
Gordon Wu Hall, Princeton University, New Jersey, 1980–83
First-floor plan. Pencil and transfer letters on vellum, 35 ½ x 42" (90.2 x 106.7 cm). Dated 1983
Collection of Venturi, Scott Brown and Associates, Inc.

Figure 131
Gordon Wu Hall, Princeton University, New Jersey, 1980–83
Main stair

[4] Research notes compiled by Joseph Blanco in 1999 document the chronology of the commission; they are filed in the Architectural Archives of the University of Pennsylvania. These notes were supplemented by additional information compiled by William Whitaker.

[5] Robert Venturi, "Robert Venturi's Response at the Pritzker Prize Award Ceremony at the Palacio de Iturbide, Mexico City, May 16, 1991," in *Iconography and Electronics*, p. 101.

Figure 132
Gordon Wu Hall, Princeton University, New Jersey, 1980–83
South facade

Figure 133
Lee D. Butler Memorial Plaza, Princeton University, New Jersey, 1980–83
Elevation study. Pencil and colored pencil on yellow tracing paper, 12 x 27½" (30.5 x 69.9 cm) Robert Venturi. Signed and dated August 10, 1982
Collection of Venturi, Scott Brown and Associates, Inc.

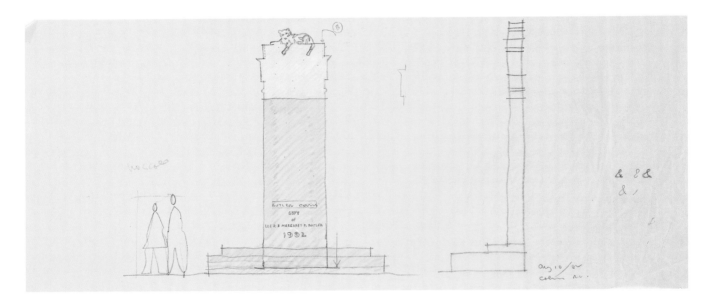

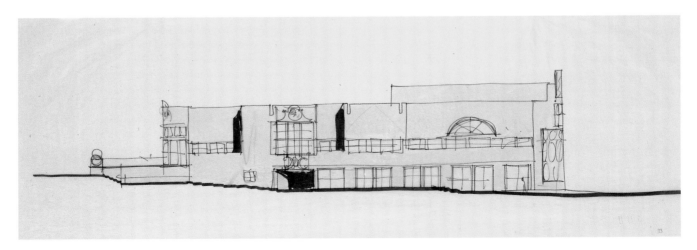

Figure 134
Gordon Wu Hall, Princeton University, New Jersey, 1980–83
Elevation study. Marker and colored pencil on yellow tracing paper, 12 x 34" (30.5 x 86.4 cm) Robert Venturi
Collection of Venturi, Scott Brown and Associates, Inc.

Figure 135

**Gordon Wu Hall, Princeton
University, New Jersey, 1980–83**

Elevation study. Marker on
yellow tracing paper, 18 x 16¾"
(45.7 x 42.5 cm). Robert Venturi

Collection of Venturi, Scott Brown
and Associates, Inc.

Figure 136
Sebastiano Serlio, Rusticated Gate, c. 1537

From *Tutte l'opera d'architettura*, book 7 (Venice, 1584). Engraving, 9 x 7½″ (22.9 x 19.1 cm)

Gift of the Estate of Alfred H. Gumaer Anne and Jerome Fisher Fine Arts Library, University of Pennsylvania Library

of the architects Venturi most admires. The entrance lobby and a grand, ceremonial stair occupy residual space between the exterior profile of the building and partitioned rooms within (fig. 131), and this residual space is marked on the outside by a projecting bay window. At the opposite end of the building, a second bay window rises two floors to light both the dining hall and the lounge above; from the outside, it effects a gentle presence at one end of a major pedestrian route of the campus—College Walk (fig. 132). Characteristic of the Venturis' approach, it does so not by terminating this walk, as a more conventional design might have done, but rather by reinforcing its continuation as it bends, a bit like light waves pulled by gravitational force. A freestanding, flattened column, a memorial to Lee D. Butler (1980–83), adds to the composition; together with designs for its surrounding plaza, it had been shown in early presentations (fig. 133), and Venturi had taken care to explain its importance to the project: "As a vertical element which is non-directional, it would have an important spatial function as well as its symbolic and memorial functions—that is to create a focus for Butler College, to create a plaza and meeting place at the center of the complex, and to help unify the three rather disparate buildings that make up the college as they come together."[6]

Although the majority of Princeton's older buildings are stone and generally medievalizing in character, Wu Hall is located in an area of predominantly brick buildings, and these limestone-trimmed structures carry a mixture of historicizing elements. Numerous elevation studies record Venturi's concern with details that would relate to this setting (fig. 134). Of special focus was the main doorway, which was to form the ceremonial entrance to Butler College itself. The final design (fig. 135) derives from Elizabethan motifs, particularly of the sort inspired by Sebastiano Serlio (1475–1555), whose influential books, much circulated in Europe, affected English architecture just as it was evolving from a late-medieval to an early Renaissance mentality (fig. 136). Venturi skillfully adapted such sources through

[6] Robert Venturi to Neil Rudenstine, June 2, 1981, "2.1 Client Correspondence," VSB box 84 (Venturi, Scott Brown and Associates, Inc.; hereafter VSBA archives).

[7] Quoted in Peter Eisenman, "Interview: Robert Venturi and Peter Eisenman," *Skyline*, July 1982, p. 15.

flattening, simplification, and exaggerated scale, appropriately evoking a period of stylistic transition within an area of varied stylistic motifs. Decorative bands and other flattened elements, diverse window shapes, and gently modeled wall planes further complicate one's first impression of the building as a basically rectangular shape. As with all the firm's designs, perception shifts. Through reasoned complication, the seemingly obvious becomes something extraordinary, imparting new and unexpected meaning to the basic form itself. As Venturi once explained to the architect Peter Eisenman, "Essentially what we do is try to enrich life, not clarify it."[7]

The design for Wu Hall defined a building typology that is essential to understanding much of their later work: what they have more recently come to call a "generic loft." Scott Brown has likened these to a flexible mitten as opposed to a constricting glove.[8] The approach of creating an adaptable, yet expressive, building can be traced back to early examples of their work, such as the Lieb house (1967–69) or the Humanities (1968–73) and Social Sciences (1970–78) buildings for the State University of New York at Purchase. With Wu Hall, all of the critical ingredients of the generic loft are fully in place.

The first of these ingredients is a simple, understated structural system of columns and unpartitioned floor plates, in its stripped form not unlike Le Corbusier's famously influential Domino prototype of 1914 (fig. 137). This modernist approach of beginning with open spaces underlies the work of Mies van der Rohe as well, a source acknowledged by the Venturis: "We're evolving from Modernism . . . we learned a lot from Mies . . . But it's Mies with signs."[9] It is also Mies with relaxed divisions, for in place of strictly ordered partitions that echo the uncompromised shapes of his buildings, the partitioning of these open spaces, accommodates disparate functions with looser arrangements more in the manner of Aalto.

Two other ingredients critical to the typology of the generic loft, the decoration of exterior surface and the

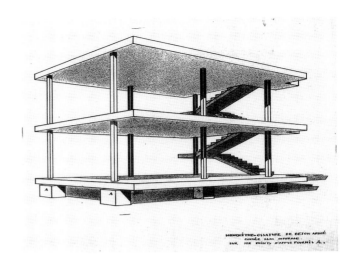

Figure 137
Le Corbusier, Domino House, c. 1914
Prototype. Ink, pencil, and colored pencil, 18 ½ x 22 ½" (47 x 57 cm)
Fondation Le Corbusier, Paris
© 2001 Artists Rights Society (ARS), New York/ADAGP, Paris/FLC

[8] Paula D. McIntyre, "Maps as Muse: First Phase of Campus Plan Released for Comment," *Michigan Alumnus*, vol. 105 (Fall 1998), pp. 20–23.

[9] Quoted in Mary McLeod, "On Artful Artlessness: A Conversation," in Stanislaus von Moos, *Venturi, Scott Brown & Associates: Buildings and Projects, 1986–1998* (New York: The Monacelli Press, 1999), p. 349.

modification of external regularity, illustrate how the Venturis radically and creatively transformed the very modernism from which their work initially evolved. While their decorative surfaces—richly rendered in their play with color and pattern—depart from the look of modernism, they sustain its rational spirit. For in regarding the exterior surface of a neutral structure as essentially arbitrary, their substitution of what they define as symbolic imagery for a dated modernist vocabulary justifiably provides meaning that would otherwise be absent. Sylvia Lavin was among the first to appreciate this critical position: "If the Modern facade is not integrally structural, then it is applied, and if its two-dimensionality is only metaphorical, then the modern facade is the epitome of applied decoration."[10] Through such devices as flattening and exaggerated scale, familiar images—related in some specific way to a building's context, but significantly changed by the Venturis—proclaim their own time as surface decoration. And intentions remain high, never descending to a duplication of the truly ordinary, as Scott Brown said in a reference to such decoration: "Although we may try to make the shed seem artless, it's artfully artless."[11]

The Venturis' modifications to exterior form offer a significant rebuttal to an imposed order so essential to conventional modernism. For in every example of these adaptable buildings, as seen clearly in the design of Wu Hall, the regular shape of the Domino prototype or a Mies van der Rohe building has been altered, or eroded, not only reflecting different interior needs, but more significantly in response to exterior forces, such as those generated by adjacent buildings or patterns of external movement. The Venturis describe such modifications as inflections responsive to some specific condition of place. This approach can be traced back to the early work of the firm, such as the North Penn Visiting Nurses Association building of 1961–63 (see fig. 24).

The Venturis' "contextualism"—a term they did much to initiate and popularize—is now described as conven-

Figure 138
Giambattista Nolli, Plan of Rome, 1748
Etching on 16 combined sheets, detail
Pace Master Prints, New York

[10] Sylvia Lavin, "Artistic Statements," *Interiors*, vol. 147 (November 1987), p. 136.

[11] Quoted in McLeod, "On Artful Artlessness," in von Moos, *Venturi, Scott Brown & Associates*, p. 349.

[12] For example, Herbert Muschamp, "Living Up to the Memories of a Poetic Old Skyline," *New York Times*, August 13, 2000; and Herbert Muschamp, "How Modern Design Remains Faithful to Its Context," *New York Times*, August 6, 2000.

tional, for in recent years the idea of context has been so broadened that almost anything can be described as having it, even the most sculptural of buildings by Frank Gehry or the purest examples of early modernism.[12] Manifestations of contextualism abound. Frank Lloyd Wright, for example, related his early buildings to perceived patterns of natural topography, while Peter Eisenman attempts to evoke an imagined archaeology in his recent buildings.[13] Yet contextualism as conceived by the Venturis has a very specific meaning, dealing as it does with tangible manifestations of place as well as broader cultural concerns, and their evocations remain distinct.

A final ingredient of the Venturis' adaptable buildings, and perhaps the most dynamic, deals with the juncture of internal and external realms. This is the place where the accommodating form of the internally functioning parts meets the inflected, contextually responsive profile of the outer enclosure. Like the collision of differently charged particles, here flashes occur. Often they are signaled on the exterior by explosionlike flourishes of shape, something the Venturis describe as "fanfares." Venturi had alluded to this as early as 1961, and he reinforced it thirty years later: "We design from the inside out *and* the outside in . . . this act can create valid tensions where the wall, the line of change between inside and out, is acknowledged to become a spatial record—in the end, an essential architectural event."[14]

Almost always this critical juncture of inside and outside houses major elements of public circulation—complicated, gallerylike areas rich in architectural form as housing compacted functions. In many instances, these galleries parallel and amplify corresponding routes of circulation outside, as seen earlier in the buildings at Purchase (see fig. 59). The importance of these routes, which the Venturis describe as symbolic streets and trace back to the plan of the Vanna Venturi house, has been much discussed, especially by Stanislaus von Moos. He identifies them as "their prime architectural theme," one that relates to the juncture of private and public space somewhat in the manner of

Giambattista Nolli's famous plan of Rome, first published in 1748.[15] In that plan, Nolli depicted significant interiors as continuous with the public streets they adjoined, thus rendering an expanded scale of civic space (fig. 138). Surely a deeper meaning of the Venturis' parallel enrichment of places for circulation, and their location at critical junctures of internal and external realms, deals with their own sense of social responsibility, with an attempt to establish meaningful public space, even in private buildings. Such architectural celebration of an otherwise mundane function ensures a life-giving vitality through the movement it is meant to stimulate.

In January of 1983, as Wu Hall was nearing completion, Princeton announced plans for a new facility for molecular biology, what would become the Lewis Thomas Laboratory.[16] In this the university joined a growing national trend toward the creation of such facilities, a trend supported by coveted grants from private institutions as well as the federal government. Believing speed was essential to maintain a competitive standing, the university moved quickly to engage two firms already working on campus projects to create the laboratories: Payette Associates and Venturi, Rauch and Scott Brown.[17] As agreed by March 1983, Payette Associates, highly regarded for their technical designs of laboratory facilities, were to be the architects of record, responsible for the program and planning; Venturi, Rauch and Scott Brown were responsible for site planning and were to design the exterior, or decoration, of what was to be essentially a shed, for they had little say regarding its interior arrangement. The relationship proved highly workable and led to several later, similarly arranged, commissions.

By the summer of 1983, Payette's proposals were sufficiently advanced so that work could begin on exterior cladding. The building was to be a simple rectangle in plan, with ranges of windows lighting open laboratories along each side. On the long sides, regularly spaced, thin columns were to alternate with wider mechanical shafts, which together defined individual bays. Located parallel to

[13] On Wright in this regard, see David G. De Long, ed., *Frank Lloyd Wright: Designs for an American Landscape, 1922–1932* (New York: Harry N. Abrams in association with the Canadian Centre for Architecture, the Library of Congress, and the Frank Lloyd Wright Foundation, 1996), esp. pp. 118–20. One of the many examples by Eisenman is the Aranoff Center of Design and Art at the University of Cincinnati, discussed in Joseph Giovannini, "Campus Complexity," *Architecture*, vol. 85 (August 1996), pp. 114–25.

[14] Venturi, "Response at the Pritzker Prize Award Ceremony," in *Iconography and Electronics*, p. 97. For the earlier mention of inside out/outside in, see Jan C. Rowan,

"Wanting To Be: The Philadelphia School," *Progressive Architecture*, vol. 42 (April 1961), pp. 130–63.

[15] Von Moos, *Venturi, Scott Brown & Associates*, p. 39; see also pp. 40–42.

[16] Research notes compiled by Gregory Saldana in 1999 document the chronology and other details of the commission; they are filed in the Architectural Archives of the University of Pennsylvania.

[17] A detailed account from Payette's perspective can be found in James Collins Jr., "The Design Process for the Human Workplace," in Peter Galison and Emily Thompson, eds., *The Architecture of Science* (Cambridge and London: The MIT Press, 1999), pp. 399–412.

Figure 139

**Lewis Thomas Laboratory,
Princeton University, New Jersey,
1983–86**

Preliminary elevation. Marker on
yellow tracing paper, 12 x 22 ¼"
(30.5 x 56.5 cm). Robert Venturi

Collection of Venturi, Scott Brown
and Associates, Inc.

Figure 140

**Lewis Thomas Laboratory,
Princeton University, New Jersey,
1983–86**

Elevation sketch. Marker on yellow
tracing paper, 12 x 16" (30.5 x 40.6 cm)
Robert Venturi

Collection of Venturi, Scott Brown
and Associates, Inc.

College Walk not far from Butler College, this building also fell within the area of Princeton's brick-and-limestone buildings, and these materials, greatly enriched with diaper and checkerboard patterns, became Venturi, Rauch and Scott Brown's as well. Sketches record many variations that were tried (fig. 139), with particular emphasis given to the main entrance, on College Walk (fig. 140), and to the ends of the building, where they added minor variations to the otherwise regular plan (fig. 141). Lounges, essential to the program, were to be located at each end, where they related to the major circulation system linking the functionally planned laboratories and became the escaping sparks that defined the link between shared and private, or planned and informal, space. On the west, facing Butler College, the end wall curves out (fig. 142), and on the east, it angles in.

As refined during late 1983 and early 1984, the main entrance was given a special emphasis that signaled a third communal area near the center of the building: a lobby and generously scaled stair. As seen from the outside, it illustrates the firm's evolving mannerism, for its apparently idiosyncratic details derive from circumstance rather than whim (fig. 143). At first, it appears that structural columns rising above the entrance have been illogically removed from the first floor, leaving the simplified Tudor arches immediately over the entrance suspended in space. Yet what rises above are not really columns, but instead enclosures for mechanical shafts. The actual columns—efficiently thinner, and thus less structural in appearance—remain firmly in place, but further to the sides (fig. 144). Thus what at first seems whimsical comes to have an underlying logic of its own, giving voice to complicated reality.

The Lewis Thomas Laboratory was dedicated in April 1986. Over a decade later, when changing fashions inclined toward a late-modernist perspective, James S. Ackerman, a noted architectural historian at Harvard, sounded an odd note, pejoratively describing the exterior as "a wrapping comparable to the Neo-Classical disguises of the early welfare hospitals."[18] What does he mean? Is such wrapping

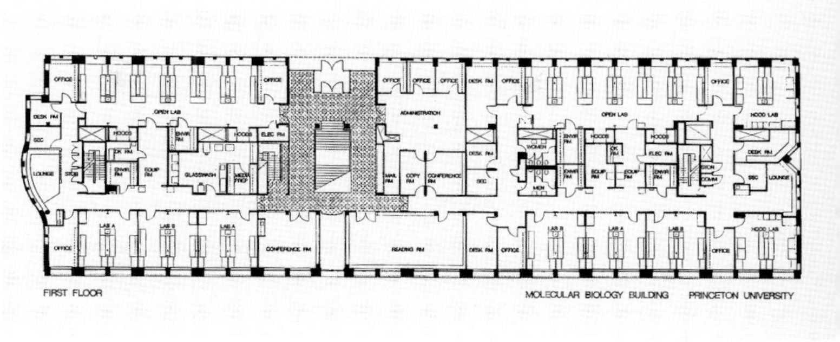

Figure 141
Lewis Thomas Laboratory,
Princeton University, New Jersey,
1983–86
First-floor plan
Whereabouts unknown

Figure 142
Lewis Thomas Laboratory,
Princeton University, New Jersey,
1983–86
North and west facades

[18] James S. Ackerman, review of *The Architecture of Science,* by Peter Galison and Emily Thompson, eds., *Harvard Design Magazine,* Fall 1999, p. 97.

Figure 143

**Lewis Thomas Laboratory,
Princeton University, New Jersey,
1983–86**

Elevation. Airbrush on photomechanical
print, 42 x 29" (106.7 x 73.6 cm)

Collection of Venturi, Scott Brown
and Associates, Inc.

Figure 144
**Lewis Thomas Laboratory,
Princeton University, New Jersey,
1983–86**
Entrance

Figure 145
**Clinical Research Building,
University of Pennsylvania,
Philadelphia, 1985–89**

wrong? Are people in welfare hospitals, and by inference, in laboratories, expected to suffer from undisguised plainness?

By the time the Lewis Thomas Laboratory had opened, the firm was engaged in two additional laboratory designs, again in association with Payette, and again similar in their simple plans and their flat, decorated facades: the Clinical Research Building at the University of Pennsylvania (1985–89; fig. 145) and the Gordon and Virginia MacDonald Medical Research Laboratories at the University of California at Los Angeles (1986–91; figs. 146–48). Site plans for the laboratories in Los Angeles indicate the presence of a second building that would complete the human-scaled, urbanistic composition of connecting stairs and terraces (fig. 149); this was later realized as the Gonda (Goldschmied) Neuroscience and Genetics Research Center (1993–98; figs. 150, 151, 153). At one end of the Gonda Research Center, oriented toward the adjacent intersection, a faceted glass projection breaks free of the masonry enclosure of the building. Designed to contain lounges, this element, which becomes a true fanfare of the design (fig. 152), sustains a pattern of emphasizing that space between defined interior areas and a separated exterior wrapping. It was also meant to signal an entry to the campus and thus be visible from afar.

At Princeton, the firm's next designs were for Fisher and Bendheim halls (1986–91; fig. 154), connected buildings for the Department of Economics and the Center of International Studies attached at one end to an older structure. Their angled wings, clad in brick and limestone, enlivened with flattened contextual references and with gentle bays, bring a seamless unity to that area of the campus (figs. 155, 156). While work on these buildings was under way, they began designs (once again with Payette Associates) for yet another Princeton building: the George LaVie Schultz Laboratory for the Department of Biology (1988–93; fig. 157). Now the urbanistic unity they created was in relation to their own earlier work, for the Schultz Laboratory was angled against Guyot Hall (to which it is joined) so that it paralleled their Lewis Thomas Laboratory across the way,

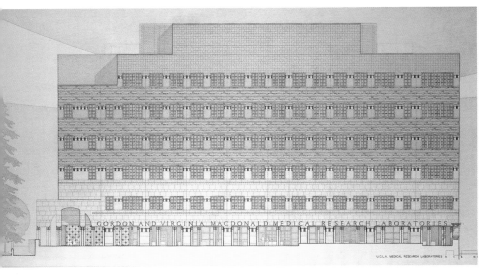

Figure 146

Gordon and Virginia MacDonald Medical Research Laboratories, University of California at Los Angeles, 1986–91

Elevation. Marker and colored pencil on diazo print, 36 x 65½" (91.4 x 166.4 cm). Ronald Evitts and Douglas Hassebroek

Collection of Venturi, Scott Brown and Associates, Inc.

Figure 147

Gordon and Virginia MacDonald Medical Research Laboratories, University of California at Los Angeles, 1986–91

Entrance

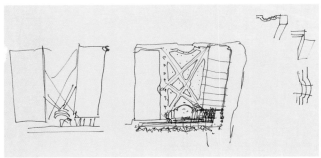

Figure 149

Gordon and Virginia MacDonald Medical Research Laboratories, University of California at Los Angeles, 1986–91

Preliminary site plans including what would later be called the Gonda (Goldschmied) Neuroscience and Genetics Reseach Center. Marker on yellow tracing paper, 12 x 23¾" (30.5 x 60.3 cm). Robert Venturi

Collection of Venturi, Scott Brown and Associates, Inc.

Figure 148

Gordon and Virginia MacDonald Medical Research Laboratories, University of California at Los Angeles, 1986–91

Entrance facade, detail

Figure 150

Gonda (Goldschmied) Neuroscience and Genetics Research Center, University of California at Los Angeles, 1993–98

Elevation. Cut paper on foam core, 31 x 12″ (78.7 x 30.5 cm). Eva Lew and Thomas Purdy

Collection of Venturi, Scott Brown and Associates, Inc.

Figure 151

Gonda (Goldschmied) Neuroscience and Genetics Research Center, University of California at Los Angeles, 1993–98

Exterior, detail

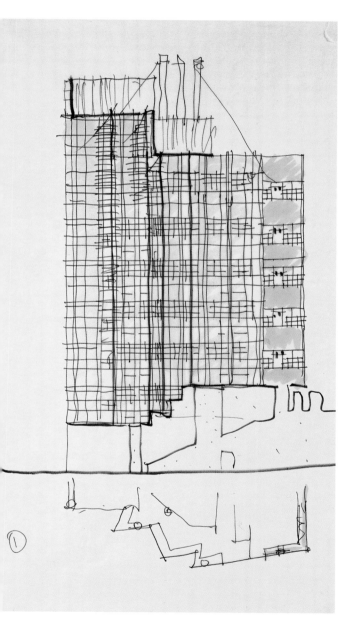

Figure 152

Gonda (Goldschmied) Neuroscience and Genetics Research Center, University of California at Los Angeles, 1993–98

Elevation and plan. Marker and colored marker on yellow tracing paper, 31½ x 18″ (80 x 45.7 cm) Robert Venturi

Collection of Venturi, Scott Brown and Associates, Inc.

Figure 153

Gonda (Goldschmied) Neuroscience and Genetics Research Center, University of California at Los Angeles, 1993–98

Figure 154
**Fisher and Bendheim Halls,
Princeton University, New Jersey,
1986–91**

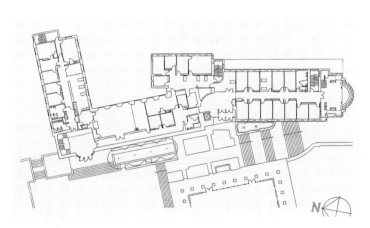

Figure 155
**Fisher and Bendheim Halls,
Princeton University, New Jersey,
1986–91**
Podium floor plan
Whereabouts unknown

Figure 156
**Fisher and Bendheim Halls,
Princeton University, New Jersey,
1986–91**
Podium-level entrance of Bendheim
Hall

Figure 157

George LaVie Schultz Laboratory, Princeton University, New Jersey, 1988–93

Figure 158

Roy and Diana Vagelos Laboratories, University of Pennsylvania, Philadelphia, 1990–97

Figure 159
**Charles P. Stevenson Jr. Library, Bard
College, Annandale-on-Hudson,
New York, 1989–93**

reinforcing that connection as well as defining College Walk, which lay between.

With Payette Associates they next designed the Roy and Diana Vagelos Laboratories at the University of Pennsylvania (1990–97; fig. 158), which further demonstrated the Venturis' urbanistic approach. Here the problem was complicated by a need to acknowledge two quite different elements of place, for the Vagelos Laboratories were to be connected at their narrow end to the neutral, undistinguished 1973 Chemistry Laboratories, yet the building also lay directly across from the strongly expressive University Library (1888–91) by Philadelphia's great architect Frank Furness. Long before, while faculty members at Penn, the Venturis had helped save the library from demolition, and they had just restored it as the Fisher Fine Arts Library. Few architects could have achieved the balance they did with this project, persuasively relating the color and detail of their cladding to the library while managing to make the chemistry building look better rather than worse.

The Charles P. Stevenson Jr. Library at Bard College (1989–93) presented an even greater problem of connection, for the original library, Hoffman Hall, built in the early nineteenth century to emulate a Greek temple, was notoriously difficult to expand in an aesthetically pleasing manner.[19] As Venturi noted, "almost by definition you can't add to it."[20] Yet it already had an addition. In 1970 Bard had contacted the office with regard to an addition to Hoffman Hall, but then chose another firm instead for this work, which was completed in 1976. In 1989, Venturi prepared schematic designs for a second addition, submitted to Bard in May in competition with other architects seeking the commission. The Venturis were selected as architects in July, and by May of the following year had almost completed their design. The production of working drawings, along with ongoing refinements to the design, delayed the onset of construction until early 1992, and the completed building was dedicated in May 1993 (fig. 159).

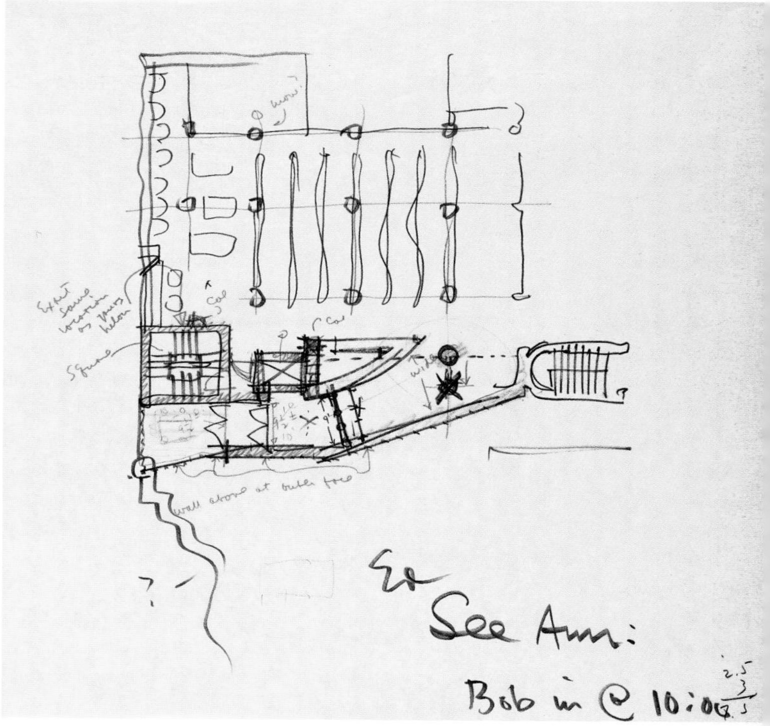

Figure 160

Charles P. Stevenson Jr. Library, Bard College, Annandale-on-Hudson, New York, 1989–93

Plan. Marker, colored marker, pencil, and colored pencil on yellow tracing paper, 18 x 23½" (45.7 x 59.7 cm)
Robert Venturi

Collection of Venturi, Scott Brown and Associates, Inc.

[19] Research notes compiled by Matthew E. Pisarski in 1999 document the chronology and other details of the commission; they are filed in the Architectural Archives of the University of Pennsylvania.

[20] Robert Venturi, "Dedication of the Charles P. Stevenson Jr. Library, Bard College," May 28, 1993, "89.10 0.2.5 Robert Venturi's File," VSB box 218 (VSBA archives).

Figure 161

Charles P. Stevenson Jr. Library, Bard College, Annandale-on-Hudson, New York, 1989–93

South elevation. Cut paper, marker, and tape on yellow tracing paper mounted on photomechanical print Robert Venturi. Dated June 1, 1990

Whereabouts unknown

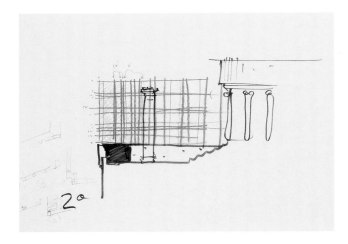

Figure 162

Charles P. Stevenson Jr. Library, Bard College, Annandale-on-Hudson, New York, 1989–93

Preliminary elevation. Marker, pencil, and colored pencil on yellow tracing paper, 18 x 33" (45.7 x 83.8 cm) Robert Venturi

Collection of Venturi, Scott Brown and Associates, Inc.

In concept the Stevenson Library is again an adaptable, loftlike building (fig. 160), placed so it mostly screens the 1976 addition when the original library is seen from the front. Respectful of context, each of its three exposed facades differs in response to the area overlooked. That adjacent to Hoffman Hall angles protectively out, embellished with a bright, colorful pattern of syncopated metallic stripes that partly echo the freestanding columns of the original building while greatly enlivening its monochromatic palette. Venturi described them as "a crescendo of modern pilasters" (fig. 161).[21] A narrow portion of the 1976 addition, effectively exposed on this side, defines a clear joint. On the opposite side, to the north, the new wall is detailed in sympathy with the 1976 addition it adjoins. Linking these two facades is a wall of patterned brick; it rises above a limestone base and is visually stabilized by horizontal stringcourses, bringing an element of calm to the composition.

Early designs included a freestanding Ionic column (fig. 162), which again echoed the similar columns of Hoffman Hall but was larger and placed to mark the new, smaller-scaled entrance at the corner of the proposed addition. Changes of grade and a constricted site complicated this important outdoor area, and it was studied with special care. In July 1990, Venturi exchanged the column for a small, freestanding, columned pavilion, which they came to call a "tempietto," and which better suited the scale of the small entrance plaza. As finally built, raised over angled retaining walls and suggesting a propylon to the temples beyond, the pavilion adds immeasurably to the composition (fig. 163). Within the low entrance to which it leads, again at the juncture of inner and outer configurations of plan, a tall volume, glazed on both sides so it becomes a light source for the library within, defines an active lobby.

Letters from faculty and staff document enthusiastic reactions to the library addition, as did published articles.[22] Building on their success with the Allen Memorial Art Museum at Oberlin College (1973–77), the Venturis again demonstrated how additions to historic buildings need not

[21] Ibid.

[22] For example, M. Lindsay Bierman, "Arcadian Acropolis," *Architecture*, vol. 83 (February 1994), pp. 78–85.

Figure 163
**Charles P. Stevenson Jr. Library,
Bard College, Annandale-on-
Hudson, New York, 1989–93**
South facade with tempietto

Figure 164

**Fisher Fine Arts Library, University
of Pennsylvania, Philadelphia,
1985–91**

Reading room

Figure 165

**Memorial Hall, Harvard University,
Cambridge, Massachusetts,
1992–96**

Dining hall (Annenberg Hall)

Figure 166

**Memorial Hall, Harvard University,
Cambridge, Massachusetts,
1992–96**

Elevation of Loker Commons
Cut paper collage, 4¼ x 39¼"
(10.8 x 99.7 cm). Daniel McCoubrey
and Kimberley Jones

Collection of Venturi, Scott Brown
and Associates, Inc.

be slavish imitations, but could in fact better distinguish those buildings through discerning, clearly contemporary, variations. But at the very beginning of construction, the President's Advisory Council on Historic Preservation, in Washington, D. C., threatened to withhold federal funding because of preservation concerns. Accustomed to more conservative additions, the council failed to appreciate the Venturi design and questioned the validity of the tempietto, which seemed to them disrespectful to Hoffman Hall.[23] Ultimately they released the promised government funding, but not before angering those involved with the design. How ironic that such problems occurred, for the Venturi office excels in additions that brilliantly differentiate their work from the historic fabric they adjoin (the very quality federal guidelines seek to encourage,)[24] and they do so with a degree of wit and sensitivity too often missing in such projects!

Happily problems of official judgment have not constrained the Venturis' preservation of other notable academic buildings, including their restoration of the Fisher Fine Arts Library at the University of Pennsylvania (1985–91; fig. 164) and Ware and Van Brunt's Memorial Hall at Harvard (1992–96; fig. 165). In addition to treating the main volumes of each building with museological accuracy, they reclaimed unused portions of their lower levels, at Harvard fashioning a lively place of "good food and good atmosphere"[25] known as Loker Commons (fig. 166). At Memorial Hall, the critic Robert Campbell wrote, "A team led by Robert Venturi . . . has created a new masterpiece out of the drab, neglected hulk of an old landmark."[26] But to judge from their masterful recovery of original colors and details, they knew from the outset that neither building had ever really been drab; they only appeared so through indifferent use.

Larger in scope is Perelman Quadrangle at the University of Pennsylvania, begun with preliminary studies in 1989 and completed in 2000.[27] There, four historic buildings, sensitively rehabilitated, are linked to form a new student precinct (figs. 167, 168). It developed out of early planning studies undertaken by Denise Scott Brown, a pattern repeated with

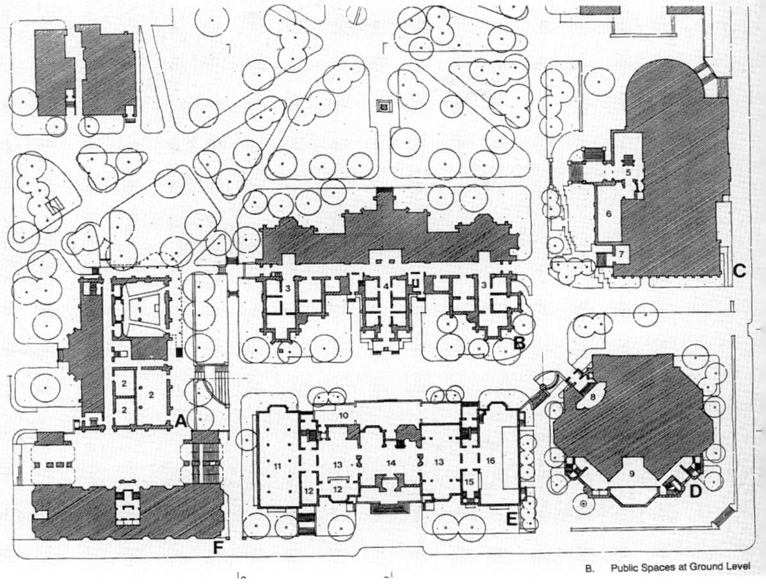

Figure 167

University of Pennsylvania Master Plan, Philadelphia, 1989–93

Site plan of campus center. From "Preliminary Site and Capacity Considerations in the Design of Campus Center," October 10, 1989

Collection of Venturi, Scott Brown and Associates, Inc.

Figure 168

Perelman Quadrangle, University of Pennsylvania, Philadelphia, 1993–2000

Perspective. Airbrush on photo-mechanical print mounted on board, 23 x 27¾" (58.5 x 70.5 cm). Elizabeth Hitchcock, Don Jones, and R. Michael Wommack

Architectural Archives, University of Pennsylvania, Philadelphia

[23] Ann Trowbridge to Robert Venturi, October 28, 1992, "89.10 0.2.1 Memos," VSB box 218 (VSBA archives). See also, research notes compiled by Matthew E. Pisarski in 1999; they are filed in the Architectural Archives of the University of Pennsylvania.

[24] *The Secretary of the Interior's Standards for Rehabilitation and Guidelines for Rehabilitating Historic Buildings*, rev. ed. (Washington, D.C.: Government Printing Office, 1990), esp. pp. 5–11.

[25] Editorial, "An Excellent Student Center," *Harvard Crimson*, December 12, 1995.

[26] Robert Campbell, "Harvard's Great Room," *Boston Globe*, January 28, 1996.

[27] Schematic plans are included in a planning document by Venturi, Scott Brown and Associates, "The Perelman Quadrangle Campus Center, University of Pennsylvania," December 14, 1994. Earlier reports show the plan established by 1989.

Figure 169
**Trabant Student Center,
University of Delaware,
Newark, 1992–96**

Figure 170
**Trabant Student Center, University
of Delaware, Newark, 1992–96**

Interior of "pedestrian street"

some frequency beginning in the 1980s, especially in academic settings. Scott Brown usually leads her firm in these efforts, as Venturi does in developing building designs. She clearly perceives how planning—at least good planning—is as creative as architecture,[28] and her role in demonstrating this fact is beginning to be more widely recognized.[29]

Other student centers by the Venturis have incorporated older structures, but with major additions that again work variations on adaptable, loftlike plans. Among these is the Trabant Student Center at the University of Delaware at Newark (1992–96; figs. 169, 170). Its low, awkwardly large enclosure dictated by programmed uses is articulated as a series of connected units, and these incorporate smaller buildings on the site, so its visible mass seems lessened overall. Within the main unit, a long gallery along one edge provides a pedestrian street that angles in response to the jogged street outside, providing a parallel, but smoother, route inside linking dormitories at one end to new classroom buildings at the other.

At Princeton, the Venturis created the Frist Campus Center by converting what they described as an older generic loft—Palmer Hall, completed in 1918—and adding to it along the rear (fig. 171). Schematic designs were completed by late 1996,[30] and the facility opened in late 2000 (fig. 172). The Venturis understand the special potential of such adaptive use, explaining that students today "tend to be at ease in kinds of discovered spaces . . . whose juxtapositions embrace old and new associations and forms."[31]

The Berry Library addition to Baker Library at Dartmouth College, scheduled for completion in 2001, clearly illustrates the importance of planning to design. Studies begun in 1989 examined options for expansion of the campus, focusing on the reuse of medical buildings to the north.[32] Baker Library, dating from 1918 and positioned at the north edge of the older campus, was identified as "the pivotal center of the new campus."[33] Site plans showed how a needed addition to the library could be shaped in response to this function, anchoring a new northern axis

[28] As evidenced in Denise Scott Brown, "The Hounding of the Snark," in Galison and Thompson, *Architecture of Science*, pp. 375–80.

[29] For example, Martin Filler, "Beyond All Right," review of *Urban Concepts*, by Denise Scott Brown, *Design Quarterly*, no. 154 (Winter 1992), p. 36.

[30] As included in their office report, Venturi, Scott Brown and Associates, "Princeton Campus Center, Pre-Design Phase Report," December 9, 1996.

[31] Quoted in ibid.

[32] The first schematic study by Venturi, Scott Brown and Associates, "A Concept Plan: Dartmouth College," was issued on June 5, 1989.

[33] Quoted in Venturi, Scott Brown and Associates, "Interim Report: A Concept Plan, Dartmouth College," August 11, 1989.

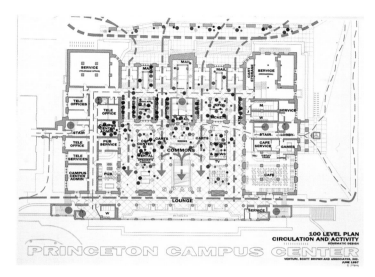

Figure 171

Frist Campus Center, Princeton University, New Jersey, 1996–2000

Circulation and activity plan. Computer plot mounted on foam core, 35 x 48" (88.9 x 121.9 cm). Dated June 1997

Collection of Venturi, Scott Brown and Associates, Inc.

Figure 172

Frist Campus Center, Princeton University, New Jersey, 1996–2000

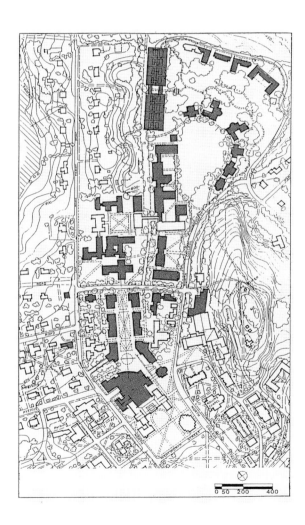

Figure 173

Dartmouth College Master Plan for North Campus, Hanover, New Hampshire, 1988–93

Site plan. From "A Concept Plan, Mary Hitchcock Memorial Hospital Acquisition and Adjacent Properties Interim Report, Dartmouth College," August 11, 1989

Collection of Venturi, Scott Brown and Associates, Inc.

Figure 174

Dartmouth College Master Plan for North Campus, Hanover, New Hampshire, 1988–93

Page from "A Concept Plan, Mary Hitchcock Memorial Hospital Acquisition and Adjacent Properties Interim Report, Dartmouth College," August 11, 1989

Collection of Venturi, Scott Brown and Associates, Inc.

Figure 175

Baker / Berry Library, Dartmouth College, Hanover, New Hampshire, 1995–2001

Model. Computer plot on foam core, 21 x 48 x 36" (53.3 x 121.9 x 91.4 cm)

Collection of Venturi, Scott Brown and Associates, Inc.

Figure 176

Fondren Library, Rice University, Houston, 1999–2000

Perspective. Computer rendering, 13½ x 38½ (34.3 x 97.8 cm). John Bastian, John Izenour, and Ian Smith

Collection of Venturi, Scott Brown and Associates, Inc.

that could be reinforced by future buildings aligned to create a formal quadrangle (fig. 173). Schematic diagrams of the library further defined its component parts (fig. 174). When the Venturis were commissioned to undertake the design of the library addition in 1995, these studies were put into effect, and plans that refined the schematic diagrams were completed within a relatively short time (fig. 175). In this instance, the context of their new building is not so much that which exists as that which is to come, for its scale relates to still larger structures yet unbuilt, but firmly projected. Unable to grasp the image of this future, some faculty have complained that the Venturis' building seems too big, yet when the projected structures are built, that size will seem very much of its place.[34]

An equally strong insertion at Rice University might have demonstrated a similar fusion of planning and architecture had it been built. The firm's proposed addition to Fondren Library (1999–2000; fig. 176), done in association with Shepley, Bulfinch, Richardson and Abbot, featured an arcaded facade that mediated between the older building behind and the more formal quadrangle that lay in front. Positioned effectively to complete that quadrangle, it was detailed with flattened arches and a stepped parapet that brilliantly paraphrased nearby buildings by Ralph Adams Cram (on which Cram, Goodhue and Ferguson's Boston office had worked from 1909 to 1941).

Unassuming Elegance for the Display of Art

During the 1980s and 1990s, the firm received a number of museum commissions, for which the Venturis continued to explore flexible building shapes with adaptable plans, now varied to reflect denser urban settings and more refined contents. Although far fewer in number than those for academic institutions, these buildings generated more publicity and greatly enhanced the international standing of the firm.

The Laguna Gloria Art Museum in Austin, Texas (unbuilt, 1982–89), was their first museum commission. Like the Berry Library and the Perelman Quadrangle, it,

too, developed as part of a planning study, although in a slightly different sequence. The Venturis submitted qualifications for the museum commission in October 1982, and the firm was selected as architects the following April, just as work on the Lewis Thomas Laboratory was beginning at Princeton.[35] The museum was to be a joint enterprise between the city and Watson-Casey Companies, private developers involved with redevelopment of the city, who had agreed to donate land for the site. The firm was retained by Watson-Casey as planners for their development as well, allowing designs for the museum to be realistically developed as part of a much larger scheme.

The Republic Square District development plan, completed in May 1984, stressed the need to develop a coherent public realm in the district and emphasized the importance of the museum to the project: "Public sector projects were seen as anchors to the private development. In particular, the Laguna Gloria Art Museum's plan to establish a downtown presence on a site donated by the Watson-Casey Companies was considered a key to the initial development of the project."[36] The museum was prominently sited across from Republic Square and shown in plan as a long, narrow rectangle with stepped corners, corresponding with preliminary building designs then under way. Various housing prototypes were suggested for a cluster of blocks to the east, along a meandering creek, and a grand pedestrian boulevard, to be called the Rambla after its counterpart, Las Ramblas, in Barcelona, was to provide an active link within the envisioned district. Comparative city-block studies showed how retail development could revitalize the area. One drawing (fig. 177), rendered in the manner of Nolli's eighteenth-century plan of Rome (see fig. 138), defined public space as a continuum, with outside areas joined to accessible spaces within the buildings.

The museum was to be part of a mixed-use complex, and early elevations showed it with a varied profile suggestive of its multiple functions (fig. 178). Problems of funding the complicated partnership slowed things considerably, but the Venturis continued to design the museum, arriving at a

[34] Plans were described as complete in J. Andrew Culp and Arthur J. Monaco, "Library Expansion: Sooner Than You Think," *Dartmouth Review*, vol. 16 (April 10, 1996), pp. 8–10, and cover. The scheduled beginning of construction in 1998 is mentioned in Kristina Eddy, "College Library Design Decried," *Valley News*, November 4, 1997, and it is in this article that concerns regarding the scale of the addition—one required by programmatic needs—are voiced.

[35] Research notes compiled by Rachel Iannacone in June 2000 document the chronology and other details of the commission; they are filed in the Architectural Archives of the University of Pennsylvania.

[36] Venturi, Rauch and Scott Brown, "A Plan for the Republic Square District, Austin, Texas," May 1984, p. 9.

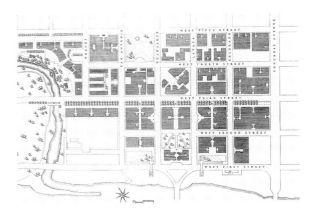

Figure 177
**Republic Square District
Development Plan, Austin, Texas,
1982–84**

Plan. Pencil on vellum, 23¼ x 31⅛"
(59.1 x 79.1 cm). Miles Ritter. Dated
May 1984

Collection of Venturi, Scott Brown
and Associates, Inc.

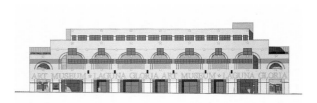

Figure 178
**Laguna Gloria Art Museum,
Austin, Texas, 1982–89**

Preliminary elevation. Marker, pencil,
and cut paper mounted on foam
core, 18¾ x 40" (47.6 x 101.6 cm)
Miles Ritter and Margo Angevine

Collection of Venturi, Scott Brown
and Associates, Inc.

Figure 179
**Laguna Gloria Art Museum,
Austin, Texas, 1982–89**

Model. Chipboard, diazo print,
construction paper, pencil, and
tape, 10 x 14 x 40" (25.4 x
35.6 x 101.6 cm)

Collection of Venturi, Scott Brown
and Associates, Inc.

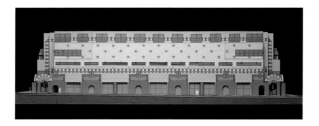

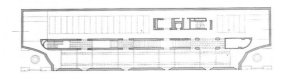

Figure 180
**Laguna Gloria Art Museum,
Austin, Texas, 1982–89**

Second-floor plan. Dated
October 3, 1985

Whereabouts unknown

final scheme in February 1985 (fig. 179). Large openings at ground level activate the long facade, recalling the arcaded openings of their earlier schemes, and a diaper pattern of widely spaced insets activates the planes above. Elements that step in plan—some curved, some straight—soften the ends of the building so it relates more informally to its setting (fig. 180). These elements call attention as well to the juncture between interior and exterior order. Further disputes between the city and the developers, which caused another pause from 1986 to 1987, were sufficiently resolved so working drawings could be produced in 1988, but the developer's bankruptcy later that year led to the project's demise. Venturi lamented that it was "particularly sad for us because there is the beautiful set of working drawings that we slaved over and what is perhaps the best facade ever to come out of our office." [37]

Long before the Laguna Gloria museum project ended, the firm had been selected to design three other museums, all of which were built: the Seattle Art Museum (1984–91), the Sainsbury Wing of the National Gallery in London (1985–91), and the addition to the Museum of Contemporary Art in La Jolla, California (1986–96). They were designed almost simultaneously, just when final drawings for Laguna Gloria were being completed, and this added great pressure to an already busy office. During this time, in 1987 and 1988, the number of people working for the firm soared briefly to nearly one hundred.

The Seattle Art Museum realizes much of the promise of Laguna Gloria, which it resembles. An architect selection committee appointed by the Seattle museum in April 1982 had begun its work early, but at first concentrated on the building's program and on selecting its site, so that negotiations with prospective architects did not begin until much later.[38] Alert to the pending commission, Venturi had contacted this committee in August 1982 and submitted qualifications in February 1983, but it was only in August 1984 that Venturi, Rauch and Scott Brown was named as one of the three finalists and in September was selected as

[37] Robert Venturi to Robert T. Renfro, February 22, 1989, "Laguna Gloria Art Museum 1989," VSB box 274 (VSBA archives). Renfro had previously worked for the Venturi office; his firm, Renfro, Steinbomer, and Petty, Associated Architects (later RioGroup), were associated architects for the Austin project.

[38] "Report to New Museum Committee & Museum Executive Committee, Architect Selection Committee," September 19, 1984, "Seattle Art Museum Correspondence from Post-Interview to Selection," VSB box 291 (VSBA archives). Preliminary research notes compiled by Christopher Redmann in 1999 are filed in the Architectural Archives of the University of Pennsylvania. Additional research was conducted by William Whitaker.

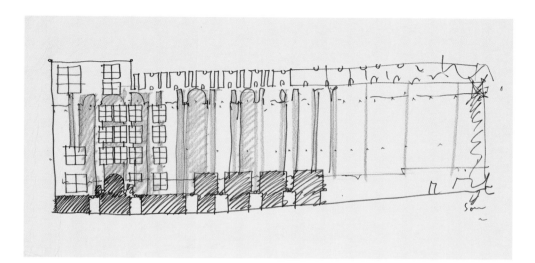

Figure 181
Seattle Art Museum, 1984–91
Preliminary elevation. Marker and colored pencil on yellow tracing paper, 12 x 27½" (30.5 x 69.9 cm) Robert Venturi

Collection of Venturi, Scott Brown and Associates, Inc.

Figure 182
Seattle Art Museum, 1984–91
Perspective. Marker and colored marker on yellow tracing paper, 24 x 41" (61 x 104.1 cm) Robert Venturi

Collection of Venturi, Scott Brown and Associates, Inc.

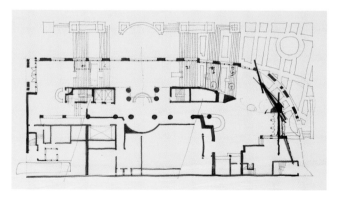

Figure 183
Seattle Art Museum, 1984–91
Plan. Marker and pencil on yellow tracing paper, 24 x 40" (61 x 101.6 cm). Robert Venturi

Collection of Venturi, Scott Brown and Associates, Inc.

Figure 184
Seattle Art Museum, 1984–91

Figure 185
Seattle Art Museum, 1984–91
Gallery

architect.[39] Drawings show that design activity was most intense during 1986, when there was a pause on the Laguna Gloria project (figs. 181, 182). Final design drawings were completed the next year, but construction drawings were not ready for bids until March 1989. The building was completed by December 1991.

The firm developed the Seattle Art Museum in a manner similar to their academic buildings, but for different uses, with individually defined galleries above and public amenities below, all arranged within a perimeter shaped more in response to its site than to the divisions within (fig. 183). The building occupies one end of a rectangular block within the dense commercial core of the city, just a few blocks uphill from the harbor, with the long facade pulled back in observance of a city-imposed view corridor toward Puget Sound. At its lower end, near the harbor, the facade gently steps back, then curves, to open that corridor further. Thus the imposed order of a Cartesian grid is relieved by a reflection of circumstance, and the building defers to its surroundings in a manner quite unlike that of the conventional museum.

On that same long side, stairs lead down from the street above (fig. 184), balanced within by a grand stair that leads up from the main entrance. Evocative of a public street, these stairs lead past a coffee shop along a route articulated by monumental sculpture. Suspended from the ceiling above, a row of decorative flattened arches defines a vaulted profile, obvious stagecraft supporting a gentle monumentality (fig. 186). A glazed arcade links the inner and outer stairs, its exterior enlivened by varied profiles that incorporate segmental, triangular, and even ogee arches. These play on the arcaded ground floors of nearby commercial buildings, bringing them into active context with the museum. Quantities of sketches document intensive study of this element (fig. 187). Venturi had applauded the selection of this downtown site and early noted "the richness of the 10-12 story office buildings built [mainly] in the teens and '20s that are characteristic of downtown Seattle. . . . We can make something truly new that reinforces the older tradition."[40] Above this contextual

Figure 186
Seattle Art Museum, 1984–91
Interior stair

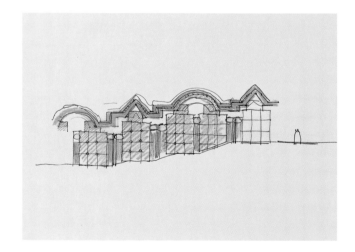

Figure 187
Seattle Art Museum, 1984–91
Elevation study. Marker and colored pencil on yellow tracing paper, 18 x 26 ½" (45.7 x 67.3 cm)
Robert Venturi
Collection of Venturi, Scott Brown and Associates, Inc.

[39] R[obert] V[enturi] to JR, DVSB, SI and MK, August 16, 1982, "Seattle Art Museum Corres. + Memos from 1982 to Interview July '84," VSB box 291 (VSBA archives); Robert Venturi to Dr. Solomon Katz, February 24, 1983, "Seattle Art Museum Corres. + Memos from 1982 to Interview July '84," VSB box 291 (VSBA archives); "Report to New Museum Committee & Museum Executive Committee, Architect Selection Committee," September 19, 1984, "Seattle Art Museum Correspondence from Post-Interview to Selection," VSB box 291 (VSBA archives). The other two finalists were Henry Cobb of I. M. Pei and Partners and William Pedersen of Kohn Pederson Fox Associates.

[40] Robert Venturi to Dr. Solomon Katz, August 23, 1984, "Seattle Art Museum Correspondence from Post-Interview to Selection," VSB box 291 (VSBA archives).

Figure 188
**Sainsbury Wing, National Gallery,
London, 1985–91**

Figure 189
**Ahrends Burton and Koralek,
Architects, National Gallery
Extension Scheme, 1987**

arcade, faceted panels of stone, almost like pleated fabric, enclose the galleries on the second and third floors. A glazed band lighting administrative offices at the top is quietly detailed, relieving the weight of the building below. On each of the gallery floors, a long, slightly curving corridor, again a symbolic street, leads toward a concave window (fig. 185), which adds another element of fanfare to the exterior.

So unpretentious, relaxed, and welcoming a museum confused critics expecting formal bombast, and some unthinkingly argued for the very things the firm had avoided. One found it a "rather klutzy box"; another termed the effect of the arcade as "neo-Romper Room."[41] Others, more perceptively, found much to praise in the design, with one describing it as "unpretentiously cosmopolitan" and another saying it "appears both big and small, monumental yet inviting."[42] With time, many have finally come to appreciate better its many strengths. *Seattle* magazine even demanded that any future addition "celebrate and protect the artistic integrity of the Venturi and Scott Brown building as a masterwork, part of the museum's collection of 20th century art."[43]

The Sainsbury Wing of the National Gallery in London expands upon themes of the Seattle Art Museum in its scale, complexity, and unassuming elegance (fig. 188). Together with the Vanna Venturi house (1959–64), it emerges as one of the great buildings of the last half of the twentieth century. It stands in marked contrast to the other two renowned museums of the period: Richard Meier's J. Paul Getty Museum in Los Angeles (1984–97) and Frank Gehry's Guggenheim Museum in Bilbao (1991–97), both of which exploit early twentieth-century vocabularies to achieve an undeniably grand, yet coldly impersonal, monumentality. In their Sainsbury Wing, that monumentality was eschewed in favor of focusing more on aspects of urban relationship and appreciable scale, and on aspects of meaningful symbol and enlivening detail.

The firm's involvement with the Sainsbury commission began just after they received the Seattle commission, but

[41] Susan M. Kahn, "The Seattle Art Museum: A Post-Modernist Architecture of Ironic Self-Denial," *Open House West: Museum Architecture and Changing Identity* (Los Angeles: Fisher Gallery, University of Southern California, 1999), p. 42; and Roger Kimball, "Elitist Anti-elitism: Robert Venturi Does Seattle," *New Criterion*, vol. 10 (April 1992), p. 6.

[42] Kurt Anderson with reporting by Daniel S. Levy, "Pioneer's Vindication: The Founder of Postmodern Architecture Adds the Seattle Art Museum to His String of Triumphs," *Time*, February 17, 1992, p. 84; Aaron Betsky, "Complexity and Contradiction at New Seattle Art Museum," *Architectural Record*, vol. 180 (February 1992), p. 17.

the building was finished several months before, so the chronology sometimes seems inverted. Theirs was not the first proposal for a new addition to the original building by William Wilkins (1832–38), which had already been twice expanded and was about to be again. A competition for a third addition (in which the museum was to be in partnership with a private development and the new wing was to contain mixed uses) had been won in 1981 by the British firm of Ahrends Burton and Koralek. The final version of their design (fig. 189) was famously denounced by Britain's Prince Charles in May 1984 as "like a monstrous carbuncle on the face of a much loved and elegant friend."[44] The unhappy situation was resolved in March 1985, when the Sainsbury brothers gave money to fund the new addition, which freed it from the complications of private development. This felicitous change of program necessitated a new design, and a selection committee met during the next few months to identify architects for consideration. The firm of Venturi, Rauch and Scott Brown was one of six announced as contenders in October 1985.[45] By the following month, sketches show the Venturis' scheme beginning to take shape, for each of the firms was expected to present a schematic design in January. Their early parti with relaxed perimeter and angled galleries, and with a low exterior profile (figs. 190, 191), remained remarkably constant during its rapid development, and their scheme as submitted was judged best (fig. 192). In an interview shortly after winning the commission, Venturi expressed his feelings: "You are looking at the happiest architect in the world—and the most privileged. . . . I can think of no greater opportunity or challenge than to design for the National Gallery. . . . I had never hoped to be so personally involved in two of my great loves— Italian painting and English architecture—let alone have the opportunity to combine that involvement in one building."[46]

The commission claimed much of the Venturis' time even though the firm was also engaged with drawings for Seattle. By July some adjustments had been made to the front facade (fig. 193), and by October the plan had been

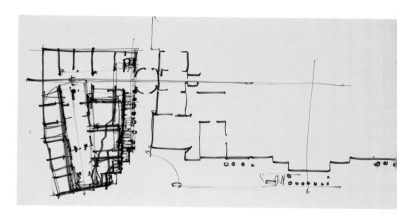

Figure 190
Sainsbury Wing, National Gallery, London, 1985–91
Preliminary plan. Marker on yellow tracing paper, 20½ x 36" (52.1 x 91.4 cm). Robert Venturi
Collection of Venturi, Scott Brown and Associates, Inc.

Figure 191.
Sainsbury Wing, National Gallery, London, 1985–91
Preliminary elevation. Marker on yellow tracing paper, 12 x 21¾" (30.5 x 55.2 cm). Robert Venturi
Collection of Venturi, Scott Brown and Associates, Inc.

Figure 192
Sainsbury Wing, National Gallery, London, 1985–91
Perspective. Pencil on vellum, 42¼ x 35" (107.3 x 88.9 cm). Garreth Schuh
Collection of Venturi, Scott Brown and Associates, Inc.

[43] Glenn Weiss, "In Praise of SAM," *Seattle*, vol. 8 (December 1999), p. 79.

[44] Quoted in Colin Amery, *The National Gallery Sainsbury Wing: A Celebration of Art & Architecture* (London: National Gallery, 1991), p. 49. A full history of the commission is detailed in this book.

[45] Ibid., p. 58. The firms as reported were Henry Nichols (Harry) Cobb of I. M. Pei Partnership; Colquhoun and Miller; Jeremy Dixon/BDP; Piers Gough of Campbell, Zogolovitch, Wilkinson and Gough; James Stirling, Michael Wilford and Associates; and Venturi, Rauch and Scott Brown.

[46] Robert Venturi, "Robert Venturi: Learning from Trafalgar Square?" *Art & Design*, vol. 2 (March 1986), p. 6.

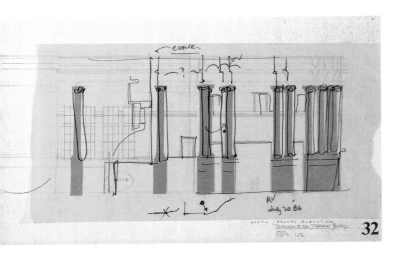

Figure 193
**Sainsbury Wing, National Gallery,
London, 1985–91**
South elevation, column study. Marker
and colored marker on yellow tracing
paper mounted on diazo print, 24¼ x
42½″ (61.6 x 108 cm). Robert Venturi
Signed and dated July 20, 1986; diazo
print dated July 11, 1986
Collection of Venturi, Scott Brown
and Associates, Inc.

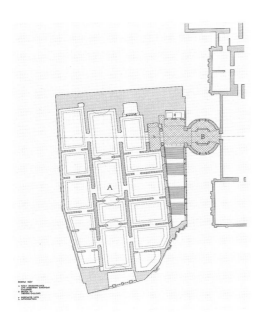

Figure 194
**Sainsbury Wing, National Gallery,
London, 1985–91**
Gallery level plan
Whereabouts unknown

refined, but essentially the scheme remained the same.[47] A public exhibition of their developed scheme was held in London in April 1987, marking the design as nearly complete. By then the firm was completing their designs for the Seattle Art Museum as well as schematic designs for the La Jolla Museum of Contemporary Art. During the next few months, as demands by the National Gallery's building committee seemed to them increasingly unreasonable, the Venturis considered withdrawing from the prestigious commission. But adjustments were made and work continued. Final design refinements were complete by December, working drawings were started in January 1988, and construction began a year later. The installation of paintings began in April 1991, and in July of that year, the Sainsbury Wing was officially opened by Queen Elizabeth.

The building was indeed a grand yet unpretentious gesture. The plan of the top-lit galleries brilliantly adjusts to the original building, with a slight shift in axial alignment so that views through the new galleries are invested with a different energy, and the rigid formality of the old order gives way to a different, yet still sympathetic, spatial flow (fig. 194). Elsewhere doorways are shifted to energize the volume further, and carefully shaped moldings, together with engaged columns and clearly articulated doorways, modulate each differentiated space (figs. 195–97). At their perimeter, the galleries are held back from the outer wall, allowing it to be shaped in response to surrounding streets and buildings. Along one side, as had been shown in the 1987 exhibition of the design (fig. 198), a grand stair rises from the entry lobby below, lit by a glass curtain wall that separates the addition from the original building while providing full views toward it, a juncture of great clarity (fig. 199). This arrangement parallels that of the Seattle Art Museum, as would the plans for a window at one end of the galleries, where it would have defined that charged point of connection between interior and exterior realms. The London client failed to grasp the importance of this window to the overall scheme, objecting to what seemed an unnecessary distraction; it was not built,

[47] Research notes compiled by Rachel Iannacone in June 2000 document the chronology and other details of the commission; they are filed in the Architectural Archives of the University of Pennsylvania.

Figure 195

Sainsbury Wing, National Gallery, London, 1985–91

Interior perspective. Marker on yellow tracing paper, 18 x 22″ (45.7 x 55.9 cm). Robert Venturi

Collection of Venturi, Scott Brown and Associates, Inc.

Figure 196
Sainsbury Wing, National Gallery, London, 1985–91
Gallery interior

Figure 197
Sainsbury Wing, National Gallery, London, 1985–91
Gallery interior

Figure 198
**Sainsbury Wing, National Gallery,
London, 1985–91**

Interior perspective of main stair
Pencil on vellum, 42 x 33½" (106.7 x
85.1 cm). Maurice E. Weintraub and
Matthew Schottelkotte

Collection of Venturi, Scott Brown
and Associates, Inc.

Figure 199
**Sainsbury Wing, National Gallery,
London, 1985–91**

Main stair

Figure 200
**Sainsbury Wing, National Gallery,
London, 1985–91**

Exterior, detail of "Egyptian" columns

Figure 201
**Sainsbury Wing, National Gallery,
London, 1985–91**
Exterior, detail of columns and cornice

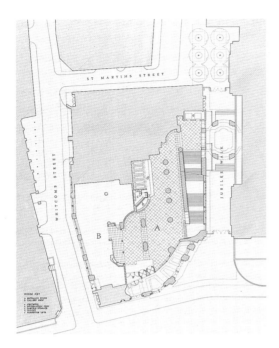

Figure 202
**Sainsbury Wing, National Gallery,
London, 1985–91**
Ground-floor plan
Whereabouts unknown

Figure 203
**Sainsbury Wing, National
Gallery, London, 1985–91**
Entrance lobby and main stair

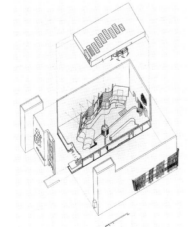

Figure 204
**Alvar Aalto, Finnish Pavilion,
New York World's Fair,
Queens, 1938–39**
Axonometric perspective by
Peter MacKeith with Laura Mark
Museum of Finnish Architecture,
Helsinki, Finland

resulting in a certain anticlimax in the sequential experience of the galleries and causing the Venturis considerable agony; yet they managed to imprint its outline within the building's frame so that one day it can be accurately recovered.

In response to Trafalgar Square, the main facade of the Sainsbury Wing is broken back in a series of facets that describe a gentle, irregular curve (figs. 200, 201), conceived a few months earlier than its less complicated Seattle counterpart. At the corner nearest the original National Gallery building, the elaborate entablature and Corinthian pilasters appear at first to repeat Wilkins's design, yet a richer, more complicated layering distinguishes the addition from the earlier building. These elements are repeated, then allowed to feather out, effecting a smooth transition to a more distant area of the site. Near the end of the angled portion of this wall, an engaged Corinthian column appears to mediate between the corresponding columns of Wilkins's entrance portico and Nelson's giant freestanding column in Trafalgar Square, a relationship Venturi described as a "poignant juxtaposition" and emphasized in drawings exhibited in 1987.[48] Large, unglazed openings lighten the monumentality of the facade, leading to an angled glass wall behind that opens to the main lobby (fig. 202). The elegant, asymmetrically curved enclosure of that lobby (fig. 203) recalls Alvar Aalto's famed Finnish pavilion at the 1939 New York World's Fair (fig. 204), both clear statements of an informal, unassuming monumentality.

The other facades of the wing are varied in response to adjacent buildings and to the smaller scale of their streets, with brick taking the place of limestone and columns reflecting specific aspects of adjacent structures (figs. 205, 206). The effect is far from casual, as Sylvia Lavin has observed: "The whole is an inversion of the Modernist notion of transparency: one does not simply see through to the interior or its structure, but through the revealingly transparent collage of the exterior, one sees and understands the surrounding context."[49] Here, as effectively as anywhere, the firm made art of context, finding meaningful expression through its

[48] In his remarks on the opening of the April 1987 exhibition of the design; quoted in John Russell, "A Fine Scottish Hand," *New York Times Magazine*, July 22, 1990, p. 42.

[49] Lavin, "Artistic Statements," p. 134.

[50] Gavin Stamp, "The Battle of Trafalgar Square," *Times* (London), May 4, 1991.

[51] Simon Jenkins, "Triumph for a Modern Master," *Times* (London), May 4, 1991.

[52] Martin Filler, "An American in London," *House & Garden*, vol. 163 (April 1991), pp. 126–27.

[53] HRH The Prince of Wales, preface to Amery, *The National Gallery*, p. 13.

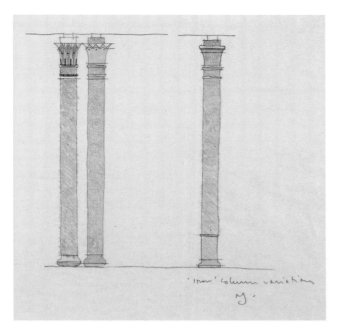

Figure 205
**Sainsbury Wing, National Gallery,
London, 1985–91**

"Iron" column variations. Pencil and
colored pencil on yellow tracing
paper, 16½ x 13¼" (41.9 x 33.7 cm)
Robert Venturi

Collection of Venturi, Scott Brown
and Associates, Inc.

Figure 206
**Sainsbury Wing, National Gallery,
London, 1985–91**
Rear facade

symbolic representation. This has nothing to do with simple replication, such as Kevin Roche's addition to New York's Jewish Museum (1992), but rather with intelligent interpretation, with distortions and unexpected juxtapositions of shape and scale, all recognized as means of twentieth-century artists. The feathering, or gradual diminution of applied detail, is critical as well. It helps reveal the representational nature of the imagery and aids in deconstructing what could otherwise be seen as regular geometry, steadfastly avoiding numbing, life-constricting prettiness.

Little wonder that the building proved to be controversial! One London observer writing in the *Times* called it "the cruellest disappointment I have ever suffered as an architectural critic,"[50] but in the same issue another exclaimed, "No praise is too great for the most exciting new galleries I have ever seen. The Sainsbury Wing . . . is a marvel."[51] The American critic Martin Filler, writing for a London audience, described it as "a triumphant culmination," continuing, "this is a rich and profound piece of architecture, a virtuoso demonstration of space, light, volume, and proportion brought together through the consummate understanding of a designer with great instincts reinforced by great learning."[52] Prince Charles also formally responded: "The debate will now rage, I'm sure," adding "about how good a building Mr. Venturi has given us. I will leave that to others to decide—though I *will* say that I think the interiors very promising as spaces in which to reflect upon art."[53]

How much easier it must have seemed to design the Museum of Contemporary Art, San Diego (fig. 207)! Known originally as the Art Center in La Jolla, it had been established in 1941 in the former Ellen Browning Scripps house (1915–16), one of the acknowledged masterpieces of the California architect Irving Gill (1870–1936), whose clean-lined, concrete buildings seemed to prefigure modernism. Additions in 1950, 1959, and 1976–80, all by the San Diego firm of Mosher & Drew, had progressively obscured that core until nothing of the original was visible.[54] Hugh Davies, the director of the museum, who would

[54] Information on the museum is drawn from Ann Jarmusch, "80-Year-Old Home Now Museum," *San Diego Union-Tribune*, March 10, 1996; also, Hugh M. Davies and Anne Farrell, *Learning from La Jolla: Robert Venturi Remakes a Museum in the Precinct of Irving Gill* (San Diego: Museum of Contemporary Art, San Diego, 1996). Research notes compiled by Amanda Hall in 1999 provide additional documentation; they are filed in the Architectural Archives of the University of Pennsylvania.

Figure 207
**Museum of Contemporary Art,
San Diego, La Jolla, California,
1986–96**

Figure 208

**Museum of Contemporary Art,
San Diego, La Jolla, California,
1986–96**

Perspective view from Prospect Street
Marker, acetate, and tape on yellow
tracing paper, 18 x 24" (45.7 x 61 cm)
Dated March 7, 1994

Collection of Venturi, Scott Brown
and Associates, Inc.

Figure 209

**Museum of Contemporary Art,
San Diego, La Jolla, California,
1986–96**

Rear perspective. Ink on vellum,
18 x 38" (45.7 x 96.5 cm)
Robert Venturi. Signed and dated
July 10, 1994

Private collection

Figure 210

**Museum of Contemporary Art,
San Diego, La Jolla, California,
1986–96**

Rear facade

prove to be a sympathetic and well-focused client, recommended further expansion in 1984, and by the fall of 1985 some forty firms were being considered. Venturi, Rauch and Scott Brown found themselves among the four finalists in May 1986 and following their presentation in La Jolla were selected that June, during a time of intense work for both the Seattle and London museums. Their preliminary design for La Jolla was accepted in October 1986, and after further refinements, a more developed design was approved in April 1988, while working drawings for the other two museums were being completed. The need for additional funding brought a providential pause of several years, and work did not resume until 1992. Final drawings were complete by 1994, and construction, which began that year, was completed by March 1996.

Portions of the later additions were removed so that the original Gill facade could be restored, establishing the spirit of the partly new and partly remodeled whole. Along the front, its gentle curve responds to the adjoining street (fig. 208), and its arched openings, muscular Tuscan columns, and trellis-covered entry court honor the spirit of Gill, particularly his Women's Club of 1912–14 just across the way, with which the La Jolla museum now engages in a mutually supportive dialogue. At the back of the building, facing the ocean, the blocky additions of the 1950s are treated respectfully and even celebrated in a manner that makes them seem equally distinguished, a reflection of the Venturis' sympathy for ordinary buildings as well as for such singular examples as those by Gill. Few, if any, could achieve such a remarkable union (figs. 209, 210).

Circulation patterns within the museum were clarified and some galleries reconfigured. Central to the scheme was a new entrance lobby, conceived as a place for receptions and other special events; as a central atrium from which all radiates, it brings dynamic unity to the scheme (fig. 211). This lobby, as a largely residual space tightly enclosed by other portions of the building, has no real shape of its own, and instead becomes a place of interface between interior

135

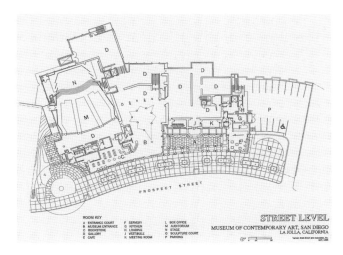

Figure 211
**Museum of Contemporary Art,
San Diego, La Jolla, California,
1986–96**
Street-level plan. Dated May 1996
Whereabouts unknown

Figure 212
**Museum of Contemporary Art,
San Diego, La Jolla, California,
1986–96**
Lobby

Figure 213
**Museum of Contemporary Art,
San Diego, La Jolla, California,
1986–96**

Figure 214
"I Am a Monument." From
Learning from Las Vegas, **1972**

galleries and exterior perimeter. The pressure of a spark, or fanfare, at this juncture could only expand upward, and from the beginning, Venturi had planned such an event to enliven the space below. First he proposed a low dome, then a ribbed dome contained within an exterior drum. La Jolla's building height restrictions led to further modifications, and in 1992 an extraordinary clerestory in the unexpected form of an irregular, seven-pointed star with flattened ribs and edges outlined in neon was substituted for the dome (fig. 212).

Some critics have questioned what may seem like an ambiguous entrance to the museum,[55] for the restored doorway of the original Scripps house is sealed, and the new entrance appears partly hidden within the newly configured courtyard (fig. 213). But this ambiguity, the result of reexposing the Scripps house and mediating the various layers of the building, was embraced by the Venturis as a means of engendering the experience of those layers and of celebrating the unique history and situation of the museum. Otherwise, response to this brilliant essay in addition and consolidation was enthusiastic, as suggested by one critic's praise on the occasion of the building's opening: "Venturi has added dash, order and some comfort to the sprawling, formerly forlorn museum building and its urban and coastal surroundings."[56] Writing for the *New York Times*, Paul Goldberger claimed, "This is an exquisite project, overflowing with those qualities that make Mr. Venturi a designer of extraordinary gifts."[57]

Two smaller and much simpler museums designed by the firm are the Children's Museum of Houston (1989–92) and the Children's Garden and entrance building in Camden (1996–2000), which is essentially a landscaped garden that is part of the New Jersey State Aquarium. In Houston, a playfully detailed temple front embellishes an angled entry, and flattened images of children mix as caryatids and telamones to support a low roof over an adjacent walkway. Similarly playful images enliven the New Jersey setting.

Gentle Monuments for Civic Institutions

Other civic works designed by the Venturis in these years dealt less with a physical context than with a cultural one. These buildings related not so much to specific elements of their surroundings as to monumental aspirations of place inherent in the commission. Each of these designs seems to illustrate Venturi's diagram "I Am a Monument," published in *Learning from Las Vegas* (fig. 214), in which a simple built shape is given public identity through exterior signage rather than through some specially invented form.

The monumental Iraqi State Mosque came first. A component of President Saddam Hussein's program of massive redevelopment, it was allotted a site in a largely undeveloped area of Baghdad, within surroundings lacking any sense of immediate context, at least in terms of preexisting buildings. In July 1982, Venturi, Rauch and Scott Brown was one of twenty-two firms invited to submit dossiers for the competition. The program requirements enclosed with the invitation were impressive: this was to be the largest mosque in the world, capable of holding 30,000 people, with space for an additional 4,000 in an open court. Parking for 1,200 cars and 120 buses, a library for 150,000 books and manuscripts, along with other residential and meeting facilities, added greatly to its enormous state.[58]

In September 1982, the firm learned that they had been selected as one of seven finalists.[59] They were to participate in a hundred-day competition, beginning in October and ending in January, and they quickly developed their scheme (fig. 215). Although the jury reached its decision by early February, the results remained confidential, and in August, the still-hopeful finalists were invited to participate in an international symposium on their designs. At the symposium, held in October 1983, the jury results were at last announced. Although the firm did not place,[60] Saddam Hussein (who attended the symposium) reportedly liked their design, and the firm was asked to collaborate on the mosque with the Spanish architect Ricardo Bofill (who had

55 For example, Paul Goldberger, "Robert Venturi, Denise Scott Brown: Museum of Contemporary Art, San Diego, La Jolla, California, 1986–1996," in Vittorio Magnago Lampugnani and Angeli Sachs, eds., *Museums for a New Millennium: Concepts, Projects, Buildings* (Munich and New York: Prestel, 1999), pp. 56–61.

56 Ann Jarmusch, "Art Upstaged by Architectural Flourishes," *San Diego Union-Tribune*, March 10, 1996.

57 Paul Goldberger, "Refashioning the Old, with All Due Respect," *New York Times*, May 5, 1996.

58 Research notes compiled by William Whitaker in August 2000 document the chronology and other details of the commission; they are filed in the Architectural Archives of the University of Pennsylvania.

59 The others were Maath Alousi/ TEST (Iraq); Kahtan Al-Madfai (Iraq); Makiya Associates (London, Iraqi based); Minour Takeyama (Japan); Rasem Badran (Jordan); and Ricardo Bofill (France).

60 The three firms given top ranking were Badran, Bofill, and Alousi.

Figure 215
State Mosque, Competition, Baghdad, Iraq, 1982–83
Preliminary elevation. Marker and colored marker on yellow tracing paper, 12 x 31¼" (30.5 x 79.4 cm) Robert Venturi
Collection of Venturi, Scott Brown and Associates, Inc.

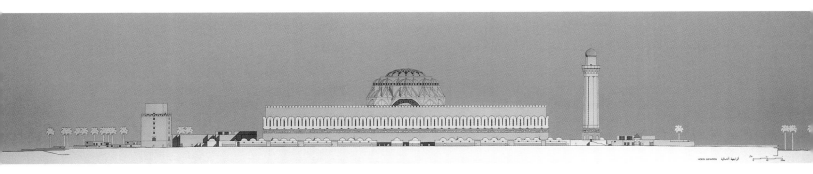

Figure 216
State Mosque, Competition, Baghdad, Iraq, 1982–83
North elevation. Airbrush on photo-mechanical print, 25¼ x 119" (64.1 x 302.3 cm). Rick Buckley, Miles Ritter, and Daniel McCoubrey
Collection of Venturi, Scott Brown and Associates, Inc.

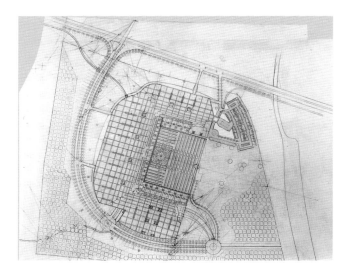

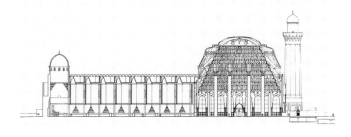

Figure 218
State Mosque, Competition, Baghdad, Iraq, 1982–83
Section. Ink, acetate, and tape on mylar, detail. Rick Buckley, Daniel McCoubrey, and John Hayes
Collection of Venturi, Scott Brown and Associates, Inc

Figure 217
State Mosque, Competition, Baghdad, Iraq, 1982–83
Site plan. Pencil on vellum, 42 x 33¼" (106.7 x 84.5 cm). Christine Matheu
Collection of Venturi, Scott Brown and Associates, Inc.

Figure 219

State Mosque, Competition, Baghdad, Iraq, 1982–83

Interior arches and mihrab. Airbrush on photomechanical print, 35½ x 40½" (90.2 x 102.9 cm). David Marohn, James Bradberry, and Miles Ritter

Collection of Venturi, Scott Brown and Associates, Inc.

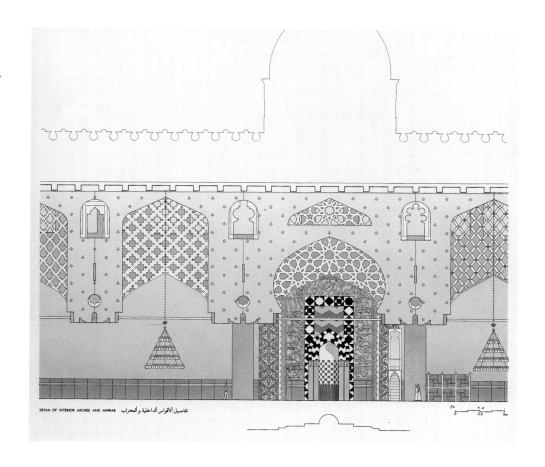

Figure 220

State Mosque, Competition, Baghdad, Iraq, 1982–83

Interior perspective toward qibla Pencil, colored pencil, acetate, and tape on vellum, 30 x 42" (76.2 x 106.7 cm). Simon Tickell and John Hayes

Collection of Venturi, Scott Brown and Associates, Inc.

placed second), but they were unwilling to compromise design authority, and the project went no further.

The firm based their mosque on the hypostyle model, an Islamic prototype of unassailable lineage in the Middle East, and in its basics, one of the world's first true lofts (fig. 216). In accord with this model, its interior was shown as a vast, open, nondirectional space. The entire structure was to rise from a gigantic terrace that covered underground parking (fig. 217). The outer shape of the congregational area was outlined as a squat U, and within the U they placed the open court. A large domic structure was to shade most of the courtyard, its surfaces faceted both within and without by elements that resembled the traditional *muqarnas*, or stalactites, of Islamic buildings (fig. 218). Its structure was unexpected, for the dome was not to be supported at its edge, as would be customary, but instead by a series of slim columns that rose up within its canopy; the resulting unencumbered perimeter would have facilitated connections to adjoining areas. Exterior surfaces of the mosque were to be richly embellished with patterns that also recalled Islamic motifs (fig. 219), and honoring long-standing tradition, phrases from the Koran were to be incorporated into its facade. Huge trusses were to span the wide interior, detailed with a fretted lower profile that suggested the low ceiling and multiple supports of typical hypostyle mosques (fig. 220).

Oleg Grabar, a leading scholar of Islamic architecture, praised the design, relating it to historic prototypes and noting that "old mosques have inspired the designers in such a way that, while sources are quoted, the building is in reality something quite new and different."[61] Venturi had said something similar on the occasion of the Baghdad symposium: "There are two ways to be creative: to invent new forms, and to use old forms in new ways. We have chosen to emphasize the latter approach in our design."[62]

The Philadelphia Orchestra also wanted a building with major civic presence, but first its members, then city officials, and finally a strong-willed donor disagreed as to what might constitute that presence, and the Venturis' proposal

foundered. They had been selected as architects in July 1987 following a long and wide-ranging search.[63] Early sketches for the building (figs. 221, 222) show various facades masking the large concert hall within, its plan dictated by functional concerns. Yet from the start, the Venturis added a sense of flexibility to its shape, with a monumental front facing Broad Street and a harborlike indentation on the side to serve as a court of vehicular arrival. By the summer of 1988, the facade had assumed a plainer shape with broad, generously scaled windows (fig. 223). It was further refined the next year to include a huge pedimented window at its center (fig. 224), which responded to an adjacent landmark by John Haviland, the temple-fronted building that serves as the main building of Philadelphia's University of the Arts (1823). To those with more grandiose expectations, the Venturis explained that Philadelphia was not Paris, nor Broad Street, the Champs Elysées. They saw their design as being in rhythm with the historic grid of Philadelphia's streets, and they likened its calm facade to that of a Friends meeting house, again evocative of Philadelphia's history.[64] There seemed never to have been debate regarding the interior of the concert hall itself (fig. 225), which had firmly established requirements that absorbed most of the allotted funds, leaving little for exterior embellishment.

Work on the project paused from 1989 until November 1992, while the orchestra sought funds for its construction. Efforts revived with Mayor Edward Rendell's ambitious plans to develop Broad Street as the Avenue of the Arts, for which the new hall was to be a centerpiece. Striving to heighten the building's presence while adding only minimally to its cost, the Venturis proposed a more varied palette of materials. By 1995, drawings show a vibrant facade indeed, with greater expanses of glass in rhythmically syncopated frames (fig. 226). As seen at night, the second-floor lobby would have become an active extension of the avenue itself, a moving celebration of the building's social presence. Giant notes atop a musical staff were proposed as a decorative band above the doors, a sign of its special function.

[61] Oleg Grabar, "From the Past into the Future: On Two Designs for State Mosques," *Architectural Record*, vol. 172 (June 1984), p. 151.

[62] Robert Venturi, "Remarks Delivered to the President of Iraq and Assembled Guests at the Symposium to Present and Discuss the Entries in the Competition for the State Mosque of Iraq," October 1983, "1.0 Mosque Client Proposal Agreements," VSB box 91 (VSBA archives).

[63] Research notes compiled by Isabel Taube in July 2000 document the chronology and other details of the commission; they are filed in the Architectural Archives of the University of Pennsylvania.

[64] Diane M. Fiske, "Architects Discuss Designs for Orchestra Hall," *Art Matters* (Philadelphia), June 1997, pp. 6–7.

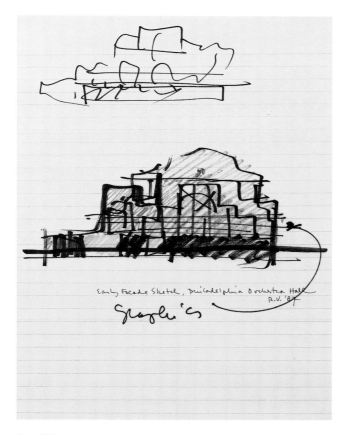

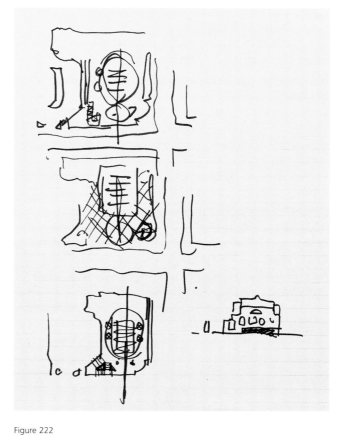

Figure 221
**Philadelphia Orchestra Hall,
1987–96**

Early facade sketch. Marker, colored
marker, and colored pencil on yellow
lined paper, 11 x 8½" (27.9 x 21.6 cm)
Robert Venturi. Signed and dated 1987

Collection of Venturi, Scott Brown
and Associates, Inc.

Figure 222
**Philadelphia Orchestra Hall,
1987–96**

Plan and elevation sketches. Marker
on yellow lined paper, 11 x 8½"
(27.9 x 21.6 cm). Robert Venturi

Collection of Venturi, Scott Brown
and Associates, Inc.

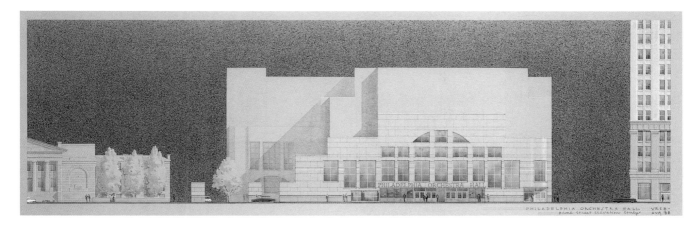

Figure 223
**Philadelphia Orchestra Hall,
1987–96**

Preliminary elevation. Watercolor,
gouache, pencil, and ink on paper,
14¼ x 33⅞" (36.2 x 86 cm). Miles
Ritter. Signed and dated August 1988

Collection of Venturi, Scott Brown
and Associates, Inc.

Figure 224
**Philadelphia Orchestra Hall,
1987–96**

Perspective from Broad Street
Airbrush on photomechanical print
mounted on foam core, 32 x 46½"
(81.3 x 118.1 cm). Don Jones and
R. Michael Wommack

Collection of Venturi, Scott Brown
and Associates, Inc.

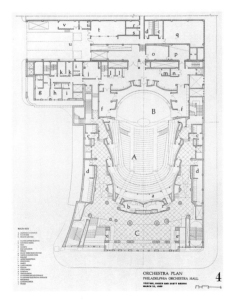

Figure 225
**Philadelphia Orchestra Hall,
1987–96**

Orchestra-level plan. Panchromatic
film on photomechanical print,
48 x 36" (121.9 x 91.4 cm). Dated
March 22, 1989

Collection of Venturi, Scott Brown
and Associates, Inc.

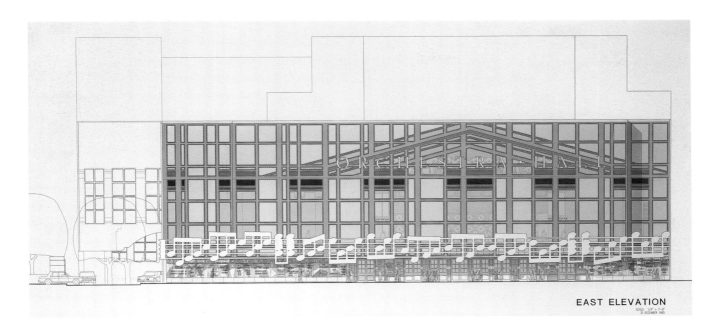

EAST ELEVATION

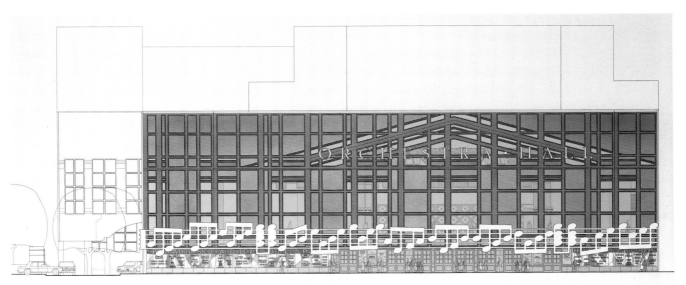

EAST ELEVATION

Figure 226

**Philadelphia Orchestra Hall,
1987–96**

East elevation, day and night. Airbrush
on photomechanical print mounted
on foam core, 34½ x 65½" (87.6 x
166.4 cm). Amy Noble and R. Michael
Wommack. Dated December 21,
1995

Collection of Venturi, Scott Brown
and Associates, Inc.

Figure 227
Whitehall Ferry Terminal, Competition, New York, 1992–96

Model, first scheme. Plexiglass, paint, photographic print, foam, and cast aluminum, 33 x 16 x 36½" (83.8 x 40.6 x 92.7 cm)

Collection of Venturi, Scott Brown and Associates, Inc.

Figure 228
Whitehall Ferry Terminal, Competition, New York, 1992–96

Perspective of proposed LED with image of the New York City Marathon Computer rendering

Collection of Venturi, Scott Brown and Associates, Inc.

By then a major donor had come forward, and at this point the project took on a new life, although it was moving in a different direction.[65] Others on the building committee came to agree with a concern, that the design that the Venturis had developed had too commercial an appearance. At the same time, they also determined upon a new and more ambitious program, one necessitating an entirely new design, for which they added the requirement that its architect must have had previous experience in designing a concert hall; this eliminated the Venturis from further consideration.[66] The commission thus went from "Philadelphia's greatest architect, Robert Venturi," as a writer in the *New Yorker* later lamented, to the Argentinian architect Rafael Viñoly.[67]

A somewhat similar fate befell the Whitehall Ferry Terminal in New York City (1992–96). The firm had won a competition in 1992, yet almost immediately the president of the Borough of Staten Island, Guy Molinari, whose approval was necessary before any construction could proceed, objected to its design.[68] On the harbor side of their straightforward, vaulted structure, the Venturis proposed a giant clock, to be animated by the tesserae of LED pixels, a perfect joining of conventional iconography and advanced electronics, and one meaningfully expressive of its time and of the building's function (figs. 227, 228). Regarding its civic presence, a statement by the firm explained: "In an era when civic place has been supplanted by shopping centers, the new Whitehall Ferry Terminal is an unparalleled opportunity to create a civic setting that celebrates New York City and enhances the daily routine of 70,000 commuters."[69] A curtailment of funds in September 1994 required major changes to the design, and the Venturis attempted with these changes also to placate Molinari. By June of 1995, drawings show the building had been reduced in size and the great clock replaced by an electronic LED signboard that would carry moving images of a timely sort. It was most often shown with a billowing American flag (fig. 229), recalling their 1989 competition entry for the United States

Figure 229
Whitehall Ferry Terminal, Competition, New York, 1992–96
Perspective, second scheme. Computer rendering. John Izenour
Collection of Venturi, Scott Brown and Associates, Inc.

Figure 230
United States Pavilion, Expo '92, Competition, Seville, Spain, 1989
Elevation. Cut paper, panchromatic film, and airbrush on photograph mounted on foam core, 30 x 60" (76.2 x 152.4 cm). Erik Aukee and R. Michael Wommack. Dated April 1990
Collection of Venturi, Scott Brown and Associates, Inc.

65 Peter Dobrin, "A Change in Plans for Exterior Design of Orchestra Hall," *Philadelphia Inquirer*, May 10, 1995.

66 Stephen Seplow, "Clothes Made the Man: And Then Sidney Kimmel Took the Millions He Made and Put Them to Good Use," *Philadelphia Inquirer Sunday Magazine*, January 31, 1999, p. 14.

67 Nicholas Lemann, "Letter from Philadelphia: No Man's Town," *New Yorker*, vol. 76 (June 5, 2000), p. 46.

68 Research notes compiled by Rachel Iannacone in 2000 document the chronology and

other details of the commission; they are filed in the Architectural Archives of the University of Pennsylvania.

69 Venturi, Scott Brown and Associates, "Whitehall Ferry Terminal: Return to New York (via Las Vegas)," *Casabella*, vol. 62 (July/August 1998), p. 12.

Figure 231

**The Big Apple at Times Square
Center, New York, 1984**

Perspective. Airbrush on photomechanical print, 40 x 48¾"
(101.6 x 123.8 cm). Frederic Schwartz

Collection of Venturi, Scott Brown
and Associates, Inc.

Pavilion at Expo '92, in Seville (fig. 230). Still Molinari objected, the Venturis resigned from the commission in September 1996, and New York lost what would have been a major landmark.

Urban Gestures for Public Places

Large-scale planning projects, including such comprehensive schemes as the Westway Park for the New York State Department of Transportation (1978–85, unbuilt), Center City Development Plan for Downtown Memphis (1984–87), and the North Neighborhood Master Plan for Battery Park City in New York (1992–93), formed a counterpoint to commissions for individual buildings in these years, while designs for public plazas illustrated the Venturis' approach to creating civic spaces with distinctive identity. In 1984, for Times Square in New York, they proposed the Big Apple (fig. 231). It was commissioned for the Park Tower Realty Corporation in an effort to add some distinctive feature to their planned development of sober, mansard-roofed towers designed by Philip Johnson; neither the towers nor the apple were built. In 1985, for a monument in an ill-defined park known as Marconi Plaza that straddled Broad Street in South Philadelphia, they designed two flat, billboardlike masonry walls that would have established a needed edge to the park while also framing views to City Hall in the distance (fig. 232). Generalized images of Italian palaces depicted on the facades alluded to its intended function of honoring both the five-hundredth anniversary of Columbus's voyage to America and the local Italian-American community, while the device of framing would have also symbolized that community's unity with the city.

In a comprehensive study for the Civic Center Cultural Complex in Denver (1991–95, not implemented), Scott Brown suggested a giant arc to define an urban forecourt so as to "establish a common setting and context" for the three collaborating institutions, the Colorado Historical Society, Denver Public Library, and Denver Art Museum (fig. 233).[70] Its sense of grand scale could have been realized with

[70] As described in the booklet submitted by Venturi, Scott Brown and Associates, "Schematic Design, Civic Center Cultural Complex, Denver, Colorado," June 17, 1993, p. 3

Figure 232
Monument for Marconi Plaza, Philadelphia, 1985
Marconi Plaza looking north
Cut paper on photograph, 34½ x 68"
(87.6 x 172.7 cm). Steven Izenour and David Schaaf. Dated June 1, 1985
Collection of Venturi, Scott Brown and Associates, Inc.

Figure 233
Civic Center Cultural Complex Master Plan, Denver, 1991–95
Site plan. From "Schematic Design, Civic Center Cultural Complex, Denver, Colorado," June 17, 1993
Collection of Venturi, Scott Brown and Associates, Inc.

Figure 234
Civic Center Cultural Complex Master Plan, Denver, 1991–95
Perspective. From "Schematic Design, Civic Center Cultural Complex, Denver, Colorado," June 17, 1993
Collection of Venturi, Scott Brown and Associates, Inc.

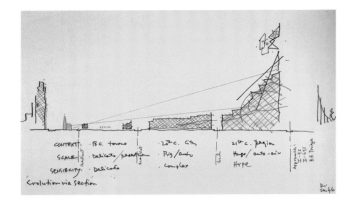

Figure 235

**Gateway Visitor Center and
Independence Mall Master Plan,
Philadelphia, 1996**

Site section. Marker and colored
marker on yellow tracing paper,
11 x 16½" (27.9 x 41.9 cm). Robert
Venturi. Signed and dated February
1996

Collection of Venturi, Scott Brown
and Associates, Inc.

Figure 236

**Gateway Visitor Center and
Independence Mall Master Plan,
Philadelphia, 1996**

Interior perspective. Colored marker
on yellow tracing paper, 19 x 20¾"
(48.3 x 52.7 cm). Robert Venturi
Signed and dated April 24, 1996

Collection of Venturi, Scott Brown
and Associates, Inc.

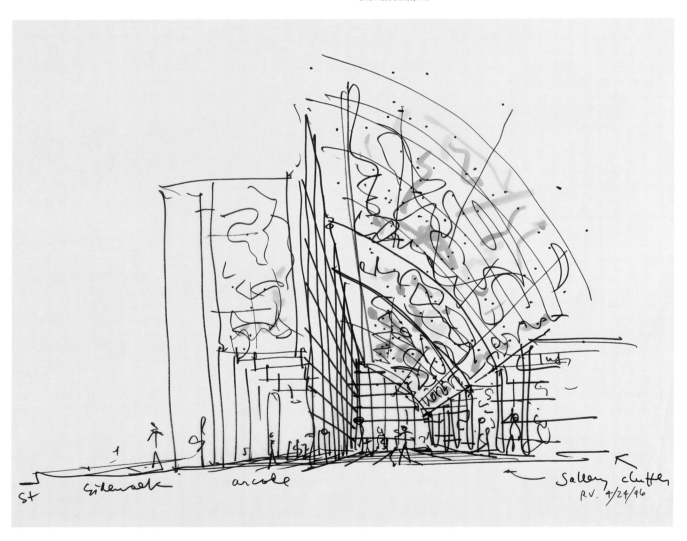

modest means: twenty slender, open-work spires of sand-blasted stainless steel, each 110-feet tall, would have outlined the arc in plan and formed a diaphanous monument responsive to its setting (fig. 234).

For Independence National Historical Park in Philadelphia, they proposed a Gateway Visitor Center that was meant to mediate the vast scale of Independence Mall (1996). The planning effort of which it was a part had been supported by a grant from the Pew Charitable Trusts to the National Park Service, given with the intent of stimulating improved design for the area.[71] The Venturis proposed a pavilion that would be placed across the axis of the mall to help reduce its length, maintaining a low profile toward the small-scaled Independence Hall and defining an area more in league with Philadelphia's other squares, such as Rittenhouse and Logan. Toward the larger-scaled, more commercial ambience of Market Street, they made their facade appropriately taller. The vaulted surface inside—a transitional band linking the two facades—was to be animated by electronic images (figs. 235, 236), not unlike their National Collegiate Football Hall of Fame designed in 1967 (see fig. 52).

Critical Images for Business

Given their enthusiastic study of commercial buildings, commissions for such enterprises would seem particularly well suited to the Venturis' talents, as was proved by their showrooms from the late 1970s for Best and BASCO (see figs. 107, 109). Yet since 1980 they have received comparatively few such opportunities, and fewer still have been built. Among unbuilt proposals are some of their rare studies for office towers, part of a 1985 project in Jacksonville, Florida, prepared for Rouse & Associates. Some of the studies suggest Spanish colonial profiles (fig. 237), others jazzy Art Deco crestings, almost like a Saul Steinberg drawing (fig. 238). More finished drawings for the Jacksonville project are harder edged, but with sunburst-like attachments (fig. 239). An unpremiated competition entry for the Ernest and Julio Gallo Winery visitors' center in Modesto, California (1989–90),

Figure 237
Office Tower Development, Jacksonville, Florida, 1985
Perspective. Marker on yellow tracing paper, 18 x 23" (45.7 x 58.4 cm)
Robert Venturi
Collection of Venturi, Scott Brown and Associates, Inc.

Figure 238
Office Tower Development, Jacksonville, Florida, 1985
Perspective sketch of cresting. Marker and colored pencil on yellow tracing paper, 12 x 17" (30.5 x 43.2 cm)
Robert Venturi
Collection of Venturi, Scott Brown and Associates, Inc.

[71] Editorial, "A Fresh Eye," *Philadelphia Inquirer*, January 26, 1996.

Figure 239
**Office Tower Development,
Jacksonville, Florida, 1985**

Elevation. Cut paper, panchromatic
film, and pencil on paper mounted on
foam core, 53 x 32" (134.6 x 81.3 cm)
Steven Izenour and Ivan Saleff

Collection of Venturi, Scott Brown
and Associates, Inc.

151

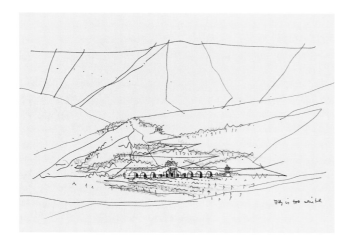

Figure 240
Rural Wine Center for the E. & J. Gallo Winery, Competition, Modesto, California, 1989–90

Aerial perspective. Marker and colored pencil on yellow tracing paper, 24 x 36½" (61 x 92.7 cm) Robert Venturi. Dated January 1990

Collection of Venturi, Scott Brown and Associates, Inc.

Figure 241
Rural Wine Center for the E. & J. Gallo Winery, Competition, Modesto, California, 1989–90

Front elevation. Marker and colored pencil on yellow tracing paper, 18 x 54¼" (45.7 x 137.8 cm). Robert Venturi. Dated January 1990

Collection of Venturi, Scott Brown and Associates, Inc.

Figure 242
Hotel and Convention Complex, Walt Disney World Resort, Competition, Lake Buena Vista, Florida, 1986

Elevation and sections. Marker and colored pencil on yellow tracing paper, 9 x 55½" (22.9 x 141 cm) Robert Venturi

Collection of Venturi, Scott Brown and Associates, Inc.

© Disney Enterprises, Inc.

Figure 243
Hotel and Convention Complex, Walt Disney World Resort, Competition, Lake Buena Vista, Florida, 1986

Aerial perspective site plan. Marker and colored pencil on yellow tracing paper, 30¾ x 48½" (90.8 x 123.2 cm) Robert Venturi

Collection of Venturi, Scott Brown and Associates, Inc.

© Disney Enterprises, Inc.

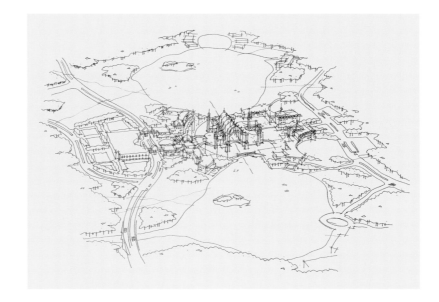

Figure 245
Reedy Creek Improvement District Emergency Services Headquarters and Fire Station, Walt Disney World Resort, Lake Buena Vista, Florida, 1992–93
© Disney Enterprises, Inc.

Figure 246
Bank of Celebration, Celebration, Florida, 1993–96
© The Celebration Company

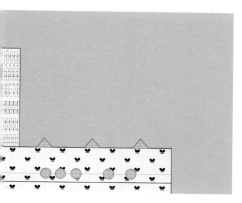

Figure 244
Fantasia Hotel, Disneyland Paris Resort, Marne-la-Vallée, France, 1988

Elevation. Cut paper, panchromatic film, and marker on foam core, 13½ x 57½" (34.3 x 146.1 cm)
Matthew Schottelkotte and Melanie Swick

Collection of Venturi, Scott Brown and Associates, Inc.

© Disney Enterprises, Inc.

with arcaded walls and extensive terracing, evokes ancient Roman as well as Italian Renaissance villas (fig. 240), while a gigantic representation of a bunch of grapes, dominating the entrance, would have signaled the building's purpose (fig. 241).

The Walt Disney Company would seem to be an ideal client for Venturi, Scott Brown and Associates. They submitted several proposals, four of which were realized. One large-scale design, a 1986 competition entry for a Disney hotel and convention complex in Orlando, however, went no further than preliminary sketches, which show an interrelated group of richly profiled buildings (figs. 242, 243). The more exuberant Fantasia Hotel, a 1988 competition entry for Disney's site at Marne-la-Vallée in France (also unbuilt), is one of the most striking facades ever designed by the Venturis, a giant, almost explosive, sunburst of color (fig. 244).

Three commissions for Disney buildings were constructed in Florida: the fire station (or Reedy Creek Improvement District Emergency Services Headquarters, as it is officially known) in Lake Buena Vista for The Walt Disney Company (1992–93); the Bank of Celebration, also for The Walt Disney Company (1993–96); and the Pleasure Island Exxon gas station in Lake Buena Vista for Disney Development Company (1993–96). These designs reflect the lively presence of Steven Izenour. The fire station, described as "one a child might have drawn,"[72] takes its imagery from overscaled red bricks and the spots of a dalmatian, a dog generally associated with American firehouses (fig. 245). Its Aalto-like plan and exaggerated patterns parallel the firm's other work of the time, notably the much larger Mielmonte resort hotel in Japan. The Bank of Celebration, with flattened, angled planes suggestive of the subdued classicism of the 1930s, strikes some as being "as much a building of today as yesterday" (fig. 246).[73] Its total lack of specific historic references seems almost to mock the sweetened classicism that otherwise abounds in this designed place. The more commercial gas station, realized in a subdued form

Figure 247
Pleasure Island Exxon Gas Station, Walt Disney World Resort, Lake Buena Vista, Florida, 1993–96

© Disney Enterprises, Inc.

[72] Beth Dunlop, *Building a Dream: The Art of Disney Architecture* (New York: Harry N. Abrams, 1996), p. 171.

[73] Beth Dunlop, *Downtown Celebration: Architectural Walking Tour* (Celebration, Fla: Disney, 1996), p. 10.

Figure 248
Frank G. Wells Building, Walt Disney Studios, Burbank, California, 1994–98

Preliminary elevation. Airbrush and cut paper mounted on foam core, 21⅜ x 18¼" (55.2 x 46.4 cm). Amy Noble and R. Michael Wommack

Collection of Venturi, Scott Brown and Associates, Inc.

© Disney Enterprises, Inc.

Figure 249
Frank G. Wells Building, Walt Disney Studios, Burbank, California, 1994–98

Elevation. Cut paper on foam core, 18 x 12" (45.7 x 30.5 cm)

Collection of Venturi, Scott Brown and Associates, Inc.

© Disney Enterprises, Inc.

Figure 250
Frank G. Wells Building, Walt Disney Studios, Burbank, California, 1994–98

© Disney Enterprises, Inc.

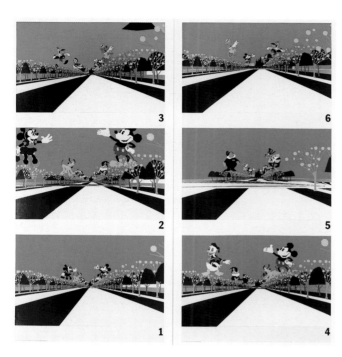

Figure 251
EuroDisney Entrance Boulevard, Disneyland Paris Resort, Marne-la-Vallée, France, 1988

Perspective. Computer plot mounted on foam core, 14 x 19⅜" (35.6 x 49.2 cm). Pablo Meninato

Collection of Venturi, Scott Brown and Associates, Inc.

© Disney Enterprises, Inc.

that dispensed with the BASCO-like 30-foot-high letters and 75-foot-high sign that was first proposed, sits in relative tranquility behind a screen of representational trees, a true decorated shed (fig. 247).

In Burbank, California, Venturi, Scott Brown and Associates realized their largest Disney commission, the Frank G. Wells Building for Walt Disney Imagineering (1994–98). Large-scale images of Mickey Mouse and Goofy were originally planned for the facade (fig. 248) but were dropped from the final scheme, an adaptable loftlike space enclosed by walls patterned to recall reels of film (figs. 249, 250). Speaking of an earlier, similar component of the Venturis' plans for Disneyland Paris Park (an entrance boulevard lined with 150-foot-high representations of Disney characters, fig. 251), Frank Gehry offers a clear explanation for its rejection: "It was Bob Venturi at his pinnacle, just the best. There is an essence and a truth in Venturi's portrayal of this whole thing. . . . That's why he could not do work for them."[74] In fact, the Venturi office subsequently designed their four projects for Disney, more than most other firms working for the company. In such situations, the Venturis force a confrontation never uncritically endorsing commercial values, but instead extracting and reshaping selected images from them. Thus they position their designs in a broader cultural context so they, too, become art rather than submissive accessories to the consumerism they serve. Yet some might mistake such art as satire.

Tailored Houses for Special Sites

Between 1980 and 2000, Venturi as chief designer for his firm undertook only about one-quarter as many commissions for houses as he had from 1957 to 1979. Partly this resulted from a reluctance to accept such time-intensive responsibilities when so much other work was at hand. When the firm did accept such commissions, Venturi expanded upon themes of earlier buildings, which were now realized with an increasing assurance that reflected a maturing aesthetic.

[74] Quoted in Karal Ann Marling and Phyllis Lambert, "Interview with Frank Gehry, January 6, 1996," in Karal Ann Marling, ed., *Designing Disney's Theme Parks: The Architecture of Reassurance* (Montreal: Centre Canadien d'Architecture/Canadian Centre for Architecture; Paris and New York: Flammarion, 1997), p. 211.

Figure 252
Dream Village for the Sunshine Foundation, Loughman, Florida, 1985–89

Perspective. Pencil and transfer letters on vellum, 30 x 42" (76.2 x 106.7 cm). Dated November 1985

Collection of Venturi, Scott Brown and Associates, Inc.

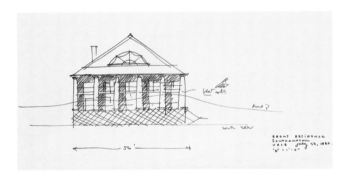

Figure 253
Brous House, Southampton, New York, 1980

Elevation. Marker on yellow tracing paper, 12 x 22¾" (30.5 x 57.8 cm) Dated July 22, 1980

Collection of Venturi, Scott Brown and Associates, Inc.

Figure 254
Hubbard House, Nantucket, Massachusetts, 1981–86

Front elevation. Pencil and transfer letters on vellum, 15 x 21" (38.1 x 53.3 cm). Robert Venturi Signed and dated December 12, 1981

Collection of Venturi, Scott Brown and Associates, Inc.

The houses themselves, located in rural or suburban settings, stood apart as independent structures, and issues of context became more generalized. They related more to elements of landscape than to other buildings, and their forms were essentially complete in themselves rather than inflected toward some preexisting structure; in this they contrast with most of the Venturis' contemporaneous work. Drawings depicting these houses in splendid isolation tend to emphasize a picturesque quality of varied facades, as had the 1977 series of Eclectic House studies showing alternate elevations for a single plan (see fig. 115), studies that recall similar presentations in such tracts as John Claudius Loudon's 1833 *Encyclopaedia of Cottage, Farm, and Villa Architecture*.[75] Several observers have noted the resemblance and sought to compare their work to the Picturesque point of view, a movement that flourished in the late eighteenth and early nineteenth centuries, its popularity epitomized by Loudon's even-handed catalogue of innumerable, interchangeable designs. Von Moos correctly notes parallels, for in their easy adaptability of various stylistic modes, and in the flexible manner with which specific conditions imposed by clients and sites are made an expressive part of the design, the Venturis indeed sustain the tradition of the Picturesque.[76] Yet they differ in one very important way: they resist the pictorial, artificialized comfort essential to the Picturesque. Indeed, they seek to upset it. In this their work stands apart.[77] Rare exceptions exist, as the Sunshine Foundation's Dream Village near Orlando, Florida (1985–89; fig. 252). The circumstances of this design set it apart, however, for the Venturis donated their services to this foundation, which seeks to realize the last wishes of terminally ill children, and were not involved in the execution of a generalized image that they had only suggested.

If one were to group the early houses according to categories that could have appeared in a Picturesque tract,

Figure 255
Petrie House, Wainscott, New York, 1980–83

Figure 256
Kalpakjian House, Glen Cove, New York, 1983–86

Figure 257
Kalpakjian House, Glen Cove, New York, 1983–86

Elevation sketch. Marker on yellow tracing paper, 15 x 23½" (38.1 x 59.7 cm). Robert Venturi

Collection of Venturi, Scott Brown and Associates, Inc.

[75] John Claudius Loudon, *An Encyclopaedia of Cottage, Farm, and Villa Architecture and Furniture* (London: Longman, Reese, Orme, Brown, Green, and Longman, 1833). According to Denise Scott Brown in an interview with the author, Philadelphia, March 24, 2001, she and Robert Venturi first became aware of Loudon through an article by George Hersey, "J. C. Loudon and Architectural Associationism," *Architectural Review*, August 1968, pp. 88–92.

[76] Von Moos, *Venturi, Scott Brown & Associates*, pp. 52–53.

[77] For sources of the Picturesque and its relationships to twentieth-century American architecture, particularly the work of Frank Lloyd Wright and Bruce Goff (both much closer to the Picturesque than the Venturis), see David G. De Long, "Bruce Goff and the Evolution of an Architectural Ideal," in Helen Searing, ed., *In Search of Modern Architecture: A Tribute to Henry-Russell Hitchcock* (New York: The Architectural History Foundation; Cambridge and London: The MIT Press, 1982), pp. 338–59.

Figure 258
House on the Coast of Maine, 1986–90

Figure 259
De Havenon House, East Hampton, New York, 1985–91

they might, with some stretching, have been labeled temple (or pedimented-front) villas (Vanna Venturi house); porticus (or linear) villas (Brant house in Tucker's Town); towered villas (Carll Tucker house in Katonah); and curved-bay villas (Brant house in Greenwich). Yet, as seen elsewhere, first impressions inevitably give way to more complex perceptions, and seemingly simple outlines are disrupted by unexpected breaks and intersections, by layered openings and vertical shifts of space, by fragmented references to historic detail. These qualities persist in the later houses, but the generalized forms they modify become less subject to even such fanciful categorizations as those suggested above.

In the early 1980s, the Brous house in Southampton, New York (1980, unbuilt; fig. 253), and the Hubbard house in Nantucket (1981–86; fig. 254) work variations on the pedimented front. The Petrie house in Wainscott, New York (1980–83), and the Kalpakjian house in Glen Cove, New York, (1983–86), both of which overlook bays off Long Island, are more extended in plan, their gabled roofs opened by long shed-roofed dormers. Donald Petrie asked Venturi to relate his design to shingled turn-of-the-century houses nearby, and this was accomplished without resorting to imitative devices (fig. 255). The adjacent garage (with boat storage loft above), angled to the main house, develops a composition not unlike that of the Brant house in Tucker's Town.[78] The Kalpakjian house sits dramatically on a point of land extending out into Long Island Sound (fig. 256). A large apsed bay, oriented toward this view, terminates the end of the house almost like a ship's pilot house. Early sketches emphasize this quality, making the house itself appear to be an approaching vessel (fig. 257). The most linear house of all, situated on the coast of Maine (1986–90), also overlooks an expansive bay (fig. 258).

The De Havenon house in East Hampton, New York (1985–91), on an inland site without dramatic views, is roughly square in plan and opens equally on all four sides, roofed by intersecting gables and hipped intersections so it is somewhat pyramidal in form (fig. 259). Here, expansive views

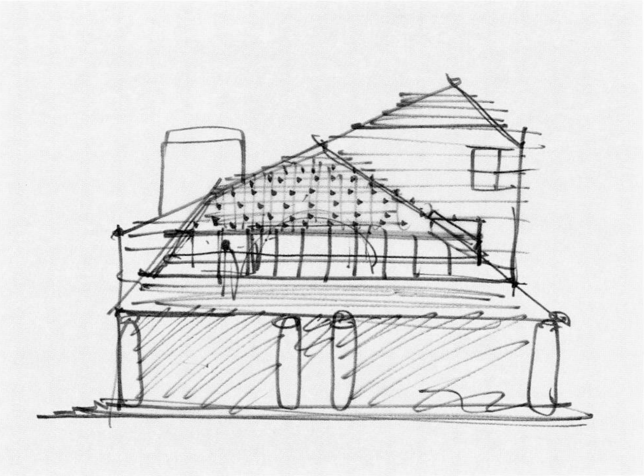

Figure 260
Hanks House, Tuxedo Park, New York, 1987–90

Elevation. Marker on yellow tracing paper, 18 x 24" (45.7 x 61 cm)
Robert Venturi

Collection of Venturi, Scott Brown and Associates, Inc.

Figure 261
Adler House, Williamstown, Massachusetts, 1999

Model. Chipboard, diazo print, foam core, and stainless-steel pins, 10 x 40 x 32" (25.4 x 101.6 x 81.3 cm)

Collection of Venturi, Scott Brown and Associates, Inc.

[78] Leland M. Roth, in *Shingle Styles: Innovation and Tradition in American Architecture, 1874 to 1982* (New York: Harry N. Abrams, 1999), claims Petrie was drawn to the Venturis because of the Trubek-Wislocki and Coxe-Hayden houses. When the authors interviewed Mr. Petrie in August 2000, however, he said this was not true. Rather, his first wife, a Philadelphian, made the suggestion. He had not heard of the office at the time. A small, undetectable addition was designed in consultation with the Venturis by Frederic Schwartz with Ronald Evitts, both of whom had worked for the Venturis; working drawings in Mr. Petrie's possession are dated August 18, 1999.

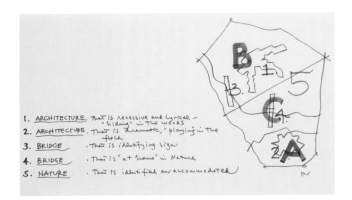

Figure 262
Hotel Mielmonte Nikko Kirifuri,
Nikko, Japan, 1992–97
Preliminary site plan. Marker on yellow
tracing paper, 11¼ x 17" (28.6 x 43.2 cm)
Robert Venturi. Signed
Collection of Susumu Yamagiwa

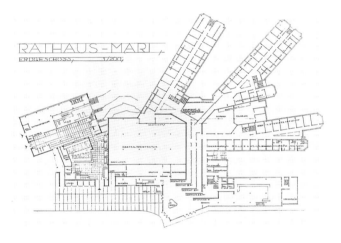

Figure 263
Alvar Aalto, Marl Town Hall, 1957
Plan. Pencil on sketch paper, 94⅛ x
14¼" (240.3 x 36.2 cm)
Alvar Aalto Archives, Helsinki, Finland

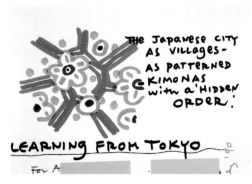

Figure 264
"Learning from Tokyo," 1990
Sketch. Marker and colored marker
on paper, 11 x 17" (27.9 x 43.2 cm)
Robert Venturi. Dated July 1990
Collection of Akio Izutsu

occur within, where double-height windows emphasize vertical shafts of space. A similar parti informs the smaller Hanks house design for Tuxedo Park, New York (1987–90, unbuilt; fig. 260). The Adler house in Williamstown, Massachusetts (1999, unbuilt), reactivates the theme of a pedimented front, but with such unexpected scale and elaborate variation that it enlarges upon its prototypes (fig. 261).

Buildings That Make Streets

Because of the remarkable consistency of the later work of the Venturis as well as extended, overlapping periods of project development, it is difficult to describe its chronological trajectory. Yet in two recently completed works, each large in scale, public in nature, and built overseas—in Japan and France—a shift in the definition of context not only develops earlier themes but also may indicate a subtle change of direction.

The Venturis' involvement in Japan seems especially to have energized the office, which benefited as well from the Venturis' own energies, clearly renewed by their enthusiasm for a material culture they found much to their liking. For them it was the commercial vitality of Japan and the vibrant ambience of ordinary shops and their contents that held special appeal, so much so that an exhibition of the objects they had collected there was held at the Philadelphia Museum of Art in 1994.[79] Just as Frank Lloyd Wright, in 1905, found in vernacular Japanese architecture a reinforcement of his own ideas, so the Venturis, in 1990, extracted from ordinary Japanese objects an affirmation of their own beliefs.

The Mielmonte Nikko Kirifuri hotel and spa (part of the Mielparque chain), near Nikko, Japan (1992–97), stands as the firm's most important commercial building to date, and at 328,000 square feet (almost three times the area of the Sainsbury Wing of the National Gallery), their largest. It was commissioned by Japan's Ministry of Posts and Telecommunications as an investment of postal savings capital.[80] The ministry's detailed program for the facility

[79] For the Venturis' enthusiastic response to Japan, see Robert Venturi and Denise Scott Brown, "Two Naifs in Japan," in Venturi, Scott Brown and Associates, *Architecture and Decorative Arts: Two Naifs in Japan* (Tokyo: Kajima Institute Publishing Co., 1991), pp. 8–24.

[80] Preliminary research notes compiled by Joyce Cheng in May 1999 help document the chronology and other details of the commission; they are filed in the Architectural Archives of the University of Pennsylvania. Additional information was gathered in Japan in May 1999 in meetings David Brownlee, William Whitaker, and the author

had been completed before a competition for its design was announced in April 1992. In May, Marunouchi Architects & Engineers, a Tokyo firm, invited Venturi, Scott Brown and Associates to collaborate on a submission.[81] They had been led to the Venturis by Akio Izutsu, the former president of Knoll International in Japan and a longtime admirer of their work. He had met them in 1984 and later, in 1990, had served as guide during their first trip to Japan.[82] In June 1992, Marunouchi sent the competition prospectus to the Venturis; it included a site plan diagramming two tightly restricted areas within the extensive property where buildings would be permitted. In July, Robert Venturi traveled to Japan to study the site and begin work on their firm's competition entry.[83] By late July, scarcely ten days after leaving Japan, Venturi submitted a draft of the firm's proposal in which he explained: "We would juxtapose diverse elements, sometimes harmonious, sometimes dissonant . . . that truly reflect the genius of Japan today and contribute to the vitality of its culture. . . . The design should acknowledge not only the natural context but also a cultural ethos."[84] Diagrams located the major structures, and these were refined for the formal submission in August (fig. 262). The hotel is shown in the upper parcel of land where building would be allowed, approached by a bridge that he had explained "could work as a form of sign . . . could symbolize this place."[85] As notes on the drawing indicate, the hotel was to be "recessive and lyrical—'hiding' in the woods"; the spa, located on the lower parcel of the site, was to be "dramatic, 'playing' in the field." A second bridge, to be "'at home' in nature" as it led through the forest, was meant to provide a path between the two.

The hotel in the diagram, with its stepped, angled wings, is like no other building designed by the firm. It first seems to resemble Aalto's competition entry for the town hall in Marl, Germany, of 1957 (fig. 263), but it also recalls a sketch Venturi had made during that first visit to Japan in 1990 titled "Learning from Tokyo" (fig. 264). On its margin, he wrote: "The Japanese city as villages—as patterned

Figure 265
Hotel Mielmonte Nikko Kirifuri, Nikko, Japan, 1992–97
Section through "Village Street"
Marker and colored marker on yellow tracing paper, 18 x 23½" (45.7 x 59.7 cm). Robert Venturi
Signed and dated 1994
Collection of Venturi, Scott Brown and Associates, Inc.

had with representatives of the Ministry of Posts and Telecommunications, with Akio Izutsu, and Susumu Yamagiwa, president of Marunouchi Architects & Engineers.

81 Yoshitaka Taguchi, president and regional director, Marunouchi Architects & Engineers, to Robert Venturi, May 11, 1992. Courtesy of Marunouchi Architects & Engineers.

82 I am grateful to Mr. Izutsu for sharing this information with me and for showing me those sites in Tokyo that had particularly fascinated the Venturis.

83 The prospectus by the General Affairs Division, Building Department, The Ministry of Posts and Telecommunications,

is titled, "'Nikko Kirifuri Resort Facilities' Design Commissioning Specifications," June, 1992. I am grateful to Susumu Yamagiwa, currently the president of Marunouchi, for sharing this prospectus with me and for confirming the dates of Venturi's visit in his office diary.

84 The signed draft is dated July 27, 1992; Venturi had left Japan on July 16. Again, I am grateful to Mr. Yamagiwa for sharing this information.

85 Robert Venturi, draft submission, July 27, 1992. Courtesy of Marunouchi Architects & Engineers.

Figure 266
**Hotel Mielmonte Nikko Kirifuri,
Nikko, Japan, 1992–97**
"Village Street"

Figure 267
Photographs taken in Japan

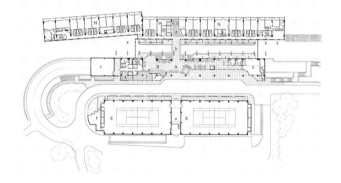

Figure 268
**Hotel Mielmonte Nikko Kirifuri,
Nikko, Japan, 1992–97**
Entry-level plan of hotel
Whereabouts unknown

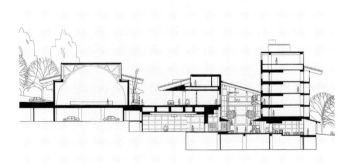

Figure 269
**Hotel Mielmonte Nikko Kirifuri,
Nikko, Japan, 1992–97**
Transverse section of hotel. Dated
December 1996
Whereabouts unknown

kimonos with a 'hidden order.' " First impressions of Tokyo that Venturi and Scott Brown recorded elsewhere reinforced this perception, for they described the future Tokyo as "an overlaid pattern of different scales and types of urban configuration, reminiscent somehow of the patterns of a kimono."[86] This sense of the hotel as being like a village, and Tokyo as being like a collection of villages with a complex order like that of a patterned kimono, remained paramount in the firm's development of the scheme and a featured part of its description.[87] Thus what they learned from Tokyo remained a force in their design, recalling how London had affected work by the New Brutalists long before, but with quite different results befitting a quite different city.

The firm was announced as winner of the competition in August 1992, and they embarked upon a long campaign. Conceptual designs were complete by February 1993, final designs by December of that same year, and working drawings by April 1995. Site work had begun in March 1994, the groundbreaking held a year later, and the formal opening in April 1997.[88]

The early diagram of the hotel had quickly given way to a composition of two long wings joined by a tall lobby. A glazed roof over the lobby emphasizes the separateness of the wings and amplifies the imagery below, for the lobby is inspired by traditional Japanese streets, lively places recalled with flattened images of utility poles, telephones, utility wires, hanging bouquets, and the like (figs. 265, 266). Close parallels can be found in the village-scaled shopping streets of Tokyo today. Along the side walls, photographic murals depict actual images found in Japanese streets (fig. 267). As Venturi and Scott Brown later wrote, "we have aimed for a scenographic architecture where generic forms are adorned with signs and the conventionally ordinary is made aesthetically extraordinary."[89] Restaurants, a bar, a library, a shop, and other amenities line the sides of the lobby, and at each end, views continue through glazed walls to the forest beyond. The outer wing, six stories tall, contains almost one hundred hotel rooms together with Japanese baths on its top floor.

86 Venturi and Scott Brown, "Two Naifs in Japan," p. 21.

87 For example, see von Moos, *Venturi, Scott Brown & Associates*, p. 270.

88 Both Mr. Yamagiwa and Shiro Nitani of the Facilities Department of the Ministry of Posts and Telecommunications and one of the judges (whom I interviewed in May 2000) confirmed details of the competition; fourteen firms submitted portfolios for consideration, and four were selected as finalists. Names of the other finalists were not revealed. Dates of various phases were recorded by the project's manager, David Marohn; "Design Phases and Site Construction Phase Summary," February 7, 1997, "92.11 Nikko-Phases and Dates," VSB box 500 (VSBA archives).

89 Robert Venturi and Denise Scott Brown, "Toward a Scenographic Architecture for Today: Generic Form with Ordinary=Extraordinary Signs . . . [1995]," in Venturi, *Iconography and Electronics*, p. 191.

Figure 270
**Hotel Mielmonte Nikko Kirifuri,
Nikko, Japan, 1992–97**

Perspective. Marker and colored
marker on yellow tracing paper,
24 x 57" (61 x 144.8 cm). Robert
Venturi. Signed

Collection of Venturi, Scott Brown
and Associates, Inc.

Figure 271
**Hotel Mielmonte Nikko Kirifuri,
Nikko, Japan, 1992–97**
Bridge

Figure 272
**Hotel Mielmonte Nikko Kirifuri,
Nikko, Japan, 1992–97**
Plan of spa. Marker, colored pencil,
and pencil on yellow tracing paper,
12 x 22″ (30.5 x 55.9 cm). Robert
Venturi. Dated November 29, 1992
Collection of Venturi, Scott Brown
and Associates, Inc.

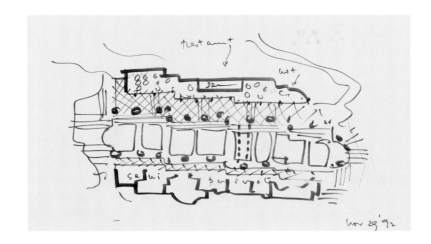

Figure 273
**Hotel Mielmonte Nikko Kirifuri,
Nikko, Japan, 1992–97**
Longitudinal section of spa. Marker,
colored marker, and colored pencil
on yellow tracing paper, 12 x 24½″
(30.5 x 62.2 cm). Robert Venturi
Dated November 2, [1992]
Collection of Venturi, Scott Brown
and Associates, Inc.

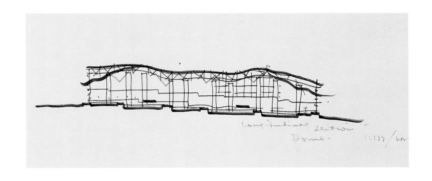

Figure 274
**Hotel Mielmonte Nikko Kirifuri,
Nikko, Japan, 1992–97**
Spa with hotel in background

Figure 275
**Hotel Mielmonte Nikko Kirifuri,
Nikko, Japan, 1992–97**
Spa

The inner wing houses the main entrance and meeting facilities; it opens to the main approach drive, which is bordered on its opposite side by enclosed tennis courts to complete the definition of a formal court of arrival (figs. 268, 269).

The soberly detailed exterior is meant to recall anonymous village architecture, an impression conveyed mainly by flattened, decorative rafters affixed to the ends of the wings and projecting along the sides of the flat-roofed structure. At first the flat roofs had not been so embellished. But in September 1993 Venturi had been notified that the local prefecture required buildings to have sloped roofs,[90] and these decorative elements were added to convey the mandated image (fig. 270). This proved a felicitous compromise. At first sight, the buildings offer a familiar, comforting image, yet one quickly revealed as representational, like a stage set perceived from the real world backstage rather than from the imaginary world of the audience, consciously avoiding any Disney-like illusion (fig. 271).

The spa, with a vast swimming pool as its primary feature, was conceived as a basilica-like volume with loosely defined walls (fig. 272). As sketched in section, its undulating roof suggested the waves of the water below (fig. 273). Its shapes were later simplified, and ultimately it was given a pitched roof that was real rather than representational. But the concrete trees with giant plum blossoms that playfully decorate screens along its base remained (fig. 274). Inside, decorative festoons made to resemble large bunches of leaves were suspended from trusses that span the pool (fig. 275). Similar decorations can be found in the Tokyo shopping streets that the Venturis had admired; here, they allude to surrounding forest, and like that forest, change color (at least in a sense), for they are green on one side and yellow on the other.

Like the hotel, the spa, too, creates its own place, for in an area lacking any sort of built context, the firm provided their own. The "cultural ethos" Venturi had promised to acknowledge in the firm's proposal of 1992 guides that creation even more fully than it had with the State Mosque in Baghdad. This is best seen in the hotel, which, as in so much of the firm's work, relates to streets and to patterns of movement. Yet the streets had to be created first, defined by the buildings that enclose them. This is the first specific example of what might be called a "streetmaker" building, providing clarified patterns of movement through architectural imposition, like a Beaux-Arts product of a century before, but without that product's predictable, unrelieved order. At Nikko, landscape provides that larger sense of order, but one attuned to ecological concerns. These had been effectively accommodated by Andropogon Associates, world-famous landscape architects who worked with the Venturis to refine the siting of individual elements and maintain the ecology of the area as part of their landscape plan.

Published reactions to Nikko, although fewer than one would expect with so prominent an achievement, were consistently positive. Typically, one Taipei observer noted that the "decorations in [the] 'Village Street' connote festivity and relieve people's minds from everyday stress."[91] Negative views, if they exist at all, have not been openly expressed. But one statement by Akio Izutsu, the Venturis' loyal supporter and mentor in Japan who did so much to secure the commission, suggests all may not have been easy: "The first presentation of construction appearance by VSBA embarrassed a concerned people" (quickly adding that the second presentation was "well received").[92] And in the photographic murals that adorn the lobby street, those taken by Venturi emphasize commercial subjects, while those by Izutsu focus more on tranquil images of scenic or architectural beauty.[93] Art made from the ordinary, so different from what might be called "calendar art," clearly demands a flexible response.

The government building in Toulouse, officially, the Hôtel du Département de la Haute-Garônne, which opened in the summer of 1999, also makes its own streets. It stands as the Venturis' most important civic building to date, and also their largest undertaking, at 866,000 square feet. Its very size, as well as its prominence in this major French city,

[90] Akio Izutsu to Robert Venturi, September 24, 1993. Courtesy of Akio Izutsu.

[91] Noriyuki Yasuyama, "From 'Ugly' to 'Beautiful'–Mielparque Nikko Kirifuri," *Dialogue: Architecture +*

Design + Culture, October 1997, p. 34. Other positive accounts include Martin Filler, "Shogun Wedding," *House Beautiful*, vol. 140 (May 1998), p. 76; and Juanita Dugdale, "*Learning from* Nikko," *Print*, vol. 52 (July/August 1998), pp. 56–63.

[92] Akio Izutsu, "Learning from Robert Venturi and Denise Scott Brown (Summary)," *Research Journal of the Cultural Institute of Northern Region Hokkaido Tokai University*, no. 23 (1998), p. 2.

[93] I am grateful to Mr. Izutsu for identifying these photo murals for me during my visit to Nikko in May 2000.

Figure 276
Hôtel du Département de la Haute-Garônne, Toulouse, France, 1990–99

Plan and elevation sketches. Marker on yellow lined paper, 11 x 8½" (27.9 x 21.6 cm). Robert Venturi

Collection of Venturi, Scott Brown and Associates, Inc.

signals this as no ordinary provincial office, and indeed it is not, for the role of départements in the government of France is substantial. Haute-Garônne is one of nearly one hundred départements, each governed by a general council whose members are elected to six-year terms; each council, in turn, elects its own president. Roughly analogous to large, populous counties in the United States, departments oversee a myriad of programs that include welfare, health, the administration of local regulations, and the management of public property.[94] They are large-scale operations.

Like the Mielmonte resort, the Toulouse commission resulted from a competition in which the Venturis were allied with local architects. Françoise Blanc, an independent practitioner and part of a consortium of Toulouse architects Hermet-Blanc-Lagausie-Mommens (formed to collaborate on the project), related that she had met the Venturis in Rome several years earlier, when she was a fellow at the French Academy and they were visiting the city. In the years that followed she became an enthusiastic admirer of their work.[95] When a competition for the projected building was announced in 1990, she persuaded the Venturis to submit a design in association with the consortium.[96] Resulting sketches by Venturi record the building's basic footprint: a diagonal pedestrian street linking a bridge at one corner to new development below, its shape defined by two parallel wings incorporating a great crescent (fig. 276). This was to remain essentially unchanged throughout the long course of work. The firm was among four finalists announced in early 1991, and after several months' delay, while site issues were resolved by government officials, they began the second phase of the competition in November. The drawings and model they submitted show a refined design (fig. 277), and they were judged the winners in June 1992.[97] Schematic designs were approved in August 1993, final designs in July 1994, and working drawings in March 1995. Construction began that year and was completed in the summer of 1999. During the nearly decade-long project, which was tormented by the sorts of disputes and reversals that might be expected

[94] The départements were originally formed in 1790; since 1964, they have been grouped together in twenty-two regions to facilitate economic planning. For detailed information, see Anne Stevens, *The Government and Politics of France* (New York: St. Martin's Press, 1992).

[95] I am grateful to Mlle. Blanc for sharing much information with me during my visit to Toulouse in May 2000, and for showing me not only the Venturis' building but also Robert Venturi's favorite buildings.

[96] Further assisting the Venturis in later phases of the commission was Anderson/Schwartz Architects, New York, with whom they were also in association.

[97] Research notes compiled by Rachel Iannacone document much of the chronology of the commission; they are filed in the Architectural Archives of the University of Pennsylvania.

Figure 277

**Hôtel du Département de la
Haute-Garônne, Toulouse, France,
1990–99**

Aerial perspective. Pencil on vellum,
30 x 42" (76.2 x 106.7 cm)

Collection of Venturi, Scott Brown
and Associates, Inc.

Figure 278

**Hôtel du Département de la
Haute-Garônne, Toulouse, France,
1990–99**

Figure 279
**Hôtel du Département de la
Haute-Garônne, Toulouse, France,
1990−99**

Figure 280
**Hôtel du Département de la
Haute-Garônne, Toulouse, France,
1990−99**

Figure 281
**Hôtel du Département de la
Haute-Garônne, Toulouse, France,
1990–99**
Exterior of council chamber

Figure 282
**Alvar Aalto, Rovaniemi City
Library, 1961–68**
Plan. Ink on tracing paper
Alvar Aalto Archives, Helsinki, Finland

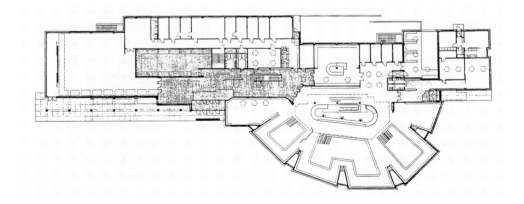

Figure 283
**Pont des Minimes, Toulouse,
France, 1900**
Archives de la Départementales de la
Haute-Garônne, Toulouse, France

Figure 284
**Hôtel d'Assézat, 1555–56,
Toulouse, France**

from so complicated a bureaucracy, Blanc remained stead-fastly loyal to the Venturis' proposals, defending them as their representative to the demanding clients.

The footprint of parallel wings related to planning analysis undertaken by the Venturis at the very beginning of the project, which had inspired them to define a pedestrian street enclosed by the two wings (fig. 278). Near the center of the building facing the canal, one wing bows out to form the monumental crescent (fig. 279), and a generously scaled, piazzalike space is shaped inside (fig. 280). The council assembly chamber projects asymmetrically from the opposite side (fig. 281), recalling Aalto's favored configuration for such auditoriumlike rooms (fig. 282).[98] Two glass-enclosed pedestrian bridges join the wings at the points of the crescent, completing the form of the piazza and modulating views down the pedestrian street to the new commercial center beyond.

There is not much in the way of intimate context on the expansive site. Older houses along the avenue Honoré Serres that might have provided some near the council chamber were removed in November 1995 despite the Venturis' wish to retain them. A few houses remain near the back corner of the complex, but as odd fragments, they offer little. Thus, as in the Mielmonte resort, the firm resorted to other means to establish context, referring not to indigenous building as they had in Japan, but to buildings at the outer perimeter and to nobler elements of Toulouse's history, as befits a civic building of this prominence.

Most apparent of the Venturis' contextual references are the flattened, freestanding columns that mark the approach to the pedestrian street (see fig. 278); they were inspired by ceremonial columns that once marked the entrance to north Toulouse at almost the same location, but were destroyed in 1940 (fig. 283). On the ends of the building's wings—framing the entrances to the pedestrian street within and forming, in a sense, the ceremonial entrance to the complex as a whole—is a split and flattened representation of a French architectural frontispiece, one of the most

[98] Among other examples by Aalto, see the auditorium in the House of Culture, Helsinki, 1952–58, as illustrated in Göran Schildt, *Alvar Aalto: The Complete Catalogue of Architecture, Design and Art* (New York: Rizzoli, 1994), p. 93, fig. 142.

characteristic elements of French architecture with a history that stretches back at least to the sixteenth century. It relates specifically to one of Toulouse's historic buildings, the Hôtel d'Assézat (1555–56; fig. 284), which Venturi admired on an early visit to the city when beginning work on the competition. Other historic references that establish a context for the building include its brick and limestone facades, which echo the materials of Toulouse, and the exuberant pattern in the glazed exterior of the council chamber, evocative of the rainbow image that was once used as a promotional symbol for the city of Toulouse. Scott Brown refers to this image-creating technique as "painting with steel and glass."[99] Taken together, these references indicate the Venturis' broad concept of appropriate context, one that can even recall missing fragments, as Franklin Court had done long before (see fig. 97).

Ceremonial spaces within the building evoke a quite different past: that of the early twentieth century. The public entrance from the piazza to the wing housing the council chamber leads through a rotunda reaching the full height of the six-story building; linear patterns embellishing its balconies (fig. 285) recall architectural motifs of Czech cubism, and Scott Brown confirms that during their visit to Prague in 1991 she and Venturi were drawn to such details.[100] Elsewhere, references to Aalto abound, especially in the lobby and an adjoining stair leading up to the public gallery of the council chamber (fig. 286). These areas manifest the same easy, angled informality of such Aalto interiors as the foyer of Finlandia Hall in Helsinki (1960–69; fig. 287). The continuing relationship to Aalto is important, and worth repeating, for it helps explain an essential approach in their respect for modernism, as Venturi had written: "Aalto himself has become an Andrea Palladio of the Modern movement—a mannerist master, but in a low key. Among the complexities and contradictions I see in his work are its conventional architectural elements organized in unconventional ways, its barely maintained balance between order and disorder, and its effects of plain and fancy, of the modest and the

Figure 285
Hôtel du Département de la Haute-Garônne, Toulouse, France, 1990–99
Entrance rotunda

Figure 286
Hôtel du Département de la Haute-Garônne, Toulouse, France, 1990–99
Entrance lobby

Figure 287
Alvar Aalto, Finlandia Hall, Helsinki, Finland, 1960–69
Foyer

99 Denise Scott Brown, interview with the author, Philadelphia, March 24, 2001.

100 Denise Scott Brown, interview with the author, Philadelphia, March 29, 2001. For published images, see Alexander von Vegesack, ed., *Czech Cubism: Architecture, Furniture, and Decorative Arts, 1910–1925* (New York: Princeton Architectural Press, 1992).

Figure 288

**Hôtel du Département de la
Haute-Garônne, Toulouse, France,
1990–99**

Council chamber

Figure 289

**University of Michigan Master
Plan, Ann Arbor, 1997–**

Options for an arts-science axis.
From "Presentation to the Regents,
Selected Illustrations," May 20, 1999

Collection of Venturi, Scott Brown
and Associates, Inc.

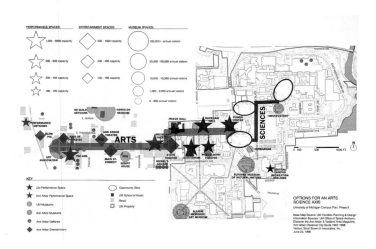

monumental at the same time."[101] Blanc relates that such references as those to Czech cubism and Aalto sometimes failed to please the president of the Conseil Général, Pierre Izard, who gradually assumed the role of the client.[102] He wanted something more orthodox in its modernity. His objections to other details were evidently many, and they raised tensions. He blocked the proposal for a luminous rainbow mural in the council chamber (fig. 288) and demanded complicating changes in the delegates' lobby. The choice of ordinary streetlights for wall sconces along the pedestrian street particularly irritated him, but there the Venturis prevailed.[103] Blanc reports that public response in Toulouse, however, has been strongly positive.[104]

A third "streetmaker" design that largely defines its own context is the Life Sciences Laboratory for the University of Michigan, where planning again provided a solid base for design. Work began in the fall of 1997, when university president Lee C. Bollinger (who had been provost at Dartmouth during the Venturis' planning efforts there) commissioned the firm to prepare a master plan for the campus.[105] Actually it was to be a master plan for six interrelated campuses, for over time the university had spread across Ann Arbor and into the region, and direction was needed to unify these disparate elements and relate them better to the surrounding community.[106]

By the fall of 1998, proposed linkages included among others two exterior corridors of activity: one related to performing arts, the second to the sciences (fig. 289)[107] By the spring of 1999, the place where these two corridors met assumed special prominence as the site for a complex of proposed buildings that would incorporate a parking structure below as part of a pedestrian bridge. This complex became critical to both the academic and physical plans for the university in its provision for life sciences and the arts as well as for a commons building and related facilities. As dia-

grammed, the buildings were shaped to define pedestrian routes: life sciences, angled to effect a transitional shift, and the "L-Shaped" building, reinforcing the arts corridor as it linked to the sciences (figs. 290, 291). The firm's statement described these buildings as a "bridge between the Medical Center and the Central Campus, through facilities that incorporate disciplines of both campuses and through a network of pedestrian walkways."[108] They continued to focus on this element; schematic drawings for the Life Sciences Laboratory, which maintained the profile suggested by their master plan, were approved by university regents in April 2000,[109] and study models show it taking form (fig. 292). By 2001 it was under construction.

Parting Words

Few architectural firms achieve fame equal to that of the Venturis. Yet they remain frustrated by commissions left unbuilt and irritated by superficial criticism, things that no great architects escape, and the Venturis seem to have experienced no higher proportion of these than any other. But like Frank Lloyd Wright between waves of hard-earned adulation, they are impatient for the next appraisal to come. Also like Wright, their work remains controversial, an extraordinary achievement in itself after more than forty years of practice.

An incident at the University of Michigan offers one clue as to how their situation might differ slightly from that of other architects. Asked to add new rows of seats at the top of the University of Michigan Stadium, they backed them with the school's colors overlaid with such icons as helmets and shields and with giant quotations from Michigan's Wolverine fight song. When their iconographic scheme was announced in November 1997, it was praised as giving the stadium a "festive image,"[110] yet when completed

101 Robert Venturi, "Alvar Aalto," *Arkkitehti*, vol. 73 (July/August 1976), p. 66, reprinted at least four times; in Venturi, "Learning from Aalto," *Iconography and Electronics*, p. 77.

102 Françoise Blanc, interview with the author, Toulouse, May 2000.

103 When I met M. Izard in May 2000, he seemed much more at peace with the building.

104 For an enthusiastic American response, see Ned Cramer, "Power Outage," *Architecture*, vol. 89 (May 2000), pp. 138–45.

105 Roger Green, "Renowned Architects to Design U-M Master Plan," *Ann Arbor News*, October 1, 1997; and Heather Kamins, "Bollinger Commissions Master Plan," *Michigan Daily*, October 1997.

106 Grace Shackman, "Venturi Scott Brown and Associates Embrace the Wandering Campus: Master Architect/Master Plan," *Michigan Today*, vol. 30 (Spring 1998), pp. 12–14.

107 As described in McIntyre, "Maps as Muse," pp. 20–23.

108 Venturi, Scott Brown and Associates, "Draft: The University of Michigan Campus Plan, Phase 2," July 21, 1999. The angled shape of what would become identified as a building for life sciences had appeared in their March 8, 2000, draft, and was shown in a model presented in June, as described in Susan Carney, "Officials Get Update on U-M Plan," *Ann Arbor News*, June 5, 1999.

109 Jane R. Elgass, "Life Sciences Building Project Approved," *University Record*, April 17, 2000, <http://www. umich.edu/~ure-cord/9990/Apr17_00/3.htr>.

110 Janet Adamy and Heather Kamina, "The Victors: 'U' Breaks Ground for Expansion of Big House," *Michigan Daily*, November 24, 1997.

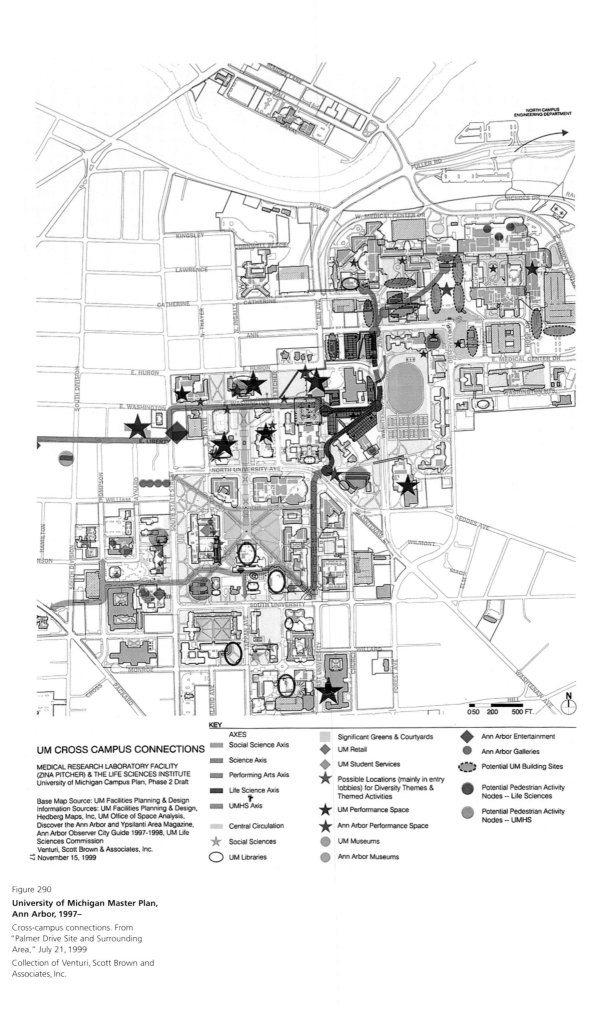

KEY

UM CROSS CAMPUS CONNECTIONS

MEDICAL RESEARCH LABORATORY FACILITY
(ZINA PITCHER) & THE LIFE SCIENCES INSTITUTE
University of Michigan Campus Plan, Phase 2 Draft

Base Map Source: UM Facilities Planning & Design
Information Sources: UM Facilities Planning & Design,
Hedberg Maps, Inc, UM Office of Space Analysis,
Discover the Ann Arbor and Ypsilanti Area Magazine,
Ann Arbor Observer City Guide 1997-1998, UM Life
Sciences Commission
Venturi, Scott Brown & Associates, Inc.
17 November 15, 1999

AXES

- Social Science Axis
- Science Axis
- Performing Arts Axis
- Life Science Axis
- UMHS Axis
- Central Circulation
- Social Sciences
- UM Libraries

- Significant Greens & Courtyards
- UM Retail
- UM Student Services
- Possible Locations (mainly in entry lobbies) for Diversity Themes & Themed Activities
- UM Performance Space
- Ann Arbor Performance Space
- UM Museums
- Ann Arbor Museums

- Ann Arbor Entertainment
- Ann Arbor Galleries
- Potential UM Building Sites
- Potential Pedestrian Activity Nodes -- Life Sciences
- Potential Pedestrian Activity Nodes -- UMHS

Figure 290

University of Michigan Master Plan, Ann Arbor, 1997–

Cross-campus connections. From "Palmer Drive Site and Surrounding Area," July 21, 1999

Collection of Venturi, Scott Brown and Associates, Inc.

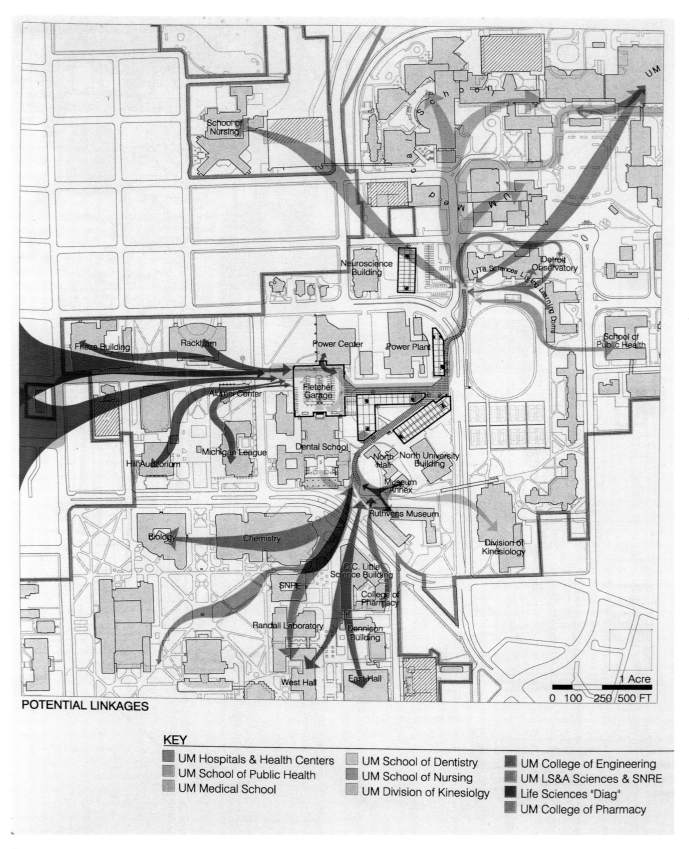

POTENTIAL LINKAGES

KEY

UM Hospitals & Health Centers
UM School of Public Health
UM Medical School

UM School of Dentistry
UM School of Nursing
UM Division of Kinesiolgy

UM College of Engineering
UM LS&A Sciences & SNRE
Life Sciences "Diag"
UM College of Pharmacy

Figure 291

**University of Michigan Master
Plan, Ann Arbor, 1997–**

Potential linkages for Palmer Drive site
From "Linkages and Programming,
Possibilities for the Palmer Drive
Complex," July 21, 1999

Collection of Venturi, Scott Brown
and Associates, Inc.

in time for the 1998 football season, reaction to it was mixed (fig. 293). Some thought it went against Michigan's "understated tradition"; others were more outspoken in their negative criticism.[111] President Bollinger remained strongly supportive, but ongoing criticism of what had come to be called "the halo" led eventually to the removal of the appliqué of images and words in January 2000.[112] Sometimes, it seems, people shrink from confronting real aspects of what they admire—in this case, perhaps the highly competitive, brutally physical reality of intercollegiate football—preferring to imagine it as being on a higher plane. Those real aspects are what the Venturis reveal in their work, and not everybody likes it, especially those who would rather not see themselves too clearly, as people who hide their television sets in cabinets and stash their popular novels under the bed, where nobody will see them.

Often such reactions seem based on wrongful first impressions that focus on the seemingly simplistic shape of a building's design without adequately recognizing the subtle modifications that would make that shape special. Something of the sort seemed to have happened with the Philadelphia Orchestra Hall, for apparently few, if any, perceived the intelligent layers of refinement that lay beneath the deceptively simple facades of the various proposals. Other clients evidently mistake the Venturis' accommodating manner, and their language born out of accessible sources, as invitation to make their own unilateral design decisions, believing themselves capable like those who claim they can paint as well as Jackson Pollock. Often this client design effort may focus on apparently small details, like the light sconces at Toulouse, yet these details the Venturis will fiercely defend.

When the Venturis' work is considered as a whole, and tiresome distractions are set aside, the full measure of how they forever changed architecture becomes more readily apparent. Like Louis Kahn, with whom both had ties, and in the spirit of an evolving art, they sought not to reject

modernism but to expand upon it. As Venturi had said in 1978, "I shall talk as an architect, not as a theoretician, but as a Modern architect—not a Postmodern or neo-Beaux-Arts architect. Our work evolves from the recent past."[113] In the end, the Venturis went further. Both they and Kahn questioned the cold abstraction and undifferentiated interiors of modernism, and both reconnected architecture with history, although in different ways.[114] Yet Kahn never really questioned other long-proclaimed principles of modernism: architecture deals primarily with space, with universal order, and with the clear definition of form. Today, buildings that cling to these principles offer comforting images, for they have become an admired part of our own history. In questioning and ultimately rejecting these very principles as of another time, Robert Venturi and Denise Scott Brown wrought more radical change, and as a consequence, some reject their work, a problem affecting any genuinely new art. Also unlike Kahn, they seek the particular over the universal, and the universal in the particular, inclining their work away from any classic, balanced resolution of its parts. Many architects now deal with similar values: more with image and flatness than space, more with an artful reworking of reality that better reflects our own, less conventionally ordered time. In this way the Venturis have led in helping define our post-modern culture.

Beginning in the 1980s, critics increasingly identified the Venturis as the parents of post-modernism, referring not to post-modern culture that is an inescapable condition of our time, but to a revival of historicism that flourished as fashion in just those years.[115] This reflects a misinterpretation of their work, for while they did much to inspire this fashion, they should not be blamed for what they never intended. Their allusions to historic motifs, which stimulated an entire generation of architects, were symbolic rather than literal, manipulated in ways that never deceived, that never fostered combined with other, equally symbolic references to popular culture, further anchoring their work within its own time. Yet

[111] Susan Carney, "Nothing Heavenly about Stadium's Halo, Some Gripe," *Ann Arbor News*, November 8, 1998, <http://www.aa.mlive.com/news/index.ssf?/news/stories/halo.frm>.

[112] Bollinger's support is expressed in Maryanne George, "Halo May Get Sacked," *Detroit Free Press*, September 6, 1999, <http://www.

freep.com/sports/umich/9halo6.htr>; its removal is pictured under the caption, "Deconstructing Halo," *Michigan Daily*, January 18, 2000.

[113] Robert Venturi, "Learning the Right Lessons from the Beaux-Arts [1978]," in Venturi and Scott Brown, *View from the Campidoglio*, p. 70.

[114] Kahn's role in this regard is discussed in David B. Brownlee and David G. De Long, *Louis I. Kahn: In the Realm of Architecture* (Los Angeles: The Museum of Contemporary Art; New York: Rizzoli, 1991), esp. pp. 55–70.

[115] For example, Martin Filler, "Personal Patterns," *House & Garden*, vol. 156 (January 1984), pp. 90–99; William H. Jordy, "Robert Venturi and the

Decorated Shed," *New Criterion*, vol. 3 (May 1985), pp. 58–68; Christian Norberg-Schulz, "The Two Faces of Post-Modernism," *Architectural Design*, vol. 58, no. 7/8 (1988), pp. 11–15. Seeing differences between work by the Venturi firm and standard post-modernism is Lavin, "Artistic Statements," pp. 131–37, 166.

Figure 292
**Palmer Drive Development,
University of Michigan, Ann
Arbor, 1999–**

Model. Chipboard, 6 x 36 x 23½"
(15.2 x 91.4 x 59.7 cm)

Collection of Venturi, Scott Brown
and Associates, Inc.

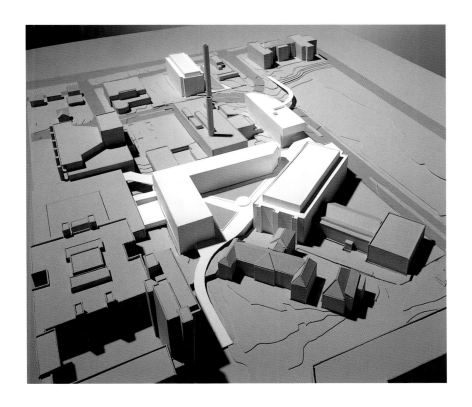

Figure 293
**Stadium, University of Michigan,
Ann Arbor, 1997–98**

to their immediate followers, the lure of a simple, romantic historicism proved irresistible. As Martin Filler explained, "a number of Venturi's essential concepts—especially the reuse of traditional motifs in a simplified but recognizable manner—are all too easily mimicked. Thus over the four decades of his career, many lesser talents—most notably Philip Johnson, Michael Graves, and Robert A. M. Stern—have been able to profit from Venturi's ideas and designs more than he has, thereby obscuring the importance of their true originator."[116] Perhaps none of their followers has had a greater impact in this regard than Elizabeth Plater-Zyberk, a former member of the firm, who with Andres Duany is a leading force of what is called "New Urbanism." No less an architectural historian than Vincent Scully has celebrated this revival of traditional values as a triumphant accomplishment,[117] yet it draws from only a single dimension of the Venturis' vastly more complicated work.

Alert to the misdirected influence their work could exert, the Venturis sought early on to distance themselves from post-modernism. Venturi did this in 1981: "The symbolism being adopted—I refer particularly to that of the historicist Classical vocabulary of the Postmodernists—is in my opinion at once too pure and too consistent. It does not allow a diversity that is sensitive and adaptable to the plurality of taste cultures which our architecture must acknowledge if it is to be real and broad in its scope."[118] In 1982 he spoke even more emphatically: "The Postmodernists, in supplanting the Modernists, have substituted for the largely irrelevant universal vocabulary of heroic industrialism another largely irrelevant universal vocabulary—that of parvenu Classicism, with its American manifestation, a dash of Deco and a whiff of Ledoux."[119] More recently, Denise Scott Brown has further differentiated their own approach: "Contextual borrowings should never deceive; you should know what the real building consists of beneath the skin. For this reason our allusions are representations

rather than copies of historic precedents. The deceit is only skin deep."[120]

Meanings suggested by these surface images imbue individual buildings with special relevance, expressing our postindustrial age in a way distinct from most other architects, as Venturi later attested: "Is it not time for architects to connect with some new revolution, perhaps the electronic one? The existing commercial Strip with moving lights and signs involving representation and symbolism and meaning, and elements far apart in space to accommodate cars moving and parked, is as relevant to us now as were the factories with their industrial processes and functional programs several generations ago."[121] They had earlier distinguished such symbolism from modernist perceptions of space and structure, describing theirs as "antispatial; it is an architecture of communication over space," and explaining that "the symbol systems that electronics purveys so well are more important than its engineering content."[122]

In recent years, the Venturis have welcomed the decline of a bland, unthinking historicism as a reigning architectural fashion. But just as their reputations were earlier buoyed by that fashion, however ironically, so they have suffered from its decline, a consequence of close association. For example, Roger Kimball, managing editor of the *New Criterion*, revealed an all-too-common misinterpretation: "Venturi is in a class of postmodernists whose buildings pretend to be something that they aren't. Like Philip Johnson, like Michael Graves and so on, he's engaged in a kind of production of stage sets."[123] Others have likened the firm's work to that of Charles Moore.[124] But Moore himself, indeed an early adherent of historicism, had seen clear differences, describing Venturi's work as more artful, and his own as "easier and perhaps floppier."[125]

Largely overlooked in the Venturis' work is their contribution to another, more current, architectural fashion: that of distorted geometries. For by questioning conventional

[116] Martin Filler, "Fantasia," review of *Iconography and Electronics upon a Generic Architecture: A View from the Drafting Room*, by Robert Venturi, *New York Review*, vol. 44, no. 16 (October 23, 1997), p. 10.

[117] For example, Vincent Scully, "The Architecture of Community," in Peter Katz, *The New Urbanism: Toward an Architecture of Community* (New York: McGraw Hill, 1994), pp. 221–30.

[118] Robert Venturi, "The RIBA Annual Discourse [1981–82]," in Venturi and Scott Brown, *View from the Campidoglio*, p. 104.

[119] Robert Venturi, "Diversity, Relevance and Representation in Historicism, or *Plus ça Change . . . Plus a Plea for Pattern All Over Architecture with a Postscript on My Mother's House* [1982]," in Venturi and Scott Brown, *View from the Campidoglio*, p. 113.

[120] Denise Scott Brown, "Talking about the Context," *Lotus International*, vol. 74 (1992), p. 128.

[121] Robert Venturi, "A Definition of Architecture as Shelter with Decoration on It, and Another Plea for a Symbolism of the Ordinary in Architecture [1978]," in Venturi and Scott Brown, *View from the Campidoglio*, p. 66.

[122] Robert Venturi, Denise Scott Brown, and Steven Izenour, *Learning from Las Vegas* (Cambridge and London: The MIT Press, 1972), pp. 4, 102.

[123] Quoted in James S. Panero, "Bob Venturi and Postmodernism; An Interview with Roger Kimball," *Dartmouth Review*, April 10, 1996.

[124] Anthony Vidler, "Architectural Awakenings," *UCLA Magazine*, vol. 6 (Summer 1994), p. 42.

[125] Charles Moore, "Moore Is More," *RIBA Journal*, ser. 3, vol. 88 (November 1981), p. 36.

order from the very beginning, they also helped initiate a revived expressionism, or "deconstructivism," as it is more often termed.[126] Yet the Vanna Venturi house was described in deconstructivist terms well before the celebrated deconstructivist buildings of Frank Gehry, Peter Eisenman, and others were even conceived. In 1965, in what must be the first perceptive, positive analysis of that house, Ellen Perry wrote: "The whole, in its studied disjointedness, appears to express the discontinuity and fragmented quality that characterizes contemporary life."[127] Venturi continues to support this interpretation of the firm's work,[128] yet feels as distanced from recent buildings by Frank Gehry as from those by the neohistoricists. Again, from his perspective, fundamental principles have been misapplied, leading to the creation of arbitrary form: "Classical order that is broken—that is there, so to speak, to be broken—that admits contradiction—that is MANNERIST. But broken by circumstance—not for the picturesque or arty reasons that are characteristic today of Decon, for instance, but by circumstance—a manifestation of order that acknowledges the ultimate complexity and contradiction in experience. Mannerism that pragmatically acknowledges the limitations of universal order in terms of form and symbol—that acknowledges urban context and promotes aesthetic tension—and in the end exalts the element of dissonance."[129]

With justification, Robert Venturi and Denise Scott Brown identify the architectural fantasies of early twentieth-century German Expressionist designs—now made buildable by computer technology—as a major visual source for deconstructivism. From their perspective, the supposedly new is thus no more original than work by the late modernists, such as Richard Meier, who more obviously mine early twentieth-century vocabularies. Who, then, is the most original? Certainly it is not the post-modernists, nor the late modernists. But not the deconstructivists, either. In such ways, the Venturis find themselves uniquely positioned.

Deeper issues lie beneath such questions of style. One relates to the Venturis' long commitment to their social responsibilities as architects, and to functionalism as a moral and aesthetic mandate, things too easily ignored by an affluent society drawn to private ostentation.[130] Current planning studies by the Venturis sustain this commitment. Another issue that transcends questions of style deals with their refusal to invent new forms, designing instead what Venturi describes as "buildings that look like buildings."[131] This relates back to the question of originality, and forward to an appreciation of their more recent work: "I think that there is still on the part of architects the desire to be original—that old Romantic ideal of the architect as an original genius. Yet probably the greatest art is conventional; you can reach greater heights by combining the original with the not original. The idea of being new with every building is simply nonsense. It's harder to be good than it is to be original."[132]

They are indeed good, but hardly conventional, except on their own terms. For in the end, the Venturis remain firmly independent, anti-authoritarian, and rebellious in the best American tradition, a tradition that extends back through Wright, Sullivan, and Furness to Downing. Their banner could very well be one of their currently favored phrases: "Viva mannerism—generic, iconographic, electronic."[133] In these ways, coming out of modernism but rejecting its dictates, seeking to identify and express essential qualities of their own era, the Venturis make personal, time-defining art out of the ordinary.

[126] See, Philip Johnson and Mark Wigley, *Deconstructivist Architecture* (New York: The Museum of Modern Art, 1988).

[127] Ellen Perry [Berkeley], "Complexities and Contradictions," *Progressive Architecture*, vol. 46 (May 1965), p. 168. Herbert Muschamp, critic for the *New York Times*, is one of the few who seems to understand this; see Muschamp, "Ground Up,"

Artforum, vol. 27 (January 1989), pp. 14–15.

[128] Robert Venturi to Ellen Perry Berkeley, November 4, 1998; I am grateful to Ellen Perry Berkeley for sending me a copy of that letter.

[129] Robert Venturi, "Notes for a Lecture Celebrating the Centennial of the American Academy in Rome . . . [1993]," in *Iconography and Electronics*, p. 51.

[130] Denise Scott Brown comments on this in her essay, "Pop Off: Reply to Kenneth Frampton [1971]," in Venturi and Scott Brown, *View from the Campidoglio*, pp. 34–37.

[131] During the past three years, from 1997 to 2000, Venturi has used this phrase in countless conversations with David Brownlee and me.

[132] Quoted in McLeod, "On Artful Artlessness," in von Moos, *Venturi, Scott Brown & Associates*, p. 348.

[133] Robert Venturi, inscription in the author's copy of von Moos, *Venturi, Scott Brown & Associates*, on March 25, 2000.

Figure 294
**Duke House, New York University,
1958–59**
Work study room

DECORATIVE ART AND INTERIORS

Kathryn B. Hiesinger
Curator of European Decorative Arts
Philadelphia Museum of Art

Interior design has been a service provided to clients from the earliest days that Robert Venturi worked as an architect, and it continues to the present, as part of the architectural commissions of Venturi, Scott Brown and Associates. The design of furniture, decorative arts, and textiles for manufacture, on the other hand, occupied only a short, concentrated period within the history of the firm, from about 1978 to 1993, during the commercial peak of architect-designed boutique products in the United States and abroad. The firm's design of interiors and objects can be seen as an extension and reflection of its architectural theory and practice; like the architecture, it is both deeply indebted to historical precedent and deeply modern.

In its historical referencing, this work is distinguished from contemporary post-modernist design by the distance it maintains from its historical source. Never an essay "in the style of," it is rather a commentary on that style. In the historically inspired decorative arts, for example, shaped by a mannerist discipline, qualities of appearance are selected, condensed, and arbitrarily revised, creating in the process an aesthetic more abstract and artificial, more subtle and complex, than that of the antecedent style. It is the contrast and contradiction between these qualities that gives this work its distinctive energy.

Eclecticism Was Essentially Out

In his earliest interior designs, including the renovation of the James B. Duke house for New York University's Institute of Fine Arts (1958–59), Robert Venturi set the theoretical and aesthetic course his firm would follow, sympathetically combining disparate elements, most noticeably and originally, the modern with the historical. Scrupulously preserving the eighteenth-century-style interior paneling of the Duke house, Venturi furnished the Institute of Fine Arts with standard metal shelving and with bentwood chairs originally designed in 1929 by Josef Frank for Thonet (fig. 294). "Our approach was to touch the inside as little as possible," he explained, "and to create harmony between the old and the

Figure 295
**Vanna Venturi House,
Philadelphia, 1959–64**
Dining room

new through contrasting juxtapositions . . . to consider the new elements furniture rather than architecture and to use furniture and equipment which is commonplace and standard but enhanced by its uncommon setting. These elements are the bentwood chairs, and steel library shelving by Remington Rand whose rectangular geometry was superimposed on that of the wall panels, but separated from them."[1] Venturi's Mother's House (1959–64) presented the young architect with the opposite problem, that of placing traditional furnishings within a modern architectural space (fig. 295). "I designed the house," Venturi later wrote, "so my mother's old furniture (c. 1925, plus some antiques) would look good in it. In those days interiors were expected to be purely modern. Although you could scatter some very old antiques about (and the Italians were masters at this), eclecticism was essentially out."[2] Promoting the "messy vitality"[3] of eclecticism and ornament over uniformity, Venturi's interiors, nevertheless, remained modernist in their impression of openness and light and in the distinctive, discrete identities of the individual objects that furnished them. The two years he had spent in the office of Eero Saarinen (1951–52) working on the General Motors Technical Center had reinforced his interest in aspects of interior space planning (seeing its purpose as to "enclose rather than direct space"[4]) as well as in industrial processes and products, although not in the reductive aesthetic that distinguished the interiors of the Technical Center.

Venturi was most profoundly influenced in his approach to the furnishing of interior spaces by the writing and examples of Le Corbusier and Charles and Ray Eames. Vincent Scully, in his preface to *Complexity and Contradiction in Architecture*, compared Venturi's book to Le Corbusier's *Towards a New Architecture* (1923).[5] He could also have compared it to Le Corbusier's *The Decorative Art of Today* (1925). Venturi borrowed Le Corbusier's literary style (his use of aphorisms) as well as his use of the term "decorative art," a nineteenth-century designation for applied arts current then as now in France and in the nomenclature of art museums.

[1] Robert Venturi, *Complexity and Contradiction in Architecture* (New York: The Museum of Modern Art, 1966), pp. 104, 106.

[2] Robert Venturi, "Mother's House 25 Years Later," in Frederic Schwartz, ed., *Mother's House:*

The Evolution of Vanna Venturi's House in Chestnut Hill (New York: Rizzoli, 1992), p. 37.

[3] Venturi, *Complexity and Contradiction*, p. 22.

[4] Ibid., p. 72.

[5] Ibid., p. 11.

The Decorative Art of Today is organized as a series of discontinuous chapters (reprinted from articles published earlier), each prefaced by an aphoristic key, such as "modern decorative art is not decorated"[6] and "decorative art can no longer exist any more than can the 'styles' themselves."[7] Le Corbusier's fundamental argument was that domestic furnishings are "tools," or equipment, not decorative art; they reflect standard, universal needs and therefore should be standardized and rationalized in their manufacture and limited in number and type: "tables for working at and eating; chairs for eating and working; armchairs . . . for resting; and *cabinets* for storing the objects we use."[8] In the Esprit Nouveau pavilion, which he designed for the Exposition Internationale des Arts Décoratifs et Industriels Modernes, in Paris in 1925, Le Corbusier included furniture that he thought fulfilled these basic requirements: Thonet's B 39 chair (for dining and working), an English-type traditional club armchair custom-made in France (for relaxing), tables assembled from industrial components, and specially made modular storage units—*casiers*, or cabinets—with standard exterior dimensions and variable interior fittings (fig. 296). Such an eclectic combination of nineteenth- and twentieth-century ready-made and custom designs, all produced by modern industrial methods, broke radically with the prewar coordinated interior of suites of matching furniture, still guided by the ideals of the Arts and Crafts movement.

In *Complexity and Contradiction*, Venturi praised Le Corbusier for juxtaposing "commonplace elements, such as the Thonet chair, the officer's chair, cast iron radiators, and other industrial objects."[9] Le Corbusier had in fact said that the Thonet chair was not only commonplace ("banal") and "humble" but also "noble"; he admired the fact that it was an inexpensive industrial product sold "by the millions," and made of processed wood, a modern material.[10] Venturi went on to comment on his own use of Thonet chairs in Grand's restaurant in 1962 "which are also almost anonymously designed objects, although now perhaps becoming chi-chi" (fig. 297).[11] For Le Corbusier, the Thonet chair was a type-

Figure 296
Le Corbusier and Pierre Jeanneret, Esprit Nouveau Pavilion, for the Exposition Internationale des Arts Décoratifs et Industriels Modernes, Paris, 1925
Musée des Arts Décoratifs, Paris
© 2001 Artists Rights Society (ARS), New York / ADAGP, Paris / FLC

[6] Le Corbusier, *The Decorative Art of Today*, trans. and intro. James I. Dunnett (1925; London: The Architectural Press, 1987), p. 81.

[7] Ibid., p. 115.

[8] Le Corbusier, *Precisions on the Present State of Architecture and City Planning*, trans. Edith Schreiber Aujame (1930; Cambridge and London: The MIT Press, 1991), p. 108.

[9] Venturi, *Complexity and Contradiction*, p. 50.

[10] Le Corbusier, *Almanach d'architecture moderne* (Paris: Editions Crès, 1925), p. 145.

[11] Venturi, *Complexity and Contradiction*, p. 111.

Figure 297
**Grand's Restaurant, Philadelphia,
1961–62**

Figure 298
**Adolf Loos, Villa Müller, Prague,
1928–30**

Dining room

© 2001 Artists Rights Society (ARS),
New York/VBK, Vienna

object—a typology—universal in its beauty, simplicity, method of manufacture, and popularity. For Venturi, Thonet was also decorative and artful as well as a conscious historicism. Throughout his career, and distancing himself from Le Corbusier and the modern movement in general, Venturi introduced historical or traditional furnishings, or both, in his interiors for their rich and varied appearance and for their associative properties, writing that he even considered classic earlier twentieth-century modern furniture "historical."[12]

Venturi found historicizing precedent as well as examples of the stylistic eclecticism that he pursued in two early twentieth-century architects, Edwin Lutyens and Adolf Loos, whose work also interested Le Corbusier. Venturi wrote that he had learned method, if not specific content, from Lutyens, claiming that his picturesque "period" buildings and mixing of stylistic elements were "valid again in our own pluralist, mobile, pop, mass culture . . . period."[13] A more direct, if unexpected, parallel to Venturi was Adolf Loos, a pioneer of modern architecture most famous for his antiornament polemic, who selected for his residential interiors in Vienna and elsewhere, chairs in eighteenth- and nineteenth-century English styles—Queen Anne, Hepplewhite, Chippendale, Windsor—and leather-upholstered club armchairs, all reproduced locally by Austrian craftsmen (fig. 298). Such traditional-style furnishings represented to Venturi, as they did to Loos, personal possessions that might have been acquired by the client over time, not Le Corbusier's standard "equipment." Historical models have been a constant presence in Venturi's interiors, and his few perspective drawings of interiors—such as one for the renovation of the Gambescia house and office (1957–59; fig. 299)—typically include some variant of a late-eighteenth-century Pennsylvania ladder-back chair. This was a type of chair Venturi had grown up with, and the dining room in his mother's house had been carefully designed to accommodate it (see fig. 295).

In addition to following Loos's use of historical models, and Le Corbusier's preference for an eclectic combination

12 Robert Venturi, Project statement, Furniture for Knoll, October 10, 1978, "PR/Press Info.," VSB box 422; Mary Nomecos (for Robert Venturi) to Nan Swid, October 10, 1978, "Correspondence," VSB box 421 (VSBA archives).

13 Robert Venturi and Denise Scott Brown, "Learning from Lutyens," *Journal of the Royal Institute of British Architects*, vol. 76 (August 1969), p. 354.

Figure 299

**Gambescia House and
Professional Office, Philadelphia,
1957–59**

Perspective of waiting room
Pencil and colored pencil on tracing
paper, 18 x 24" (45.7 x 61 cm)
Robert Venturi

Collection of Venturi, Scott Brown
and Associates, Inc.

Figure 300
**Herman Miller Furniture Company
Showroom, Los Angeles, c. 1955**
Photograph by Charles Eames

of off-the-rack, ready-made furnishings, custom-made equipment, and built-ins, Venturi was also influenced by the aesthetic of Charles and Ray Eames. Their widely published Case Study House (1945–49), showroom displays for Herman Miller, and exhibitions were distinguished by careful juxtapositions of disparate objects that provided richness of pattern, color, and texture in otherwise economical interiors (fig. 300). Their personal vocabulary of decorative furnishings, including plants, Mexican masks, paper flowers, toys, and other winsome objects they had collected on their travels, expressed a mood of wit and informality then largely unknown in modern interiors. These objects were intended to define the character of the interior, as the Eameses specified for their house in 1945, with a "large unbroken area for pure enjoyment of space in which objects can be placed and taken away . . . driftwood, sculpture, mobiles, plants, constructions, etc."[14] Venturi applauded the Eameses for "reinvent[ing] good Victorian clutter. Modern architects wanted everything neat and clean and they came along and spread eclectic assemblages over an interior."[15] It was less the clutter, however, and more the principles of complex and unconventional juxtapositions, the change of scale, and the expression of wit "to surprise the mind and the eye" that Venturi seemed to absorb from the work of Charles and Ray Eames.[16]

University Projects

As the architectural practice grew, most of the firm's decisions concerning interior furnishings and surface color between the mid-1960s and the late 1980s were made in collaboration with Dian Boone, an interior designer practicing independently in Philadelphia. Boone had met Venturi when she was a graduate student in the Department of Fine Arts at the University of Pennsylvania. According to Boone, their philosophy was to use off-the-rack, production furniture whenever possible, and to make the best of it. In the Penn State Faculty Club of 1973–76, for example, the dining-room chairs were commercial "Country Chippendale"

[14] "Case Study Houses 8 and 9, by Charles Eames and Eero Saarinen, Architects," *Arts and Architecture*, vol. 62 (December 1945), p. 46.

[15] Quoted in Esther McCoy, "An Affection for Objects," *Progressive Architecture*, vol. 8 (August 1973), p. 67.

[16] Ibid.

Figure 301

Faculty Club, The Pennsylvania State University, University Park, Pennsylvania, 1973–76

Dining hall

Figure 302

Faculty Club, The Pennsylvania State University, University Park, Pennsylvania, 1973–76

Reception room

maple chairs, made in Denmark, Maine, by the firm of Douglas Campbell (fig. 301). These chairs with pierced splats took a third of the total budget for the interior-design project, their style alluding to the nearby Georgian-revival Nitanny Lion Inn.[17] Their reductive flatness and simplicity are features that Venturi would recall when he designed his own Chippendale chair for Knoll a decade later.

The specifications for furnishings prepared by the firm for the Penn State Faculty Club on December 22, 1975, included other eighteenth-century reproduction furniture: a hickory-frame Windsor "Letchworth" settee with simple stick back for the foyer, a mahogany "Salisbury" tea table with a round top and tripod base for the reception room and balcony, and a mahogany "Weston" English country-style Chippendale side chair to be used in the foyer, reception room, and balcony (fig. 302). These pieces were all ordered from the Philadelphia firm Saybolt & Cleland, a maker of high-quality reproduction furniture much admired by Venturi.[18] In addition, the firm used reissued "historical" classics of international modernism in the reception room, but embellished them with patterned upholsteries; these included Ludwig Mies van der Rohe's tubular-steel Brno armchair (1929–30), made by Knoll, and Josef Hoffmann's upholstered Keller house armchair (1911) from ICF. Like Le Corbusier's component tables, the Faculty Club dining tables were assembled from commercial ready-made elements, the oak tripod bases and plastic laminate tops produced by two institutional/restaurant-supply firms, Buckstaff in Oshkosh, Wisconsin, and Falcon in Saint Louis, respectively. Finally, the firm provided custom designs for the Faculty Club, most notably, the dining-room chandeliers and a built-in upholstered banquette in the reception room, a reception desk for the foyer, and a serving station for the dining room. Originally the firm had intended to use off-the-rack eighteenth-century reproduction brass chandeliers for the dining room but by May 1975 had decided to design a special fixture.[19] In August, Venturi presented a preliminary design for a wooden chandelier,[20] and by November,

schematic drawings were being reviewed by the fabricator, Wood-Mountain Makings, in Dallastown, Pennsylvania. The chandelier was made of wood jacketed around steel tubes, which were used for support and as an electrical raceway. Venturi designed the chandelier as an open structure of flat intersecting planes (see fig. 301), paraphrasing both the abstract composition of Gerrit Rietveld's hanging lamp from 1922 made of bare, suspended, standard lighting tubes and the detailing of one of Edwin Lutyens's painted-wood electric chandeliers, designed for the nursery at Viceroy's House, New Delhi (1929). Like Lutyens, Venturi defined the form as silhouetted, descriptive segments (from which incandescent bulbs were hung like Christmas ornaments), an idea that appeared first in Venturi's work in the coffee-cup signboard of Grand's restaurant in 1961–62, which according to his description in *Complexity and Contradiction*, "attracts the eye by being unifying and disrupting at once" (fig. 303).[21] This format would continue virtually unchanged in numerous lighting fixtures designed by the firm, and it was later applied to furniture and objects.

The eclectic mix of furnishings in the Faculty Club thus included traditional reproductions of eighteenth-century wooden furniture, both high style and vernacular; modern reproductions and editions of twentieth-century classic furniture of metal and upholstery; furniture assembled from ready-made components; and specially designed custom and built-in fittings. In a letter of April 1979, John Rauch, Venturi's partner, described the firm's interior-design philosophy to a prospective client: "Many of our projects have involved the careful blending of existing furniture and collections with new objects and materials. In instances where everything is new, as in our project for a Faculty Club for the Pennsylvania State University, fabric patterns and furniture of different periods were used to create a warm, dignified setting, as if the rooms had developed over time and the objects in them were part of an evolving collection, not all-bought-at-once."[22] The practice of combining such different elements has consistently distinguished the firm's design

[17] Venturi and Rauch, Architects and Planners, Penn State Faculty Club Furnishings Budget Allocations, September 18, 1975, "6.4.1 Interior Correspondence-Construction Phase," VSB box 71 (VSBA archives).

[18] Venturi and Rauch, Architects and Planners, "Specifications for Furnishings: The Faculty Club,

the Pennsylvania State University, University Park, Pennsylvania," December 22, 1975, "6.4.1 Interior Correspondence-Construction Phase," VSB box 71 (VSBA archives).

[19] Robert T. Renfro to J. P. Jackson, May 28, 1975, "10.5.5 Correspondence," VSB box 72 (VSBA archives).

[20] Venturi and Rauch, Architects and Planners, Meeting minutes, "Faculty Club, Penn State University, University Park, Pa. 16802," August 21, 1975, "6.4.1. Interior Correspondence-Construction Phase," VSB box 71 (VSBA archives).

[21] Venturi, *Complexity and Contradiction*, p. 112.

[22] John Rauch and Dian Boone to John C. Rettew, signed by John Rauch, April 20, 1979, "Butler Wilson Furniture Budget," VSB box 85 (VSBA archives).

Figure 303
**Grand's Restaurant, Philadelphia,
1961–62**

Figure 304
**Gordon Wu Hall, Princeton
University, New Jersey, 1980–83**
Lounge

Figure 305
**Gordon Wu Hall, Princeton
University, New Jersey, 1980–83**
Dining hall

work in its university, commercial, and residential interiors, even to the present day.

For the interior of Gordon Wu Hall, Butler College, at Princeton University (1980–83), the firm specified furnishings similar to those at Penn State. They included Windsor armchairs in oak from Krug in Kitchener, Ontario, to be used in the lounge, reception room, offices, conference room, and library (later changed to a similar model from Nichols & Stone, fig. 304); a modern sofa and lounge chair with mohair upholstery from David Edward in Baltimore, for the lounge; and modular seating units with vinyl upholstery designed by the Italian architect Menilio Taro for Stendig, to be used in the television rooms.[23] As at Penn State, the dining-room tables were assembled from commercial components, the oak bases again from Buckstaff and the laminated plastic tops from Johnson, an institutional supply firm in Elgin, Illinois (fig. 305). Early seventeenth-century-style oak chairs, inspired by those that furnished the Princeton Commons but abstracted and simplified, were used in the dining hall; these were made by Oneida Furniture in Oneida, New York. Custom designs included the dining booths (with laminated plastic tops from Johnson) and the dining-room chandelier. Venturi sent a preliminary sketch of the chandelier to the fabricator, Design Lighting, in Ivyland, Pennsylvania, in October 1982. Its design was developed from an industrial channel-strip fixture (albeit with an inverted crown molding profile); this added a modern element to the space, although the layout of tables and chairs along the length of the dining hall was intended to recall traditional dining halls at Princeton, and, as it had been at Penn State, the medieval English refectories on which they were based.[24]

Residential Projects

The firm's residential projects bear out the same design philosophy and eclectic furnishing pattern as their university projects. The living room of the Trubek house on Nantucket, for example, was furnished by Boone and

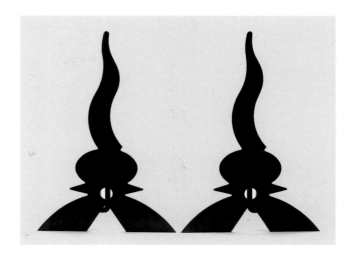

Figure 306
Andirons, 1989–90
For the Kalpakjian House, Glen Cove, New York, 1983–86. Wrought iron, 32 x 21 x 23" (81.3 x 53.3 x 58.5 cm)
Made by Solebury Forge, Wycombe, Pennsylvania
Collection of Mr. and Mrs. Gary Kalpakjian

[23] Venturi, Rauch and Scott Brown, "Furnishing Specifications: Social Dining Facility, Butler College, Princeton University, Princeton, New Jersey, 08544," October 25, 1982, "Furniture Specs.," VSB box 85 (VSBA archives).

[24] Venturi, Scott Brown and Associates, Project description, Gordon Wu Hall, Butler College, Princeton University (VSBA archives).

Figure 307
**Flint House, Greenville, Delaware,
1978–80**
Dining room

Figure 308
**Flint House, Greenville, Delaware,
1978–80**
Music room

Venturi in the summer of 1972[25] with nineteenth-century-style wicker furniture from Charles Schober in Philadelphia, and the Universal plastic chair of 1965–67 by the Italian designer Joe Colombo. By the mid-1980s, the firm's new furniture for Knoll began to appear in their residential commissions, such as the sofa, tables, and chairs ordered from Knoll in 1986 for the Kalpakjian house in Glen Cove, New York (1983–86). They accompanied custom designs, including lighting fixtures and andirons by Venturi (fig. 306) and bedroom furniture and rugs by Boone.

Even earlier, a dining-room table had been custom made by the Lititz Planing Mill Company in Lititz, Pennsylvania, for the Flint house in Greenville, Delaware (1978–80; see fig. 116). This was described in a letter of July 1983 as a version of Venturi's urn table then still being finalized for Knoll (fig. 307).[26] The Flints said they chose Venturi, Rauch and Scott Brown because they saw in the firm's work "a lot of warmth, and the use of design that makes it friendly and comfortable."[27] This sentiment was borne out by the interior of the music room, a high, light, open space with colorful ornamental "Carpenter Gothic" trusses, flat and silhouetted like the signature chandelier that hangs there (fig. 308). The organ, which dominates the music room, reflects the source of the house design in eighteenth-century domestic and farm architecture. Fritz Noack of the Noack Organ Company, Georgetown, Massachusetts, wrote Venturi about it in December 1978: "I hope you will be pleased with the way the organ fits in—there is a certain 'farm art' quality about the work of the 1700 North German organ builders (such as Arp Schnitger, who provides the model)."[28] The late-seventeenth-, early eighteenth-century-style baluster-back armchairs with openwork scrolls on the cresting selected for the room again evoke historical tradition in an otherwise abstract space.

Commercial Projects

The firm's largest and most important commercial interior project to date is the Mielmonte resort hotel complex (see fig. 271), which opened in 1997 near Nikko National Park

[25] Dian Boone to Mr. and Mrs. David Trubek, April 27, 1972, "70.23 Furnishings," VSB box 39 (VSBA archives).

[26] Maurice Weintraub to Mr. and Mrs. Peter Flint, July 6, 1983, "78.06 Flint Table," VSB box 133 (VSBA archives).

[27] Quoted in Michael J. Crosbie, "Friendly House Full of Surprises," *Architecture*, vol. 74 (May 1985), p. 228.

[28] Fritz Noack to Robert Venturi, December 19, 1978, "78.06 G-4 Organ," VSB box 133 (VSBA archives).

and the temple town of Nikko just north of Tokyo. Built by the Japanese Ministry of Posts and Telecommunications, the resort was described in the Ministry's program of 1990 as a "space in nature where city dwellers could enjoy a relaxed atmosphere."[29] In July 1992, Venturi and Denise Scott Brown, his wife and partner, defined their overall design approach for Nikko as "an architecture of wellbeing" that would respond not only to the specific site and program, but "to values and lifestyles of work and leisure, tourism and nature and to a heritage, cultural and religious—that truly reflect the genius of Japan today and contribute to the vitality of its culture."[30] An addendum to that statement in December 1992, which accompanied the first conceptual sketches for the resort, described ideas for "an architectural whole but one that is rich in its contemporary and contrasting expressions of rural tradition and of modern technology" (see fig. 262).[31] By the following spring, Venturi had developed the schematic design as a cluster of small buildings that suggested but did not replicate a rural Japanese village. Two parallel streets, one vehicular at the entrance, the other, pedestrian, in the lobby, define the hotel. The pedestrian street is decorated with colorful, abstracted, two-dimensional signs and murals drawn from Japanese sources both urban and rural, contemporary and historical, "to give an effect of rich clutter . . . combined in the tense manner of Pop Art" (fig. 309).[32]

Venturi's furnishings in the public spaces similarly favored an effect of density, variety, and richness, an aesthetic order founded on disparate relationships, as he articulated in a statement of March 1994: "The inspiration for this design approach derives from the particular layout of chairs as I happened to see them displayed in a showroom a long time ago. This arrangement consisted of rich juxtapositions of various chairs of Modern design—current and classic, original and conventional in their imagery—all of high quality. The effect was rich. . . . With furniture like this the spaces will look lively even at those times when they are sparsely populated."[33] In contrast to the vibrant furnishings

Figure 309
**Hotel Mielmonte Nikko Kirifuri,
Nikko, Japan, 1992–97**
"Village Street" lobby

Figure 310
**Hotel Mielmonte Nikko Kirifuri,
Nikko, Japan, 1992–97**
Family guest room

[29] Japanese Ministry of Posts and Telecommunications, Report, September 30, 1990, "9211: Nikko Kirifuri Program 3.1 Programs and Reports," VSB box 440 (VSBA archives).

[30] Robert Venturi, Project statement, "Draft Submission: An Architecture of Wellbeing for the Kirifuri Resort Project," July 16, 1992, "9211: Nikko Kirifuri Contracts 1.1 Pre-Contract Job Development," VSB box 440 (VSBA archives). The title was derived from a studio on "the architecture of wellbeing" given by Denise Scott Brown at Harvard in September 1989.

[31] Robert Venturi, Project statement draft, "Addendum to Nikko Kirifuri Project Statement," December 9, 1992, "Fax File," VSB box 442 (VSBA archives).

[32] Robert Venturi, Project statement, "Nikko Kirifuri Project: Schematic Design, General Architectural Approach," May 12, 1993, "Village Street," VSB box 441 (VSBA archives).

[33] Robert Venturi, Project statement, "Nikko Kirifuri Project: A General Approach to the Furnishings of the Public Rooms (Not the Bedrooms) in the Hotel of the Kirifuri Project," February 28, 1994; revised March 15, 1994, "Furnishings Nikko 12/95," VSB box 441 (VSBA archives).

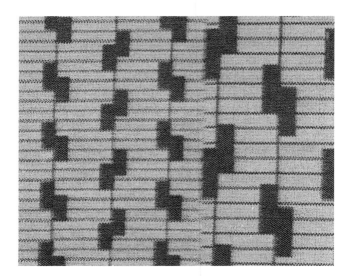

Figure 311

Hotel Mielmonte Nikko Kirifuri, Nikko, Japan, 1992–97

Guest-room carpet sample with pattern in two sizes. Nylon. Made by Lees Commercial Carpets, Greensboro, North Carolina

Collection of Venturi, Scott Brown and Associates, Inc.

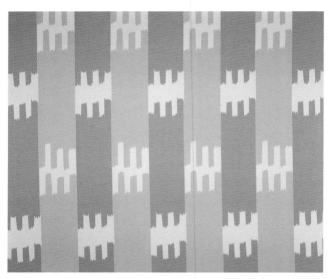

Figure 312

Hotel Mielmonte Nikko Kirifuri, Nikko, Japan, 1992–97

Guest-room drapery and bedspread fabric. Polyester. Made by DesignTex, New York

Collection of Venturi, Scott Brown and Associates, Inc.

Figure 313

Hotel Mielmonte Nikko Kirifuri, Nikko, Japan, 1992–97

Guest-room upholstery fabric. Polyester Made by DesignTex, New York

Collection of Venturi, Scott Brown and Associates, Inc.

of the public spaces, particularly the "Village Street" lobby, the guest rooms were intended to provide "a very soothing and welcoming environment" with a "quiet and cooler color scheme," as David Marohn, the project architect, explained in May 1996.[34] The rooms were filled with light-colored, warm, maple plywood furniture; blue-gray wallpaper; and warm tan carpeting (fig. 310). The predominantly blue patterns of the soft furnishings—carpets, wallpapers, draperies, bedspreads, and upholsteries—were adapted from traditional indigo textiles that Venturi and Scott Brown had seen in the book *Japanese Indigo Design: The Collection of Sadako Fukui* (Kyoto, 1991). Fukui lent textiles from her collection for design review; she noted that the small-scale pattern the firm had adapted for the carpets (fig. 311) was originally woven for kimonos, while the larger patterns used for the draperies, bedspreads, and wallpapers (fig. 312) had originally been created for futons.[35]

The references to traditional Japanese cultural images, patterns, and even colors, so central to Venturi and Scott Brown's idea of design at Nikko, sometimes ran afoul of Japanese custom. The indigo patterns, for example, were associated with rural poverty and frugality since they originally decorated tough cotton fabrics worn for durability in the countryside. These negative associations—particularly apparent to elderly clients—were noted but ultimately ignored by Knoll International Japan, responsible for producing the hotel furnishings.[36] The Ministry of Posts and Telecommunications warned that the grayish-blue tonality of the wallpapers might give a "strict and gloomy impression."[37] A green colorway suggested for the upholsteries, draperies, and bedspreads was vetoed because of its militaristic associations.[38] Finally, the ume (Japanese apricot) blossom pattern developed for the hotel upholsteries had to be replaced at the last minute when Knoll International Japan pointed out that the ume blossom was used traditionally in the crests of courtly and samurai families and that some Japanese, especially local elders, might feel uneasy about sitting on such a noble pattern (fig. 313).[39]

The design and production of the furniture and soft furnishings for Nikko was extremely complicated, as it involved both Japanese and American suppliers. For the public spaces, Venturi, Scott Brown and Associates mostly selected products from Knoll International Japan; however, custom furnishings included the leather sofa, loveseat, and chair that Venturi designed for the hotel lobby in the summer of 1995 (fig. 314) and the Swirl plywood chair (fig. 315) he designed for the "dry" restaurant in the spa in 1994–95 (fig. 316). The "Village Street" lobby was furnished with such modern design classics as Marcel Breuer's Wassily armchair and Laccio table of 1925 (which were also used in the elevator lobbies) as well as with the Toledo aluminum chairs and tables of 1986–88 by the Spanish designer Jorge Pensi. The "wet" restaurant in the spa featured steel-wire chairs of 1952 by the American Harry Bertoia (fig. 317) while the "fancy" restaurant in the hotel was furnished with Mies van der Rohe's Brno armchair of 1929–30. The guest-room furniture was adapted by Venturi from standard American hotel product lines and modified in Japan by Masahiro Saito, production designer for Knoll International Japan, who produced plywood samples with colorful laminates. Venturi acknowledged its "standard principles of design," and character of "quality . . . in the details . . . furniture that works as tranquil background and that stands up sturdily to use over time. . . . The light natural wood surfaces of this plywood furniture are contrasted with their edges whose exposed laminations contain layers of plastic laminate in contrasting colors—blue, black, and white . . . analogous to the blue and white hues of the wallpaper, textiles, and carpets of the guest rooms and promote thereby aesthetic harmony."[40] In addition to this custom furniture, which was made by Itoki, the guest rooms included Eero Saarinen's upholstered armchair developed from a design of 1940 with Charles Eames but upholstered in the firm's Japanese-inspired indigo pattern.

The Ministry of Posts and Telecommunications intended that Venturi, Scott Brown and Associates be responsible for

[34] David Marohn to Susumu Yamagiwa, May 16, 1996, "Chronological Fax File, April 4, 1995 to February 12, 1997," VSB box 442 (VSBA archives).

[35] Communicated by Masahiro Saito to Robert Venturi and Denise Scott Brown, September 12, 1995, "Furnishings Nikko 7/95," VSB box 441 (VSBA archives).

[36] Asuka Sasayama to David Marohn, April 28, 1995, "Chronological Fax File, April 4, 1995 to February 12, 1997," VSB box 442 (VSBA archives).

[37] Hiroshi Nomura to Robert Venturi, May 14, 1996, "Furnishings-Meeting Notes Manufacturers June 1996," VSB box 441 (VSBA archives).

[38] Venturi, Scott Brown and Associates, Meeting minutes, "Nikko Kirifuri Resort Meeting at VSBA, Philadelphia," June 17, 1995, "Chronological Fax File, April 4, 1995 to February 12, 1997," VSB box 442 (VSBA archives).

[39] Masahiro Saito to David Marohn, May 22, 1996, "Furnishings/Saito/ Akio, June 1996," VSB box 441 (VSBA archives).

[40] Robert Venturi, Project statement, "Nikko Kirifuri Project: A Proposal for the Design Concept of the Guest Room Furniture in the Hotel of the Nikko Kirifuri Project," August 23, 1996, "Furnishings Sept./Oct. 1996," VSB box 441 (VSBA archives).

Figure 314
**Hotel Mielmonte Nikko Kirifuri,
Nikko, Japan, 1992–97**
Lobby

Figure 315
Swirl Chair, 1994–95

For Hotel Mielmonte Nikko Kirifuri,
Nikko, Japan, 1992–97. Molded ply-
wood, birch veneer, and upholstery,
33 x 18½ x 22¼" (83.8 x 47 x 56.5 cm)
Made by Knoll International Japan,
Tokyo

Philadelphia Museum of Art. Gift
of the Japanese Postal Savings
Promotion Society

Figure 316
**Hotel Mielmonte Nikko Kirifuri,
Nikko, Japan, 1992–97**
Dry restaurant

Figure 317
**Hotel Mielmonte Nikko Kirifuri,
Nikko, Japan, 1992–97**
Wet restaurant

all the interior design work in the resort complex whether the furnishings were selected or specified from off-the-rack products, adapted by the firm from standard materials and furnishings, or custom designed. It was not common Japanese practice for the design firm to be involved in furniture layout (which was usually left up to the client),[41] but Venturi went to Nikko in March 1997 to make final layout adjustments because he had become concerned during a site meeting in November 1996 that the fancy restaurant was too empty looking and that the location of certain furnishings throughout the resort needed to be changed or refined.[42] The participation of Japanese and American manufacturers varied over the course of the project as a result of the worsening, hence more protectionist, Japanese economy and for practical considerations, such as fabricating the vinyl wallcovering, which after considerable research, could not be produced economically in the United States or meet the Japanese fire-rating requirements on schedule. The six Japanese-style tatami guest rooms were entirely furnished by Marunouchi Architects & Engineers, who obviously were qualified to do so. The simplest collaboration concerned the carpeting, which was produced by an American firm with a Japanese counterpart, Lees Commercial Carpets, a division of Mitsubishi Burlington. DesignTex, for whom Venturi and Scott Brown had designed a series of fabrics in 1990–91, produced the guest-room textiles from designs developed by the firm in the spring of 1995; the fabrics were shipped to Japan by fall 1996, where they were manufactured into bedspreads, draperies, and upholsteries.

Coordinating the entire process was Akio Izutsu, president of Knoll International Japan, who made a final site inspection in September 1996, writing to Venturi that he thought it finally a "tranquil building well matched with the natural environment." "The Nikko Kirifuri resort facilities," he continued, "are scheduled to be completed in three months. The time, seven years, that has passed away since your first visit to Japan in 1990, seems to me to be (both) long (and) short."[43]

The Design of Objects Interests Me at Least as Much as Architecture

As the principal designer for the decorative-arts projects that occupied the firm from about 1978 to 1993, Robert Venturi was inspired in his imagery and forms by the history of furniture, decorative arts, and architecture. Yet Venturi's understanding of historical process and style has never been fussily academic, but rather overridingly visual. Guided by the look of historic buildings or objects, Venturi took liberties with these visual sources and proved himself a modernist by abstracting and simplifying them. The character of Venturi's modernism was often inflected by his fondness for pop art: its cartoon graphics, flatness, large size, references to commercial art, and the "contradictions of scale and context" he championed in *Complexity and Contradiction.*[44] Venturi's designs were also modernist in their reliance on industrial processes and materials. He designed, with the support of Knoll's technical design and development team, for example, a lightweight, overstuffed sofa, with a structured shell like a car body made of fiberglass pieces, and cushions filled with a combination of dacron, foam, and down.

Venturi has been an unusually literate product designer. He typically defined his theoretical approach to every project either in his correspondence or with a formal project statement, usually written early in the design process and often in collaboration with Scott Brown. While these statements were sometimes used by the firm and clients alike for marketing purposes, they were an important, nonvisual means by which the architect expressed and communicated his ideas. These statements sometimes were revised during the course of a project, just as Venturi continued to modify and refine certain designs even after they were produced.

Most of the firm's commercial furniture and product designs were done for three principal clients: Knoll, Alessi, and Swid Powell. In addition, the firm designed a series of "lowboys" for Arc International, fabrics for DesignTex, and rugs for V'Soske, as well as several other products, including jewelry for Cleto Munari. Maurice Weintraub, the project

[41] Akio Izutsu to Robert Venturi, December 5, 1996, "Furnishings January 1997," VSB box 441 (VSBA archives).

[42] Venturi, Scott Brown and Associates, Meeting minutes, "Furnishing Review Meeting Notes," November 26, 1996, "Chronological Fax File, April 4, 1995 to February 12, 1997,"

VSB box 442; David Marohn to Masahiro Saito, December 17, 1996, "Chronological Fax File, April 4, 1995 to February 12, 1997," VSB box 442 (VSBA archives).

[43] Akio Izutsu to Robert Venturi, September 4, 1996, "Accent Ptg.," VSB box 441 (VSBA archives).

[44] Venturi, *Complexity and Contradiction*, p. 103.

manager for nearly all of the firm's decorative-arts work, explained that in the office, such product designs were viewed as serious "fun," and although Venturi found the projects very rewarding, he was generally too busy with architectural work "to spend the time he would [have liked] to on them."[45] Venturi said as much in a letter to Alberto Alessi in August 1989, complaining of his "frustration in not having the time to focus on the design of objects which interests me at least as much as architecture."[46]

Knoll

Design for Knoll was and remains the firm's most important decorative-arts project. It resulted in nine historically inspired chairs: Queen Anne, Chippendale, Sheraton, Hepplewhite, Empire, Biedermeier, Gothic Revival, Art Nouveau, Art Deco; three tables (two high tables, cabriole leg and urn, and one low table); one sofa; and two surface designs, Grandmother (fig. 318) and Tapestry. More sketches and hardline drawings by Venturi survive for the Knoll furniture than for any other decorative-arts project; these include numerous full-scale, front elevations of the chairs. In addition, there are production drawings, colored-paper collages on blue-line prints, and color separations. In an interview with Judith Weinraub of the *Washington Post* when the furniture was introduced in 1984, Venturi stated that he had initiated the project with Knoll in order to realize "very specific ideas about the chairs, table and sofa,"[47] and these remained essentially unchanged in later development. The earliest mention of the project is a proposal for the furniture series sent by Venturi to Nan Swid, a design director at Knoll, in October 1978: "I think it is time for an evolutionary change in Modern furniture," he wrote in a kind of manifesto.

> What I propose is chairs, tables, and bureaus that adapt a series of historical styles involving wit, variety, and industrial process, and consisting of a flat profile in a decorative shape in a frontal dimension. Like a building with a "false" facade, you see the "real" structure from the side and you attribute a symbolic rather than an authentic quality to the ornamental surface in front. For

Figure 318
Chippendale Chair for Knoll, 1978–84
Bent laminated wood and plastic laminate, 37⅜ x 25½ x 23¼" (94.9 x 64.8 x 59.1 cm)
Philadelphia Museum of Art. Gift of Collab: The Group for Modern and Contemporary Design at the Philadelphia Museum of Art

[45] Quoted in Kim Kopple, Maurine Dooley, and F. Cinne Morgan, "The Object Is . . . ," *Philadelphia Architect*, nos. 10–11 (December 1988/January 1989), p. 9.

[46] Robert Venturi to Alberto Alessi Anghini, August 9, 1989, "Alessi," VSB box 420 (VSBA archives).

[47] Quoted in Judith Weinraub, "Breaking Boundaries: Robert Venturi's Unorthodox Designs," *Washington Post*, May 24, 1984.

Figure 319
Alvar Aalto, Armchair, 1930–33

Laminated birch and birch plywood,
26 x 23 x 29" (66 x 58.5 x 73.7 cm)
Made for Artek Oy, Helsinki

Philadelphia Museum of Art
Purchased with funds contributed by
Collab: The Group for Modern
and Contemporary Design at the
Philadelphia Museum of Art in honor
of Cynthia W. Drayton, and the
Fiske Kimball Fund

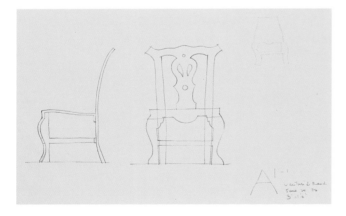

Figure 320
Chippendale Chair, 1976

Pencil and colored pencil on yellow
tracing paper, 18 x 28" (45.7 x 71.1 cm)
Robert Venturi. Dated June 24, 1976

Collection of Venturi, Scott Brown
and Associates, Inc.

this reason I consider this furniture to be a variety of Modern furniture, an evolution within the Modern movement. I think of this furniture as wood although other materials are possible; the exact methods of construction also must be developed. Color can be an important element in the design.[48]

What Venturi meant by "modern" furniture was defined elsewhere in his proposal as furniture that reflected industrial process, not historical style; was original, not traditional; serious, not witty; and spare, not ornamental. Venturi's solution was to reinvent modern furniture on his own terms by applying a historical facade to a modern, processed material—molded, laminated plywood—and leaving the laminate layers exposed in profile. Thus, he conformed, at least sideways, to the modernist tradition of openly expressing materials and process. As his precedent, Venturi claimed Alvar Aalto's use of plywood, as in the same way he had earlier paid homage to Aalto in some of his buildings (fig. 319). In Venturi and Scott Brown's architectural terms, the design and construction of the Knoll chairs was equivalent to the decoration of a modernist shed. The sofa, too, presented a traditional facade over a modern structure, in this case, overstuffed soft upholstery over a lightweight fiberglass shell (fig. 321).

Venturi was thinking about a historical series of chairs as early as June 1976, when he drew a number of models, including Queen Anne, Chippendale (fig. 320), and Arts and Crafts. Some of the drawings show careful study of published examples; the firm's library includes, for example, a well-thumbed edition of Wallace Nutting's *Furniture Treasury: (Mostly of American Origin)* originally published between 1928 and 1933, and frequently reprinted (figs. 322, 323). At the same time, Venturi and Scott Brown were deeply involved in furnishing the historic "Art Nouveau" house built in 1909 that they had purchased in Mount Airy in 1972. They used the traditional furniture Venturi inherited at his mother's death in 1975 (including her eighteenth-century-style ladder-back chairs) and bought other pieces, among them, some highly original Chinese-style chairs designed in 1914–15 by

[48] Mary Nomecos (for Robert Venturi) to Nan Swid, October 10, 1978, "Correspondence," VSB box 421; Robert Venturi, Project statement, Furniture for Knoll, October 10, 1978, "PR/Press Info.," VSB box 422 (VSBA archives).

Figure 321
Sofa for Knoll, 1978–84
Wood, fiberglass, polyurethane foam,
and upholstery, 33¾ x 87 x 43½"
(85.7 x 221 x 110.5 cm)

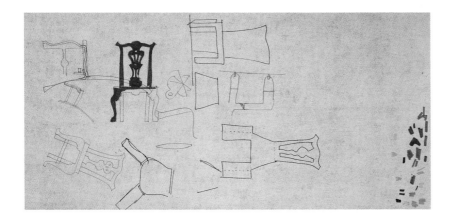

Figure 322
Chippendale Chair for Knoll, 1978–84
Study sketches. Pencil, ink, and
colored marker on diazo print,
24 x 12" (61 x 30.5 cm)
Collection of Venturi, Scott Brown
and Associates, Inc.

Figure 323
Page from Wallace Nutting,
Furniture Treasury: (Mostly of
American Origin), **1928 [New**
York, 1948]

Figure 324
Cabriole Leg Table for Knoll, 1978–84
Birch, laminated birch, and plastic laminate, 28½ x 48 x 48″ (72.4 x 121.9 x 121.9 cm)
Collection of Mr. and Mrs. Gary Kalpakjian

Figure 325
Biedermeier Chair for Knoll, 1978–84
Bent laminated wood and plastic laminate, 34½ x 23⅜ x 22¾″ (87.6 x 59.4 x 57.8 cm)
Collection of Venturi, Scott Brown and Associates, Inc.

Figure 326
Biedermeier Chair, Vienna, c. 1825–30
Walnut and walnut veneer with modern upholstery, 36¼ x 18½ x 16⅞″ (92 x 47 x 43 cm)
MAK – Austrian Museum for Applied Arts, Vienna

Figure 327
Art Nouveau Chair, from
1900 in Barcelona, **1967**

Figure 328
Art Nouveau Chair for Knoll,
1978–84

Bent laminated wood and plastic
laminate, 37⅜ x 23⅞ x 24⅜"
(94.9 x 58.1 x 61.9 cm)

Collection of Venturi, Scott Brown
and Associates, Inc.

Figure 329
Sheraton Chair
Photocopy from Venturi, Scott
Brown and Associates Archive
Collection of Venturi, Scott Brown
and Associates, Inc.

Figure 330
Sheraton Chair for Knoll, 1978–84
Bent laminated wood, plastic
laminate with applied pattern, and
upholstery, 33½ x 23⅛ x 23⅞"
(85.1 x 58.7 x 60.6 cm)
Philadelphia Museum of Art. Gift
of Collab: The Group for Modern
and Contemporary Design at
the Philadelphia Museum of Art

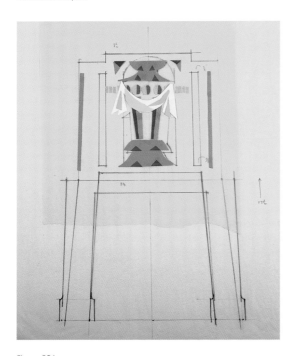

Figure 331
Sheraton Chair for Knoll, 1978–84
Elevation. Marker, cut paper, and tape
on yellow tracing paper, 42½ x 38¾"
(108 x 98.4 cm). Robert Venturi
Collection of Venturi, Scott Brown
and Associates, Inc.

the architect William Price for the Traymore Hotel in Atlantic City, New Jersey.

Venturi's interest in past styles of furniture corresponded to the most historicist phase of the firm's work. But as in their architecture, such as the house based on Mount Vernon designed for the Brants in 1978–79 (see fig. 119), Venturi accented the eccentricities of the original and then played with them. The cabriole table, for example, has appropriately curved, eighteenth-century-style cabriole legs, but they are entirely flat and set alternately in front and side elevation as if they cannot determine the direction in which they are headed (fig. 324). Venturi also took inspiration from examples that were themselves anomalies, such as his Biedermeier chair (fig. 325). For his version, Venturi appropriated the unusual, fancifully scrolled, back of a model like that in the Austrian Museum for Applied Arts in Vienna (fig. 326), but steamrolled it into a simpler, broader, more regular, and consequently, more comfortable form. The most literal borrowing in the Knoll series is the back of an odd, provincial Art Nouveau chair from a private collection that Venturi found illustrated in the book *1900 in Barcelona* (Barcelona, 1967) (fig. 327). What appealed to him was the flat, swooping asymmetrical curve of the cresting rail that Venturi finally set upon a broader, more solid, and again more comfortable back-panel frame (fig. 328). The approach in these designs was consistently graphic and linear, derived from Venturi's drawing board or the printed images he studied or from both (fig. 329); it sometimes defined surface patterns in which the spaces around or through the back panels could read as shapes in their own right. Venturi's process of translating carved ornament into flat, two-dimensional pattern could produce gentle parody, as in the square-back Sheraton chair. Its characteristic vase-shaped splat, narrow banisters, decorative swag, and Prince-of-Wales feathers compose a cartoon composition of elementary lines, shapes, and colors (figs. 330, 331). One might also argue that a stenciled pattern like this allowed for more decorative detail than would otherwise be economically viable today.

Summarizing their approach to the reuse of historical forms in a statement of May 1983, "Process and Symbol in the Design of Furniture for Knoll," Venturi and Scott Brown explained: "Our historical referents are intended to be used symbolically and representationally, not accurately. The historic representation is a picture of a style. It is not intended to fool you. The profile is abstracted and generalized to stress silhouette. Our aim is exemplification and representation, not reproduction."[49]

Venturi refined his design concept for the chairs, tables (figs. 332–34), and sofa in drawings throughout 1979 while Knoll fabricated prototypes of the Queen Anne model chair. The base of the urn table was made of four pairs of silhouettes, following the Grand's coffee-cup format, each pair linked at the bottom with a metal shoe. At the same time, the firm was involved with the design and construction of Knoll's new showroom in New York, which opened in November. After the contract between Knoll and the firm was signed for the furniture in April 1980, research and development continued through 1981. Prototypes of the Chippendale (fig. 335) and Empire chairs and cabriole and urn tables were made along with a model of the sofa. The seat and back pieces of the Queen Anne, Chippendale, and Empire chairs were molded with individual press blocks and jigsawed into their particular outlines afterward, so that they not only looked but also sat differently from each other. All of the other chairs were eventually made from a fourth press block because it was more cost-effective. Technical problems were studied during 1982, when it was felt that the chairs still needed to be revised from both a visual and comfort standpoint. These revisions included thickening the wood laminate layers where needed for structural integrity and tapering them elsewhere, and creating a simple but effective joint between the seat and the back.

Following these revisions, by March 1983, Knoll froze the design of all nine chairs (figs. 336–41), as well as the color scheme and pattern of appliqué on the Sheraton and Art Deco models, and the design of the three tables. At the

49 Robert Venturi and Denise Scott Brown, Project statement, "Process and Symbol in the Design of Furniture for Knoll," May 4, 1983, "PR/Press Info.," VSB box 422 (VSBA archives).

Figure 332
Urn Table for Knoll, 1978–84
Plan and elevation. Pencil on vellum, 21 x 30" (53.3 x 76.2 cm). Dated September 1979
Collection of Venturi, Scott Brown and Associates, Inc.

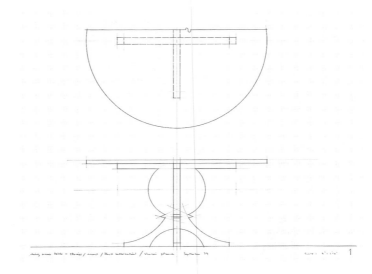

Figure 333
Urn Table for Knoll, 1978–84
Laminated wood and plastic laminate, 28½ x 60" (72.4 x 152.4 cm)

Figure 334
Low Table for Knoll, 1978–84
Elevations and plans. Pencil on vellum, 21 x 30" (53.3 x 76.2 cm) Dated September 1979
Collection of Venturi, Scott Brown and Associates, Inc.

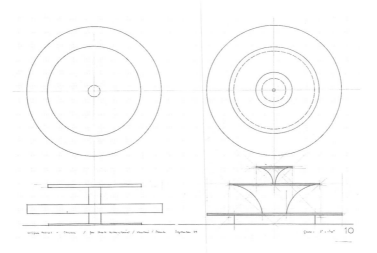

Figure 336
Chippendale Chair for Knoll, 1978–84

Bent laminated wood and plastic laminate, 37⅜ x 25½ x 23¼" (94.9 x 64.8 x 59.1 cm)

Philadelphia Museum of Art. Gift of Collab: The Group for Modern and Contemporary Design at the Philadelphia Museum of Art

Figure 337
Queen Anne Chair for Knoll, 1978–84

Bent laminated wood and painted plastic laminate, 38½ x 26¼ x 23½" (97.8 x 66.7 x 59.7 cm)

Collection of Venturi, Scott Brown and Associates, Inc.

Figure 338
**Hepplewhite Chair for Knoll,
1978–84**

Bent laminated wood, plastic laminate,
and upholstery, 35⅝ x 23 x 22¾"
(90.5 x 58.5 x 57.8 cm)

Collection of Venturi, Scott Brown
and Associates, Inc.

Figure 339
Empire Chair for Knoll, 1978–84

Bent laminated wood, plastic laminate,
and upholstery, 32½ x 24¼ x 23⅛"
(82.6 x 61.6 x 59.4 cm)

Collection of Venturi, Scott Brown
and Associates, Inc.

211

Figure 340
Gothic Revival Chair for Knoll, 1978–84

Bent laminated wood and painted plastic laminate, 40½ x 20¼ x 23" (102.9 x 51.4 x 58.5 cm)

Philadelphia Museum of Art
Gift of Marion Boulton Stroud

Figure 341
Art Deco Chair for Knoll, 1978–84

Bent laminated wood and plastic laminate with applied pattern, 32½ x 23⅜ x 21½" (82.6 x 60 x 54.6 cm)

Collection of Venturi, Scott Brown and Associates, Inc.

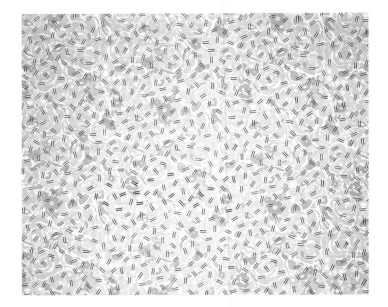

Figure 342
Grandmother Fabric for the Fabric Workshop, Philadelphia, 1981–84
Printed cotton

Philadelphia Museum of Art
Gift of Collab: The Group for Modern and Contemporary Design at the Philadelphia Museum of Art

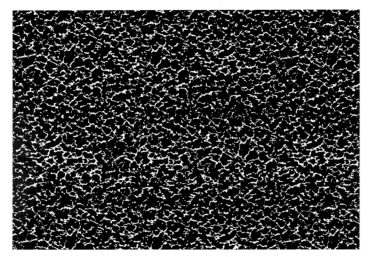

Figure 343
Notebook Fabric for the Fabric Workshop, Philadelphia, 1981–84
Printed cotton

Philadelphia Museum of Art
Gift of Collab: The Group for Modern and Contemporary Design at the Philadelphia Museum of Art

Figure 344
Tapestry Fabric for Knoll, 1978–84
Cotton

Collection of Venturi, Scott Brown and Associates, Inc.

same time, various surface finishes for the furniture were under trial, from plain maple veneers to solid-color and patterned laminates. These included a bold, multicolored abstract pattern derived from television static by Paola Navone, an Italian designer, who was conducting research on plastic laminates for the Milanese company Abet Laminati, and the Grandmother floral pattern newly created by Venturi with Scott Brown. Venturi's treatment of the finishes paralleled the firm's increasing commitment to patterned surfaces in their architecture, dating from the checkerboard addition to the Allen Memorial Art Museum at Oberlin College (1973–77), to the floral facade of the Best Products showroom in Langhorne, Pennsylvania (1973–79; see fig. 107), and the abstract composition of the Institute for Scientific Information in Philadelphia (1977–79; see fig. 108).

The Grandmother design was adapted from a flowered tablecloth that had belonged to an associate's grandmother, over which a pattern of black dashes inspired by the conventional lining of business envelopes was superimposed (fig. 342). The original concept for Grandmother, "contrasting a dark, geometric pattern on a sentimental floral one,"[50] as Venturi and Scott Brown put it, came to the designers in 1981 from the historic collections of the Paley Design Center at the Philadelphia College of Textiles (now Philadelphia University), where they saw fabrics with combined patterns and skillfully juxtaposed colors. Venturi later elaborated on its conception: "We wanted a pattern here that was explicitly pretty in its soft, curvy configurations and sweet combinations of colors, and represented as well something with nice associations, those of flowers. By juxtaposing the two patterns, the dashes and grandmother-tablecloth, we achieved design involving dramatic contrasts of scale, rhythm, color, and association, and one that is usable in many ways."[51] The Grandmother pattern, as well as a separate Notebook pattern, unrelated to Knoll (fig. 343) were developed with the firm largely during 1982–83 by the Fabric Workshop in Philadelphia, where prototypes were hand-printed on cotton sateen. Founded in 1977 by Marion

Boulton Stroud as a studio and laboratory of new design in fabric printing, the workshop was an experimental laboratory for the realization of the patterns. For Grandmother, matching the pale colors of the hand-printed pigments to the plastic laminate finish developed for the furniture, and superimposing the black dashes, proved to be particularly challenging exercises. Stroud offered Venturi the assistance of her technical staff of master printer, assistant printers, and construction technicians, as she had done for the workshop's earlier visiting artists and artists in residence, among them Scott Burton, Richard DeVore, Sam Gilliam, Robert Kushner, and Roy Lichtenstein. The Grandmother pattern was completed and copyrighted by Robert Venturi in 1983 and licensed to Knoll the following year.

Like Grandmother's dashes, the Notebook pattern was inspired by standard stationers' supplies, but according to Denise Scott Brown, who proposed the design, it evolved "to look more like the black-and-white blobs on the covers of composition notebooks that American children use in school."[52] Another textile pattern—the Tapestry fabric designed for the Knoll sofa (fig. 344)—was conceived from the first as a floral pattern like Grandmother. Like Grandmother also, the floral ground of Tapestry was overlaid with an abstract geometric pattern, of rotated white squares in purple ones. The pattern initially resembled the flowers designed in 1977 for the Best Products facade (fig. 345), a pattern itself inspired by the French commercial wallpaper "Matin" made by Paule Marrot that Venturi and Scott Brown were using in their Mount Airy bedroom. The Best Products pattern was studied by the firm for Knoll in 1982, when it was printed on fabric as a prototype, but never developed, by the Fabric Workshop (fig. 346).

In August 1983, Knoll recommended that the Queen Anne, Chippendale, Sheraton, Empire, and Art Deco chairs, the three tables, and the sofa be standard order items, while the Hepplewhite, Biedermeier, Gothic Revival, and Art Nouveau chairs were to be produced only on special order. The numerous possible veneers and Formica finishes

[50] Robert Venturi and Denise Scott Brown, "Architecture, Design, Fabric," in Marion Boulton Stroud, ed., *An Industrious Art: Innovation in Pattern & Print at the Fabric Workshop* (Philadelphia: The Fabric Workshop; New York: W. W. Norton & Company, 1991), p. 29.

[51] Robert Venturi, Project statement, "Grandmother Pattern," July 19, 1990, "Canon: Contract & Coordination," VSB box 425 (VSBA archives).

[52] Quoted in Venturi and Scott Brown, "Architecture, Design, Fabric," p. 29.

Figure 345
Showroom, Best Products Company, Langhorne, Pennsylvania, 1973–79

Composite facade study. Ink and gouache on paper, 6¼ x 28¼" (15.9 x 71.8 cm). Robert Venturi

Collection of Sydney and Frances Lewis

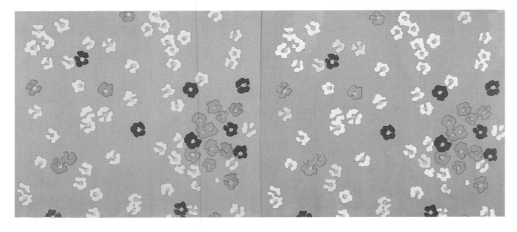

Figure 346
Flowers Fabric for the Fabric Workshop, Philadelphia, 1982

Prototype. Screen-printed cotton, 17½ x 54" (44.5 x 137.2 cm)

The Fabric Workshop and Museum, Philadelphia

were reduced to natural maple; dark gray stained maple; Grandmother pattern (Navone was eliminated, but was represented in the initial exhibition in hand-painted models); and plastic laminate in black, surf, yellow, and burgundy. This left about 150 permutations, including the fabric options for the seat cushions. Jeffrey Osborne, vice-president of design at Knoll, reiterated the necessity of providing a variety of surface treatments for the series despite the large financial commitment this would mean for Knoll: "Bob Venturi's design premise is one of pluralism," he wrote, "not one of an aesthetic ideal. . . . Bob Venturi has designed a collection with the intention of offering many varieties of the same basic product. To provide that variety a wide selection of finishes is essential. When describing his intentions for the opening exhibition of the collection, Bob used the analogy of a flower garden teeming with variety."[53]

When the furniture was finally introduced to the public in May 1984, after more than five years of development, the critical reception was positive, like that of Paul Goldberger, writing in the *New York Times*:

> They are not like the work of any other architect, even in this age when architects seem as prolific in the design of chairs as of buildings. Mr. Venturi's furniture, like his buildings, cannot be easily categorized, save to say it is generally startling on first viewing and far more comfortable after some extended exposure. It is willfully eccentric, like the architect's buildings, but its eccentricity has a deeply ingenuous quality. . . . It is the dining chairs that are the thing here, the most unusual element in the collection and the one by which the Venturi furniture will be known . . . these chairs have a great deal of panache. They also have a certain cartoonlike quality. They are, after all, plays on "real" chairs, affectionate puns done with great skill. They are bright and not a little brash, and like a good cartoon they have an unbeatable wit and self-assurance. What is most important is that they are, in the end, convincing as chairs.[54]

Despite their critical acclaim, the chairs were not a commercial success, reaching their peak of sales in 1985–86 and selling in diminishing numbers afterward. Targeted as residential "objects," the chairs, tables, and sofa never crossed over to Knoll's more lucrative corporate market. In 1990, when Knoll was purchased by Westinghouse, the furniture was discontinued, although the possibility of reintroducing the Queen Anne, Chippendale, and Sheraton models was discussed sporadically during 1990–91. Venturi looked forward to the reintroduction as an opportunity to resolve two design problems that he felt persisted in the chairs, namely that they were still "too heavy and thick in section, and they should be shrunk in size a little bit."[55] These revisions were finally made not in the United States but in Japan when the furniture was reintroduced by Knoll International Japan in 1991. In their thinner form, the chairs had the springiness and lightness that Venturi had intended. The reintroduction of the furniture in Japan was accompanied by an exhibition (and publication) of the firm's architecture and decorative arts, which opened in the Knoll Tokyo showroom and traveled to Kyoto, Kanazawa, and Sapporo in 1991.[56]

Arc International and the Triennale

During 1984, just after the Knoll furniture was inaugurated, Venturi designed the "bureaus" he had proposed but never realized for Knoll: a series of chests of drawers in historic styles for Arc International (figs. 347, 348, 350) and a William and Mary chest of drawers for the Triennale exhibition in Milan. Like the Knoll chairs, these pieces were inspired by historic forms and decoration, and were similarly simplified, abstracted, and cartooned. The chests were made of plywood and decorated with hand-painted patterns, much in the way the Paola Navone pattern had been applied to a limited group of furniture for the opening exhibition at Knoll. Michael Wommack, a decorative painter working in Philadelphia, painted the Navone chairs for Knoll freehand and the decorations for the Arc International chests using masking and stenciling techniques. The William and Mary chest was similarly hand-painted by craftsmen in Lissone, Italy, for Renzo Brugola, the furniture firm that produced the piece.

[53] Jeffrey Osborne to Trevor Eke, September 2, 1983, Untitled folder, VSB box 421 (VSBA archives).

[54] Paul Goldberger, "Design Notebook," *New York Times*, May 3, 1984.

[55] Robert Venturi to Andrew Cogan, July 3, 1989, "Correspondence," VSB box 425 (VSBA archives).

[56] Venturi, Scott Brown and Associates, *Architecture and Decorative Arts: Two Naifs in Japan* (Tokyo: Kajima Institute Publishing Co., 1991).

Figure 347
**Queen Anne Lowboy for Arc
International, 1984–89**

Elevation mock-up. Panchromatic
film on plywood, 30 x 25½"
(76.2 x 64.8 cm)

Collection of Venturi, Scott Brown
and Associates, Inc.

Figure 348
**Louis XV Lowboy for Arc
International, 1984–89**

Elevation mock-up. Panchromatic
film on plywood, 29¼ x 22½"
(74.3 x 57.2 cm)

Collection of Venturi, Scott Brown
and Associates, Inc.

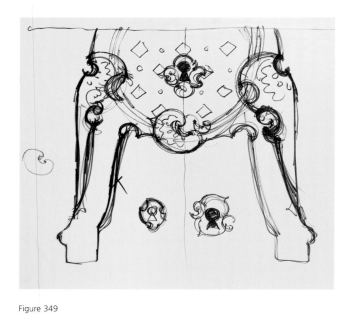

Figure 349
**Louis XV Lowboy for Arc
International, 1984–89**

Elevation. Black marker on
yellow tracing paper, 36 x 45"
(91.4 x 114.3 cm). Robert Venturi

Collection of Venturi, Scott Brown
and Associates, Inc.

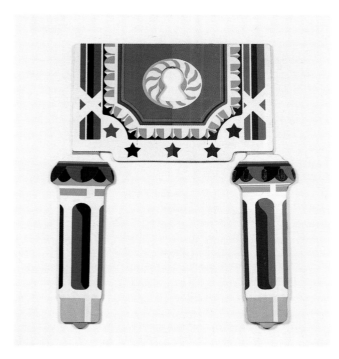

Figure 350
Louis XVI Lowboy for Arc International, 1984–89
Elevation mock-up. Panchromatic film on plywood, 30 x 25″ (76.2 x 63.5 cm)
Collection of Venturi, Scott Brown and Associates, Inc.

Between May 1984, when the contract was signed, and the following July, Venturi sent drawings of the Queen Anne, Louis XV, and Louis XVI "lowboys" to Louis Goodman, partner of Joseph Duke and Jennifer Johnson, who owned Arc International (fig. 349). The Queen Anne and Louis XVI models were first shown in prototype at Goodman's Gallery of Applied Arts when it opened in October of that year in New York. Goodman, trained as an architect at the University of Pennsylvania, where he studied with Venturi and Louis Kahn, exhibited Venturi's lowboys together with an eclectic collection of interior objects commissioned from such craftsmen and artists as Wendell Castle, Robert Graham, and Marisol. While the lowboys were offered for sale on special order at the gallery and by Arc International, Venturi continued to refine their designs in drawings of February 1985, August 1986, May 1987, and July–August 1988, the last in advance of the opening of Arc's new showroom in New York in 1989. For that occasion, Venturi described the chests as "practical and witty . . . they explicitly evoke stylistic associations when you see them but there is no doubt they are not literally Queen Anne, Louis XV or XVI. They do not replicate these styles, they *represent* them . . . like . . . signs or in the false fronts of stores in Western towns."[57]

Venturi was one of twenty-one international architects and designers invited to participate in an exhibition titled "Le Affinità Elettive," or "Elective Affinities," at the XVII International Triennale in Milan. The XVII Triennale, in fact, comprised several cycles of exhibitions held at the Palazzo dell'Arte between 1983 and 1986. "Le Affinità Elettive" opened the third cycle in February 1985. The twenty-one designers were paired with furniture craftsmen in Lissone who produced their work, focusing attention on the skilled makers of a then-depressed local industry. Each project was to include a marketable piece of furniture made in Lissone, displayed on a platform over the personal or historical sources—the "affinities"—that informed its design. Although Venturi initially had declined the invitation to participate in the Triennale because he had so little time to

[57] Robert Venturi, Project statement, Lowboys for Arc International, June 5, 1989, "Current Arc," VSB box 420 (VSBA archives).

Figure 351

William and Mary Bureau for XVII International Triennale, Milan, 1984

Elevation. Cut paper and pencil on paper, 30 x 40½" (76.2 x 102.9 cm)
Maurice E. Weintraub

Collection of Venturi, Scott Brown and Associates, Inc.

Figure 352

William and Mary Bureau for XVII International Triennale, Milan, 1984

Painted plywood, gilded brass, and plastic, 40½ x 30 x 20½" (102.9 x 76.2 x 52.1 cm). Made by Renzo Brugola, Lissone, Italy

Collection of Sydney and Frances Lewis

realize the project, by July 1984, drawings for the William and Mary bureau were completed (fig. 351). The following month Venturi traveled to Italy to discuss finishes.

In the exhibition, the bureau was installed on a platform supported by a stepped pyramid decorated with aphoristic statements. These aphorisms announced the designer's commitment to visual and historical complexities, for example: "Viva ornamental surface over articulated form, pattern over texture and sometimes pattern all over"; "Viva a symbolism of cultural relevance"; "Don't name styles, evolve them"; "If you use historical symbolism, look for the elemental"; and "Post-modern is Lost-modern." In a statement written for the exhibition catalogue, Venturi described the bureau as "a piece of furniture . . . that employs symbolism involving historical association—that of the style of William and Mary. . . . This kind of symbolism involves exaggerated scale, color, and pattern further to promote the sense of representation, to promote tension among the elements with the design and to accommodate the exaggerated stimuli our modern sensibilities are attuned to" (fig. 352).[58] With its oversized bun feet, drop handles, overhanging top, fictive signature, and surface pattern that alludes to figured veneer, Venturi parodied and abstracted elements of late-seventeenth- and early eighteenth-century American chests of drawers in the William and Mary style (fig. 353). The William and Mary bureau was one of the more commercially viable and functional designs at the Triennale, and appeared on the April 1985 cover of the design magazine *Domus*. By contrast, the designer Emilio Ambasz created a tiny house formed of vine-covered bookcases, and the architect John Hejduk designed a high chair complete with library steps and canopy.

Swid Powell

Work for Swid Powell, the firm's second most important decorative-arts client, was closely linked to that for Knoll, which had been purchased by Stephen Swid and Marshall Cogan in 1977 as a subsidiary of General Felt Industries. Its

Figure 353
Chest of Drawers, early eighteenth century
American. Maple, pine, and walnut, 34 x 38 x 21¾" (86.4 x 96.5 x 55.2 cm)
National Museum of American History, Division of Social History, Smithsonian Institution, Washington, D.C.

[58] Quoted in Carlo Guenzi, *Le affinità elettive: Ventuno progettisti ricercano le proprie affinità* (Milan: Electa, 1985), p. 157.

Figure 354
Grandmother Dinner Service for Swid Powell, 1982–84
Plate. Porcelain with overglaze transfer-printed decoration, diameter 12¼"
(31.1 cm)
Collection of Venturi, Scott Brown and Associates, Inc.

Figure 355
Notebook Dinner Service for Swid Powell, 1982–84
Plate. Porcelain with overglaze transfer-printed decoration, diameter 12¼"
(31.1 cm)
Collection of Venturi, Scott Brown and Associates, Inc.

principals were committed to positioning Knoll "at the leading edge of design."[59] Swid and Cogan invested in designs by a number of internationally known architects and designers, including Niels Diffrient, Charles Gwathmey and Robert Siegel, Richard Meier, Richard Sapper, and Venturi as well. They sought to create new lines of furniture with name recognition that would update the modern classics by Mies van der Rohe, Marcel Breuer, Eero Saarinen, and Harry Bertoia that the firm continued to sell.

Swid Powell was created in 1981 when Swid's wife Nan, a design director at Knoll, decided to establish a tablewares firm with Addie Powell, a Knoll sales vice-president. Swid and Powell based the idea for their firm on the same principle, commissioning well-known architects and designers to design domestic products. Venturi, Gwathmey and Siegel, and Meier overlapped with the Knoll program, while Swid and Powell added Michael Graves, Steven Holl, Arata Isozaki, Laurinda Speer, and Stanley Tigerman to their roster of designers. In late 1982, Swid and Powell presented their concept of bringing modern design to the conservative tabletop industry to Venturi and the other architects. They were asked to apply decorative patterns to standard tableware forms, and were given three months to produce sketches. Since the Grandmother and Notebook patterns were already developed, Swid Powell agreed to reuse them for the new line (figs. 354, 355). Buffet plates, luncheon plates, cups, saucers, and mugs were produced in both patterns. In addition, glass tumblers in three sizes were etched with the Grandmother pattern and separately with just the dashes from the Grandmother pattern, both on transparent grounds. Both designs were laid out as continuous allover patterns (figs. 356, 357). A draft agreement for this collaboration was sent to the firm in June 1983 but was not actually signed until June 1984, in revised format,[60] shortly before Swid Powell's inaugural collection of some fifty items was introduced at the New York Tabletop show, the nation's largest trade show for tableware buyers. In November 1984, the Swid Powell line was launched at retail, Swid Powell

[59] Stephen Swid and Marshall Cogan quoted in Eric Larrabee and Massimo Vignelli, *Knoll Design* (New York: Harry N. Abrams, 1981), p. 268.

[60] Venturi, Rauch and Scott Brown, Agreement with Swid Powell, June 28, 1984, "Swid Powell Contracts," VSB box 421 (VSBA archives).

Figure 356
Grandmother Glassware for Swid Powell, 1984

Glass with acid-etched decoration, height 5⅛" (13 cm), diameter 2¾" (7 cm); height 4" (10.2 cm), diameter 3" (7.6 cm)

Collection of Venturi, Scott Brown and Associates, Inc.

Figure 357
Dashes Glassware for Swid Powell, 1984

Glass with acid-etched decoration, height 5⅛" (13 cm), diameter 2¾" (7 cm); height 4" (10.2 cm), diameter 3½" (8.9 cm)

Collection of Venturi, Scott Brown and Associates, Inc.

Figure 358
**Village Tea and Coffee Service
for Swid Powell, 1985–86**

Porcelain with overglaze
transfer-printed decoration;
teapot, 4⅞ x 5⅝ x 10″
(12.4 x 14.3 x 25.4 cm);
coffeepot, 9¾ x 5 x 8¾″
(24.8 x 12.7 x 22.2 cm);
creamer, 3 x 4½ x 7¼″
(7.6 x 11.4 x 18.4 cm);
sugar, 4¼ x 4½ x 3⅝″
(10.8 x 11.4 x 9.2 cm)

Collection of Venturi, Scott Brown
and Associates, Inc.

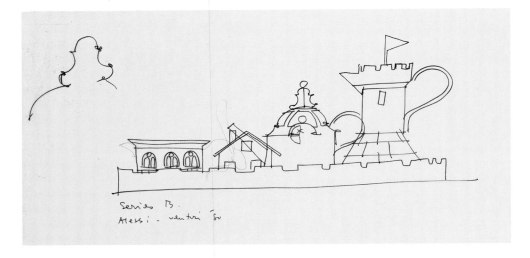

Figure 359
**Tea and Coffee Service for Alessi,
1980–83**

Elevation. Marker and pencil on
yellow tracing paper, 12 x 23½″
(30.5 x 59.7 cm). Robert Venturi
Signed and dated 1980

Collection of Venturi, Scott Brown
and Associates, Inc.

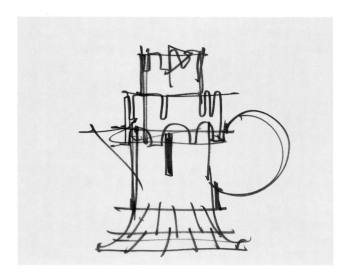

Figure 360
Tea and Coffee Service for Alessi, 1980–83

Coffeepot elevation. Marker on yellow tracing paper, 12 x 20" (30.5 x 50.8 cm). Robert Venturi

Collection of Venturi, Scott Brown and Associates, Inc.

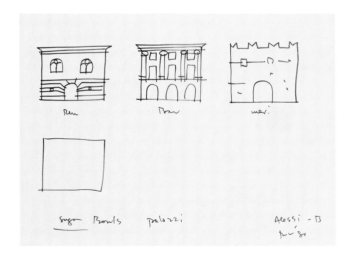

Figure 361
Tea and Coffee Service for Alessi, 1980–83

Sugar bowls. Marker on yellow tracing paper, 12 x 14½" (30.5 x 36.8 cm). Robert Venturi Signed and dated 1980

Collection of Venturi, Scott Brown and Associates, Inc.

having obtained a license from Venturi a month earlier to use the Grandmother and Notebook patterns on their products. The collection was an instant success, and the first production run was sold out by Christmas. Writing in *House & Garden*, Martin Filler included the Notebook series among those Swid Powell pieces "destined to become classics" and called Venturi's skill in handling complex pattern "more highly developed than any other member of his architectural generation."[61] Grandmother and Notebook, which were in production from 1984 to 1990, became the firm's best-sellers for Swid Powell.

In 1986, Venturi added new designs to the Swid Powell line: the four-piece Village tea and coffee service in porcelain (fig. 358) and a silver-plated candlestick. Venturi had developed the original ideas for these pieces in the summer of 1980 for Alessi, the Italian metalwares manufacturer. In August of that year, in response to an invitation from Alberto Alessi, Venturi sent proposals for two tea and coffee services, one with each piece inspired by a silver form from a different historical period, the other, an architectural service with each piece in the shape of a different building type (fig. 359). The latter included a crenellated tower (coffeepot, fig. 360), baroque church later described as the Pantheon (teapot), palace (creamer), and rustic house (sugar bowl, fig. 361). Alessi replied in September of that year that while both the miniature buildings proposal and what he called the "stylized traditional" service (which he went on to produce) were interesting, he felt that the former presented "insuperable technical difficulties" for industrialized production in metal.[62] But Venturi continued to pursue the idea. Casting in complex shapes and applying color decoration were less problematic and less expensive in porcelain, and shifting mediums, he sent revised drawings for the service to Swid Powell in November of 1985. Marc Hacker, Swid Powell's vice-president of design and development, accepted the proposal, and by April 1986, he was able to write that the first polychrome decorated samples of what was known as the Village tea set looked "splendid."[63] Venturi's process of

[61] Martin Filler, "The Architectural Tabletop," *House & Garden*, vol. 156 (October 1984), pp. 96, 98.

[62] Alberto Alessi Anghini to Robert Venturi, September 24, 1980, "Correspondence," VSB box 419 (VSBA archives).

[63] Marc Hacker to Maurice Weintraub, April 21, 1986, "SP Sugar and Cream," VSB box 424 (VSBA archives).

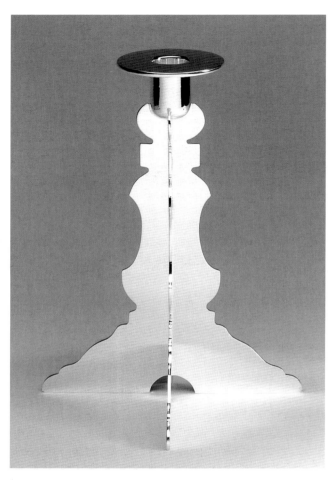

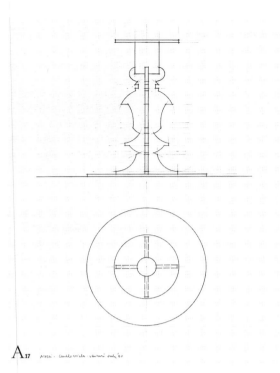

Figure 362
Candlestick for Swid Powell, 1985–86

Silver plate, 9 x 4 x 4"
(22.9 x 10.2 x 10.2 cm)
Made by Cleto Munari, Vicenza, Italy

Collection of Venturi, Scott Brown
and Associates, Inc.

Figure 363
Candlestick for Alessi, 1980

Elevation and plan. Pencil and
transfer letters on vellum, 24 x 18"
(61 x 45.7 cm). Robert Venturi
Signed and dated July 1980

Collection of Venturi, Scott Brown
and Associates, Inc.

Figure 364
Candlestick, 1712–13

Possibly made by Lewis Mettayer,
English. Silver, height 4⅜" (11.1 cm),
depth 2⅞" (7.3 cm)

Philadelphia Museum of Art
Gift of Samuel Rea

Figure 365
Nouveau Sugar Bowl and Creamer for Swid Powell, 1986

Prototypes. Porcelain with overglaze transfer-printed decoration; sugar bowl, height 5½" (14 cm), depth 5" (12.7 cm); creamer, 3⅞ x 4¼ x 6¾" (9.8 x 10.8 x 17.1 cm)

Collection of Venturi, Scott Brown and Associates, Inc.

Figure 366
Vegas Dinner Service for Swid Powell, 1986–87

Porcelain with overglaze transfer-printed decoration; buffet plate, diameter 12¼" (31.1 cm); dinner plate, diameter 11" (27.9 cm); cup, 2¼ x 3¼ x 4½" (5.7 x 8.3 x 11.4 cm); saucer, diameter 6¼" (15.9 cm)

Collection of Venturi, Scott Brown and Associates, Inc.

Figure 367
**Dashes Bedlinens for Swid Powell,
1988–90**

Printed cotton and polyester. Made by
Fieldcrest Cannon, Eden, North Carolina

abstracting and simplifying the design of these objects as well as his iconography drawn from the culture of architecture transformed them into intellectual objects. At the same time, the bright colors and sweet, childlike rendering made the set look almost toylike in its ingenuousness. Although the Village tea set was discontinued in 1988, Venturi sporadically revised the design until 1990, when the set was recolored in blue, but never marketed.

The silver-plated candlestick (fig. 362), also proposed for Alessi in 1980 (fig. 363), originated with an early eighteenth-century knopped baluster form (fig. 364), which Venturi abstracted and segmented into flat, two-dimensional silhouettes, like the coffee-cup signboard from Grand's restaurant (see fig. 303) and the base of the urn table for Knoll (see fig. 333). The candlestick remained in production between 1986 and 1989. Another group, also first conceived for Alessi in 1980, the Nouveau sugar bowl and creamer (fig. 365), was introduced with the Village tea set and candlestick in 1986 but never marketed. Based loosely on historical prototypes, the pieces proved difficult to realize as designed until the last version, in which the legs of both pieces were released from the underside of their spherical bodies to facilitate fabrication. In the fall of 1986, when these products were being retailed, Venturi had the idea for another dinnerware pattern, made of random dots imposed on a circle (fig. 366). The dots were variously referred to in the correspondence as "Dalmatian" and the "St. Valentine's Day Massacre," but were renamed "Vegas" when the pattern was introduced by Swid Powell in 1987. Like the Grandmother and Notebook services, Vegas was produced as a four-piece place setting, which included two plates, a cup, and a saucer.

Beginning in 1988 Venturi became involved with two new projects, a line of bed linens and towels for Fieldcrest Cannon, a sublicensee of Swid Powell, and a silver-plated serving set for Reed & Barton, another Swid Powell sublicensee. An agreement between Swid Powell and the firm was signed in December 1990, granting Swid Powell a license to develop and sublicense products to Fieldcrest

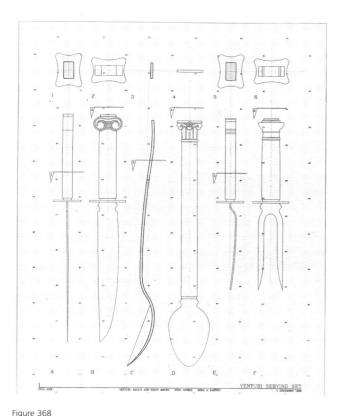

Figure 368
Carving Set and Serving Spoon for Swid Powell, 1988–89
Computer plot, 30 x 42" (76.2 x 108 cm). Maurice E. Weintraub
Dated December 4, 1989
Collection of Venturi, Scott Brown and Associates, Inc.

Figure 369
**Carving Set for Swid Powell,
1988–89**

Silver plate and stainless steel; knife,
length 13" (33 cm); fork, length 10"
(25.4 cm). Made by Reed & Barton,
Taunton, Massachusetts

Philadelphia Museum of Art. Gift of
Robert Venturi

Figure 370
**Flatware for Swid Powell,
1990–92**

Stainless steel; knife, length 9½"
(24.1 cm); fork, length 8" (20.3 cm);
salad fork, length 7" (17.8 cm);
teaspoon, length 6¼" (15.9 cm);
soup spoon, length 7" (17.8 cm)
Made by Reed & Barton, Taunton,
Massachusetts

Philadelphia Museum of Art. Gift of
Swid Powell and Reed & Barton

Cannon. Following Swid Powell's lead, Fieldcrest Cannon made sample bed linens in the Grandmother pattern and both linens and towels in the dashes from the Grandmother pattern (fig. 367). "The dashes design," Venturi wrote, "comes from our wanting a bold overall pattern that is abstract but . . . recalls and indeed derives from a conventional pattern . . . a lining in an envelope, but at a bigger scale. We like being abstract on one hand and adapting the conventional on the other."[64] Despite interest in the bed linens and towels at the October 1990 market when the two lines were introduced, only the bed linens were produced.

An agreement between Venturi and Swid Powell for the Reed & Barton serving set was signed in June 1989. The set, including carving knife, fork, and serving spoon, was designed with handles based on the architectural orders of columns. The forms of the Doric, Ionic, and Corinthian orders the firm had been developing for the serving pieces (fig. 368) were studied from published sources, among them Charles Normand's *Parallel Orders of Architecture: Greek, Roman and Italian*, which originally appeared in Paris in 1819. Venturi's desire to shape the handles with architecturally correct entasis (that is, a bulging outward between the base and capital of the column) caused a problem during the summer of 1989 because it would have been too expensive, placing the products outside Reed & Barton's target market. One suggested solution was to make the handles straight, but Venturi opposed this. He was able to retain the entasis with thicker, stronger handles that could support the tapering process. The carving set was introduced in the fall of 1989 (fig. 369), with the serving spoon following a year later. In January 1991, the set won the International Tabletop Award for design excellence.

During the summer of 1990, the firm was approached by Swid Powell / Reed & Barton about the possibility of designing a five-piece stainless-steel place setting that would be part of the same "ordered" program as the serving set (fig. 370). The firm agreed and Venturi reviewed prototypes early in 1991. A chief area of concern was shaping the inci-

[64] Robert Venturi, Project statement,
"Grandmother Pattern," July 19,
1990, "Canon: Contract &
Coordination," VSB box 425
(VSBA archives).

sions to give the clearest definition and greatest consistency of detail, and matching the columnar orders to the length of the cutlery, for example, using the more intricate Corinthian capital on the longer handle of the forks, and the Doric capital on the shorter handle of the spoons. During the winter of 1991–92, the design phase of the flatware, as well as that of a five-piece "hostess" set of serving pieces, was completed. Entasis was again an issue, and Reed & Barton tried to make the curve more dramatic, as Venturi had wished, by narrowing the handles as they approached the capitals and reducing the size of the capitals. But Reed & Barton finally decided that the capitals seemed undersized and the handles too long and drawn out, so they returned the capitals to the original size while emphasizing the curve of the entasis slightly. The flatware and hostess set were introduced in the fall of 1992.

In October 1991, Swid Powell proposed including the flatware in a large, integrated collection of tabletop products based on the capitals theme. The series would involve the firm in a major product-design program that was to range from porcelain dinnerware to candlesticks, picture frames, and desk accessories. Such a themed program was intended to make the products understandable and immediately accessible to the consumer. The firm responded a few weeks later with several "Adam"-style classical dinnerware patterns, decorated with anthemion and other motifs suitable to the capital program, which thereafter were progressively refined. Drawings were also produced in the months that followed for other capital pieces. While design continued into 1993, only one dinnerware pattern, Classical, was introduced that year, for which Venturi drew the floral anthemion in a sketchy fashion (fig. 371). Marc Hacker of Swid Powell explained in a pre-production letter that Venturi's drawings in black marker were so compelling that he wanted to use them to capture the "hand spirit" of the design.[65]

In 1993 Swid Powell introduced another dinnerware pattern, Flowers (fig. 372), which was completely unrelated to the capital program. The design was reminiscent of the

Figure 371
Classical Dinner Service for Swid Powell, 1991–93
Plate. Porcelain with overglaze transfer-printed decoration, diameter 12¼" (31.1 cm)
Collection of Venturi, Scott Brown and Associates, Inc.

Figure 372
Flowers Dinner Service for Swid Powell, 1993
Porcelain with overglaze transfer-printed decoration; buffet plate, diameter 12¼" (31.3 cm); cup 2¼ x 3¼ x 4½" (5.7 x 8.3 x 11.4 cm); saucer, diameter 6¼" (15.9 cm)
Philadelphia Museum of Art
Gift of Swid Powell

65 Marc Hacker to Robert Venturi and Denise Scott Brown, March 31, 1993, "Swid Powell Flowers & Classic," VSB box 423 (VSBA archives).

Figure 373

Borromini Dinner Service for Swid Powell, 1987

Prototype, plate. Porcelain with overglaze transfer-printed decoration, diameter 11″ (27.9 cm)

Collection of Venturi, Scott Brown and Associates, Inc.

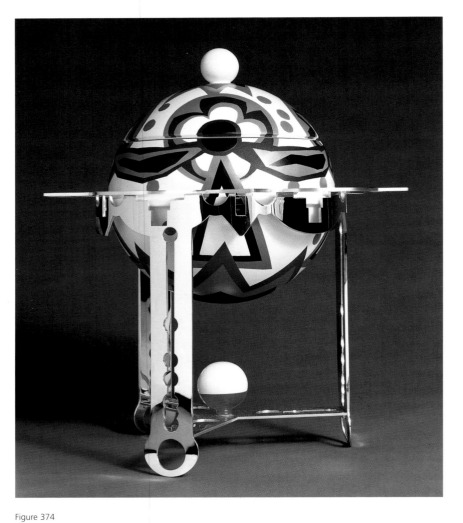

Figure 374

Centerpiece for Swid Powell, 1990–91

Prototype. Hand-painted porcelain and silver plate, height 14¾ (37.5 cm), depth 13″ (33 cm)

Collection of Venturi, Scott Brown and Associates, Inc.

large, loosely drawn flowers on the facade of the Best Products showroom (1973–79) and the prototype printed after it by the Fabric Workshop. Here, however, the flowers are hand drawn in black outline, the bright colors superimposed and deliberately misaligned with the outlines as if inexpertly applied by a child. Unlike the earlier allover patterns, both Flowers and Classical were conceived as border designs on white grounds, and were offered in sets that included two plates, soup bowl, and cup and saucer. While these patterns were going into production, Swid Powell asked Venturi to add a white canister set and storage jar, which could be decorated with the Flowers pattern or in other ways. Venturi had the idea of putting letters on the top and in free form down the face of the canisters, which were otherwise to be sparsely decorated with small "Laura Ashley flowers." Typical of Venturi's practice, therefore, the canister set combined a modern graphic idea, the letter forms, with a descriptive, "ordinary" one, the flowers.[66] The lettered canisters were introduced in Swid Powell's 1993 catalogue along with the two dinnerware patterns, and remained in production with Flowers for two seasons; Classical was produced until 1996. The firm's collaboration with Swid Powell and its intense activity of product design ended in 1993. Although only a handful of products were ever marketed by Swid Powell, about two dozen projects were designed and developed. In 1988 an internal project status report listed nineteen projects, of which only five were actually realized.[67] Among those suspended in various stages were Borromini dinnerwares decorated with an illusionistic coffering pattern inspired by the dome of Francesco Borromini's church of San Carlo alle Quattro Fontane in Rome (fig. 373); Dalmatian candlestick and salt-and-pepper shakers related to the Vegas series; and a centerpiece for a proposed collection of tabletop objects to be designed by different architects (fig. 374). Such lavish investment in research and development was not typical of the market; rather, it reflected both Swid Powell's admiration for its designers and those same designers' tendency to seek perfection in their work.

Alessi

The third of Venturi's most important decorative-arts clients was Alberto Alessi, head of a family-owned company that had manufactured high-quality metal housewares in Crusinallo, Italy, since the 1920s. When Alessi took over the company in 1979, he, like Knoll and Swid Powell, decided to emphasize the role of design. The architect Alessandro Mendini, who was also editor of the design magazine *Domus*, was brought in as consulting designer, and he, in turn, engaged a group of international architects and designers to sell their names as well as their distinctively styled products. In 1980 Venturi was invited to participate in Alessi's first "research" program, a series of eleven silver tea and coffee services by such architects as Mendini himself, Michael Graves, Hans Hollein, Charles Jencks, Richard Meier, Aldo Rossi, and Stanley Tigerman. Venturi's set was one of the few that could really be used (fig. 375). Jencks's service, for example, in the form of a picturesque classical ruin consisting of four columns, lacked handles and in some cases, spouts. When Venturi's proposal of a miniature "village" of traditional building types was judged too difficult to produce in metal (see above), Alessi moved ahead with Venturi's alternate idea, what Venturi described as a tea and coffee service based on "historical precedent abstracted and simplified" (fig. 376).[68] On sending the first drawings in August 1980, Venturi said that the designs also depended on surface pattern.[69] Each of the pieces was intended to be decorated differently according to its historical model, as well as colored. "You will see that I have kept the historical symbolism," Venturi wrote to Alessi and Mendini in March 1981, "but made the aesthetic involve a more disparate eclecticism with a more or less Rococo coffee pot, a Queen Anne tea pot, a Neo-Classical sugar bowl and Art Nouveau cream pitcher. The Piazza Campidoglio remains the tray."[70]

The coffeepot was based on a popular mid-eighteenth-century Continental silver form distinguished by its swirled fluting (fig. 378), which was realized in relief through repoussé and chasing. In a preparatory drawing, Venturi

66 Robert Venturi et al., Meeting notes, Swid Powell, [June 1993], "Swid Powell," VSB box 423 (VSBA archives).

67 Swid Powell/Venturi, Rauch and Scott Brown, Project status report, September 29, 1988, "Correspondence," VSB box 420 (VSBA archives).

68 Robert Venturi to Alessandro Mendini, August 5, 1980, "Correspondence," VSB box 420 (VSBA archives).

69 Ibid.

70 Robert Venturi to Alberto Alessi Anghini and Alessandro Mendini, March 31, 1981, "Correspondence," VSB box 419 (VSBA archives).

Figure 375

Tea and Coffee Service for Alessi,
1980–83

Silver with gilt decoration;
coffeepot, 8¾ x 7¾ x 6″ (22.2 x 19.7 x 15.2 cm);
teapot, 6 x 10¼ x 5¾″ (15.2 x 26 x 14.6 cm);
creamer, 3 x 4¾ x 4″ (7.6 x 12.1 x 10.2 cm);
sugar, height 5¼″ (13.3 cm), depth 3½″ (8.9 cm);
tray, width 16¾″ (42.5 cm), depth 14″ (35.6 cm)
Made in 1985

Philadelphia Museum of Art
Purchased with the Richardson Fund

Figure 376

**Tea and Coffee Service for Alessi,
1980–83**

Elevation of coffeepot and
teapot. Marker on yellow tracing
paper, 18 x 27" (45.7 x 68.6 cm)
Robert Venturi

Collection of Venturi, Scott Brown
and Associates, Inc.

Figure 377

**Tea and Coffee Service for Alessi,
1980–83**

Plan and elevation of coffeepot
Lithograph, 19½ x 27½"
(49.4 x 69.9 cm). Robert Venturi
Signed and dated March 1981

Collection of Venturi, Scott Brown
and Associates, Inc.

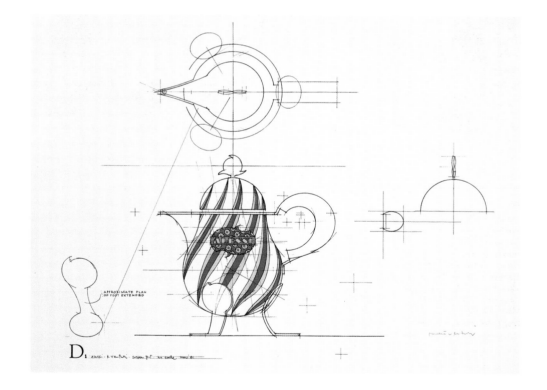

Figure 378
Chocolate Pot, 1783–84

Made by Joseph-Théodore Vancombert, French. Silver and wood, height 8⅛ (20.5 cm), depth 4⅞" (12.5 cm)

Musée des Arts Décoratifs, Bordeaux

Figure 379
Teapot, c. 1720

Made by Paul de Lamerie, English
Silver and wood, 4¼ x 8 x 4⅛"
(10.8 x 20.3 x 10.5 cm)

Philadelphia Museum of Art
Gift of Samuel Rea

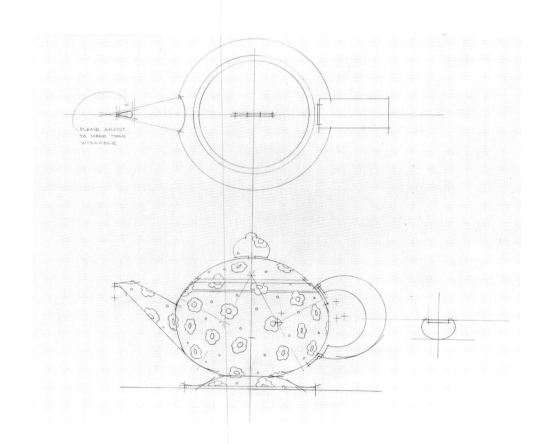

Figure 380
Tea and Coffee Service for Alessi, 1980–83

Plan and elevation of teapot
Pencil and transfer letters on vellum,
18 x 24" (45.7 x 61 cm)
Robert Venturi. Signed and dated
March 1981

Collection of Venturi, Scott Brown and Associates, Inc.

reduced the fluting in the original to a two-dimensional pattern in bright, modern colors, albeit with illusionistic shading (fig. 377). Venturi's drawing captures the sense of movement and love of display of the rococo prototype as well as the crispness and quality of its finish. Something is lost, however, in the translation from the design to the actual silver coffeepot, where owing to technical problems, the fluting had to be represented by engraved lines, and the color by gold plate. The teapot was based on the extremely simple, often undecorated, English forms current around the reign of Queen Anne (fig. 379), which Venturi modernized with an allover floral pattern. The flowers were finished in gold plate, the stems and leaves left as engraved lines (fig. 380). While Venturi's teapot decoration was entirely invented, the decoration of the sugar bowl and creamer was based on historical models, a neoclassical festoon for the sugar bowl, and a band of small, gold-plated rectangles in the style of the Wiener Werkstätte for the creamer. The decoration of the tray was drawn from the history of urban design rather than the decorative arts; it represents a simplified, bird's-eye view of the paving pattern designed by Michelangelo for the Piazza del Campidoglio in Rome (fig. 381). Venturi's tea and coffee service was exhibited with the other architects' work in the fall of 1983 in Milan at the former church of San Carpoforo and in New York at the Max Protetch gallery. In a brief statement written in September of that year, Venturi explained: "The basis of the design of the Alessi Collection is its symbolism and eclecticism—its aesthetic which promotes richness and ambiguity over unity and clarity—and its reliance on surface pattern as well as form."[71]

The tea and coffee set was the first of Venturi's products to be introduced into the retail market; it preceded the Knoll furniture by about nine months. Alessi hoped to make the services available in stainless steel for the general market, as well as in silver, but only the Campidoglio tray (fig. 382) was introduced in steel, in 1985. During 1984–85 the firm continued to provide revised drawings for a stainless-steel version of the tea and coffee set, in which Venturi stressed the

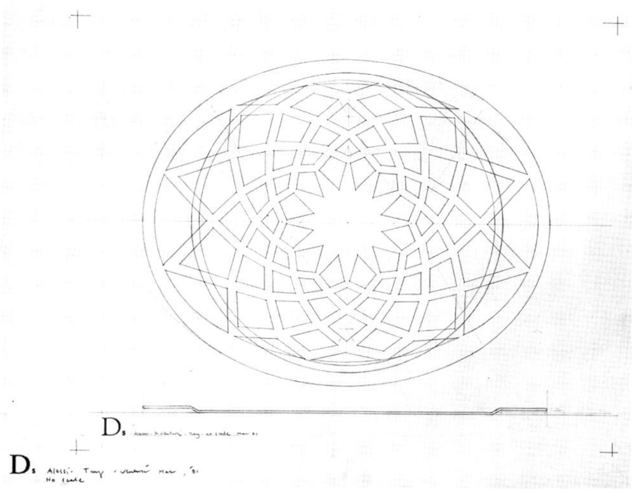

Figure 381
Campidoglio Tray for Alessi, 1980–83

Plan. Pencil, colored pencil, and transfer letters on vellum, 21 x 30" (53.3 x 76.2 cm). Robert Venturi Signed and dated March 1981

Collection of Venturi, Scott Brown and Associates, Inc.

Figure 382
Campidoglio Tray for Alessi, 1980–83

Silver with gilt decoration, width 16¾" (42.5 cm), depth 14" (35.6 cm) Made in 1985

Philadelphia Museum of Art Purchased with the Richardson Fund

[71] Robert Venturi, Project statement draft, Alessi tea and coffee service, September 2, 1983, "Correspondence," VSB box 419 (VSBA archives).

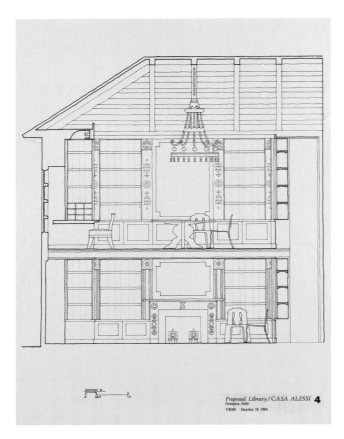

Figure 383
**Alberto Alessi Anghini House,
Omegna, Italy, 1984–88**

Section of library. Marker, pencil,
and acetate on yellow tracing paper,
41 x 30" (104.1 x 76.2 cm). Robert
Venturi. Dated October 19, 1984

Collection of Venturi, Scott Brown
and Associates, Inc.

importance of color in the overall design. The more brilliant color treatment Venturi envisioned exceeded the technological and economic limits of silver and stainless-steel finishes; he also considered trying to add color with plastic handles and in other plastic parts.

At the same time, Venturi was involved with an architectural project for Alessi designing the library for Alessi's house complex in Omegna, which Mendini had planned (fig. 383). In addition, in June 1985, Venturi designed for the library an Empire-style sofa that was also to be brilliantly colored.

In 1986, as part of a new clocks-and-watches series, Alessi asked Venturi to design a cuckoo clock, "a real architecture miniature," as Alessi wrote (fig. 384). "An historical and stylistical reference," he continued, "could be the swiss-chalet, very typical for the cuckoo clocks, however we don't want to reject the possibility of a house of completely different style."[72] The first prototype of the clock was ready early in 1987, when Venturi prepared a written statement about its design: "Everyone knows what cuckoo clocks are and almost everyone loves them. It was a nice challenge to take what is at once a familiar form and a vivid symbol and retain its lovable qualities and make it new and fresh at the same time. We did this by diminishing its usual hand-craft quality, and abstracting its form, increasing its scale, and intensifying its colors—to create a bold kind of image appropriate for our time."[73] The clock was introduced in 1988 (fig. 385), but Venturi continued to request color changes and offer suggestions about its workmanship.

Munari

In his ambition to market silver objects designed by internationally known architects and designers, Cleto Munari's approach was most similar to that of Swid Powell. Beginning in 1976 with a centerpiece by the Italian architect Carlo Scarpa, Munari's firm in Vicenza issued a series of designer silverwares in editions much more limited than a large manufacturer like Alberto Alessi would have been able

[72] Alberto Alessi Anghini, Proposal, "Robert Venturi, Design of a Cuckoo Clock," [1986], "Alessi Clock Sketches," VSB box 419 (VSBA archives).

[73] Robert Venturi, Project statement draft, March 1987, "Alessi Clock Correspondence," VSB box 419 (VSBA archives).

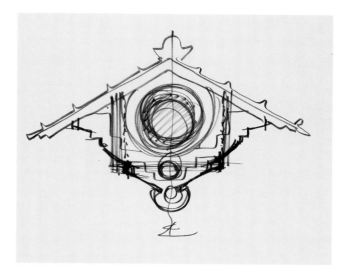

Figure 384
Cuckoo Clock for Alessi, 1986–88
Elevation. Marker on yellow tracing
paper, 20 x 24″ (50.8 x 61 cm)
Robert Venturi

Collection of Venturi, Scott Brown
and Associates, Inc.

Figure 385
Cuckoo Clock for Alessi, 1986–88
Lacquered wood, 11⅛ x 16 x 4⅝″
(28.3 x 40.6 x 11.7 cm)

Collection of Venturi, Scott Brown
and Associates, Inc.

to produce economically. In March 1984, Munari invited
Venturi to design either domestic objects in silver, or jewelry,
"something like a ring, earrings, bracelet or a pendant."[74]
Venturi replied that in principle he would be delighted, but
that he was "overwhelmed with architectural obligations"
and hoped that Munari would allow him several months to
create something.[75] It was not, however, until June 1985 that
Venturi sent Munari sketches for a pendant or earrings, or
both, in the form of a building that resembled Palladio's
Villa Rotonda with a pearl as the dome. Marc Hacker of
Swid Powell actually delivered the drawings to Munari, since
Munari was then involved in having Venturi's silver-plated
candlestick made for Swid Powell. The following month
Venturi sent additional sketches for jewelry that continued
his architectural theme, including a ring and earrings with
pendant miniatures of the Tower of Pisa and an obelisk
(fig. 386). Further sketches of rings and necklaces were sent
in April 1986. In the fall of 1986 Venturi saw the finished
jewelry, which included two necklaces, three rings, and three
earrings, among them the Villa Rotonda model (fig. 387).
These were exhibited in Vienna at the Belvedere gallery in
November of that year and elsewhere in Europe, the
United States, Canada, and the Far East through 1987.

V'Soske

The firm's decorative-arts commissions continued into the
early 1990s, when Robert Venturi and Denise Scott Brown
created three rugs for the V'Soske company and five fabric
patterns for DesignTex in New York. All of these textile
designs were influenced by the trip Venturi and Scott
Brown made to Japan and Korea in 1990, their first to Asia.
The V'Soske and DesignTex projects were initiated by
Steven W. Kroeter, whose New York firm, Archetype Associates, assisted Venturi and Scott Brown in marketing their
product designs from 1989.

V'Soske, a manufacturer of high-quality rugs since 1924,
had a long tradition of collaborating with architects. It had
produced rugs designed by Frank Lloyd Wright and Stuart

[74] Cleto Munari to Robert Venturi,
March 5, 1984, "Munari," VSB
box 424 (VSBA archives).

[75] Robert Venturi to Cleto Munari,
April 17, 1984, "Munari," VSB
box 424 (VSBA archives).

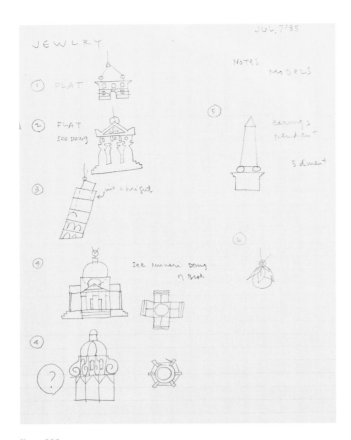

Figure 386
Jewelry for Cleto Munari, 1984–86
Study sketches. Pencil on yellow-lined paper, 8½ x 11″ (21.6 x 27.9 cm)
Robert Venturi. Dated July 7, 1985
Collection of Venturi, Scott Brown and Associates, Inc.

Figure 387
Jewelry for Cleto Munari, 1984–86
Villa Rotonda earring
Gold and agate, 1⅛ x ⅞ x ⅞″ (2.9 x 2.22 x 2.22 cm)

Davis in the 1930s and 1940s, and from 1978 developed a new program of designer collaborations that eventually included architects Michael Graves, Charles Gwathmey, Steven Holl, Billie Tsien, and Tod Williams. In late 1989, V'Soske's design and marketing directors, Roger McDonald and Ellen Hertzmark, invited Venturi and Scott Brown to join that program. Throughout 1990, Venturi and Scott Brown created about ten rug designs of which three—later named "Kimono," "Dots," and "Spots"—were actually developed and produced. Kimono (fig. 388), with its pattern of bright colors, illusion of folded cloth, and stylized flowers that seemed to float throughout the piece, was the first to be approved by V'Soske in July 1990 and was targeted for high-end residential or corporate use. By December 1990, the first woven samples of the rugs were being developed from the drawings submitted by the architects, although it was not until February 1991 that all the drawings were recorded as being approved. From April 1991, when the contract was signed, through 1992, samples were modified and reworked: an important issue for Dots was resolving the border on one side with the design at the other three edges (fig. 389). For the introduction of the rugs in the summer of 1993, Venturi wrote a formal project statement: "Symbolically these designs derive from our fascination with aspects of Japanese art—a fascination acknowledging the long tradition in which inspired Western artists interpret and adapt Japanese art and architecture—although we admittedly are focusing on a humble manifestation of Japanese art."[76] Dots is, in fact, a graphic translation of a stitching pattern that typically strengthened and decorated traditional Japanese peasant clothing. An example of this pattern can be found in a late-nineteenth-century cotton vest in the Japan Folkcrafts Museum in Tokyo, which is ornamented with the same design of diamonds filled with *sashiko*, or running stitches, and a border pattern at the edges. The rug design, however, is larger in scale than its source, and transposed in its construction, texture, and use.

[76] Robert Venturi, Project statement, "Some Thoughts on the Design of Our Rugs for V'Soske," July 12, 1993, "V'Soske," VSB box 423 (VSBA archives).

Figure 388
**Kimono Rug for V'Soske,
1989–93**
Silk and wool, 84 x 90"
(213.4 x 228.6 cm)
V'Soske, New York

Figure 389
Dots Rug for V'Soske, 1989–93
Wool, 66 x 90" (167.6 x 228.6 cm)
V'Soske, New York

Figure 390
**Dots Fabric for DesignTex,
1989–91**
Cotton, width 54" (137.2 cm)
Philadelphia Museum of Art
Gift of Francine and
Stuart Gerstein

DesignTex

Venturi and Scott Brown created five fabrics in similarly Japanese-inspired designs for DesignTex in 1990–91: Dots, Gingham Floral, Raku, Staccato, and Yukata (figs. 390–92). These fabrics were part of DesignTex's architect-designed Portfolio collection, the other participating architects being Richard Meier and Aldo Rossi. Founded in New York by Ralph Saltzman and Harry Paley, DesignTex had produced and marketed upholstery and drapery fabrics for office and commercial use since 1961. After Steelcase acquired the firm in 1988, Saltzman, DesignTex president, and Susan Lyons, the firm's new design director, concentrated on product development. The following year, they introduced a custom-product design studio and the idea for the architects' collection. Venturi and Scott Brown were approached by DesignTex for the architects' collection in December 1989, and the first ideas for the fabrics were already sketched by Venturi in April 1990: a version of Gingham Floral annotated as "geometric and soft"[77] (fig. 393), and Staccato, a pattern of stripes with a dot-screen overlay, as "hard and soft" (fig. 394).[78] These designs followed Venturi and Scott Brown's familiar preference for contrasting and juxtaposing patterns. In May 1990, nine concepts, including Gingham Floral and Staccato as well as versions of Yukata, Dots, and Raku, were approved for development. During the summer of that year, various design problems were studied: the scale of the Yukata pattern did not, for example, fit gracefully into a standard repeat size, while the composition of Gingham Floral required a greater proportion of flowers to checkerboard, in order for the flowers to read more distinctly as clumps rather than as an allover pattern. When the contract between the firm and DesignTex was signed in December 1990, it stipulated that the collection would consist of some three to five designs "inspired by traditional patterns and themes such as those found in Oriental woodcuts and kimonos."[79] Some of the designs abstracted and cartooned their Japanese sources, while others translated them more literally. In Dots, for example,

[77] Robert Venturi, Annotated sketch number one for DesignTex, April 22, [1990], "Sketches," VSB box 423 (VSBA archives).

[78] Robert Venturi, Annotated sketch number three for DesignTex, April 22, [1990], "Sketches," VSB box 423 (VSBA archives).

[79] License agreement between Venturi, Scott Brown Design, L.P. and DesignTex Fabrics Inc., November 26, 1990, "DesignTex Correspondence and Contract," VSB box 418 (VSBA archives).

Figure 391
**Yukata Fabric for DesignTex,
1989–91**
Cotton, width 54″ (137.2 cm)
Collection of Venturi, Scott Brown
and Associates, Inc.

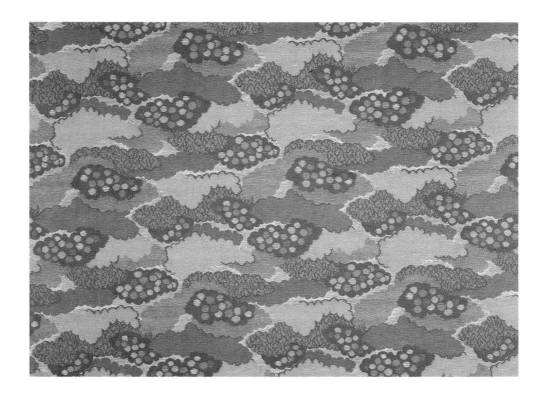

Figure 392
**Gingham Floral Fabric for
DesignTex, 1989–91**
Cotton, width 54″ (137.2 cm)
Philadelphia Museum of Art
Gift of DesignTex

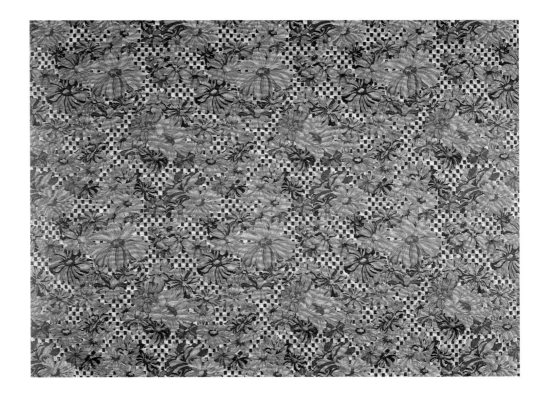

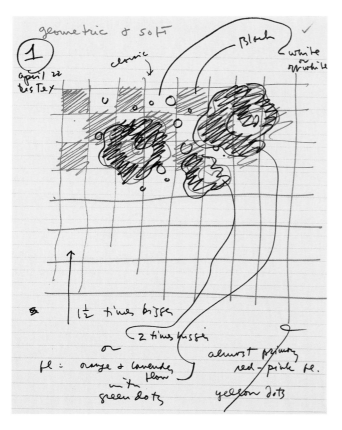

Figure 393
**Gingham Floral Fabric for
DesignTex, 1989–91**

Study sketch. Marker and
colored marker on yellow lined
paper, 11 x 8½" (27.9 x 21.6 cm)
Robert Venturi. Dated April 22 [1990]

Collection of Venturi, Scott Brown
and Associates, Inc.

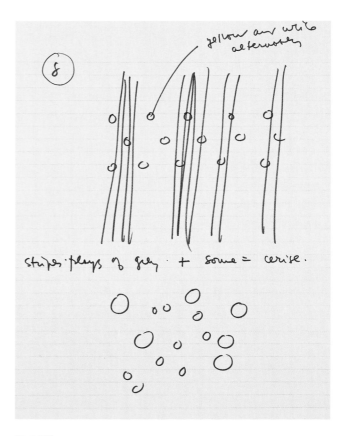

Figure 394
**Staccato Fabric for DesignTex,
1989–91**

Study sketch. Marker on yellow lined
paper, 11 x 8½" (27.9 x 21.6 cm)
Robert Venturi

Collection of Venturi, Scott Brown
and Associates, Inc.

Venturi and Scott Brown adapted a traditional obi pattern, the *janome*, or snake's-eye design, but altered it by adding an extra ring of color around the eye and enlarging the scale.

Samples of the fabrics were developed in the fall and winter of 1990, while other designs continued to be revised, including Staccato, for which the relationship of the dots to the edges of the stripes was still at issue in January 1991. The fabrics were introduced by DesignTex in March 1991 at the Pacific Design Center during WestWeek, Los Angeles's annual contract furnishings market. As did Meier and Rossi, Venturi and Scott Brown designed the exhibition of their fabrics at WestWeek, which they centered around an oversized, overstuffed, chair cutout wrapped in Gingham Floral. *Architectural Record* reported that DesignTex's Portfolio collection "stole the show" at WestWeek,[80] while *Interior Design*—which featured the Venturi and Scott Brown installation on the cover of its March 1991 issue—commented on the richness of the Venturi/Scott Brown fabrics and also their combination of contrasting elements, such as the small-scale black-and-white checkerboard grid interwoven with colorful flowers in Gingham Floral. "We like the juxtaposition of things to promote a certain dissonance," Denise Scott Brown said in the same article, " . . . [and] combining scales and patterns as an architectural expression."[81] Following WestWeek, the various colorways were selected and the fabrics were put into production during the fall of 1991. Raku proved to be the most successful of the five fabrics. It represented in the first quarter of 1992 over forty percent of the fabrics' sales, and remained longest in production, until December 1997.

Notwithstanding such success, by the mid-1990s, the economy and climate for architect-designed signature products had changed, while manufacturers also sought different creative talent, often from the field of industrial design. At the same time, fashion designers were developing their own "home" collections. Swid Powell, for example, was principally occupied in creating table- and giftwares for Calvin Klein. DesignTex's most important collaboration was with the architect/environmentalist William McDonough, who in 1995 launched a line of environmentally responsible fabrics. A general slowdown in the furniture industry during the 1990s caused Knoll to retreat from the risky, expensive design projects they had sponsored so heavily in the 1980s; they promoted instead their more conservative—and more profitable—office systems for which the firm had been traditionally known. Product development at Knoll, like that of other firms, became more market driven in the 1990s, an exception being the furniture Knoll commissioned from the architect-sculptor Maya Lin in 1998 to celebrate Knoll's sixtieth anniversary. Finally, as Venturi, Scott Brown and Associates took on simultaneously in the 1990s a number of large-scale architectural projects—from Nikko and Toulouse to university buildings and academic planning studies throughout the United States—Venturi's chronic complaint of lack of time for product design became a literal reality.

[80] Karen D. Stein, "Meier, Rossi, Scott Brown and Venturi Add Fabrics to Their Futures," *Architectural Record*, vol. 179 (May 1991), p. 21.

[81] Quoted in Peter Blake, "3 Directions in 3 Dimensions: Rossi, Meier and Venturi & Scott Brown, Design an Environment for WestWeek," *Interior Design*, vol. 62 (March 1991), p. 125.

CHRONOLOGY

Diane L. Minnite

Robert Venturi, 1926

Denise Lakofski with her parents, Shim and Phyllis Lakofski, in 'Nkana, Northern Rhodesia, 1931

1925

June 25 Robert Charles Venturi is born in Philadelphia, the first and only child of Vanna (née Luisi) and Robert Venturi. Robert, Sr., born in Atessa, Italy, and owner of a produce business, had dreams of becoming an architect. Vanna, the daughter of Italian immigrants, was the dominant parent, "whose sound but unorthodox positions," Venturi would later recall, "worked to prepare me to feel almost all right as an outsider."[1]

1930

Vanna, a non-practicing Catholic like her husband, joins the Society of Friends and enrolls Robert in Lansdowne Friends School in order to expose him to the Quaker ideals that reflect her own concerns with pacifism and social justice.

1931

October 3 Denise Lakofski is born in 'Nkana (now Kitwe), Northern Rhodesia (now Zambia), the first child of Shim and Phyllis (née Hepker) Lakofski. Two sisters and a brother would be born into the family. Shim, the descendant of Lithuanian Jews, is a young businessman who owns a trading store. Phyllis, whose Jewish family is Latvian, is described as a free spirit, a lover of the outdoors who, as a teenager, spent five years working in and around the small mines operated by her father before studying architecture in Johannesburg, South Africa.

1933

The Lakofski family moves to Johannesburg, where, at the insistence of Phyllis, they build an International Style house of glass and concrete designed by her classmates the South African architectural partners Norman Hanson, Tomkin and Finkelstein.

1935

Robert enters Episcopal Academy in Merion in suburban Philadelphia.

1937

Denise attends Kingsmead College, a liberal-minded primary and secondary school for girls.

1944

Venturi enters Princeton University, where his instructors include Donald Drew Egbert, a social and art historian, and Jean Labatut,

[1] Robert Venturi, "Robert Venturi's Response at the Pritzker Prize Award Ceremony at the Palacio de Iturbide, Mexico City, May 16, 1991," in *Iconography and Electronics upon a Generic Architecture: A View from the Drafting Room* (Cambridge and London: The MIT Press, 1996), p. 99.

the Beaux-Arts–trained chair of graduate studies, from whose combined direction he evolves an understanding of modernism in the context of history.

1947

Venturi is elected to Phi Beta Kappa and graduates *summa cum laude* with a bachelor's degree in architecture. He spends the summer as the sole draftsman for Robert Montgomery Brown, a Philadelphia architect who works in association with George Howe. In the fall he enters the master's program at Princeton's Graduate School of Architecture.

1948

Lakofski enrolls in the liberal arts program at the University of the Witwatersrand, Johannesburg, where her mother spent two years studying architecture. In her second year she switches to the architecture program, which stresses technical proficiency over recent architectural history or theory, but where a respected tradition of early modern architecture prevails and social questions in architecture and politics are of intense concern.

Venturi travels to Europe for the first time, touring sites around London and Paris, as well as numerous locations throughout Italy.

1949

Lakofski meets architect Robert Scott Brown, a fellow architecture student at Witwatersrand.

1950

Venturi submits his M.F.A. thesis to Princeton titled "Context in Architectural Composition," a design for a new chapel for the Episcopal Academy. Among the critics on his thesis jury are Louis Kahn and George Howe.

Upon receiving his degree, Venturi enters the office of Oscar Stonorov, a German-born architect practicing socially responsible architecture in Philadelphia. Venturi contributes to the designs of the Cherokee Apartments in Chestnut Hill, Philadelphia, as well as to the design of an exhibition on the work of Frank Lloyd Wright, which was organized by Stonorov and shown in Gimbel's department store in Philadelphia and the Strozzi Palace in Florence.

1951

Venturi is employed for the next two years in the office of Eero Saarinen in Bloomfield Hills, Michigan, where his colleagues

Robert Venturi around the time of his graduation from Princeton University, 1947

Denise Lakofski at age eighteen, 1949

Robert Venturi and William Shellman, a young Princeton faculty member, at Chartres Cathedral in July, 1948

Denise Lakofski in Spain, c.1953

Robert Venturi, his parents, Robert and Vanna Venturi (far left and far right), and a family friend on the porch of the Venturi home in Rosemont, Pennsylvania, c.1953

Robert Venturi at the Acropolis, 1955

include future and fellow Pritzker laureate Kevin Roche. While in Saarinen's office, Venturi works on the design of the Milwaukee War Memorial Auditorium (1948–64) and the General Motors Technical Center in Warren, Michigan (1946–57).

1952

In her fourth, or practicum, year at the University of the Witwatersrand, Lakofski travels to London and accepts a job as a draftsperson in the office of Frederick Gibberd, a modernist architect, author, and former principal at the Architectural Association (AA), whose interests include town planning and public housing. Lakofski takes the entrance exam of the AA and is subsequently admitted—she never returns to Witwatersrand to complete her degree. At the AA she admires the early work of the New Brutalist architects, attends lectures by John Summerson, and has as a studio critic Arthur Korn, a German refugee, who helps guide her professional formation in architecture and encourages her to teach.

1953

Venturi's first publication, an essay deriving from his M.F.A. thesis, appears in *Architectural Review* (May).

1954

Venturi wins the Rome Prize Fellowship to the American Academy in Rome. That spring he teaches at the University of Pennsylvania as Louis Kahn's assistant and also works sporadically in Kahn's office. In October he leaves for Rome for a two-year stay, traveling while there throughout Italy and to Egypt, Turkey, Greece, Austria, and Scandinavia.

For her thesis project at the AA, Lakofski and her partner Brian Smith design a residential neighborhood for a Welsh mining village, complete with housing, schools, recreational spaces, and health facilities. Lakofski receives her diploma from the AA.

Robert Scott Brown arrives in London, and he and Lakofski enroll in a one-year course at the AA that focuses on tropical architecture.

1955

July 21 Lakofski and Robert Scott Brown marry in London. After a honeymoon spent exploring Yugoslavia, the Scott Browns embark on three years of work and travel in Europe, England, and South Africa, where Denise gathers considerable experience, working as a draftsperson and designer in the offices of Ernö

Goldfinger and Dennis Clarke-Hall in London, then with Giuseppe Vaccaro in Rome. While in Europe the Scott Browns attend the CIAM summer school in Venice, run by Franco Albini, Ignazio Gardella, and Gino and Nani Valle. Back in Johannesburg in 1957, Denise works in the firm of Cowen, deBruyn and Cook.

1956

Upon his return from Rome, Venturi goes back to work for Louis Kahn for a period of seven months, contributing drawings for a number of projects, including the Research Institute for Advanced Science near Baltimore (1956–58; unbuilt), the City Tower Project in Philadelphia (1952–57; unbuilt), and the Lewis house, a town house in the city's Rittenhouse Square neighborhood (1957; unbuilt).

1957

Venturi resumes his teaching position at Penn (1957–65), first as an instructor and assistant to Kahn, then as an assistant (1961), and later as associate (1964) professor.

Venturi leaves Kahn's office and begins independent architectural practice.

1958

Heeding the advice of Peter Smithson, an instructor at the AA from 1955 to 1960, and with his wife Alison, an influential member of the New Brutalist movement, the Scott Browns apply to the University of Pennsylvania's planning department to study under Louis Kahn. Although disappointed once there to discover that Kahn teaches not in the land and city planning program but in the architecture department, the couple enroll in courses on housing, economics, urban land economics, statistical analysis, and urban sociology. Sociologist Herbert Gans; planners William Wheaton, Robert Mitchell, David Crane, and Paul Davidoff; and historian Malcolm Campbell become mentors.

Venturi forms an association with Paul Cope and his partner Mather Lippincott in their architectural office on North 17th Street in Philadelphia.

1959

Robert Scott Brown is killed in an automobile accident in June.

In July, Venturi executes the first designs for his parents' house to be built on a newly purchased lot in Chestnut Hill. Venturi's father, Robert, dies in December.

1960

Scott Brown, in her final semester, takes her first and only studio with Louis Kahn. She receives a master's degree in city planning from Penn and becomes an instructor and then assistant professor (1961) at Penn's Graduate School of Fine Arts (through 1965), teaching city planning and urban design studios and seminars in the theories of city planning, urban design, architecture, and landscape architecture. While a member of the faculty, Scott Brown enrolls in Penn's advanced master's program in architecture.

Denise Scott Brown and Robert Venturi meet during a faculty meeting in which Scott Brown convincingly argues against the proposed demolition of a campus library designed by Frank Furness. Venturi is one of the few sympathetic faculty members in attendance.

Venturi goes into architectural practice with a new partner, William H. Short, a classmate from Princeton, setting up an office on South 16th Street. The two are joined by John Rauch, a 1957 graduate of the University of Pennsylvania whom Venturi met when both were working in the office of Cope and Lippincott.

1962

At the University of Pennsylvania, Venturi and Scott Brown begin collaborating on the course in architectural theory that Venturi had recently begun teaching, which they continue to teach together through 1964.

Scott Brown's first published article, "Form, Design, and the City," appears in the *Journal of the American Institute of Planners* (November).

1963

In March, Venturi submits an early manuscript of *Complexity and Contradiction in Architecture* to the Graham Foundation, which had awarded Venturi a research grant.

In the spring, Venturi is a visiting critic at Yale University's School of Art and Architecture, overseeing a master's class studio on precast concrete, which he teaches with the chair of the department, Paul Rudolph.

The Headquarters and Clinic of the North Penn Visiting Nurses Association (begun 1961) is Venturi's first completed building.

1964

William Short resigns as Venturi's partner and is replaced by John Rauch. The firm becomes known as Venturi and Rauch.

In April, after five years of planning and nearly eight months of construction, Venturi and his mother move into the house he designed for her.

1965

Scott Brown receives a Master's of Architecture from Penn.

Both Venturi and Scott Brown cease teaching at Penn. Venturi returns to Yale as a visiting lecturer for the spring term.

Venturi travels and lectures in the U.S.S.R. as a recipient of a U.S. State Department travel grant. He is sent along with Paul Rudolph to accompany an exhibition on American modern architecture, which opens in Moscow on September 17. After a few weeks traveling through the Soviet Union, including several days in Leningrad, Venturi stops briefly in Finland to view the work of Alvar Aalto, visiting both Helsinki and Imatra.

On her way to California to teach in the School of Environmental Design at Berkeley for the spring semester, Scott Brown stops off in Las Vegas. That summer she travels in the Southwest. In September, Scott Brown moves to Los Angeles and accepts the position of co-chair of the Urban Design Program at UCLA, where she remains through 1967. She recruits Venturi to act as a visiting critic.

Just a year into the partnership, the Architectural League of New York features the firm in an exhibition titled "New Talent – The Work of Venturi and Rauch."

The Vanna Venturi house receives honorable mention in the Art and Architecture Awards competition of the Architectural League of New York.

1966

During the fall, Venturi serves as architect in residence at the American Academy in Rome.

Charles Moore, chairman of the Department of Architecture, names Venturi and James Stirling the first incumbents of the Charlotte Shepherd Davenport Chair of Architecture at the Yale School of Art and Architecture. Venturi remains in this position until 1970.

Scott Brown invites Venturi to visit Las Vegas with her for a four-day trip. In November the two travel the Las Vegas strip, from casino to casino, being alternately "appalled and fascinated" by what they see.[2]

Complexity and Contradiction in Architecture is published by the Museum of Modern Art as the first in an intended series of occasional papers addressing issues of architecture and design (actual distribution is not until March 1967). Subsequent studies were never produced. In the introduction, Vincent Scully proclaims the study "the most important writing on the making of architecture since Le Corbusier's *Vers une Architecture*, of 1923."[3] Over the years *Complexity and Contradiction* will be published in seventeen languages, and currently remains in print.

1967

July 23 Scott Brown and Venturi marry in Santa Monica, California.

Scott Brown serves as visiting professor of urban design at Yale University (1967–70) with Venturi. Together they develop and teach three important architectural design and research studios, the New York City subway (1967), Las Vegas (1968), and Levittown (1970). The Las Vegas studio results in Venturi and Scott Brown's book, written with Steven Izenour, *Learning from Las Vegas*.

1968

January 22–February 18 Venturi and Rauch contribute photographs, models, and drawings for a solo exhibition held at the Philadelphia Art Alliance.

Scott Brown resigns her position at UCLA.

1969

In January and February, Venturi and Scott Brown teach the Control Game studio at Rice University in Houston.

Scott Brown becomes a partner in the firm.

1971

Venturi and Scott Brown's adopted son, James, is born in May.

In October, the Whitney Museum of American Art in New York mounts the exhibition "The Work of Venturi and Rauch, Architects and Planners."

1972

Learning from Las Vegas is published, incorporating ideas from the programs and studies of the Yale studio and articles Venturi and Scott Brown had published in 1968 and 1971.

[2] Robert Venturi, "Notes for a Lecture Celebrating the Centennial of the American Academy in Rome, Delivered in Chicago [1993]," in *Iconography and Electronics*, p. 54.

[3] Vincent Scully, introduction to Robert Venturi, *Complexity and Contradiction in Architecture* (New York: The Museum of Modern Art, 1966), p. 11.

Venturi and Scott Brown move into a new home in West Mount Airy, the former Adelbert Fisher house, designed in the "Art Nouveau" style in 1909 by Philadelphia architect Milton Medary.

1973

Venturi receives the Arnold W. Brunner Memorial Prize in Architecture from the American Academy of Arts and Letters.

1976

"Signs of Life: Symbols in the American City," an exhibition born of Scott Brown and Venturi's Levittown studio at Yale, opens at the Smithsonian Institution's Renwick Gallery in Washington, D.C.

1977

Complexity and Contradiction is reissued, and a revised edition of *Learning from Las Vegas* is published.

1978

Venturi receives the AIA Medal of Honor for *Complexity and Contradiction in Architecture*.

Venturi proposes a group of furniture to Knoll for development, the first decorative-arts commission undertaken by the firm, introduced by Knoll in 1984. Important decorative-arts commissions follow in the 1980s and early 1990s for such manufacturers as Alessi and Swid Powell.

1980

The firm name officially changes to Venturi, Rauch and Scott Brown and the office moves from South 16th Street in Center City Philadelphia to its current location on Main Street in Manayunk, an industrial neighborhood on the northwestern edge of the city.

1982

Scott Brown returns to Penn's School of Fine Arts as a visiting professor for the 1982–83 school year.

At Harvard University's Graduate School of Design, Venturi delivers the twentieth annual Walter Gropius Lecture titled "Diversity, Relevance and Representation in Historicism, or Plus ça Change . . . ," in which he articulates his response to post-modernism.

Denise Scott Brown in Las Vegas with her students from Yale, 1968

John Rauch, Gerod Clark, Robert Venturi, and Denise Scott Brown in their office in Philadelphia, 1968

Denise Scott Brown teaching a studio at the University of Pennsylvania, 1982

1983

Venturi, Rauch and Scott Brown complete Gordon Wu Hall (1980–83), a dining and social facility for a residential college on the campus of Princeton University. It is the first in a series of significant projects the firm executes for Princeton in the 1980s and 1990s. It also marks an increase in the growing number of university commissions the firm receives in the coming decades, both for large-scale planning projects and individual buildings on the campuses of UCLA, Harvard, Dartmouth, the University of Michigan, the University of Pennsylvania, Yale, and others.

1984

Venturi and Scott Brown's *A View from the Campidoglio: Selected Essays, 1953–1984* is published.

March 21–May 20 "Venturi, Rauch, and Scott Brown: A Generation of Architecture," organized by the Krannert Art Museum at the University of Illinois, Urbana-Champaign, is the most extensive exhibition to date to deal with the firm's output. Over the next two years, it travels to small, mostly academic, venues in Chicago, Princeton, Philadelphia, Cincinnati, Albuquerque, and Los Angeles.

1985

Franklin Court is one of thirteen designs for U.S. government structures to be given the Presidential Award for Design Excellence.

After the demise of Ahrends Burton and Koralek's scheme to create an addition to the National Gallery, London, the Sainsbury brothers—Simon, John, and Timothy—privately donate the necessary funds to carry on with plans for the National Gallery's new wing. In September, Venturi and Scott Brown meet in New York with the National Gallery Selection Committee, and in the following month Venturi, Rauch and Scott Brown becomes one of six firms requested to submit a proposal for the extension.

Venturi, Rauch and Scott Brown receives the Architecture Firm Award, the highest honor that the AIA bestows on an architecture firm.

1986

January 24 The National Gallery Selection Committee announces that Venturi, Rauch and Scott Brown is their unanimous choice to design the Sainsbury Wing.

Venturi and Scott Brown are awarded the President's Medal from Architectural League of New York.

1987

Venturi and Scott Brown serve as Eero Saarinen Visiting Professors of Design at Yale's School of Art and Architecture.

John Rauch resigns from the firm in November.

1989

Scott Brown is named the Eliot Noyes Visiting Critic at Harvard's Graduate School of Design, where she leads a fall studio titled "The Architecture of Wellbeing."

After John Rauch's official resignation, the firm changes its name to Venturi, Scott Brown and Associates.

The Vanna Venturi house receives the AIA's Twenty-five Year Award.

1990

Scott Brown publishes *Urban Concepts* in the profile series of *Architectural Design* magazine.

Venturi and Scott Brown visit Japan for the first time. Akio Izutsu, head of Knoll International Japan, whom the Venturi's had first met in 1984, serves as their host. Venturi later identifies Tokyo as his "favorite city of now,"[4] where shrines sit snugly next to neon-topped commercial buildings in a dense and chaotic urban juxtaposition.

1991

May 16 Venturi is presented the Pritzker Prize in Architecture in a ceremony held at the Palacio de Iturbide in Mexico City.

In July, the Sainsbury Wing is dedicated in a ceremony presided over by Queen Elizabeth.

Knoll International Japan organizes "Venturi, Scott Brown and Associates," an exhibition that focuses on the firm's decorative-arts projects, as well as on architecture. The show travels to Tokyo, Kyoto, Kanazawa, and Sapporo.

1992

Venturi and Scott Brown are awarded the National Medal of Arts, an honor bestowed by the President of the United States in recognition of their distinguished achievements in the arts.

In August, Venturi, Scott Brown and Associates, in association with Marunouchi Architects & Engineers of Tokyo, wins the competition sponsored by Japan's Ministry of Posts and Telecommunications to design the Mielmonte Hotel and Resort in Nikko.

[4] Venturi, "Notes for a Lecture," in *Iconography and Electronics*, p. 55.

Robert Venturi, Denise Scott Brown,
and their son Jimmy, in the dining room
of their home in Mount Airy, 1983

Denise Scott Brown, Robert Venturi,
and Lady Margaret Thatcher examine
the Sainsbury Wing model at the
opening of "The Sainsbury Wing: A
Presentation of Designs by Venturi,
Rauch and Scott Brown," 1987

© National Gallery, London

Denise Scott Brown and Robert
Venturi in front of the Hôtel du
Département de la Haute-Garônne,
Toulouse, France, 1999

1993

In February, "About Architecture: An Installation by Venturi,
Scott Brown and Associates," opens at the Institute of
Contemporary Art, Philadelphia.

1996

*Iconography and Electronics upon a Generic Architecture: A View from the
Drafting Room*, a compilation of Venturi and Scott Brown's recent
writings, is published. The epilogue features Venturi's 1950
M.F.A. thesis for Princeton University, reproduced in full for the
first time.

Complexity and Contradiction receives a Classic Book Award in the
AIA's seventh annual international book awards.

1997

Scott Brown is awarded the AIA/American Collegiate Schools
of Architecture (ASCA) Topaz Medallion for Excellence in
Architectural Education.

The Mielmonte Hotel and Resort in Nikko is completed. It is the
firm's largest and most significant commercial project to date.

1999

In the summer, the Hôtel du Département de la Haute-Garônne,
a government building in Toulouse, France, opens after four
years of construction. It is the firm's third high-profile international commission and its most important civic building.

2001

Venturi is named Commandeur of the Order of Arts and Letters
and Scott Brown, Chevalier of the Order of Arts and Letters, by
the French government for distinction in the arts and literature.

In June, "Out of the Ordinary: The Architecture and Design of
Robert Venturi, Denise Scott Brown, and Associates" opens at
the Philadelphia Museum of Art, with plans to travel to Europe
and to museums in La Jolla, California and Pittsburgh.

Robert Venturi and Denise Scott Brown, 2000

PROJECT LIST

This list identifies over four hundred projects designed by Robert Venturi, Denise Scott Brown, and their associates initiated between 1957 and 2000. Based on an extensive investigation of the drawings, photographs, and papers in the Venturi Scott Brown archive, the list includes commissioned projects, hypothetical studies, and competition submissions. The list does not include proposals, teaching records, publications, or exhibitions of their work, even though such endeavors were often handled or influenced by the firm.

Projects are listed in a strict chronological order based on the earliest documented date found in the archival sources. Commissions that evolved from feasibility, area, or planning studies prepared by the firm, although listed separately in the firm's job lists, are consolidated into a single entry with dates reflecting the various phases of the project.

Illustrations are Collection of Venturi, Scott Brown and Associates, Inc. (except for Fairhill Square, 1958; Architectural Archives, University of Pennsylvania, George E. Patton Collection).

William Whitaker

With Kathryn B. Hiesinger
and research assistance by
Lisa Boettger
Dana Cloud
Angie Geist-Gaebler
Amanda T. Hall
Rachel Iannacone
Nicholas Sawicki
Isabel Taube

Mr. and Mrs. Forrest Pearson House

Fairhill Square

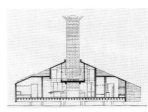

Beach House

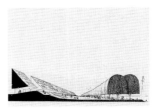

Franklin Delano Roosevelt Memorial

1957

Mr. and Mrs. Forrest Pearson House
Chestnut Hill, Philadelphia
1957; unbuilt
Robert Venturi, registered architect

Dr. and Mrs. Pasquale J. Gambescia House and Professional Office
(interior alterations)
Philadelphia
1957–59; built
Robert Venturi, registered architect

1958

Except as noted, all 1958–59 projects are by Robert Venturi, Cope and Lippincott, Associated Architects

James B. Duke House, Institute of Fine Arts, New York University
(interior alterations)
One East Seventy-eighth Street, New York
1958–59; built (removed)

Fairhill Square
(for the Fairmount Park Commission; park and service building)
Lehigh and Fourth streets, Philadelphia
1958–59; partially built
George E. Patton, landscape architect; Robert Venturi, architect

1959

Mr. and Mrs. D. Hart House
(interior renovations)
Merion, Pennsylvania
1959; built

H. Justice Williams Houses
(interior alterations and renovations to two houses)
Society Hill, Philadelphia
1959–63; built

Foulkeways at Gwynedd
(housing for the elderly)
Meeting House Road and Route 202, Gwynedd Valley, Pennsylvania
1959–60; unbuilt

Altschul House, New York University
(for the Interfaith Council; additions and alterations)
University Heights Campus, Bronx
1959–60; built

Vanna Venturi House
(Mother's House)
Chestnut Hill, Philadelphia
1959–64; built
(1975; proposed addition)
Venturi and Short, architects

Language Laboratory, New York University
(interior alterations)
University Heights Campus, Bronx
1959–62; built

Beach House
New Jersey shore
1959; unbuilt
Robert Venturi, architect

1960

Except as noted, all 1960–63 projects are by Venturi and Short, Architects

Mr. and Mrs. Bradford Mills House
(additions and alterations)
Princeton, New Jersey
1960–61; built

Mr. and Mrs. Frederick C. Carter Jr. House
(library interiors)
Bedford, New York
1960–63; built

Franklin Delano Roosevelt Memorial, Competition
Washington, D.C.
1960; honorable mention
Robert Venturi with John Rauch, George E. Patton, and Nicholas Gianopulos

Mr. and Mrs. Frank Correnty House
(additions)
Upper Darby, Pennsylvania
1960; built
Robert Venturi, architect

Mr. and Mrs. Yehndi Wyner House
(interior alterations)
Woodstock, New York
1960; unbuilt
Robert Venturi, architect

Grand's Restaurant

Mr. and Mrs. Millard Meiss House

Mr. and Mrs. F. Otto Haas House

Monumental Fountain on the Benjamin Franklin Parkway

1961

Mr. and Mrs. Dudley L. Miller House
East Hampton, New York
1961; unbuilt

Dr. and Mrs. John M. Dunn House
(alterations)
Jarrettown, Pennsylvania
1961; built
Robert Venturi, Cope and Lippincott, associated architects

Guild House
(for the Friends Neighborhood Guild)
711 Spring Garden Street, Philadelphia
1961–66; built
Venturi and Rauch, Cope and Lippincott, associated architects

Headquarters and Clinic, North Penn Visiting Nurses Association
219 Race Street, Ambler, Pennsylvania
1961–63; built (radically altered)

Grand's Restaurant
(alterations)
3627–29 Walnut Street, Philadelphia
1961–62; built (demolished)

1962

Mr. and Mrs. Millard Meiss House
Institute for Advanced Study, Princeton, New Jersey
1962; unbuilt

Mr. and Mrs. John T. Valdes House
(swimming pool and pavilion)
Princeton, New Jersey
1962; built

Mr. and Mrs. Boudinot P. Atterbury House
(renovations)
New York
1962; built

Penthouse Apartment, New York University
(alterations and additions)
Washington Square Campus, New York
1962; built

Offices, J. W. Pepper & Son
(interior alterations)
231 North Third Street, Philadelphia
1962–64; built

Dormitory and Gymnasium, The Hun School
176 Edgerstoune Road, Princeton, New Jersey
1962–64; built
Charles K. Agle, architect; Venturi and Short, associated architects

Mr. and Mrs. A. Chauncey Newlin House
(garden room)
Scarsdale, New York
1962; built

1963

District Attorney's Office and Fire Control Center
(for the City of Philadelphia; interior alterations)
City Hall, Philadelphia
1963–64; built

Mr. and Mrs. F. Otto Haas House
(alterations and additions)
Ambler, Pennsylvania
1963–84; built
Venturi and Short (with later additions by Venturi and Rauch; Venturi, Rauch and Scott Brown)

1964

Except as noted, all 1964–79 projects are by Venturi and Rauch, Architects and Planners

Mr. and Mrs. Thomas T. Fleming House
(alterations and additions)
Rydal, Pennsylvania
1964; built
Robert Venturi, architect

Poplar Street Park
(park and service building)
Poplar and Seventh streets, Wilmington, Delaware
1964; built
George E. Patton, landscape architect; Venturi and Rauch, consulting architects

Data Processing and Engineering Center
(for the U.S. Navy; renovations)
United States Naval Shipyard, Philadelphia
1964–67; unbuilt

Mr. and Mrs. J. D. Farber House
(alterations)
Society Hill, Philadelphia
1964; unbuilt

H. Justice Williams House
(interior alterations)
Queen Village, Philadelphia
1964; built

Lindbergh Park
(for the Fairmount Park Commission; park and service building)
Sixty-third Street and Eastwick Avenue, Philadelphia
1964–67; unbuilt
George E. Patton, landscape architect; Venturi and Rauch, consulting architects

Monumental Fountain on the Benjamin Franklin Parkway, Competition
(for the Fairmount Park Art Association)
Benjamin Franklin Parkway and Sixteenth Street, Philadelphia
1964; unpremiated
Denise Scott Brown, associated architect

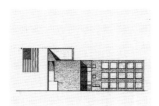

Redevelopment Plan, North Canton, City Hall

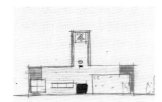

Fire Station No. 4

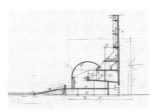

National Collegiate Football Hall of Fame

Humanities Building, SUNY, Purchase

1965

**Arts Center, University
of California at Berkeley,
Competition**
2625 Durant Avenue,
Berkeley, California
1965; unpremiated

The Footlighters Playhouse
1416 Berwyn-Paoli Road,
Berwyn, Pennsylvania
1965; unbuilt

Arthur J. Williams House
(interior alterations)
Rittenhouse Square, Philadelphia
1965; built

Offices and Hearing Rooms
(for the City of Philadelphia;
interior alterations)
City Hall Annex, Philadelphia
1965–67; built

**Research Laboratories and Offices,
Philadelphia General Hospital**
(interior alterations, 13 sites)
Civic Center Boulevard,
Philadelphia
1965–71; built

**Redevelopment Plan,
City of North Canton**
(city hall, library addition,
YMCA, commercial center,
and site planning)
Main and Maple streets,
North Canton, Ohio
1965–66; not implemented
Clarke and Rapuano, Inc.,
architects; Venturi and Rauch,
consulting architects

Cordomatic Reels Corporation
(space-use study)
1800 block of Cambria Avenue,
Philadelphia
1965; not implemented
Vinokur-Pace, engineers

Copley Square, Competition
Boston
1965–66; unpremiated

1966

**Mr. and Mrs. Bradford Mills
Pool House**
(Frug House or Teenage House)
Princeton, New Jersey
1966; unbuilt

Princeton Memorial Park
(entrance building, chapel,
tower, and mausoleum)
Gordon and Sharon roads,
Robbinsville, New Jersey
1966; unbuilt
Richard J. Cripps, landscape
architect

Medical Office Building
(for Dr. George Varga
and Dr. Frank Brigio)
351 Irving Avenue,
Bridgeton, New Jersey
1966–68; built

Fire Station No. 4
4730 East Twenty-fifth Street,
Columbus, Indiana
1966–68; built

**Mr. and Mrs. Perry Gittelson
House**
(addition)
Caldwell, New Jersey
1966–67; unbuilt

1967

**National Collegiate Football Hall
of Fame, Competition**
Sulphen and Frellnghuysen roads,
Piscataway, New Jersey
1967; honorable mention

Warehouse, Venturi Inc.
(additions and alterations)
1430 South Street, Philadelphia
1967–72; built

**Mr. and Mrs. Nathaniel Lieb
Beach House**
Barnegat Light, New Jersey
1967–69; built

Dixwell Fire Station
125 Goffe Street, New Haven
1967–74; built

James Kelly Studio
(barn renovations)
Berks County, Pennsylvania
1967–68; unbuilt

**Mr. and Mrs. George Hersey
Vacation House**
Woods Hole, Massachusetts
1967–68; unbuilt

Warehouse, Eisnor Company
(additions)
Aramingo Avenue, Philadelphia
1967–68; unbuilt

**Transportation Square Office
Building, Competition**
(for Mallory Walker and Martin
Marietta Corporation)
Maryland Avenue, between
Sixth and Seventh streets,
Washington, D.C.
1967–69; first prize, unbuilt
Caudill Rowlett Scott,
associated architects

Dr. and Mrs. Samuel Kron House
(additions)
Rittenhouse Square, Philadelphia
1967; unbuilt

**Central Business District
Planning Study**
Bethlehem, Pennsylvania
1967–68; not implemented

**Middle-Income Housing
Development for Brighton Beach,
Brooklyn, Competition**
Brightwater Court and Third
Street, Brighton Beach, Brooklyn
1967–68; third prize

1968

Betz Laboratories
(alterations)
Bensalem Township, Pennsylvania
1968; unbuilt

Law Offices, Rogers and Smith
(alterations)
820 Green Street, Norristown,
Pennsylvania
1968; unbuilt

**Rental Offices and Headquarters,
Phi Kappa Sigma Fraternity**
(renovations)
333–35 South Sixteenth Street,
Philadelphia
1966–70; built

**Humanities Building,
State University of New York
at Purchase**
Purchase, New York
1968–73; built

**Mr. and Mrs. Anthony D'Agostino
House**
(Weathervane Farm)
Clinton, New York
1968–73; unbuilt

**Philadelphia Crosstown
Community Planning Study**
(for the Committee to Preserve
and Develop the Crosstown
Community)
Philadelphia
1968–72; partially implemented

St. Francis de Sales Church
(interior alterations and
furnishings)
4625 Springfield Avenue,
Philadelphia
1968–70; built (furnishings
removed)

Mr. and Mrs. J. Roffe Wike House
Willistown, Pennsylvania
1968–69; unbuilt

Mathematics Building, Yale University

Mr. and Mrs. David Trubek and
Mr. and Mrs. George Wislocki Houses

Theater, Hartford Stage Company

1969

Dr. and Mrs. David Rosner House
(renovations)
Society Hill, Philadelphia
1969–72; built

Health Center
(for the Southeast Philadelphia
Community Corporation;
feasibility study)
310–24 Queen Street, Philadelphia
1969–75; unbuilt

Washington Square West Housing
(for the Philadelphia Housing
Development Corporation;
23 units on 3 sites)
Northwest corner of Quince
and Lombard streets; South Side
of Pine Street, between Quince
and Twelfth streets; and
Northwest corner of Lombard
and Tenth streets; Philadelphia
1969–72; unbuilt

Times Square Development
(for Peter Sharp & Co., Inc.;
theater and office tower)
1531–49 Broadway, New York
1969–71; unbuilt
Emery Roth and Sons, architects;
Venturi and Rauch, associated
architects

Mathematics Building,
Yale University, Competition
New Haven
1969–70; first prize, unbuilt

Thousand Oaks Civic Center,
Competition
Thousand Oaks Boulevard,
Thousand Oaks, California
1969; honorable mention

1970

Offices, Star Dental
Manufacturing Company
(renovations)
Fayette Street and River Road,
West Conshohocken, Pennsylvania
1970–73; built

Mr. and Mrs. Nathaniel Lieb House
(additions, alterations,
and pool house)
Penn Valley, Lower Merion
Township, Pennsylvania
1970–75; unbuilt

Social Sciences Building,
State University of New York
at Purchase
Purchase, New York
1970–78; built

Greek Taverna and Restaurant
200 South Street, Philadelphia
1970; unbuilt

Southeastern Pennsylvania
Transportation Authority Planning
(survey and analysis of subway
stations)
Lombard and South streets station,
Eighth and Market streets station,
Philadelphia
1970–72; implemented

Lawton Plaza Redevelopment
Study
(for the New York State Urban
Development Corporation;
feasibility study)
Main Street and North Avenue,
New Rochelle, New York
1970–71; not implemented

California City General Plan
(for the Great Western United
Corporation; Galileo Hill Park,
Twenty Mule Team Parkway,
sales office for the Great Western
United Corporation, MERBISC
Mart, civic center, city hall, and
cemetery)
California City, California
1970–71; not implemented

ARCO Building, Philadelphia
College of Art
(renovations and alterations)
260 South Broad Street,
Philadelphia
1970–71; unbuilt

Mural, The Children's School
3828 Spring Garden Street,
Philadelphia
1970; built

Carol M. Newman Library, Virginia
Polytechnic and State University
(additions)
Blacksburg, Virginia
1970–79; built
Vosbeck, Vosbeck, Kendrick and
Redinger, associated architects

Warehouse and Offices, BATO
Paper Company
Chestnut Street, Byram, Connecticut
1970–74; unbuilt

Mr. and Mrs. David Trubek and
Mr. and Mrs. George Wislocki
Houses
Nantucket, Massachusetts
1970–72; built

Mr. and Mrs. Peter Brant House
Greenwich, Connecticut
1970–74; built (1978–79;
proposed additions)

1971

Theater, Hartford Stage Company
(first project)
Trumbull Street, Hartford,
Connecticut
1971–75; unbuilt (see 1975)

Althouse Land Development
Study
(for the Security of America Life
Insurance Co.; feasibility study)
Bern Township, Pennsylvania
1971–72; not implemented

"Skylon" Canadian Heritage
Exhibition
(for National Heritage, Ltd.;
feasibility study for reuse
of convention center)
Niagara Falls, Ontario
1971–72; not implemented

International Bicentennial
Exposition Master Plan
(for the Philadelphia 1976
Bicentennial Corporation)
Eastwick, Philadelphia
1971–72; not implemented
Project team: Louis I. Kahn;
Bower & Fradley; Eshbach,
Glass, Kale & Associates;
Mitchell/Giurgola; Murphy Levy
Wurman; Venturi and Rauch

Dental Clinic, Thomas Jefferson
University
(interior alterations)
Philadelphia
1971; unbuilt

Frankford Arsenal
(for the U. S. Army Corps
of Engineers; renovations
to 8 buildings)
Bridge and Tacony streets,
Philadelphia
1971–73; built
Vinokur-Pace, engineers; Venturi
and Rauch, consulting architects

Offices, Women's International
League for Peace and Freedom
(interior alterations)
1213 Race Street, Philadelphia
1971–72; unbuilt

Franklin Court

Faculty Club, Penn State

Signs of Life: Symbols in the
American City

1972

Four Houses
6904 Wissahickon Avenue,
Philadelphia
1972–73; unbuilt

Franklin Court
(for the Independence National
Historical Park)
314–22 Market Street, Philadelphia
1972–76; built
John Milner, associated architect

**Mr. and Mrs. Kevin Cusack
Beach House**
(additions and alterations)
Sea Isle City, New Jersey
1972–74; built

Land Development Study
(for Partners in Housing;
feasibility study for 42 unit
low-cost housing development)
Church Lane, Germantown,
Philadelphia
1972; not implemented

Horace Bushnell Memorial Hall
(alterations and renovations)
166 Capitol Avenue, Hartford,
Connecticut
1972–73; built
George Izenour, theater consultant

**Fairmount Manor and the Poplar
Community Report**
(for the U.S. Department of
Housing and Urban Development;
area study)
Philadelphia
1972–73; partially implemented

**Celebration 76 Exposition
Master Plan**
(for the Greater Philadelphia
Cultural Alliance)
Benjamin Franklin Parkway,
Philadelphia
1972–73; not implemented

Heritage Ontario Concept Design
(for National Heritage, Ltd.;
feasibility study)
Ontario
1972–73; not implemented

**Fort William Visitor Information
Center**
(for National Heritage, Ltd.;
feasibility study and building
program)
Thunder Bay, Ontario
1972–75; not implemented

**Robert Venturi and Denise Scott
Brown House**
(interior design, furnishings,
and stenciling)
Mount Airy, Philadelphia
1972–88; built

1973

Saga Bay Development Study
(for the Saga Development
Corporation; signs and retail
development)
Biscayne Bay, Florida
1973; not implemented

**Seneca / Susquehanna Urban
Renewal**
(area study)
Harrisburg, Pennsylvania
1973; not implemented

**Allen Memorial Art Museum,
Oberlin College**
(additions)
Oberlin, Ohio
1973–77; built

East River Park
(for the New York City
Educational Construction Fund)
Catherine Slip and Robert F.
Wagner Place, New York
1973–75; unbuilt
Coffey, Levine and Blumberg,
landscape architects

**Showroom, Best Products
Company**
Redbird Mall, Arlington, Texas
1973–76; unbuilt

**Showroom, Best Products
Company**
West Covina, California
1973–76; unbuilt

**Showroom, Best Products
Company**
Oxford Valley Mall, 200
Middletown Boulevard,
Langhorne, Pennsylvania
1973–79; built

**Prototype Campus Signage
System and Street Furniture,
University of Pennsylvania,
Competition**
Philadelphia
1973; unpremiated

Schuylkill River Corridor Study
("City Edges" program, for the
National Endowment for the Arts)
Philadelphia
1973–74; partially implemented
Murphy Levy Wurman, associated
architects

**Philadelphia College of Art
Master Plan**
Philadelphia
1973–74; not implemented

**Faculty Club, The Pennsylvania
State University**
(now Executive Education Center)
University Park, Pennsylvania
1973–76; built (interior radically
altered)

**In This Academy: The
Pennsylvania Academy of the
Fine Arts, 1805–1976, A Special
Bicentennial Exhibition**
(exhibition design)
Pennsylvania Academy of the
Fine Arts, Philadelphia
1973–76; built

**Spy Lake Land Development
Study**
(for the Spy Lake Realty
Corporation)
Arietta, New York
1973–74; unbuilt

1974

NAVFAC Community Center
(for the U.S. Navy)
United States Naval Shipyard,
Philadelphia
1974–75; built

Carll Tucker III House
Katonah, New York
1974–76; built

Beach House
no site
1974; unbuilt

**Signs of Life: Symbols in the
American City**
(exhibition design)
Renwick Gallery, Smithsonian
Institution, Washington, D.C.
1974–76; built

Carefree Land Development Study
(for Frederick Henry; feasibility
study)
Carefree, Arizona
1974; not implemented

Science Museum of Virginia
(master plan and building program)
Yellow Mountain Road, Roanoke,
Virginia
1974–75; not implemented

**Education and Conference Center,
Morris Arboretum, University
of Pennsylvania**
Hillcrest Avenue, Chestnut Hill,
Philadelphia
1974–76; unbuilt

**The Strand District
Comprehensive Plan**
(for the Galveston Historical
Foundation)
The Strand, Galveston, Texas
1974–76; partially implemented

200 Years of American Sculpture
(exhibition design)
Whitney Museum of American
Art, New York
1974–76; built

Dream House
no site
1974; unbuilt

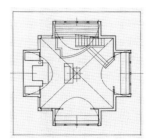

Mr. and Mrs. Peter Brant and
Jed Johnson Ski House

Discovery Place Museum

Mr. and Mrs. John Gooding House

1975

**Mr. and Mrs. Peter Brant
and Jed Johnson Ski House**
Vail, Colorado
1975–77; built

Mr. and Mrs. Peter Brant House
Windsor Beach, Tucker's Town,
Bermuda
1975–77; built
Onions, Bouchard and McCulloch,
associated architects

Theater, Hartford Stage Company
(second project)
50 Church Street, Hartford,
Connecticut
1975–77; built

**Windon / West Chester Land
Development Study**
(for Robert Olsen)
West Chester, Pennsylvania
1975; not implemented

Mr. and Mrs. Edwin Wolf House
(additions)
West Mount Airy, Philadelphia
1975; unbuilt

**Philadelphia: Three Centuries
of American Art**
(exhibition design)
Philadelphia Museum of Art,
Philadelphia
1975–76; built

1976

Downtown Mural Art Project
(for the Lackawanna County
Regional Planning Commission)
Scranton, Pennsylvania
1976–77; unbuilt

Offices, INA Capitol Management
(interior alterations)
Pennwalt Building, Three Benjamin
Franklin Parkway, Philadelphia
1976–78; built

**Heritage Plaza West
Revitalization Study**
(for the City of Salem)
Salem, Massachusetts
1976–78; partially implemented

Showroom, BASCO, Inc.
2302 Concord Pike,
Wilmington, Delaware
1976–78; built

Chapel of the Four Chaplains
(renovations to the former
Music Fund Society building)
806–20 Locust Street, Philadelphia
1976–77; unbuilt
National Heritage Corporation,
restoration architects

**Money Island Land
Development Study**
(beach house development)
Downe Township, New Jersey
1976–78; not implemented

**Discovery Place Museum
of Science and Technology**
(for the City of Charlotte)
301 South Tryon Street,
Charlotte, North Carolina
1976–81; built
Clark, Tribble, Harris and Li,
architects; Venturi and Rauch,
design consultants

Arisbe
(exhibition design)
Charles S. Peirce Museum,
Milford, Pennsylvania
1976–78; unbuilt

**Minnesota Capitol Building
Annex, Competition**
Saint Paul, Minnesota
1976–77; unpremiated

**Old City District
Comprehensive Plan**
(for the Philadelphia City
Planning Commission)
Philadelphia
1976–78; partially implemented

1977

**Showroom and Warehouse,
BASCO, Inc.**
(alterations)
Roosevelt Boulevard and
Comly Road, Philadelphia
1977–78; built (demolished)

**Showroom and Warehouse,
BASCO, Inc.**
(alterations to former
Levitz Building)
King of Prussia, Pennsylvania
1977; unbuilt

**Showroom and Warehouse,
BASCO, Inc.**
(loading dock and ramp additions)
Springfield, Pennsylvania
1977; built

Park Place Hotel and Casino
(for Reese Palley Corporation;
alterations and additions to the
former Marlborough-Blenheim
Hotel)
Ohio Avenue at Boardwalk,
Atlantic City, New Jersey
1977; unbuilt

Mr. and Mrs. John Gooding House
Absecon, New Jersey
1977; unbuilt

Palley's Jewelers
(alterations)
Atlantic and South Carolina
avenues, Atlantic City, New Jersey
1977–78; built (demolished)

**Tucker Estate Land Development
Study**
Bedford, New York
1977–78; not implemented
George E. Patton, landscape
architect

**Branch Office, County Federal
Savings and Loan Association**
(alterations)
Kings Highway Extension and Post
Road, Fairfield, Connecticut
1977; built

**Branch Office, County Federal
Savings and Loan Association**
Stratford, Connecticut
1977; unbuilt

**Historic Main Street
Planning Study**
(for the Town of Boonton)
Boonton, New Jersey
1977; not implemented

**St. Christopher's Hospital for
Children Master Plan**
Lehigh and Lawrence streets,
Philadelphia
1977–78; partially implemented

**Mr. and Mrs. F. Graham Main
Apartment**
(interior alterations)
New York
1977; unbuilt

**Lower Historic District
Planning Study**
(for the Carbon County
Planning Commission)
Jim Thorpe, Pennsylvania
1977–79; partially implemented

Freedom Plaza
(for the Pennsylvania Avenue
Development Corporation;
originally Western Plaza)
Pennsylvania Avenue,
Washington, D.C.
1977–79; built
George E. Patton, landscape
architect

**Alameda: Outdoor Advertising
on Main Street**
(for Foster, Kleiser and Eller,
Outdoor Advertising; area study)
Alameda, California
1977; not implemented

**Conservation Laboratory,
Philadelphia Museum of Art**
(alterations)
Benjamin Franklin Parkway,
Philadelphia
1977–78; built

Mauch Chunk Opera House
(alterations and renovations)
18 West Broadway, Jim Thorpe,
Pennsylvania
1977–79; partially built

**Headquarters, Institute for
Scientific Information**
3501 Market Street, Philadelphia
1977–79; built

**Hartwell Lake Regional Visitor
Center, Competition**
(for the U.S. Army Corps of
Engineers)
Scenic Highway 11 and Interstate
85, Hartwell Lake, South Carolina
1977–78; unpremiated

Furniture for Knoll, Art Deco and
Sheraton Chairs

Mr. and Mrs. Irving Abrams House

1978

**Offices, Saturday Review
of Literature**
(interior alterations)
1290 Sixth Avenue, New York
1977–78; unbuilt

**Showroom and Warehouse,
BASCO, Inc.**
(additions and alterations)
Kirkwood Highway, Newark,
Delaware
1977–78; built

Malcolm Goldstein House
Bridgehampton, New York
1977–78; unbuilt

Time Bound
(exhibition design)
The Franklin Institute,
Philadelphia
1977; unbuilt

Eclectic House Series
no site
1977; unbuilt

Jazz Club
(for Nichol's Alley Company)
Houston
1977–78; unbuilt

Mr. and Mrs. Peter Brant House
Greenwich, Connecticut
1978–79; unbuilt

Westway Urban Design Study
(for the New York State
Department of Transportation)
West Side Highway, New York
1978–85; unbuilt
Clarke and Rapuano, Inc., associated
landscape architects

Mr. and Mrs. Peter Flint House
Greenville, Delaware
1978–80; built

Settlement Music School
(alterations and additions)
6128 Germantown Avenue,
Philadelphia
1978–81; built

**Washington Avenue
Revitalization Plan**
(for the City of Miami Beach)
Miami Beach
1978–79; partially implemented

**Computer Museum, Moore
School of Engineering, University
of Pennsylvania**
(interior alterations)
200 South Thirty-third Street,
Philadelphia
1978–79; unbuilt

Showroom, BASCO, Inc.
Roosevelt Boulevard and Grant
Avenue, Philadelphia
1978; unbuilt

**Offices, Venturi, Rauch
and Scott Brown**
(interior alterations)
4236 Main Street, Philadelphia
1978–80; built

**Professional Office, Dr. Murray
Seitchik**
(alterations)
Yorktown Court of Shops,
Old York and Church roads,
Elkins Park, Pennsylvania
1978–79; built

**Central Business District Urban
Design Study**
(for the Borough of Princeton)
Princeton, New Jersey
1978–80; not implemented

**Mr. and Mrs. George Izenour
House**
Branford, Connecticut
1978–82; built

Riverloft Housing Development
(for the Reading Development
Authority; renovation of factory)
Willow and Fifth streets,
Reading, Pennsylvania
1978–79; unbuilt

**Institute for Advanced Study Land
Development Study**
(for Collins Development
Corporation)
Princeton, New Jersey
1978–79; not implemented

Furniture
(for Knoll, New York)
Queen Anne, Chippendale,
Sheraton, Hepplewhite, Empire,
Gothic Revival, Biedermeier,
Art Nouveau, Art Deco chairs;
sofa; cabriole leg, urn, low tables;
Tapestry fabric; Grandmother
laminate
1978–84 (produced 1984–90;
revised and reissued by Knoll
International Japan 1991–95)

1979

**Offices and Showroom,
Knoll International**
(alterations)
655 Madison Avenue, New York
1979–80; built

**Lackawanna Avenue
Development Study**
(for the Architectural Heritage
Association of Northeastern
Pennsylvania)
Scranton, Pennsylvania
1979; not implemented

**Central Business District
Planning Study**
(for the Borough of Jenkintown)
Old York Road, Jenkintown,
Pennsylvania
1979–80; not implemented

**United States Pavilion, Expo '82,
Competition**
Knoxville, Tennessee
1979; unpremiated

Mr. and Mrs. Irving Abrams House
Squirrel Hill, Pittsburgh
1979–81; built

Welcome Park
(for the Friends of the
Independence National
Historical Park)
Second and Sansom streets,
Philadelphia
1979–80 "Slate Roof House"
feasibility study; 1982–83; built

Chinatown Housing
(for the Philadelphia Housing
Development Corporation; 2 sites)
1006–14 Winter Street and 912–18
Spring Street, Philadelphia
1979–81; built

**Sports and Recreational Facilities
Improvements, Temple University**
(guard booth)
Philadelphia
1979–80; built
George E. Patton, Inc., landscape
architect; Venturi and Rauch,
consulting architects

**Commonwealth Parliament
House, Competition**
Canberra, Australia
1979; unpremiated

Gordon Wu Hall, Princeton University

1980

Weld Coxe and Mary Hayden House and Studio
Block Island, Rhode Island
1979–80; built

Museum für Kunsthandwerk, Competition
Frankfurt am Main, West Germany
1979–80; second prize

Penn's Light
(Proposal for the Celebration of the 300th anniversary of the founding of Philadelphia)
Belmont Plateau, Fairmount Park, Philadelphia
1979–80; unbuilt

The Shore Mall
(alterations)
Black Horse Pike, Egg Harbor Township, New Jersey
1979–80; unbuilt

Civic Center Auditorium
(for the Reading Center City Development Fund; feasibility study)
700 block of Penn Street, Reading, Pennsylvania
1979–82; not implemented

Manhattan
(for the United States Information Service; exhibition design)
Moscow, U.S.S.R.
1979; unbuilt

Except as noted, all 1980–89 projects are by Venturi, Rauch and Scott Brown

Law Offices, Abraham, Pressman, Teitz and Seidman
(interior alterations)
1530 Chestnut Street, Philadelphia
1980; unbuilt

Philadelphia Museum of Art Comprehensive Plan
Benjamin Franklin Parkway, Philadelphia
1980–81; implemented

Performing Arts Center Master Plan, University of South Carolina
Columbia, South Carolina
1980–83; unbuilt

Hennepin Avenue Transit and Entertainment Mall Study
Minneapolis
1980–81; partially implemented
BRW, Inc., associated architects; Williams, O'Brien and Associates, associated architects

Mr. and Mrs. Burton Brous House
Southampton, New York
1980; unbuilt

Prototype U.S. Retail Store
(for Dansk International)
no site
1980; unbuilt

The Metropolitan Luxury Apartments
(for Historic Landmarks for Living; renovations of U.S. Marine YMCA building)
115 North Fifteenth Street, Philadelphia
1980–83; built

Gordon Wu Hall, Butler College, Princeton University
(additions and alterations to Wilcox Hall)
Princeton, New Jersey
1980–83; built

Lee D. Butler Memorial Plaza, Butler College, Princeton University
Princeton, New Jersey
1980–83; built

John D. Rockefeller 3rd College, Princeton University
(renovations and alterations to the "Commons," Holder, Witherspoon, and Blair halls)
Princeton, New Jersey
1980–83; built

Dean Mathey College, Princeton University
(renovations and alterations to Hamilton, Campbell, Joline, and Blair halls)
Princeton, New Jersey
1980–83; built

Children's Zoo and Tree House, Philadelphia Zoological Gardens
(renovations, alterations, and additions)
3400 West Girard Avenue, Philadelphia
1980–83; built

Caesar's Palace Hotel Design Review
(for the Department of Environmental Protection, State of New Jersey)
Atlantic City, New Jersey
1980; not implemented

Social Ecology Building, University of California at Irvine
(building program)
Irvine, California
1980; implemented

Exhibition Hall, Internationale Frankfurter Messe, Competition
Frankfurt am Main, West Germany
1980; unpremiated

The Pavilions at Princeton
(office park)
Orchard Road, Montgomery Township, New Jersey
1980–81; unbuilt

Mr. and Mrs. Donald A. Petrie House
Wainscott, New York
1980–83; built (1997 addition)

Headquarters, Wheelabrator-Frye (later Signal Companies)
Liberty Lane Office Park, Hampton, New Hampshire
1980–81, 1984–85; unbuilt

Houston Hall, University of Pennsylvania
(interior alterations)
Philadelphia
1980–83; built (removed)

Park Regency Condominiums
(for Wynings and Company)
2433 Bering Drive, Houston
1980–82; built
McCleary Associates, associated architects

Mr. and Mrs. Russell P. Wynings Condominium
(interior)
Park Regency Condominiums, Houston
1980–82; built

Tea and Coffee Service
(for Alessi, Crusinallo, Italy)
1980–83; tea and coffee service, silver (produced since 1983); tray, stainless steel (produced since 1985)
Design Proposals: Village tea and coffee service (1980); Nouveau creamer and sugar bowl (1980); candlestick (1980)

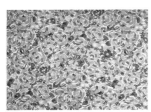

Fabrics for the Fabric Workshop,
Grandmother Pattern

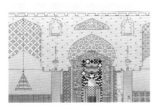

State Mosque, Baghdad

Mr. and Mrs. Gary Kalpakjian House

1981

Blair Hall, Princeton University
(alterations)
Princeton, New Jersey
1981–84; built

Hamilton Watch Factory
(feasibility study)
Lancaster, Pennsylvania
1981; not implemented
DACP Associates, associated
architects

**Lansdowne Room,
Philadelphia Museum of Art**
(restoration)
Benjamin Franklin Parkway,
Philadelphia
1981–84; built

**Contemporary American Realism
Since 1960**
(exhibition design)
Pennsylvania Academy of the
Fine Arts, Philadelphia
1981; built

**Old Main, Shippensburg State
University**
(renovations and alterations
to administrative offices)
Shippensburg, Pennsylvania
1981–86; built

**Commercial and Residential
Building**
(for Amanant-al-Assima)
Khulafa Street, Baghdad, Iraq
1981–83; unbuilt

Little Hall, Princeton University
(alterations)
Princeton, New Jersey
1981–83; built

**Mr. and Mrs. Kenneth Hubbard
House**
Nantucket, Massachusetts
1981–86; built

**Resorts International Hotels
Design Review**
(for the Department of
Environmental Protection,
State of New Jersey)
Atlantic City, New Jersey
1981–82; not implemented

Fabrics
(for the Fabric Workshop,
Philadelphia)
Grandmother and Notebook
1981–84 (produced since 1984)
Prototype: Flowers (1982)

1982

Welcome Park, see 1979

**Garage, University
of Pennsylvania**
(feasibility study)
Walnut and Thirty-eighth streets,
Philadelphia
1982; implemented

**Field House, University of
Pennsylvania**
Philadelphia
1982–83; unbuilt

**Primate Center and Discovery
House**
(for the Philadelphia
Zoological Society)
3400 West Girard Avenue,
Philadelphia
1982–86; built
(destroyed by fire 1995)
Hanna / Olin, landscape architects

**West Foyer, Philadelphia
Museum of Art**
(interior alterations and
furnishings)
Benjamin Franklin Parkway,
Philadelphia
1982–89; built

State Mosque, Competition
Rabia Street, Baghdad, Iraq
1982–83; unpremiated
Ali Mousawi and Partners,
associated architects

Laguna Gloria Art Museum
401 West Fourth Street,
Austin, Texas
1982–89; unbuilt
RIO Group, associated architects

**Republic Square District
Development Plan**
(for the Watson-Casey Companies)
Austin, Texas
1982–84; not implemented

Housewares
(for Swid Powell, New York)
Dinner Services
Grandmother 1982–84 (produced
1984–90); Notebook 1982–84
(produced 1984–90); Vegas
1986–87 (produced 1987–90);
Flowers 1993 (produced 1993–95);
Classical 1991–93 (produced
1993–96)
Glasswares
Grandmother 1984 (produced
1984–86); Dashes 1984 (produced
1984–86)
Ceramics
Village tea and coffee service
1985–86 (produced 1986–88);
Canister set and cookie jar 1993
(produced 1993–95)
Metalwares
Candlestick, silver plate 1985–86
(produced 1986–89); Carving set,
serving (platter) spoon, silver plate
1988–89; Flatware, stainless steel
1990–92; Hostess set, stainless
steel 1990–92 (produced by Reed
& Barton, Taunton, Massachusetts:
carving set, since 1989; serving
[platter] spoon, since 1990; flatware, 1992–98; hostess set,
1992–98)
Bed Linens
1988–90 (produced by Fieldcrest
Cannon, Eden, North Carolina, 1991)
Selected Prototypes
Nouveau creamer and sugar bowl
(1986); Deco creamer and sugar
bowl (1986); Vegas/Dalmatian
candlestick, salt-and-pepper shakers
(1986); Borromini plate (1987);
Fruit bowl (1987–88); Centerpiece
(1990–91); Dashes plate, mug,
(1990–91); Grandmother and
Notebook towels (developed for
production by Fieldcrest Cannon,
Eden, North Carolina, 1988–90)

1983

**College Walk Improvements
Study, Princeton University**
Princeton, New Jersey
1983; not implemented

**Memorial Lunette for
Ann Lorenz Van Zanten,
Saint Louis Museum of Art**
Saint Louis, Missouri
1983–85; unbuilt

**Lewis Thomas Laboratory,
Princeton University**
Princeton, New Jersey
1983–86; built
Payette Associates, associated
architects

**ORB Building, Graduate School
of Management, University
of California at Irvine**
Irvine, California
1983–84; unbuilt

Apartment Building
(renovations and interior
alterations)
215 Fitzwater Street, Philadelphia
1983–88; built

**Amtrak Station, Restaurant
and Railroad Museum**
(additions and alterations)
Tamarind Avenue and Datura
Street, West Palm Beach, Florida
1983; unbuilt

**New Orleans Museum of Art,
Competition**
LeLong Avenue, New Orleans
1983; unpremiated

**Winterthur Housing
Development**
(for the Acorn Construction
Company; 4 houses)
Montchanin and Rockland roads,
Montchanin, Delaware
1983–84; unbuilt

**Mr. and Mrs. Gary Kalpakjian
House**
Glen Cove, New York
1983–86; built

**National Marine Aquarium,
Competition**
(addition)
Baltimore
1983–84; unpremiated

Mirror
(for Formica Corporation,
Evendale, Ohio)
1983 (produced 1983)

Seattle Art Museum

Sainsbury Wing, National Gallery

1984

**Malcolm J. Forbes College,
Princeton University**
(alterations and additions)
Princeton, New Jersey
1984–85; built

**Tarble Student Center,
Swarthmore College**
(alterations and renovations)
Swarthmore, Pennsylvania
1984–86; built

**High Styles: Twentieth-Century
American Design**
(exhibition design)
Whitney Museum of American Art,
New York
1984–85; built

**The Big Apple at Times Square
Center**
(for the Park Tower Realty
Corporation)
Times Square, New York
1984; unbuilt

**Prospect House, Princeton
University**
(renovations)
Princeton, New Jersey
1984–89; built

**Elm Drive Entrance, Stockton
Court and Guard Booth, Princeton
University**
Princeton, New Jersey
1984–88; built
George E. Patton, Inc.,
landscape architect

**Center City Development Plan
for Downtown Memphis**
(for the Center City Commission;
planning study)
Memphis
1984–87; not implemented

Il Progetto per Roma
(reuse of the Mattatoio del
Testaccio, exposition design;
obelisk, signs, and cinema
pavilion decoration)
Rome
1984; unbuilt

Alberto Alessi Anghini House
(library interiors)
Omegna, Italy
1984–88; built
Alessandro Mendini, associated
architect

Seattle Art Museum
100 University Street, Seattle
1984–91; built

**Queen Anne, Louis XV,
and Louis XVI Lowboys**
(for Arc International,
Jacksonville, Florida)
1984–89 (produced 1984)

William and Mary Bureau
(for XVII International
Triennale, Milan)
1984 (produced 1984)

Jewelry
(for Cleto Munari, Vicenza)
1984–86; three earrings,
three rings, and two necklaces
(produced 1986)

1985

**East Campus Residential College
Study, Duke University**
Durham, North Carolina
1985; not implemented

Stony Creek Office Center
(restorations and conversion
of Scheidt's Brewing Company)
151 West Marshall Street,
Norristown, Pennsylvania
1985–86; built

Monument for Marconi Plaza
(for the Sons of Italy)
Marconi Plaza, Philadelphia
1985; unbuilt

**PATH Ventilation and Emergency
Exit Building, Competition**
(for the Port Authority of
New York and New Jersey)
New York
1985; unpremiated

**Clinical Research Building,
University of Pennsylvania**
Philadelphia
1985–89; built
Payette Associates, associated
architects

**Mr. and Mrs. Michael de Havenon
House**
East Hampton, New York
1985–91; built

**Exhibition Gallery, Tyler School
of Art, Temple University**
1619 Walnut Street, Philadelphia
1985–86; built (demolished)

**Contemporary Terra Cotta,
Competition**
(for the National Building Museum
and Ludowici Celadon Company,
Inc.; juror's submission)
Washington, D.C.
1985; unpremiated

Ponte dell'Accademia, Competition
(for the Biennale di Venezia)
Venice
1985; second prize

**Fisher Fine Arts Library,
University of Pennsylvania**
(restorations)
Philadelphia
1985–91; built

Office Tower Development
(for Rouse & Associates)
Bay and Laura streets,
Jacksonville, Florida
1985; unbuilt

**Warren Pearl Development
Houses**
(24 houses)
Breakers West, Weston, Florida
1985–89; one built

**Mr. and Mrs. Benjamin Paden
House**
(additions)
North Carolina
1985; unbuilt

**Dream Village for the Sunshine
Foundation**
5400 County Road 547 North,
Loughman, Florida
1985–89; built
Renker Eich Parks, executive
architects

**Sainsbury Wing, National Gallery,
Competition**
Trafalgar Square, London
1985–91; first prize, built
Sheppard Robson, associated
architects

**Professional Programs Facility,
University of California at Irvine**
Irvine, California
1985–87; unbuilt

Reading Terminal Market
(interior alterations and graphics)
Twelfth and Arch streets,
Philadelphia
1985–88; partially built

Museum of Contemporary Art, San Diego

Philadelphia Orchestra Hall

Dartmouth College Master Plan

1986

Fisher and Bendheim Halls, Princeton University
(additions)
Princeton, New Jersey
1986–91; built

House on the Coast of Maine
1986–90; built

Thayer School of Engineering, Dartmouth College
(additions)
Hanover, New Hampshire
1986–90; built

Gordon and Virginia MacDonald Medical Research Laboratories, School of Medicine, University of California at Los Angeles
Los Angeles
1986–91; built (see 1993 for phase 2)
Payette Associates, associated architects

Hotel and Convention Complex, Walt Disney World Resort, Competition
Lake Buena Vista, Florida
1986; unpremiated

Fan Pier Housing Development Master Plan
Boston
1986–87; unbuilt

Benjamin Franklin Bridge Lighting, Competition
(for the Delaware River Port Authority)
Philadelphia, and Camden, New Jersey
1986–88; first prize, built
George Izenour, lighting consultant

Museum of Contemporary Art, San Diego
(additions and alterations)
700 Prospect Street, La Jolla, California
1986–96; built
David Raphael Singer, associated architect

Cuckoo Clock
(for Alessi, Crusinallo, Italy)
1986–88 (produced 1988–95)

1987

Office Tower Development Study
(for the Reading Real Estate Company)
1301 Market Street, Philadelphia
1987; not implemented

Hartford Transportation Center, Competition
Hartford, Connecticut
1987; unpremiated

Philadelphia Orchestra Hall
Broad and Lombard streets, Philadelphia
1987–96; unbuilt

David Hanks House
Tuxedo Park, New York
1987–90; unbuilt

1988

Port Imperial
(for Arcorp Properties; master plan for real estate development)
Weehawken and West New York, New Jersey
1988; not implemented
Skidmore, Owings and Merrill, associated architects

EuroDisney Entrance Boulevard, Disneyland Paris Resort
(concept design)
Marne-la-Vallée, France
1988; unbuilt

George LaVie Schultz Laboratory, Princeton University
(addition)
Princeton, New Jersey
1988–93; built
Payette Associates, associated architects

Memorial Hall, Harvard University
(restoration, alterations, and additions)
Cambridge, Massachusetts
1988 feasibility study; 1992–96; built

Disney Island and Grand Boardwalk Hotel, Walt Disney World Resort
Lake Buena Vista, Florida
1988; unbuilt

Hotel, Disneyland Paris Resort
Marne-la-Vallée, France
1988; unbuilt

Christopher Columbus Monument
(for the America 500 Anniversary Corporation)
Penn's Landing, Philadelphia
1988–92; built

Roy and Diana Vagelos Laboratories, Institute for Advanced Science and Technology, University of Pennsylvania
(additions)
Philadelphia
1988 feasibility study; 1990–97; built
Payette Associates, associated architects

Dartmouth College Master Plan for North Campus
Hanover, New Hampshire
1988–93; partially implemented
North Campus / Berry Row Precinct study (1988–93); Baker / Berry Library, Rauner Special Collections Library and Department of History master planning (1988–89; implemented, see 1989 and 1990)

Massachusetts Museum of Contemporary Art Master Plan
(reuse of textile mill)
North Adams, Massachusetts
1988–89; not implemented
Skidmore, Owings and Merrill, associated architects; Frank O. Gehry and Associates, associated architects

Cedar Crest Shopping Center
(for Wargo Properties, Inc.)
Cedar Crest and Hamilton boulevards, Allentown, Pennsylvania
1988–89; unbuilt

Charles P. Stevenson Jr. Library,
Bard College

Hôtel du Département de la Haute-Garônne

Art Sales and Rental Gallery,
Philadelphia Museum of Art

1989

*Except as noted, all 1989–2000
projects are by Venturi, Scott Brown
and Associates, Inc.*

Locks Gallery
(interior alterations)
600 Washington Square South,
Philadelphia
1989–90; unbuilt

**University of Pennsylvania
Master Plan**
Philadelphia
1989–93; partially implemented
Campus master plan (1989–92;
partially implemented); Campus
Center study (1989; implemented,
see 1993 Perelman Quadrangle)

Philadelphia Maritime Museum
(feasibility study)
Penn's Landing, Philadelphia
1989; not implemented

**United States Pavilion, Expo '92,
Competition**
Seville, Spain
1989; unpremiated

**Baker / Berry Library,
Dartmouth College**
(additions and renovations)
Hanover, New Hampshire
1989–93 feasibility study;
1995–2001; built

**Charles P. Stevenson Jr. Library,
Bard College**
(additions)
Annandale-on-Hudson, New York
1989–93; built

**Park Pavilion for the Hudson River
Waterfront, Competition**
(for the Battery Park City
Authority)
Battery Park City, New York
1989; unpremiated

**Princeton Club of New York,
Princeton University**
(interior alterations)
15 West Forty-third Street,
New York
1989–91; built

Promenade at the Pikes
(for Wargo/Brandolini
Properties, Inc.; facade)
East Norriton Township,
Pennsylvania
1989; unbuilt

Children's Museum of Houston
1500 Binz Avenue, Houston
1989–92; built
Jackson and Ryan, architects;
Venturi, Scott Brown and
Associates, associated architects

Promenade at Hatfield
(for Donald Wargo; facade)
Route 463 and Funks Road,
Hatfield Township, Pennsylvania
1989; unbuilt

**Houston Museum of Fine Arts
Master Plan**
Houston
1989–90; not implemented

**Rural Wine Center for the
E. & J. Gallo Winery, Competition**
Modesto, California
1989–90; unpremiated

**Statistics / Surge Building,
Stanford University**
Stanford, California
1989–90; unbuilt

Rugs
(for V'Soske, New York)
1989–93; Kimono, Dots, and
Spots (produced 1993)

Fabrics
(for DesignTex, New York)
1989–91; Dots (produced 1991–92);
Gingham Floral (produced 1991–96);
Raku (produced 1991–97); Staccato
(produced 1991–96); Yukata
(produced 1991–92)

Mailbox
(for Marcuse Corporation,
Woburn, Massachusetts)
1989–91; not produced

Desk Accessories
(for KnollExtra, New York)
1989–90; not produced

1990

**Vagelos Laboratories,
University of Pennsylvania,**
see 1988

Mr. and Mrs. Vincent Scully House
Seaside, Florida
1990; unbuilt

Dream House
no site
1990; unbuilt

**Feature Animation Building, Walt
Disney Imagineering, Competition**
Walt Disney Studios, Burbank,
California
1990; unpremiated

**Berlin When the Wall Comes
Down, Competition**
(for the Berlin Tomorrow exhibition)
Deutsches Architektur-Museum,
Frankfurt am Main, Germany
1990; unpremiated

**Rauner Special Collections Library,
Dartmouth College**
(additions and alterations
to Webster Hall)
Hanover, New Hampshire
1990 feasibility study;
1996–99; built

**National Museum of the American
Indian, Smithsonian Institution**
(facilities program)
Washington, D.C.
1990–93; implemented

**Life Sciences Building, University
of Pennsylvania**
Philadelphia
1990–91; unbuilt
Payette Associates, associated
architects

Prototype Houses
(for Mitsui, Japan)
no site
1990–91; unbuilt

Franklin Court
(stage set for the Pennsylvania
Ballet, Philadelphia)
1990; built

**Hôtel du Département de la
Haute-Garônne, Competition**
Toulouse, France
1990–99; first prize, built
Hermet-Blanc-Lagausie-Mommens,
associated architects; Anderson/
Schwartz, associated architects

Kitchen Systems
(for Hanssem, Seoul, Korea)
1990–92; not produced

1991

**Henry R. Luce Center for
International and Area Studies,
Yale University**
New Haven
1991; unbuilt

**Mr. and Mrs. Coleman Burke
House**
Nantucket, Massachusetts
1991; unbuilt

Museum of Scotland, Competition
(additions)
Chambers Street, Edinburgh
1991; unpremiated

**Art Sales and Rental Gallery,
Philadelphia Museum of Art**
Benjamin Franklin Parkway,
Philadelphia
1991; built

**Columbus Gateway Corridor
Study**
(for the Indiana Department of
Transportation, the City of
Columbus, and the Front Door
Committee)
State Route 46 and Interstate 65,
Columbus, Indiana
1991–93; not implemented

**Center for the Study of Human
Disease, School of Medicine,
Yale University**
New Haven
1991–92; unbuilt

Perris Civic Center, Competition
Perris, California
1991; unpremiated

**Civic Center Cultural Complex
Master Plan**
Denver
1991–95; partially implemented

**Hospital of the University
of Pennsylvania, Competition**
(new entrance concept design)
Thirty-fourth and Spruce streets,
Philadelphia
1991–92; unpremiated

Watch
(for the Franklin Mint,
Franklin Center, Pennsylvania)
1991–95; not produced

Whitehall Ferry Terminal

Gonda (Goldschmied) Research Center, UCLA

1992

Memorial Hall, Harvard University,
see 1988

Ramada Inn
(alterations to facade)
2485 West Jonathan Moore Pike,
Columbus, Indiana
1992–95; built

North Neighborhood Master Plan
(for the Battery Park City
Authority)
Battery Park City, New York
1992–93; implemented
Anderson / Schwartz, associated
architects

**Reedy Creek Improvement District
Emergency Services Headquarters
and Fire Station, Walt Disney
World Resort**
651 Buena Vista Drive, Lake Buena
Vista, Florida
1992–93; built

**Market Street West Development
Study**
(for Maguire Thomas Partners)
Market Street, between Twenty-
first and Twenty-third streets,
Philadelphia
1992; unbuilt

**Cheju Resort Condominiums,
South Korea**
no site
1993; unbuilt

**Police Training Facility,
Competition**
Grand Concourse and East 153rd
Street, Bronx
1992; unpremiated
Anderson / Schwartz, associated
architects

Hotel Mielmonte Nikko Kirifuri
(for the Japanese Ministry of
Posts and Telecommunications;
hotel and spa)
1535–1 Tokorono, Nikko City,
Tochigi Prefecture, Nikko, Japan
1992–97; built
Marunouchi Architects & Engineers,
associated architects; Andropogon
Associates, associated landscape
architects

**Whitehall Ferry Terminal,
Competition**
(for the Economic Development
Corporation of New York City)
Whitehall and South streets,
New York
1992–96; first prize, unbuilt
Anderson / Schwartz, associated
architects

Stedelijk Museum, Competition
(addition)
Paulus Potterstraat 13, Amsterdam
1992–93; first prize, unbuilt

**Trabant Student Center,
University of Delaware**
Newark, Delaware
1992–96; built

Eastern State Penitentiary
(feasibility study for
administrative offices)
2124 Fairmount Avenue,
Philadelphia
1992–94; not implemented

Amazon Pier
(renovations)
Pier 36, Philadelphia
1992; unbuilt

Light Fixtures
(for Baldinger Architectural
Lighting, New York)
1992–97; not produced

1993

**Gonda (Goldschmied) Neuroscience
and Genetics Research Center,
School of Medicine, University of
California at Los Angeles**
Los Angeles
1993–98; built
Payette Associates, associated
architects

The Edison Project
(for Whittle Schools, Ltd.;
building program and concept
design for a national network
of new for-profit schools and
management of existing schools)
1993; implemented
Project Team: Venturi, Scott Brown
and Associates; Frank O. Gehry
and Associates; William Rawn &
Associates; and Billes/Manning

Barnes Foundation Museum
(restorations and additions)
300 North Latch's Lane, Merion,
Pennsylvania
1993–95; built

Bank of Celebration
(for The Walt Disney Company)
650 Celebration Avenue,
Celebration, Florida
1993–96; built

Bass Museum of Art, Competition
(additions)
2121 Park Avenue, Miami Beach
1993; unpremiated

**Mr. and Mrs. Edward Leisenring Jr.
House**
Berwyn, Pennsylvania
1993–95; unbuilt

**Pleasure Island Exxon Gas Station,
Walt Disney World Resort**
(for Disney Development Company)
300 East Buena Vista Drive,
Lake Buena Vista, Florida
1993–96; built

Prototype "Bigfoot" Gas Stations
(for Johnson Oil Company)
Columbus, Indiana
1993; unbuilt

**Perelman Quadrangle, University
of Pennsylvania**
(renovations, alterations, and
additions to Logan, College,
Williams and Houston halls, Irvine
Auditorium, and Wynn Commons)
Philadelphia
1993–94 central precinct planning;
1994–2000; built

**Environmental Science Building,
Brown University, Competition**
Providence, Rhode Island
1993; unpremiated
Payette Associates, associated
architects

St. Malachy School
(alterations)
1429 North Eleventh Street,
Philadelphia
1993–99; built

**Visual Arts Center,
Sarah Lawrence College,
Competition**
Bronxville, New York
1993; unpremiated

Frank G. Wells Building
© Disney Enterprises, Inc.

Trenton Central Fire Headquarters

McDonald's, Walt Disney World Resort
© Disney Enterprises, Inc.

1994

Perelman Quadrangle, University of Pennsylvania, see 1993

Site 7 Development Study, Competition
(for the New York State Urban Development Corporation and the New York City Economic Development Corporation)
Forty-third Street and Eighth Avenue, New York
1994; unpremiated
Development Team: Marriot International, Triarc Equities; Venturi, Scott Brown and Associates; Nobutaka Ashihara, Associates

Residence Hall, University of Cincinnati
Cincinnati
1994–96; unbuilt

Frank G. Wells Building
(for Walt Disney Imagineering)
Walt Disney Studios, Burbank, California
1994–98; built
HKS Architects, associated architects

Center for Italian American Cultural Exchange
(feasibility study)
Rockland Mansion, Fairmount Park, Philadelphia
1994–95; not implemented

Interstate 95 Welcome Center
(for The Walt Disney Company)
South Carolina
1994–2000; unbuilt

Prototype Houses
(for the Houston Chapter, Habitat for Humanity)
2901a and 2901b Gillespie Street, Houston
1994–99; built

Recigno Dental Laboratories
(concept design)
Willow Grove, Pennsylvania
1994–95; unbuilt

Skill, Care & Wit: Miscellaneous Objects from Japanese Markets
(exhibition design)
Philadelphia Museum of Art, Philadelphia
1994–95; built

1995

Baker / Berry Library, Dartmouth College, see 1989

Princeton Station
(for Princeton University; alterations and additions to train station)
Princeton, New Jersey
1995; unbuilt

Academic Support Building, Seton Hall University, Competition
South Orange, New Jersey
1995; unpremiated

Historical Society of Pennsylvania
(renovations and interior alterations)
1300 Locust Street, Philadelphia
1995–99; built

Amphitheater, Walt Disney World Resort
(concept design)
Lake Buena Vista, Florida
1995; unbuilt

Award
(for Samsung)
1995; not produced

United States Embassy, Competition
Pariser Platz, Berlin
1995; unpremiated

Trenton Central Fire Headquarters
(additions)
244 Perry Street, Trenton, New Jersey
1995–2000; built

Clinical Research Center, National Institutes of Health, Competition
Bethesda, Maryland
1995; unpremiated
Payette Associates, associated architects

1996

Rauner Special Collections Library, Dartmouth College, see 1990

Michael Foglietta Memorial
Dock and Mattis streets, Philadelphia
1996; unbuilt

Gateway Visitor Center and Independence Mall Master Plan
(for the Independence National Historical Park)
Philadelphia
1996; not implemented

Oliver Ames Free Library
(additions and renovations)
53 Main Street, North Easton, Massachusetts
1996; unbuilt

Shrine for Father Junipero Serra, Competition
Alameda and Los Angeles streets, Los Angeles
1996; unpremiated

Peabody Essex Museum, Competition
Essex Street, Salem, Massachusetts
1996; unpremiated

Frist Campus Center, Princeton University
(additions, alterations, and renovations)
Princeton, New Jersey
1996–2000; built

Bryn Mawr College Concept Plan
Bryn Mawr, Pennsylvania
1996–97; not implemented

Museum of Archaeology and Anthropology, University of Pennsylvania
(feasibility study for new entrance)
Philadelphia
1996; not implemented

Camden Children's Garden and Entrance Building
(for the Camden City Garden Club)
One Riverside Drive, Camden, New Jersey
1996–2000; built

Sun and Fun Pier
(for the Morey Organization; alterations and additions)
Wildwood, New Jersey
1996–97; unbuilt

Wild Palms Hotel
(for the Morey Organization; alterations and additions)
Ocean Boulevard, Wildwood Crest, New Jersey
1996–97; unbuilt

Acadia Summer Arts Program
(new buildings, alterations, and additions)
Mount Desert, Maine
1996–2000; built

McDonald's, Walt Disney World Resort
1596 West Buena Vista Drive, Lake Buena Vista, Florida
1996–98; built

National World War II Memorial, Competition
Washington, D.C.
1996; unpremiated

Charry Sanctuary, Germantown Jewish Centre
(Bimah restoration and alterations)
400 West Ellet Street, Philadelphia
1996; built

University of Michigan Master Plan

Biomedical Research Facility, Yale University

Mr. and Mrs. Herbert Adler House

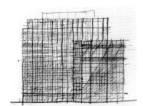
Edison School and Headquarters Building

1997

University of Michigan Master Plan
Ann Arbor, Michigan
1997–; partially implemented
Palmer Drive area study (1997–99; implemented, see 1999); Central Campus facilities management planning and facilities programming (1998–99; implemented); Health System planning (1998–); Medical Center Campus and Wall Street planning (1998–); Law School programming study (1998–2000); Walgreen Drama Center feasibility study (1998–2000; implementation stage)

Penguin Pool, New Jersey State Aquarium
(for the Cooper's Ferry Development Association)
One Riverside Drive, Camden, New Jersey
1997–98; built

Offices, Easter Fleet Center
(for Maritrans, Inc.; feasibility study)
Eastwick, Philadelphia
1997; not implemented

Stadium, University of Michigan
(additions)
Ann Arbor, Michigan
1997–98; built (partially removed)
HOK/Sport, associated architects

Dormitory, Bowdoin College
(sketch design)
Brunswick, Maine
1997; unbuilt

Visitor Center for Old Salem Village
(building program; site selection, 4 preliminary designs)
Walnut Street and Old Salem Road, Winston-Salem, North Carolina
1997–99; unbuilt

1998

Garage, Disneyland Resort, Competition
Disneyland Resort, Anaheim, California
1998; unpremiated

Biomedical Research and Teaching Facility, School of Medicine, Yale University
New Haven
1998–; construction phase
Payette Associates, associated architects

Architectural Archives, University of Pennsylvania
(feasibility study for expansion)
Philadelphia
1998–2000; partially implemented

Connelly Mill Land Development, Competition
Manayunk, Philadelphia
1998; unpremiated

Theater, Dance, Film and Arts Center, Franklin and Marshall College
Lancaster, Pennsylvania
1998–2000; feasibility study; implemented; 2000 competition; unpremiated

1999

Old Mill Storage Buildings
(for Kay Properties; signs)
Baltimore Avenue (site 1) and Shurs Lane (site 2), Philadelphia
1999; preliminary design stage

Palmer Drive Development, University of Michigan
(Life Sciences Institute Laboratory; Commons Building; parking garage; site planning; walkways; and bridge)
Ann Arbor, Michigan
1999–; design development stage Smith Group Incorporated, associated architects (laboratory); Desman Associates, associated architects (parking garage)

Penn-Asbury Infant Center, Competition
(for the University of Pennsylvania)
3300 block of Chestnut Street, Philadelphia
1999; unpremiated

Mr. and Mrs. Herbert Adler House
Williamstown, Massachusetts
1999; unbuilt

New Entrance, New Jersey State Aquarium
One Riverside Drive, Camden, New Jersey
1999; built

Fondren Library, Rice University
(additions and renovations)
Houston
1999–2000; unbuilt
Shepley, Bulfinch, Richardson and Abbot, associated architects

2000

Chicago Crown Fountain, Competition
Chicago
2000; unpremiated

Offices, Creative Technologies, New York
(interior alterations)
University City Science Center, 3535 Market Street, Philadelphia
2000; built

Train Garden, Camden Children's Garden
One Riverside Drive, Camden, New Jersey
2000; built

Edison School and Headquarters Building/Museum for African Art, Competition
Fifth Avenue and 110th Street, New York
2000–; first prize for Edison School and Headquarters

Woodmere Art Museum
(additions and alterations)
9201 Germantown Avenue, Philadelphia
2000–; preliminary design stage

Biomedical and Biological Science Research Building, University of Kentucky
(precinct plan)
Lexington, Kentucky
2000–; schematic design stage
A.M. Kinney, Inc., architects; Venturi, Scott Brown and Associates, associated architects

SELECTED BIBLIOGRAPHY

An extensive bibliography that includes all writings by and about Venturi, Scott Brown and Associates is available on the firm's website www.vsba.com.

Amery, Colin. *The National Gallery Sainsbury Wing: A Celebration of Art and Architecture*. London: National Gallery Publications, 1991.

Belluzzi, Amedeo. *Venturi, Scott Brown e Associati*. Rome: Laterza, 1992.

Davies, Hugh M., and Anne Farrell. With an essay by Robert Venturi. *Learning from La Jolla: Robert Venturi Remakes a Museum in the Precinct of Irving Gill*. San Diego: Museum of Contemporary Art, San Diego, 1996.

Mead, Christopher, ed. *The Architecture of Robert Venturi*. Albuquerque: University of New Mexico Press, 1989.

Pettena, Gianni, and Maurizio Vogliazzo. *Venturi, Rauch and Scott Brown*. Milan: Electa, 1981.

Sanmartin, A., ed. *Venturi, Rauch & Scott Brown*. London: Academy Editions, 1986.

Schwartz, Frederic, ed. *Mother's House: The Evolution of Vanna Venturi's House in Chestnut Hill*. New York: Rizzoli, 1992.

Schwartz, Frederic, and Carolina Vaccaro. *Venturi, Scott Brown and Associates: Works and Projects*. Trans. Carlos Sáenz de Valicourt and Graham Thomson. Bologna: Nicola Zanichelli, 1991.

Scott Brown, Denise. *Urban Concepts*. Architectural Design, profile 83. New York: St. Martin's Press, 1990.

Venturi and Rauch: The Public Buildings. Architectural Monographs, no. 1. London: Academy Editions, 1978.

Venturi, Rauch and Scott Brown: A Generation of Architecture. Urbana-Champaign: Krannert Art Museum, University of Illinois at Urbana-Champaign, 1984.

Venturi, Robert. *Complexity and Contradiction in Architecture*. New York: The Museum of Modern Art, 1966.

——. *The Pritzker Architecture Prize 1991: Presented to Robert Venturi*. Los Angeles: Jensen & Walker, 1991.

——. *Iconography and Electronics upon a Generic Architecture: A View from the Drafting Room*. Cambridge and London: The MIT Press, 1996.

Venturi, Robert, and Denise Scott Brown. *A View from the Campidoglio: Selected Essays, 1953–1984*. Eds. Peter Arnell, Ted Bickford, and Catherine Bergart. New York: Harper & Row, 1984.

Venturi, Robert, Denise Scott Brown, and Steven Izenour. *Learning from Las Vegas*. Cambridge and London: The MIT Press, 1972.

Venturi, Scott Brown and Associates, Inc. *Architecture and Decorative Arts: Two Naifs in Japan*. Tokyo: Kajima Institute Publishing Co., 1991.

Venturi, Scott Brown and Associates. Seoul: Plus Publishing Co., 1992.

Venturi, Scott Brown & Associates: On Houses and Housing. Architectural Monographs, no. 21. New York: St. Martin's Press, 1992.

Von Moos, Stanislaus. *Venturi, Rauch & Scott Brown: Buildings and Projects*. Trans. David Antal. New York: Rizzoli, 1987.

——. *Venturi, Scott Brown & Associates: Buildings and Projects, 1986–1998*. New York: The Monacelli Press, 1999.

ACKNOWLEDGMENTS

In studying the architecture and design of Venturi, Scott Brown and Associates over the past five years, the authors have been assisted by numerous colleagues, architects, institutions, and companies whom we warmly acknowledge and thank:

First and foremost, Robert Venturi and Denise Scott Brown, patient and wise colleagues as well as the subjects of this project, who gave us unprecedented access to their firm's archives, reviewed our work, and made themselves available to us and our students. Secondly, the Architectural Archives of the University of Pennsylvania, where the project files and papers of Venturi, Scott Brown and Associates have been organized, and its director, Julia Moore Converse, for her counsel and hospitality.

In Philadelphia, among the members of the remarkable firm that this book and exhibition celebrate: Steven Izenour and John Izenour, who offered endless help in general; Claudia Cueto, who coordinated the Nikko interiors and answered questions too numerous to count; David Marohn, project manager for Nikko; R. Michael Wommack, who supplied information on the painted furniture decorations; Judy Glass, Monica Quinn, and Susan R. Scanlon, who provided administrative help; William Rankin, who repaired a number of the architectural models for exhibition; Stephen Van Dyck.

We would also like to thank former members of the firm: most particularly Maurice E. Weintraub, former project manager for the decorative arts projects, whose advice was invaluable and who read the decorative arts portion of the manuscript in an earlier version; Dian Boone, interior designer, who advised on the development of the interior design projects on which she collaborated; John Rauch, former partner, who shared his overview of the firm's history; Linda Payne, who provided administrative help.

Also in Philadelphia, Cynthia Drayton and Grant Greapentrog, who kindly shared their knowledge of design firms, past and present; Marion Stroud Swingle as well as Maryanne Friel of the Fabric Workshop and Museum for information about the development of the fabric patterns there; Victoria Donohue for advice on the St. Francis de Sales commission; Patricia Mellet, Rectory Office, St. Francis de Sales; Morris C. Kellett, Esq. for advice on matters legal and otherwise; Patricia Conway and Roger Milgrim for special assistance; Thomas Hughes and Agatha Hughes; William Christensen and Linda Brenner of Christensen, Brenner, Kass; Joan Irving and Rondi Barracelli, the Conservation Center for Art and Historic Artifacts; and Will Brown.

In New York, Marc Hacker, formerly vice-president of design and development at Swid Powell, who patiently answered questions and reconstructed the history of the projects; Hillary Blumberg, formerly design and development at Swid Powell, for information about the history of the firm; Albert Pfeiffer, at Knoll, Curator of the Knoll Museum and knowledgeable Knoll historian; David Hanks; Roger McDonald and Ellen Hertzmark, Directors Design/Marketing at V'Soske; Kathryn Gabriel, Vice-president, Marketing, DesignTex; Steven W. Kroeter, Archetype Associates; M. Louis Goodman; Mrs. Ralph Lauren and Michèle Archambault; Mr. and Mrs. Michael de Havenon; Michael Blackwood, Michael Blackwood Productions, Inc.

Elsewhere in the United States, Kim Madden, Manager, Public Relations, Reed & Barton Silversmiths, Taunton, Massachusetts; Ruth Fox, Pillowtex, Kannapolis, North Carolina; Frederick R. Brandt, Curator, Lewis Collection, Richmond, Virginia; Vincent J. Scully Jr., New Haven; William Shea, East Greenville, Pennsylvania; Joseph Allen and Kathy Millard, Brant-Allen Industries, Greenwich, Connecticut; Peter M. Brant, Greenwich, Connecticut; Gary Kalpakjian, Garden City, New York; Mr. and Mrs. Donald Petrie, Wainscott, New York; Hugh Davies, Director, Museum of Contemporary Art, San Diego; Jeffrey D. Ryan, Jackson & Ryan, Houston; Robert Kasdin, Executive Vice President and Chief Financial Officer, University of Michigan; Sue Burnett, University of Michigan; Linda M. Baron, Photographic Archivist, Herman Miller, Zeeland, Michigan; R. Craig Miller, Curator, Architecture, Design, and Graphics, Denver Art Museum; Mr. and Mrs. Charles Weiss, Glen Cove, New York; Mr. and Mrs. Irving Abrams, Pittsburgh; Wing T. Chao and Christopher Crary, Walt Disney Imagineering, Burbank, California; Richard Spear, former director, Allen Memorial Art Museum, Oberlin College; Mary F. Daniel, Librarian, Frances Loeb Library, Harvard University Graduate School of Design; Jennifer Strobel, Domestic Life Collection, National Museum of American History, Smithsonian Institution; Scott McCoy, Pioneer New Media Technologies, Midlothian, Virginia; Kevin Jarrell, MCSI, Nashville, Tennessee.

In Europe, Francesca Appiani, Curator, Museo Alessi, Crusinallo, Italy; Cristina Ossato, Cleto Munari Design Associati, Vicenza, Italy; Paola Navone and Patrizia Valle, Paola Navone Consultant, Milan; Renzo Brugola, Lissone, Italy; Christopher Riopelle, National Gallery, London; John Harris, London; Françoise Blanc, Toulouse, France; Pierre Izard, Président, and Monique Brocard, Directeur de Cabinet, Conseil General de la Haute-Garônne, Toulouse, France; Stanislaus von Moos, University of Zurich.

In Japan, Akio Izutsu, former president, Knoll International Japan, Tokyo, for insight into the Venturis' work in Japan and information on the production of furniture there; Shigeki Kawakami, Curator of Textiles, Kyoto National Museum, Kyoto, for help on the design sources of the fabric patterns; Shiro Mitani and others, Japanese Ministry of Posts and Telecommunications; Susumu Yamagiwa, President, Marunouchi Architects & Engineers, Tokyo, for invaluable help regarding Nikko and its custom furnishings.

Finally, we would like to thank those closest to us, graduate students at the University of Pennsylvania who worked on the research project at the Architectural Archives, those who participated in seminars at the University of Pennsylvania on the architecture and design of Venturi, Scott Brown and Associates in the fall of 1998 and spring of 1999, or who assisted otherwise: Lisa Boettger; Amanda T. Hall; Rachel Iannacone; Nicholas Sawicki; Isabel Taube; as well as Joseph V. Bianco; Joyce H. Cheng; Rolando Corpus; Julianne Dunn; Seth Hinshaw; Saiko Ito; Debra Lavoie; Kelly McCullough; Matthew E. Pisarski; Christopher P. Redmann; Gregory J. Saldaña; Susanna Williams Gold; Ka-Kee Yan. At the Philadelphia Museum of Art, we are grateful to Donna Corbin, William Rudolph, Sarah Aibel, and Ann Lalley, in the Department of European Decorative Arts after 1700; Melissa S. Meighan and Sara Reiter, Conservation; William S. Hilley, Administrative Services; Betty Marmon and Linda Jacobs, Development; Felice Fischer, East Asian Art; Richard Bonk, Gretchen Dykstra, Diane Gottardi, Matthew Pimm, and Maia Wind, Editorial and Graphic Design; Danielle Rice and Elizabeth Anderson, Education; Joseph Revlock, Construction; Jack Schlechter, Installations Design; Michael A. MacFeat and Martha Masiello, Installations; Josephine Chen and Lilah Mittelstaedt, Library; Graydon Wood and Lynn Rosenthal, Photography; Gary R. Hiatt, Prints, Drawings, and Photographs; Irene Taurins, Trine Vanderwall, and Elie-Anne Chevrier, Registrar; Suzanne F. Wells and Krista Mancini, Special Exhibitions, and finally, to George H. Marcus and Nicole Amoroso, Publishing, who edited this book with infinite skill and corrected all the mistakes that we could not manage to hide from them.

INDEX OF PROPER NAMES

Note: Page numbers in italics indicate illustrations.

A

Aalto, Alvar, 34, 35, 45, 93
    armchair, 202, *202*
    Finlandia Hall, Helsinki, Finland, 173, *173*
    Finnish pavilion, 130, *130*
    Marl town hall, *160*, 161
    references to, 172, 173
    Social Security Office, Helsinki, Finland, 43
Abet Laminati (firm), 213
Abrams, Irving and Betty, 83
Abrams house, Pittsburgh, Pennsylvania, 83–85, *86*
Ackerman, James S., 101
Adam, Robert, 86
Adler house, Williamstown, Massachusetts, *159*, 160
Agriculture and forestry building for the Esposizione Universale di Roma, Rome (Brasini), 12, *12*
Ahrends Burton and Koralek, National Gallery extension scheme, *122*, 123
Alessi (firm)
    Campidoglio tray for, 235, *235*
    candlestick for, *224*, 227
    cuckoo clock for, 236, *237*
    product design for, 200, 231–36
    tea and coffee service for, *222*, 223, *223*, 231–35, *232–34*
Alessi, Alberto, 223, 231
Alessi Anghini house, Omegna, Italy, *236*
Allen Memorial Art Museum, Oberlin College, Ohio, 59–62, *60–62*, 213
Aluminum City Terrace workers housing (Gropius and Breuer), 10
Ambasz, Emilio, 219
American Architecture and Urbanism (Scully), 49
American Institute of Architects (AIA), 73
Andropogon Associates, 167
Archetype Associates, 237
Arc International (firm), product design for, 200, 215–17
Architectural Association, London, Scott Brown at, *4*, 5
Architectural League of New York, Art and Architecture Awards competition, 29
Art Deco chair for Knoll, *211*, 213
Art Nouveau chair for Knoll, *205*, 213
Austrian Museum for Applied Arts, Vienna, Biedermeier chair at, *204*

B

Bacon, Edmund, 6, 7
Baker/Berry Library, Dartmouth College, Hanover, New Hampshire, 114–17, *116*
Ballinger Corporation, 8
Bank of Celebration, Celebration, Florida, *152*, 153
Bard College, Annandale-on-Hudson, New York, Charles P. Stevenson Jr. Library, *108*, *109*, 109–13, *110*, *111*
Barnes, Edward Larrabee, 43–45
BASCO, Inc., 79–80
    showroom and warehouse, Philadelphia, *79*, 80
Bastian, John, 91
Battery Park City, New York, north neighborhood master plan for, 147
Beach house, New Jersey, *16*, 16–17
Benjamin Franklin Parkway, Philadelphia, monumental fountain on, 29–31, *30*
Bertoia, Harry, 197, 220
Best Products Company, 77–79
    showroom, Langhorne, Pennsylvania, *78*, 79, 213, *214*, 231
Biedermeier chair for Knoll, *204*, 207, 213
Big Apple at Times Square Center, The, New York, *146*, 147
Birkerts, Gunnar, 10
Blanc, Françoise, 168, 172, 175
Blenheim Hotel, Atlantic City, New Jersey (Price), 77
Bofill, Ricardo, 87, 137
Bollinger, Lee C., 175, 178
Boone, Dian, 188
Borromini, Francesco, 231
Borromini dinner service for Swid Powell, *230*, 231
Bosworth, Francis, 24
Bowen, William, 93
Brant, Peter and Sandy, 55, 64, 85
Brant house, Greenwich, Connecticut, 55–59, *56*, *57*, *59*, 159
Brant house, Tucker's Town, Bermuda, 64–66, *66*, 159
Brant-Johnson ski house, Vail, Colorado, 64, *65*
Brasini, Armando, 12, 14
    agriculture and forestry building for the Esposizione Universale di Roma, Rome, 12, *12*
Breuer, Marcel, 10, 29, 197, 220
Brighton Beach, Brooklyn, middle-income housing development for, *43*, 43–44
Brigio, Frank, 41
Brno armchair (Mies van der Rohe), 190, 197
Brous house, Southampton, New York, *156*, 159

Brown, J. Carter, 74
Buckstaff (firm), 190, 193
Bunshaft, Gordon, 43
Burton, Scott, 213

C

Cabriole leg table for Knoll, *204*, 207
California City, California, general plan for, 49, *50*, *51*
Calvin Klein (firm), 243
Campbell, Robert, 113
Campidoglio tray for Alessi, 235, *235*
Candlestick for Alessi, *224*, 227
Candlestick for Swid Powell, *224*
Carving set and serving spoon for Swid Powell, *227*, 228
Carving set for Swid Powell, 228, *228*
Case Study House (Eames), 188
Castle, Wendell, 217
Celebration 76 exposition master plan, Philadelphia, 68
Center City Development Plan, Memphis, 147
Centerpiece for Swid Powell, *230*, 231
Charles, Prince of Wales, 123, 131
Charles P. Stevenson Jr. Library, Bard College, Annandale-on-Hudson, New York, *108–11*, *109*–13
Children's Garden and entrance building, Camden, New Jersey, 137
Children's Museum of Houston, 137
Chippendale chair for Knoll, 190, *202*, *203*, 207, *209*, 213
Christoff, Stephanie, 92
City hall, North Canton, Ohio, 31, 32
City Tower, Philadelphia (Kahn), *12*, 13
Civic Center Cultural Complex, Denver, *147*, 147–49
Clark, Gerod, 22, 24, 38, 52
Classical dinner service for Swid Powell, 229, *229*, 231
Clinical Research Building, University of Pennsylvania, Philadelphia, 103, *103*
Cogan, Marshall, 219, 220
Colombo, Joe, 194
Commonwealth Parliament House, Canberra, Australia, 86, *87*
Complexity and Contradiction in Architecture (Venturi), 7, 35–36, *36*, 73, 184–85, 200
Cope, Paul, 13
Cope and Lippincott, 20, 22
County Federal Savings and Loan Association, branch office, Fairfield, Connecticut, 80, *81*
Coxe, Weld, 55

Coxe and Hayden house and studio, Block Island, Rhode Island, *54*, 55

Cram, Ralph Adams, 117

Crane, David, 6, 46

Cripps, Richard, 31

Cuckoo clock for Alessi, 236, *237*

D

D'Agostino, Anthony and Muriel, 58

D'Agostino house, Clinton, New York, 58, *58*

Dartmouth College, Hanover, New Hampshire

    Baker/Berry Library, 114–17, *116*

    master plan for north campus, *115*, 116

Dashes bedlinens for Swid Powell, *226*, 228

Dashes glassware for Swid Powell, *221*

Davies, Hugh, 131

Davis, Stuart, 237–38

Death and Life of Great American Cities (Jacobs), 7

Decorative Art of Today, The (Le Corbusier), 184–85

De Havenon house, East Hampton, New York, *158*, 159–60

Design Lighting (firm), 193

DesignTex (firm), product designs for, 200, 237, 240–43

DeVore, Richard, 213

Diffrient, Niels, 220

Discovery Place Museum of Science and Technology, Charlotte, North Carolina, 80, *81*

Disneyland Paris Resort, Marne-la-Vallée, France

    EuroDisney entrance boulevard, *155*

    Fantasia Hotel, *152–53*, 153

Dixon, John Morris, 72

Dixwell fire station, New Haven, 38, *39*

Dominican Motherhouse of Saint Catherine de Ricci, Media, Pennsylvania, 66

Dots fabric for DesignTex, *240*, 240–43

Dots rug for V'Soske, 238, *240*

Douglas Campbell (firm), 190

Downtown mural art project, Scranton, Pennsylvania, *82*, 83

Dream Village for the Sunshine Foundation, Loughman, Florida, *156*, 157

Duany, Andres, 180

Duke, Joseph, 217

Duke house, New York University, *182*, 183

Duke mansion (Trumbauer), 14–16

Dukes, George, 47

Dyckman, John, 6

E

Eames, Charles and Ray, 184, 197

    Case Study House, 188

East Pakistan capital complex, Dhaka, 34

Eclectic House series, 83, *84*

Edward, David, 193

Egbert, Donald Drew, 9

Egyed, Alex, 80

Eisenman, Peter, 45, 97, 99, 181

"Elective Affinities" (exhibition), XVII International Triennale, Milan, 215, 217–19, *218*

Emerson, Ralph Waldo, 9

Empire chair for Knoll, *210*, 213

Encyclopaedia of Cottage, Farm, and Villa Architecture (Loudon), 157

Episcopal Academy, Merion, Pennsylvania, 7

    chapel for, 9, 10, *11*

Esherick house, Philadelphia (Kahn), 18

Esposizione Universale di Roma, agriculture and forestry building, Rome (Brasini), 12, *12*

Esprit Nouveau pavilion for the Exposition Internationale des Arts Décoratifs et Industriels Modernes, Paris (Le Corbusier), 185, *185*

EuroDisney entrance boulevard, Disneyland Paris Resort, Marne-la-Vallée, France, *155*

Evitts, Ron, 92

Eyre, Wilson, 14

F

Fabric Workshop, The, Philadelphia, 213

    Flowers fabric for, 213, *214*

    Grandmother fabric for, *212*, 213

    Notebook fabric for, *212*, 213

Faculty Club, Pennsylvania State University, 62–63, *63*

    interior design, 188–90, *189*

Fairhill Square, Philadelphia, *15*, 16

Falcon (firm), 190

Fantasia Hotel, Disneyland Paris Resort, Marne-la-Vallée, France, *152–53*, 153

Fieldcrest Cannon (firm), 227–28

Filler, Martin, 131, 180, 223

Finkelpearl, Philip, 8, 13, 35

Finlandia Hall, Helsinki, Finland (Aalto), 173, *173*

Finnish pavilion (Aalto), 130, *130*

Fire station no. 4, Columbus, Indiana, 38, *39*

Fisher and Bendheim halls, Princeton University, New Jersey, 103, *106*

Fisher Fine Arts Library, University of Pennsylvania, Philadelphia, *112*, 113

Fitch, James Marston, 52

Flatware for Swid Powell, *228*, 228–29

Fleming, Thomas, 16

Flint, Peter and Karen, 83

Flint house, Greenville, Delaware, 83, 85

    interior design, 194, *194*

Flowers dinner service for Swid Powell, *229*, 229–31

Flowers fabric for the Fabric Workshop, Philadelphia, 213, *214*

Fondren Library, Rice University, Houston, *116*, 117

Foulkeways, Gwynedd Valley, Pennsylvania, 18, *18*

Frampton, Kenneth, 49

Frank, Josef, 183

Frank G. Wells Building, Walt Disney Studios, Burbank, California, *154*, 155

Franklin Court, Philadelphia, 69–71, *70*, 173

Franklin Delano Roosevelt Memorial, Washington, D.C., 20–21, *21*

Freedom Plaza, Washington, D.C., 73–75, *74*

Friedlaender, Walter, 13

Friends Neighborhood Guild, apartment building for, 22, *23*, 28

Frist Campus Center, Princeton University, New Jersey, 114, *115*

Frug House. *See* Mills pool house

Fukui, Sadako, 197

Furness, Frank, 7, 8, 109

Furniture Treasury: (Mostly of American Origin) (Nutting), 202, *203*

Futagawa, Yukio, 59

G

Gallo Winery visitor center, Modesto, California, 149–53, *151*

Gambescia house and professional office, Philadelphia, 186, *187*

Gans, Herbert, 6, 24, 47

Garfield, Eugene, 80

Gateway Visitor Center, Independence National Historical Park, Philadelphia, *148*, 149

Geddes, Robert, 35, 36

Gehry, Frank, 99, 122, 155, 181

    Guggenheim Museum, Bilbao, Spain, 122

General Felt Industries, 219

General Motors Technical Center (Saarinen), 10, 184

George LaVie Schultz Laboratory, Princeton University, New Jersey, 103–9, *107*

Gianopulos, Nicholas, 21

Giedion, Sigfried, 12

Gilbert, Cass, 59, 60

Gill, Irving

    Scripps house, 131, 134, 137

    Women's Club, 134

Gilliam, Sam, 213

Gingham Floral fabric for DesignTex, 240, *241*, *242*, 243

Girard Bank, Philadelphia (McKim, Mead & White), 9

Giurgola, Romaldo, 35, 44, 86

Glass House, New Canaan, Connecticut (Johnson), 10

Goldberg, Bertrand, 29

Goldberger, Paul, 45, 52, 55, 59, 72, 137, 215

Goldfinger, Ernö, 5

Gonda (Goldschmied) Neuroscience and Genetics Research Center, University of California at Los Angeles, 103, *105*

Goodman, Louis, 217

Gordon and Virginia MacDonald Medical Research Laboratories, University of California at Los Angeles, 103, *104*

Gordon Wu Hall, Princeton University, New Jersey, *90*, *93*, 93–97, *94*, *95*

    interior design, *192*, 193

Gore Place, Waltham, Massachusetts, 55

Gothic Revival chair for Knoll, *211*, 213

Grabar, Oleg, 140

Graham, Robert, 217

Grand, Henry and Marion, 22

Grandmother dinner service for Swid Powell, 220, *220*, 223

Grandmother fabric for the Fabric Workshop, Philadelphia, *212*, 213

Grandmother glassware for Swid Powell, *221*

Grand's restaurant, Philadelphia, *21*, 22–24, 190, *191*

    interior design, 185, *186*

Graves, Michael, 45, 79, 83, 87, 180, 220, 231, 238

Great Western United Corporation, 49

Greenberg, Allen, 79, 83, 85–87

Griffin, Walter Burley, 86

Gropius, Walter, 8, 10

Guggenheim Museum, Bilbao, Spain (Gehry), 122

Guild House, Philadelphia, 22, *23*, 28

Gwathmey, Charles, 45, 220, 238

H

Hacker, Marc, 223, 229, 237

Hanks house, Tuxedo Park, New York, *159*, 160

Harris, Britton, 6

Harrison, Wallace, 60

Hartwell Lake Regional Visitor Center, Hartwell Lake, South Carolina, 80, *81*

Harvard University, Cambridge, Massachusetts, Memorial Hall, *112*, 113

Haviland, John, 140

Hawksmoor, Nicholas, 9, 35

Hayden, Mary, 55

Hejduk, John, 45, 219

Hepplewhite chair for Knoll, *210*, 213

Herald Square subway station, 46–47

Herman Miller Furniture Company showroom, Los Angeles, California, *188*

Hermet-Blanc-Lagausie-Mommens, 168

Hersey, George, 45, 58

Hertzmark, Ellen, 238

Hess, Thomas, 71

High Hollow house (Howe), 66

Hirshorn, Paul, 92

Hoffmann, Josef, 190

Holkham Hall, Norfolk, England, 58

Holl, Steven, 220, 238

Hollein, Hans, 87, 231

Hôtel d'Assézat, Toulouse, France, *172*

Hôtel du Département de la Haute-Garônne, Toulouse, France, 167–75, *168–71, 173, 174*

Hotel Mielmonte Nikko Kirifuri, Nikko, Japan, 153, *160–66*, 160–67

   interior design, 194–200, *195, 196, 198, 199*

House on the coast of Maine, *158*, 159

Howe, George, 10, 66

Hubbard house, Nantucket, Massachusetts, *156*, 159

Hunstanton School, Norfolk, England (Smithson), 5

Hunter, John, 91

Hussein, Saddam, 137

Huxtable, Ada Louise, 52, 72

I

Iconography and Electronics upon a Generic Architecture (Venturi), 92

Independence Mall, Independence National Historical Park, Philadelphia, *148*, 149

Indian Institute of Management, Ahmedabad (Kahn), 34

Institute for Scientific Information (ISI), 80

   headquarters, Philadelphia, 78, 80, 213

Institute of Fine Arts, New York University, 14–16

International Bicentennial Exposition, Philadelphia, 67, *68*

International Tabletop Award, 228

"In This Academy: The Pennsylvania Academy of the Fine Arts, 1805–76" (exhibition design), 71

Iraqi State Mosque, Baghdad, 137–40, *138, 139*

Isozaki, Arata, 220

Itoki (firm), 197

Izard, Pierre, 175

Izenour, John, 91

Izenour, Steven, 47, 52, 67, 71, 77, 86, 91, 153

Izutsu, Akio, 161, 167, 200

J

Jacksonville, Florida, office tower development for, *149, 150*

Jacobs, Jane, 7

Jefferson Library, University of Virginia, Charlottesville, 9

Jencks, Charles, 83, 231

Jim Thorpe, Pennsylvania, lower historic district planning study for, 76, *76*

Johns, Jasper, 21

Johnson (firm), 193

Johnson, Herbert F., 9

Johnson, Jed, 64

Johnson, Jennifer, 217

Johnson, Lyndon, 3

Johnson, Philip, 10, 43, 60, 79, 147, 180

   Glass House, New Canaan, Connecticut, 10

Jordy, William, 36

K

Kahn, Louis, 6, 10, 34–35, 66–67, 178

   bathhouse for Trenton Jewish Community Center, *6, 12*, 13

   City Tower, Philadelphia, *12*

   Esherick house, Philadelphia, 18

   Goldenberg house, Rydal, Pennsylvania, 17, *17*

   Indian Institute of Management, Ahmedabad, 34

   Kimbell Museum, Fort Worth, Texas, 60

   and Venturi, 12–14, 16, 20

Kalpakjian house, Glen Cove, New York, *157*, 159

   interior design, *193*, 194

Keller house armchair (Hoffmann), 190

Kennedy, John F., 3

Kennedy, Robert, 3

Kimball, Roger, 180

Kimono rug for V'Soske, 238, *239*

King, Martin Luther, Jr., 3

Knoll International (firm), 243

   fabric design for, *212*, 213

   Hotel Mielmonte Nikko Kirifuri, Nikko, Japan, 161, 197

   offices and showroom, New York, 85–86, *87*

   product design for, 194, 200, 201–15

Koch, Carl, 10

Koetter, Fred, 52

Kolken, Jaimie, 91

Korn, Arthur, 5

Kramer, Hilton, 71

Krier, Leon, 87

Kroeter, Steven W., 237

Krug (firm), 193

Kushner, Robert, 213

L

Labatut, Jean, 8–9, 89

Laccio table (Breuer), 197

Laguna Gloria Art Museum, Austin, Texas, 117–18, *118*

Laloux, Victor, 8

Lamerie, Paul de, teapot by, *234*

Language of Post-Modern Architecture, The (Jencks), 83

Lavin, Sylvia, 98, 130

"Le Affinità Elettive" (exhibition), XVII International Triennale, Milan, 215, 217–19, *218*

Learning from Las Vegas (Venturi and Scott Brown), 37–38, *46*, 47, 52, 72, *136*, 137

"Learning from Levittown," *46*, 47

"Learning from Tokyo," *160*, 161–63

Le Corbusier, 5, 6, 35

   Decorative Art of Today, The, 184–85

   Esprit Nouveau pavilion for the Exposition Internationale des Arts Décoratifs et Industriels Modernes, Paris, 185, *185*

   Maison Citrohan, 85

   Villa Savoye, 9, 16, 57

Lee D. Butler Memorial Plaza, Princeton University, New Jersey, *94*, 96

Lees Commercial Carpets, 200

L'Enfant, Pierre Charles, 73

Lew, Eva, 91

Lewis, Frances and Sydney, 77–79

Lewis Thomas Laboratory, Princeton University, 99–103, *100–103*

Lichtenstein, Roy, 213

Lieb beach house, Barnegat Light, New Jersey, 41, *42*, 97

Lin, Maya, 243

Lippincott, Mather, 13, 22

Lititz Planing Mill Company, 194

Loos, Adolf, 186

   Villa Müller, Prague, *186*

Loudon, John Claudius, 157

Louis XV lowboy for Arc International, 216

Louis XVI lowboy for Arc International, 217, *217*

Low house, Bristol, Rhode Island (McKim, Mead & White), 16, *17*, 29

Low table for Knoll, *208*

Lumsden, Anthony, 79

Lutyens, Edwin, 35, 186, 190

Lyndon, Donlyn, 44

Lyons, Susan, 240

M

Maison Citrohan (Le Corbusier), 85

Marconi Plaza, Philadelphia, monument for, 147, *147*

Marisol, 217

Marl town hall (Aalto), *160*, 161

Marohn, David, 76, 91, 197

Marrot, Paule, 213

Marunouchi Architects & Engineers, 161, 200

Mathematics Building, Yale University, New Haven, 44, *44*, 45

McDonald, Roger, 238

McDonough, William, 243

McKim, Mead & White

   Girard Bank, Philadelphia, 9

   Low house, Bristol, Rhode Island, 16, *17*, 29

   Pennsylvania Station, New York, 8

McLuhan, Marshall, 21

Medary, Milton, 52

Meier, Richard, 29, 45, 87, 181

   J. Paul Getty Museum, Los Angeles, 122

   product design, 220, 231, 240

Meiss, Millard, 24

Meiss house, Princeton, New Jersey, 24, *25*

Memorial Hall, Harvard University, Cambridge, Massachusetts, *112*, 113

Mendini, Alessandro, 231, 236

Meyerson, Martin, 6, 80

Michelangelo, 235

Mies van der Rohe, Ludwig, 5, 97, 220

   Brno armchair, 190, 197

Mills pool house (Frug House), Princeton, New Jersey, 28, *28*, 31

Milwaukee War Memorial Auditorium (Saarinen), 10

Moore, Charles, 22, 29, 35, 44–45, 79, 87, 180

Mosher & Drew, 131

Mother's House. *See* Vanna Venturi house

Mount Vernon, house based on, 85, *86*, 207

Munari, Cleto, product design for, 200, 236–37, *238*

Museum für Kunsthandwerk, Frankfurt am Main, Germany, 86–87, *88*

Museum of Contemporary Art, San Diego, La Jolla, California, 118, 131–37, *132–36*

Museum of Modern Art, The, New York, Ecole des Beaux-Arts exhibition, 80–83

N

National Collegiate Football Hall of Fame, Piscataway, New Jersey, 38, 38–41, *40*, 149

National Farmers' Bank, Owatonna, Minnesota, 31
National Gallery, London
    Ahrends Burton and Koralek extension scheme, *122*, 123
    Sainsbury Wing, 118, 122–31, *122–31*
National Medal of Arts, 92
Navone, Paola, 213, 215
New Directions in American Architecture (Stern), 49
New York Jewish Museum (Roche), 131
New York Tabletop Show, 220
New York University
    Duke house, *182*, 183
    Institute of Fine Arts, 14–16
    renovation, 183–84
Nichol's Alley Company, Houston, jazz club for, 80, *81*
1900 in Barcelona, Art Nouveau chair from, 205
Noack, Fritz, 194
Nolli, Giambattista, plan of Rome, *98*, 99, 117
Normand, Charles, 228
North Canton, Ohio, redevelopment plan for, 31–35, *32*, *33*
North Penn Visiting Nurses Association, Headquarters and Clinic, Ambler, Pennsylvania, 18, *20*, 98
Notebook dinner service for Swid Powell, *220*, 223
Notebook fabric for the Fabric Workshop, Philadelphia, *212*, 213
Nouveau sugar bowl and creamer for Swid Powell, *225*, 227
Nutting, Wallace, *Furniture Treasury: (Mostly of American Origin)*, 202, *203*

O
Oberlin College, Ohio, Allen Memorial Art Museum, 59–62, *60–62*, 213
Oneida Furniture (firm), 193
Osborne, Jeffrey, 215
Otto, Frei, 67

P
Paley, Harry, 240
Paley Design Center, Philadelphia College of Textiles, 213
Palladio, Andrea, 173
Palley, Reese, 77
Palmer Drive development, University of Michigan, Ann Arbor, *179*
Pantheon, Rome, 9
Parallel Orders of Architecture: Greek, Roman and Italian (Normand), 228
Park Place Hotel and Casino, Atlantic City, New Jersey, 77, *77*
Patton, George, 20–21, 73
Payette Associates, 99, 103
Pearson house, Philadelphia, 14, *14*, 16

Pei, I. M., 52
Penn, William, 75
Penn Center, Philadelphia, 6
Pennsylvania State University, Faculty Club, University Park, 62–63, *63*
    interior design, 188–90, *189*
Pennsylvania Station, New York (McKim, Mead & White), 8
Pensi, Jorge, 197
Perelman Quadrangle, University of Pennsylvania, Philadelphia, *113*, 113–14
Perkins, G. Holmes, 6
Perry, Ellen, 181
Petrie, Donald, 159
Petrie house, Wainscott, New York, *157*, 159
Pevsner, Nikolaus, 13, 63
Philadelphia College of Textiles, Paley Design Center, 213
Philadelphia crosstown community planning study, 47–49, *48*
Philadelphia Museum of Art, exhibition designs for, 71
Philadelphia Orchestra Hall, 140–45, *141–43*, 178
"Philadelphia: Three Centuries of American Art" (exhibition design), 71
Piazza del Campidoglio, Rome, 9, 235
Piazza S. Ignazio, Rome, 9
Plater-Zyberk, Elizabeth, 180
Pollock, Jackson, 178
Polshek, Dean James, 72
Pont des Minimes, Toulouse, France, *172*
Powell, Addie, 220.
Powers, Hiram, 71
Price, William, 77, 207
    Blenheim Hotel, Atlantic City, New Jersey, 77
    Traymore Hotel, Atlantic City, New Jersey, 77, 207
Princeton Memorial Park, Robbinsville, New Jersey, *30*, 31
Princeton University, New Jersey
    commissions from, 89
    Fisher and Bendheim halls, 103, *106*
    Frist Campus Center, 114, *115*
    George LaVie Schultz Laboratory, 103–9, *107*
    Gordon Wu Hall, 90, *93–95*, 93–97
        interior design, *192*, 193
    Lee D. Butler Memorial Plaza, *94*, 96
    Lewis Thomas Laboratory, 99–103, *100–103*
        Venturi at, 8–9
    Witherspoon Hall, 8, *8*
Pritzker Architectural Prize, 92, 93
"Process and Symbol in the Design of Furniture for Knoll" (Venturi and Scott Brown), 207

Pruitt-Igoe housing project, Saint Louis, 3, *4*
Pyle, Nicholas, 45

Q
Queen Anne chair for Knoll, 207, *209*, 213
Queen Anne lowboy for Arc International, *216*, 217

R
Remington Rand (firm), 184
Rauch, John, 20, 29, 31, 92, 190
Ravitch, Richard, 44
Reed & Barton (firm), 227–29
Reedy Creek Improvement District Emergency Services Headquarters and Fire Station, Walt Disney World Resort, Lake Buena Vista, Florida, *152*, 153
Rendell, Edward, 140
Renwick Gallery, Smithsonian Institution, Washington, D.C., exhibition design for, 47, 67, 71–72, *72*
Renzo Brugola (firm), 215
Republic Square District development plan, Austin, Texas, 117, *118*
Research Institute for Advanced Science, Baltimore, 13
Rice University, Fondren Library, Houston, *116*, 117
Richardson, H. H., 63
Rietveld, Gerrit, 190
Roche, Kevin, 10, 44, 131
Rome Prize Fellowship, 12
Rossi, Aldo, 231, 240
Rouse & Associates, 149
Rudenstine, Neil, 93
Runtung housing estate, Leipzig, Germany, 10

S
Saarinen, Eero, 10, 29, 86, 184, 197, 220
    General Motors Technical Center, 10, 184
    Milwaukee War Memorial Auditorium, 10
Sainsbury Wing, National Gallery, London, 118, 122–31, *122–31*
Saint Andrew's Priory, Valyermo, California, 66
Saint Michel fountain, Paris, 9
Saito, Masahiro, 197
Salk Institute, La Jolla, California, 34
Saltzman, Ralph, 240
S.S. Trinità, Rome, 9
Sapper, Richard, 220
Saybolt & Cleland (firm), 190
Scarpa, Carlo, 236
Schnitger, Arp, 194
Schober, Charles, 194
Schuykill River corridor study, Philadelphia, 69, *69*

Scott Brown, Denise, 2, *91*
    at Berkeley, 35
    and historical preservation, 75–77
    personal background, 4–5
    planning studies, 113–14
    and Robert Scott Brown, 5–6
    and Robert Venturi, 3, 7, 21, 29
    Urban Concepts, 92
    at University of Pennsylvania, 6–7
    at Yale University, 46–47
    See also Venturi, Robert, and Denise Scott Brown
Scott Brown, Robert, 5–6
Scripps house (Gill), 131, 134, 137
Scully, Vincent, 35, 44, 63, 73, 83, 180, 184
    American Architecture and Urbanism, 49
    Shingle Style, 13–14, 16
    Shingle Style Today, The, 55
Sculpture in the Environment (SITE), 79
Seattle Art Museum, 118–22, *119–21*
Serlio, Sebastiano, 96, *96*
Serra, Richard, 74
Sert, Jose Luis, 29
Shepley, Bulfinch, Richardson and Abbot, 117
Sheraton chair for Knoll, 206–7, 213
Shingle Style (Scully), 13–14, 16
Shingle Style Today, The (Scully), 55
Short, William H., 20, 29
Siegel, Robert, 220
"Signs of Life: Symbols in the American City" (exhibition design), Renwick Gallery, Smithsonian Institution, Washington, D.C., 47, 67, 71–72, *72*
Simpson-Hoffman House, Salem, Massachusetts, 10
SITE (Sculpture in the Environment), 79
Skidmore, Owings & Merrill, 43
Slate Roof House, Philadelphia, 75
Smith, Brian, 5
Smith, David, 71
Smithson, Peter and Alison, 5, 6
Social Security Office, Helsinki, Finland (Aalto), 43
Society Hill Towers, Philadelphia (Pei), 52
Sofa for Knoll, *203*
Space, Time and Architecture (Giedion), 12
Spear, Richard, 59
Speer, Laurinda, 220
Staccato fabric for DesignTex, 240, *242*, 243
Stadium, University of Michigan, Ann Arbor, 175–78, *179*
State Mosque. *See* Iraqi State Mosque.

State University of New York at Purchase, Humanities building, 45, *46*, 97

Steelcase (firm), 240

Steinberg, Saul, 149

Stern, Robert, 49, 79, 83, 86–87, 180

Stirling, James, 35

Stonorov, Oscar, 10

Stoughton house, Cambridge, Massachusetts, 63

Strand District comprehensive plan, Galveston, Texas, 75–76, *76*

Stroud, Marion Boulton, 213

Sullivan, Louis, 31

Summerson, John, 5

Sunshine Foundation, Dream Village, Loughman, Florida, *156*, 157

Swid, Nan, 201, 220

Swid, Stephen, 219–20

Swid Powell (firm), 243

    product design for, 200, 219–31

Swirl chair, *198*

T

Tapestry fabric for Knoll, *212*, 213

Taro, Menilio, 193

Tate, James, 47

Thomas, Norman, 7

Thonet chair, 183, 185–86

Thousand Oaks civic center, Thousand Oaks, California, *48*, 49, 86

Tigerman, Stanley, 79, 220, 231

Times Square Center, New York, *146*, 147

Toledo aluminum chairs and tables (Pensi), 197

Trabant Student Center, University of Delaware, Newark, 114, *114*

Trainer, Nancy Rogo, 91

Transportation Square office building, Washington, D.C., *41*, 41–43

Traymore Hotel, Atlantic City, New Jersey (Price), 77, 207

Trenton Jewish Community Center bathhouse (Kahn), 6, *12*, 13

Trevi fountain, Rome, 9

Triennale Exhibition, Milan, product designs for, 215, 217–19, *218*

Trubek, David, 52–55

Trubek house, Nantucket, Massachusetts, 52–55, *53*, *54*

    interior design, 193–94

Trumbauer, Horace, 14–16

Tsien, Billie, 238

Tucker, Carll, 63

Tucker house, Katonah, New York, 63–64, *64*, 159

Twenty Mule Team Parkway, 69

"200 Years of American Sculpture" (exhibition design), 71

Tyng, Anne, 13

U

United States pavilion, Expo '92, Seville, Spain, *145*

Universal plastic chair (Colombo), 194

University of California at Berkeley, arts center, 34, *34*

University of California at Los Angeles

    Gonda (Goldschmied) Neuroscience and Genetics Research Center, 103, *105*

    Gordon and Virginia MacDonald Medical Research Laboratories, 103, *104*

University of Delaware, Newark, Trabant Student Center, 114, *114*

University of Michigan, Ann Arbor

    master plan, *174*, 175, *176*, 177

    Palmer Drive development, *179*

    stadium, 175–78, *179*

University of Pennsylvania, Philadelphia

    Clinical Research Building, 103, *103*

    Denise Scott Brown at, 6–7

    Fisher Fine Arts Library, *112*, 113

    Perelman Quadrangle, *113*, 113–14

    Robert Venturi at, 7, 13

    Vagelos Laboratories, *107*, 109

University of the Arts, Philadelphia, 140

University of Virginia, Charlottesville, Jefferson Library, 9

Urban Concepts (Scott Brown), 92

Urn table for Knoll, 207, 208

V

Vaccaro, Giuseppe, 5

Vagelos Laboratories, University of Pennsylvania, Philadelphia, *107*, 109

Vanbrugh, John, 9, 35

Vancombert, Joseph-Théodore, chocolate pot by, *234*

Vanna Venturi house (Mother's House), Philadelphia, 18, *19*, 24–29, *25*–*27*, 99, 122, 159, 181

    interior design, 184, *184*

Varga, George, 41

Vaughan, David, 52, 91

Vegas dinner service for Swid Powell, *225*, 227

Venice Biennale, 87–89, *88*

Venturi, James, 52

Venturi, Robert, 2, *91*, *92*

    Complexity and Contradiction in Architecture, 7, 35–36, *36*, 73, 184–85, 200

    and Denise Scott Brown, 3, 7, 21, 29

    and family business, 10–12

    Iconography and Electronics upon a Generic Architecture, 92

    interior design by, 183–200

    and Kahn, 12–14, 16, 20

    and modernism, 20

    personal background, 7–8

    at Princeton University, 8–9

    product design, 200–243

    project statements, 200

    in Rome, 12–13, 35

    thesis, 9–10

    work in 1950s, 13–20

    work in 1960s, 20–37, 38–45

    at Yale University, 35, 46–47

Venturi, Robert, and Denise Scott Brown

    awards, 29, 92, 228

    commercial projects, 77–80, 85–86, 149–55

        interior design, 194–200

    and deconstructivism, 181

    exhibition designs, 67, 71–72

    influence of, 178–80

    international acclaim, 73, 91, 175

    international competition designs, 86–87

    large-scale planning projects, 147–49

    Learning from Las Vegas, 37–38, 46, 47, 52, 72, *136*, 137

    museum commissions, 117–37

    and post-modernism, 4, 83, 89, 178–80

    public monument designs, 137–47

    residential projects, 52–59, 63–66, 83–85, 155–60

        interior design, 193–94

    university projects, 59–63, 93–117, 175–78

        interior design, 188–93

    urban development projects, 69–71

    View from the Campidoglio, A, 92

    work in France, 167–75

    work in Japan, 160–67

    work in late 1960s, 47–52

    work in early 1970s, 52–64, 67–72

    work in late 1970s, 64–66, 72–87

    work in early 1980s, 87–89, 91, 93–117

    work in 1980s–1990s, 117–67

Venturi, Scott Brown house, Philadelphia, 52, *92*, 202–7, 213

Viceroy's House, New Delhi, India, 190

View from the Campidoglio, A (Venturi and Scott Brown), 92

Village tea and coffee service for Swid Powell, *222*, 223–27

Villa Müller, Prague (Loos), *186*

Villa Rotonda earring, 237, *238*

Villa Savoye (Le Corbusier), 9, 16, 57

Viñoly, Rafael, 145

Von Moos, Stanislaus, 99, 157

Vreeland, Tim, 35

V'Soske (firm), product design for, 200, 237–38

W

Walker, Mallory, 41

Walt Disney Company, The, commissions from, 153–55

Walt Disney World Resort, Lake Buena Vista, Florida

    hotel and convention complex, *151*, 153

    Reedy Creek Improvement District Emergency Services Headquarters and Fire Station, *151*, 153

Warhol, Andy, 57, 64

Washington Avenue revitalization plan, Miami Beach, 76–77, *77*

Wassily armchair (Breuer), 197

Watson-Casey Companies, 117

Weinraub, Judith, 201

Weintraub, Maurice, 200

Welcome Park, Philadelphia, 75, *75*

Westway Park, New York, 147

WestWeek, Los Angeles, 243

Whitehall Ferry Terminal, New York, *144*, *145*, 145–47

Whitney Museum of American Art

    exhibition at, 52

    "200 Years of American Sculpture" (exhibition design), 71

Wike, Roffe and Penny, 58

Wike house, Willistown, Pennsylvania, 58, *58*

Wilkins, William, 123

William and Mary bureau for XVII International Triennale, Milan, 215, *218*, 219

Williams, Tod, 238

Wines, James, 79

Wingspread house, Racine, Wisconsin, 9–10

Wislocki, George, 52, 55

Wislocki house, Nantucket, Massachusetts, 52–55, *53*, 64

Witherspoon Hall, Princeton University, 8, *8*

Women's Club (Gill), 134

Wommack, Michael, 215

Wood-Mountain Makings (firm), 190

Wright, Frank Lloyd, 9–10, 13, 57, 99, 175, 237

Wu Hall. *See* Gordon Wu Hall.

Wurman, Richard Saul, 69

Y

Yale University, New Haven

    Art Gallery, 6

    Mathematics Building, 44, *44*, 45

    Venturi at, 35, 46–47

YMCA, North Canton, Ohio, 31–34, *32*, *33*

Yukata fabric for DesignTex, 240, *241*

PHOTOGRAPHIC CREDITS

Albertina, Wien / © 2001 Artists Rights Society (ARS), New York / VBK, Vienna: fig. 298

© Wayne Andrews / Esto: fig. 18

Archives Départementales de la Haute-Garonne, Toulouse, France: fig. 283

Associated Press: fig. 2

Tom Bernard: figs. 70, 82–84, 87, 91–92, 98, 101–2, 109, 125, 129, 131–132, 301–2, 304–5

Will Brown: cover, figs. 3–6, 12, 14, 21–23, 25–27, 29, 33, 36, 40–42, 44–45, 52, 54, 57, 62–67, 74, 77, 79–81, 85–86, 89, 93–95, 100, 106, 108, 110, 113–14, 118–19, 133–35, 139–40, 143, 146, 149–50, 152, 160–62, 166, 177–78, 181–83, 187, 190–93, 195, 198, 205, 208–9, 215–17, 219–22, 224–27, 230–32, 235–44, 248–49, 252–54, 257, 260, 262, 265, 272–73, 276–77, 299, 321–22, 331–32, 334, 350–51, 359–61, 363, 368, 376–77, 380–81, 383–84, 386, 393–94

David Brownlee: figs. 271, 274

Richard Bryant / Arcaid: figs. 200, 203

Mark Cohn: fig. 97

Tom Crane: fig. 88

John Donat: fig. 189

Fondation Le Corbusier, Paris / © Artists Rights Society (ARS), New York / ADAGP, Paris / FLC: fig. 137

David Graham: fig. 293

Kari Hakli: fig. 287

Courtesy of Herman Miller: fig. 300

Kouji Horiuchi: figs. 309–10, 314, 316, 317

Timothy Hursley: figs. 207, 210, 212–13

Leni Iselin: fig. 294

Luc Joubert: fig. 378

Louis I. Kahn Collection, University of Pennsylvania and the Pennsylvania Historical and Museum Commission: figs. 10–11, 19

Kawasumi Architectural Photograph Office: fig. 266

Rollin R. LaFrance: figs. 34, 295

MAK – Austrian Museum for Applied Arts, Vienna: fig. 326

Julie Marquart: figs. 127, 158, 172

Dennis McWaters: figs. 345, 352

Eric Mitchell: fig. 319

Cleto Munari: fig. 387

Musée des Arts Décoratifs, Paris / © 2001 Artists Rights Society (ARS), New York / ADAGP, Paris / FLC: fig. 296

The Museum of Modern Art, New York: figs. 15, 31

National Museum of American History, Division of Social History, Smithsonian Institution, Washington, D.C.: fig. 353

Courtesy of Pace Master Prints, New York: fig. 138

George Pohl: figs. 1, 24, 30, 35

Cervin Robinson: figs. 71, 73

Lynn Rosenthal: figs. 46, 136, 204, 214, 263–64, 282, 289, 290, 292, 323, 327, 385

Steve Rosenthal: fig. 165

Shinkenchiku-sha: fig. 275

Venturi, Scott Brown and Associates, Inc.: frontispiece, figs. 7–8, 13, 16–17, 20, 28, 32, 37–39, 43, 47–51, 53, 55–56, 58–61, 68–69, 72, 75–76, 78, 90, 96, 99, 103–5, 111–12, 115, 117, 120–23, 130, 141, 155, 167–68, 171, 173–76, 179–80, 194, 202, 211, 218, 223, 228–29, 233–34, 251, 261, 267–69, 291, 320, 329, 333, 367

Matt Wargo: figs. 107, 116, 126, 128, 142, 144–45, 147–48, 151, 153–54, 156–57, 159, 163–64, 169–70, 184–86, 188, 196–97, 199, 201, 206, 245–47, 250, 255–56, 258–59, 278–81, 284–86, 288, 307–8, 365–66, 374

Lawrence S. Williams: figs. 297, 303

Graydon Wood: figs. 306, 311–13, 315, 318, 324–25, 328, 330, 335–44, 346–49, 354–58, 362, 364, 369–73, 375, 379, 382, 388–92

CHRONOLOGY

All images are copyright by Venturi, Scott Brown and Associates, Inc., except page 251, top: J. T. Miller

PROJECT LIST

Tom Bernard: 1980

Will Brown: 1958, 1966, 1967, 1976, 1977, 1982, 1983, 1988

Mark Cohn: 1972

Stephen Hill: 1969

Timothy Hursley: 1986

Steven Izenour: 1970

Rollin R. LaFrance: 1963, 1964

Julie Marquart: 1999

George Pohl: 1962

Steven Shore: 1974

Timothy Soar: 1985

Venturi, Scott Brown and Associates, Inc.: 1957, 1959, 1960, 1965, 1968, 1971, 1973, 1975, 1979, 1987, 1992, 1995, 1997, 1998, 2000

Matt Wargo: 1978, 1984, 1989, 1990, 1991, 1993, 1994, 1996

Lawrence S. Williams: 1961

Graydon Wood: 1981